ATLA BIBLIOGRAPHY SERIES
edited by Dr. Kenneth E. Rowe

1. *A Guide to the Study of the Holiness Movement,* by Charles Edwin Jones. 1974.
2. *Thomas Merton: A Bibliography,* by Marquita E. Breit. 1974.
3. *The Sermon on the Mount: A History of Interpretation and Bibliography,* by Warren S. Kissinger. 1975.
4. *The Parables of Jesus: A History of Interpretation and Bibliography,* by Warren S. Kissinger. 1979.
5. *Homosexuality and the Judeo-Christian Tradition: An Annotated Bibliography,* by Thom Horner. 1981.
6. *A Guide to the Study of the Pentecostal Movement,* by Charles Edwin Jones. 1983.
7. *The Genesis of Modern Process Thought: A Historical Outline with Bibliography,* by George R. Lucas, Jr. 1983.
8. *A Presbyterian Bibliography,* by Harold B. Prince. 1983.
9. *Paul Tillich: A Comprehensive Bibliography . . .,* by Richard C. Crossman. 1983.
10. *A Bibliography of the Samaritans,* by Alan David Crown. 1984.
11. *An Annotated and Classified Bibliography of English Literature Pertaining to the Ethiopian Orthodox Church,* by Jon Bonk. 1984.
12. *International Meditation Bibliography, 1950 to 1982,* by Howard R. Jarrell. 1984.
13. *Rabindranath Tagore: A Bibliography,* by Katherine Henn. 1985.
14. *Research in Ritual Studies: A Programmatic Essay and Bibliography,* by Ronald L. Grimes, 1985.
15. *Protestant Theological Education in America,* by Heather F. Day. 1985.
16. *Unconscious: A Guide to Sources,* by Natalino Caputi. 1985.
17. *The New Testament Apocrypha and Pseudepigrapha,* by James H. Charlesworth. 1987.
18. *Black Holiness,* by Charles Edwin Jones. 1987.
19. *A Bibliography on Ancient Ephesus,* by Richard Oster. 1987.
20. *Jerusalem, the Holy City: A Bibliography,* by James D. Purvis. 1987.
21. *An Index to English Periodical Literature on the Old Testament and Ancient Near Eastern Studies,* Volume I, by William G. Hupper. 1987.

BLACK HOLINESS:

A Guide to the Study of
Black Participation in
Wesleyan Perfectionist and
Glossolalic Pentecostal
Movements

by
CHARLES EDWIN JONES

ATLA Bibliography Series, No. 18

The American Theological Library
Association and
The Scarecrow Press, Inc.
Metuchen, N.J., & London
1987

Library of Congress Cataloging-in-Publication Data

Jones, Charles Edwin, 1932–
   Black holiness.

   (ATLA bibliography series ; no. 18)
   Includes index.
   1. Afro-Americans--Religion--Bibliography.
2. Holiness churches--United States--Bibliography.
3. Pentecostal churches--United States--Bibliography.
4. United States--Church history--Bibliography.
I. Title.   II. Series.
Z1361.N39J66 1987   016.2708'2'08996   86-21893
[BR563.N4]
ISBN 0-8108-1948-1

To Cunningham,

my student at Tuskegee Institute

who wanted to be included

in my "book."

ACKNOWLEDGMENTS

For the bibliographer who attempts to be comprehensive, the listing of those to whom he is indebted in his work is as complex and impossible as the unfinishable task of bibliography itself. The attempt, however, provides an opportunity to retrace the process long before listing began and to thank some of those who, consciously and unconsciously, gave assistance along the way.

I was raised in a devout holiness family in Kansas City. My father, a streetcar operator and gospel team leader, was invited to conduct the Sunday afternoon service at a tent meeting in our neighborhood. I accompanied him. The tent was pitched on vacant lots separating our white area from a black one. Dad was a segregationist and upon discovery that the hosts were black insisted that they, not he, should lead the meeting. We stayed, nevertheless, and stood in the back. I can still hear the church mothers, all clad in white and standing in a line the breadth of the tent, repeat in unison: "I was glad, I was glad when they said unto me, 'Let us go up to the house of the Lord.'" There on the border of my confined universe I received a new glimpse into what it means "to worship the Lord in the beauty of holiness." Perhaps the seed planted in that experience is the origin of this book.

The debts I have incurred in this endeavor are indeed numerous. The reference librarians of the University of Oklahoma (particularly Habib Gharib and T. H. Milby) and of Bethany Nazarene College (particularly Bea Flinner) were entreated for information on many days and at many hours. Irene Owens of Howard University, Sherry DuPree of Santa Fe Community College (Florida), D. William Faupel of Asbury Theological Seminary, Robert G. Kleinhans of Saint Xavier College, and Glenn Pearl of Southwestern College of Christian Ministries (Oklahoma) demonstrated how scholarly cooperation can work. The special collections section of the library at Fisk University gave access to materials not locally available to me. And Paul William Thomas, Steven Cooley, and Margaret Muse Oden, archivists of the Wesleyan Church, the Church of the Nazarene, and the Pentecostal Holiness Church respectively, proved especially helpful. Esther Shelhamer James of Wilmore, Kentucky, provided needed material and information about the ministries of her parents and her husband among blacks. The Apostolic World Christian Fellowship provided useful publications. Allan Stifflear of the Episcopal

Divinity School (Massachusetts) made available to me materials on black Oneness Pentecostalism in Philadelphia, and Bishop James A. Forbes kindly loaned me publications relating to the United Holy Church of America and the Original United Holy Church International. The staffs of the Indianapolis Public Library and the Grace Apostolic Church of Indianapolis, and of the Church of Christ of Apostolic Faith of Columbus, Ohio, gave more than conventional assistance, as did Dr. Vinson Synan of the Pentecostal Holiness Church, Bishop Morris Golder of the Pentecostal Assemblies of the World, Bishop Alonzo Ponder of the Church of the Living God, Christian Workers for Fellowship, and the Reverend Nathaniel Irving of the Avery Chapel African Methodist Epistcopal Church of Oklahoma City. Harriet Barbour and Karen Fite, both of the Oklahoma Department of Libraries, gave indispensable assistance. Through their published works David B. Barrett, Walter Hollenweger, and James S. Tinney provided ways through many apparently impassable places. Finally, I want to thank Beverly, my wife, best friend, critic, and favorite librarian.

EDITOR'S FOREWORD

The American Theological Library Association Bibliography Series is designed to stimulate and encourage the preparation of reliable bibliographies and guides to the literature of religious studies in all of its scope and variety. Compilers are free to define their field, make their own selections, and work out internal organization as the unique demands of the subject indicate. We are pleased to publish this guide to the literature of black holiness churches as number eighteen in our series.

Charles Edwin Jones holds the Ph.D. degree from the University of Wisconsin in the field of American Religious Studies. His scholarly and bibliographical interests and writings have focused on the holiness movement in American Methodism. Dr. Jones has held library positions in Saint Paul School of Theology, Kansas City, Park College, Parkville, Missouri, the University of Michigan, Houghton College, and Brown University. He also has served as archival consultant for the Billy Graham Evangelistic Association, Bethany Nazarene College, and the Pentecostal Holiness Church. He currently resides in Oklahoma City.

Charles Jones is the author of two other distinguished titles in this series, No. 1, A Guide to the Study of the Holiness Movement (1974) and No. 6, A Guide to the Study of the Pentecostal Movement (1983).

Kenneth E. Rowe
Series Editor

Drew University Library
Madison, NJ 07940

BRIEF TABLE OF CONTENTS

---

*Indicates predominantly white denominations.

xvi

PART IV.   LEADER-CENTERED ORIENTATION

xvii

INTRODUCTION

The original plan for this book was that it should extract black-related materials that had been incorporated in A Guide to the Study of the Pentecostal Movement (Scarecrow, 1983) and incorporate a few items which surfaced after publication. It soon became clear, however, that the projected work would be strengthened if materials from A Guide to the Study of the Holiness Movement (Scarecrow, 1974) on the Wesleyan Holiness churches (the foundation upon which the other movements built) and if materials on race relations and on leader-centered bodies in Africa and North America were included as well. The desirability that black minorities within white groups be included also rapidly became apparent, the end-product being a bibliographical compendium on black participation in Wesleyan perfectionist and glossolalic Pentecostal and healing movements in Africa, the West Indies, the United States, Canada, and the United Kingdom.

At the height of the civil rights movement in the mid-1960s it was often said that the church was the most segregated institution in the United States, and that 11:00 on Sunday morning was the most segregated hour in the week. In America racism was named the culprit; in Africa, colonialism. Whatever its social or political cause, however, racial separation was and is a fact on the denominational level and, for most part, on the congregational level as well. This (together with almost universal social and economic compartmentalization) has contributed to lack of communication between blacks and like-minded believers in the white community. Their beliefs, in turn, have largely segregated black Holiness and Pentecostal churches from the rest of the black religious community.

A wide range of tongue-speaking and non-tongue-speaking groups devoted to heart-felt religion and healing are popularly called Holiness. The name, given in derision like Methodist and Dunker, has been appropriated by its recipients and is used in the title of this book in this inclusive, rather than in the exclusive Wesleyan, sense. Despite uninformed outside opinion, black Holiness encompasses a wide spectrum of doctrinal teaching. Apart from racial fraternity, there is little community among some segments of the movements included, for instance, between Oneness bodies and Wesleyan-Arminian groups. In all Pentecostal bodies the charisma of the leader is of primary importance, often of greater practical

significance than fine points of doctrine. In addition to the total
dominance of the leader in prophet-centered movements in Africa
and North America, the strong leader often appears to be the central factor in the splitting which has occurred in Oneness groups
in the United States and Holiness-Pentecostal bodies in the United
Kingdom.

The bibliography is divided into six parts. Part I is devoted
to general aspects of black Wesleyan and Pentecostal movements,
with stress on the latter. Parts II and III classify works by doctrinal emphasis: Wesleyan-Arminian (subdivided into Holiness-
Perfectionist and Holiness-Pentecostal), and Finished Work of Calvary (subdivided into Baptistic-Trinitarian and Oneness). Each section is prefaced by an introduction tracing historical development and
distinctive teachings, which is followed by nondenominational literature of the sub-movement. This introduction and bibliography is
followed, in turn, by a historical sketch for each body associated
with the particular sub-movement. The leader-centered bodies in
Part IV are treated similarly. In Parts II-IV an asterisk (*) indicates a predominantly white body. Part V includes the names,
founding and closing dates, locations, sponsorship, and related
bibliography of schools. Part VI, Biography, is devoted to materials about individuals, and includes writings on other subjects
produced by them. An asterisk (*) preceding an entry in Part VI
indicates a white subject.

The internal organization of each category in Parts I-IV is
uniform. General introductory, apologetic, and sociological works
are followed by subject bibliography in alphabetical order, i.e.,
"--Bibliography," etc. In these sections collective biography is
listed under "--Biography." The "--Controversial literature" sub-
division includes works of criticism by members of the body in question or by adherents of other Holiness groups. Under "--Doctrinal
and controversial works" are grouped works by members and other
writers proclaiming the doctrines and defending the practices of the
body or movement. Under "--History and study of doctrines" are
placed works which attempt objective analysis and are designed to
prove neither the truth nor the falsity of the teachings analyzed.
Completing the listing is a geographical sequence arranged by continent, country, province, and city.

The index provides approaches to subjects and authors not
possible through the regular organization; there, references are to
entry numbers, which precede each bibliography, directory, and
biographical listing. Page numbers which follow refer to narrative
texts. Organizations, names (personal and geographical), subjects,
occupations, and periodical titles are included.

ABBREVIATIONS

BOOKS

AMD	American medical directory.
AOHUTR	Apostolic Church of God in Christ Jesus. Our heritage: "upon this rock."
ATF	Atter. The third force.
AVOD	Anderson. Vision of the disinherited.
BCUC	Bowman. Color us Christian: the story of the Church of the Nazarene among America's blacks.
BDARB	Bowden. Dictionary of American religious biography.
BDNM	Biographical directory of Negro ministers.
BPM	Bloch-Hoell. The Pentecostal movement.
BSFH	Brumback. Suddenly from heaven.
BSIAM	Bixler. The Spirit is a-movin'.
BWTS	Brown. When the trumpet sounded.
CA	Contemporary authors.
CGH	Church of the Living God, Christian Workers for Fellowship. Glorious heritage. The golden book. Documentary-historical.
CHCCH	Cobbins. History of Church of Christ (Holiness) U.S.A., 1895-1965.
CLMA	Conn. Like a mighty army.
CP	Cornelius. The pioneer: history of the Church of God in Christ.
CPH	Crayne. Pentecostal handbook.
CPHC	Campbell. The Pentecostal Holiness Church, 1898-1948.
CSSIA	Clark. The small sects in America.
CTTR	Callen. A time to remember.
CUWS	Clanton. United we stand.
CWSHT	Conn. Where the saints have trod.
DAB	Dictionary of American biography.
DBWS	Durasoff. Bright wind of the Spirit.
DMS	Directory of medical specialists.
EPOP	Ewart. The phenomenon of Pentecost.
ERIS	Encyclopedia of religion in the South.
FTINS	Foster. Think it not strange; a history of the Oneness movement.
FVOM	Full Gospel Business Men's Fellowship International. Voices of the military.

GBPAW	Golder. The bishops of the Pentecostal Assemblies of the World, Inc.
GHPAW	Golder. History of the Pentecostal Assemblies of the World.
GLWBGTH	Golder. The life and works of Bishop Garfield Thomas Haywood.
HATAP	Harrell. All things are possible.
HGS	Heilbut. The gospel sound: good news and bad times.
HORAL	Harrell. Oral Roberts: an American life.
HP	Hollenweger. The Pentecostals.
HWSBM	Harrell. White sects and black men in the recent South.
JCITCC	Jensen. Charisma in the 20th century church.
KMIE	Kerr. Music in evangelism and stories of famous Christian songs.
KPF	Kendrick. The promise fulfilled.
KWGHW	Kulbeck. What God hath wrought.
LMGSS	Lillenas. Modern gospel song stories.
MATS	Menzies. Anointed to serve.
MAWCSM	Metcalf. American writers and compilers of sacred music.
MCAC	McLeister. Conscience and commitment: the history of the Wesleyan Methodist Church of America.
MHAFY	Mason. History and formative years of the Church of God in Christ.
MHPD	Moore. Handbook of Pentecostal denominations in the United States.
MIS	Meloon. Ivan Spencer, willow in the wind.
MLMR	Manuel. Like a mighty river.
MOM	Church of God of Prophecy. Memoirs of our ministry.
MP	Morris. The preachers.
MSBS	Martin. Sent by the Spirit.
NAW	Notable American women.
NCDCWM	Neill. Concise dictionary of the Christian world mission.
NH	The Negro handbook.
NP	Nichol. Pentecostalism.
NYT	New York Times.
PCUH	Purkiser. Called unto holiness.
PPIB	Piepkorn. Profiles in belief.
RFSTGA	Rogers. From sharecropper to goodwill ambassador.
RTU	Ringenberg. Taylor University: the first 125 years.
RWWAS	Richardson. With water and Spirit.
SAOPCO	Synan. Aspects of Pentecostal-Charismatic origins.
SBHCGRM	Smith. A brief history of the Church of God reformation movement.
SBWL	Sigsworth. The battle was the Lord's: a history of the Free Methodist Church in Canada.
SFH	Simson. The faith healer.
SGDIM	Smith. The growth and development of the interracial

	movement within the Free Methodist Church of North America.
SHPM	Synan. The Holiness-Pentecostal movement.
SOTP	Synan. The old-time power.
TBPALM	Tucker. Black pastors and leaders: Memphis, 1819-1972.
TDOOP	Thomas. The days of our pilgrimage.
TFYNM	Taylor. Fifty years of Nazarene missions.
WAB	Webster's American biographies.
WBWF	Wood. Baptized with fire.
WJ	Winley. Jesse.
WJGIG	Williamson. Julia: giantess in generosity.
WWABA	Who's who among black Americans.
WWIA	Who's who in America.
WWIACUA	Who's who in American college and university administration.
WWIAM	Who's who in American Methodism.
WWIAP	Who's who in American politics.
WWICA	Who's who in colored America.
WWIR	Who's who in religion.
WWISS	Who's who in the South and Southwest.
WWOCR	Who's who of the colored race.
WWOAW	Who's who of American women.
WWWA	Who was who in America.
WWWCH	Who was who in church history.

CHURCHES

AAChr	Apostolic Assemblies of Christ.
AAOLSJC	Apostolic Assembly of Our Lord and Savior Jesus Christ.
AC	Apostolic Church.
ACChr	Apostolic Church of Christ.
ACChr (H)	Associated Churches of Christ (Holiness).
ACChrG	Apostle Church of Christ in God.
ACJM	Apostolic Church of John Maranke.
AFCG	Apostolic Faith Church of God.
AFM	Apostolic Faith Mission.
AFMCG	Apostolic Faith Mission Church of God.
AGGC	Assemblies of God, General Council.
AGSCA	Assemblies of God in Southern and Central Africa.
AMAF	Apostolic Miracle Assembly Fellowship.
AME	African Methodist Episcopal Church.
AMEZ	African Methodist Episcopal Zion Church.
AOCGT	Alpha and Omega Church of God Tabernacle.
AOHCG	Apostolic Overcoming Holy Church of God.
AOPeC	Alpha and Omega Pentecostal Church.
AOPeCA	Alpha and Omega Pentecostal Church of America.
Ba	Baptist Church.

BACPeMA	Bethel Apostolic Church of the Pentecostal Movement Association.
BBC	Bountiful Blessings Churches.
BIC	Brethren in Christ Church.
BWCOLJCWW	Bible Way Church of Our Lord Jesus Christ World Wide.
BWPoAC	Bible Way Pentecostal Apostle Church.
CAC	Christ Apostolic Church.
CChr (H)	Church of Christ (Holiness) U.S.A.
CFBHC	Colored Fire Baptized Holiness Church.
CG (A)	Church of God (Anderson, Indiana)
CG (AP)	Church of God (Apostolic)
CG (C)	Church of God (Cleveland, Tennessee)
CG (GS)	Church of God (Gospel Spreading)
CG (SC)	Church of God (Sanctified Church)
CG (T)	Church of God (Tomlinson)
CGAFA	Church of God of the Apostolic Faith Association.
CGBF	Church of God by Faith.
CGH	Churches of God, Holiness.
CGIC	Church of God in Christ.
CGIC (A)	Church of God in Christ (Apostolic)
CGICC	Church of God in Christ, Congregational.
CGICI	Church of God in Christ, International.
CGP	Church of God of Prophecy.
ChrFB	Christian Faith Band.
CLG	Church of the Living God.
CLGCWFF	Church of the Living God, Christian Workers for Fellowship.
CLGPGT	Church of the Living God, the Pillar and Ground of the Truth.
CLJCAF	Church of the Lord Jesus Christ of the Apostolic Faith.
CMA	Christian and Missionary Alliance.
CN	Church of the Nazarene.
COLJCAF	Church of Our Lord Jesus Christ of the Apostolic Faith.
CP	Church of Pentecost.
CUTDG	Church of Universal Triumph, the Dominion of God.
DEC	Deliverance Evangelistic Centers.
EAOHCG	Ethiopian Apostolic Overcoming Holy Church of God.
ECChr (H)	Evangelical Church of Christ (Holiness)
EEB	Elim Evangelistic Band.
EF	Elim Fellowship.
EJCTPSK	Eglise de Jésus-Christ sur la terre par le prophète Simon Kimbangu.
EMA	Elim Missionary Assemblies.
EMIB	Evangelische Missionsgesellschaft in Basel.
EPeCAF	Emmanuel Pentecostal Churches of the Apostolic Faith.
EPeCOLAF	Emmanuel Pentecostal Church of Our Lord, Apostolic Faith.

FBHAA	Fire Baptized Holiness Association of America.
FBHC	Fire Baptized Holiness Church.
FBHCG	Fire Baptized Holiness Church of God.
FBHCGA	Fire Baptized Holiness Church of God of the Americas.
FCZCC	Free Christian Zion Church of Christ.
FDPM	Father Divine Peace Mission.
FGCChr	Free Gospel Church of Christ.
FGHTC	Full Gospel Holy Temple Churches.
FGTA	First Glorious Temple Apostolic.
FMCNA	Free Methodist Church of North America.
FT	Faith Tabernacle Corporation of Churches.
GCAC	Gold Coast Apostolic Church.
GCGIC	Glorious Church of God in Christ.
GEAC	Greater Emmanuel Apostolic Church.
GPC	Grace Protestant Chapels.
HAT	Holiness Association of Texas.
HC	Holiness Church.
HChrCChr	Highway Christian Church of Christ.
HCIA	Holy Church in America.
HGWCLGPGT	House of God, Which is the Church of the Living God, the Pillar and Ground of the Truth.
HLC	House of the Lord Churches.
HTCChr	Holy Temple Church of Christ.
I	Independent.
ICFG	International Church of the Foursquare Gospel.
ICG	Interdenominational Church of God.
IDC	International Deliverance Churches.
J	Jewish.
KAC	King's Apostles Churches.
KCI	Kodesh Church of Immanuel.
LHLFAPCMAF	Latter House of the Lord for All People and Church of the Mountain, Apostolic Faith.
Lu	Lutheran Church.
LWAF	Living Witness of the Apostolic Faith.
M	Methodist Church.
MBaC	Missionary Baptist Church.
MCAHPFC	Mount Calvary Assembly Hall of the Pentecostal Faith Church.
MCHCA	Mount Calvary Holy Church of America.
MCV	Macedonia Churches of Virginia.
ME	Methodist Episcopal Church.
MEL	Methodist Episcopal Church of Liberia.
MenC	Mennonite Church.
MES	Methodist Episcopal Church, South.
MHATOLJAF	Mount Hebron Apostolic Temple of Our Lord Jesus of the Apostolic Faith.
MSHCA	Mount Sinai Holy Church of America.
MSSGHC	Mount Sinai Saints of God Holy Churches.
NAAB	New Apostolic Association of Baltimore, Maryland.
NBaC	National Baptist Convention.

NDSTCCU	National David Spiritual Temple of Christ Church Union (Inc.) U.S.A.
NRDHC	New Refuge Deliverance Holiness Church.
NTCG	New Testament Church of God.
OAAOLSJC	Original Apostolic Assembly of Our Lord and Saviour Jesus Christ Faith of 31 A.D.
OBSC	Open Bible Standard Churches.
OCGSC	Original Church of God or Sanctified Church.
OCSC	Orthodox Christian Spiritual Church.
OGCGIC	Original Glorious Church of God in Christ.
OUHCI	Original United Holy Church International.
OUHCW	Original United Holy Church of the World.
PDC	Powerhouse of Deliverance Church.
PeAJ	Pentecostal Assemblies of Jamaica.
PeAJC	Pentecostal Assemblies of Jesus Christ.
PeAW	Pentecostal Assemblies of the World.
PeCAFA	Pentecostal Churches of the Apostolic Faith Association.
PeCGA	Pentecostal Church of God of America.
PeCJC	Pentecostal Church of Jesus Christ.
PECL	Protestant Episcopal Church of Liberia.
PeHC	Pentecostal Holiness Church.
PHC	Pilgrim Holiness Church.
PrCUSA	Presbyterian Church in the United States of America.
RAJCA	Redeemed Assembly of Jesus Christ, Apostolic.
SA	Salvation Army.
SAT	Shiloh Apostolic Temple.
SSS	Soul Saving Station for Every Nation Christ Crusaders of America.
TCJ	True Church of Jesus.
TCKGIC	Triumph the Church and Kingdom of God in Christ.
TFPeCA	True Fellowship Pentecostal Church of America.
TVPeCJ	True Vine Pentecostal Churches of Jesus.
TVPeHC	True Vine Pentecostal Holiness Church.
UBIC	United Brethren in Christ.
UCJA	United Churches of Jesus, Apostolic.
UCJC (A)	United Church of Jesus Christ (Apostolic)
UFMCC	Universal Fellowship of Metropolitan Community Churches.
UHCA	United Holy Church of America.
UHOPFAP	United House of Prayer for All People, Church on the Rock of the Apostolic Faith.
UM	United Methodist Church.
UPrCUSA	United Presbyterian Church in the United States of America.
UWCCChrAF	United Way of the Cross Churches of Christ of the Apostolic Faith.
WC	Wesleyan Church.
WCCChr	Way of the Cross Church of Christ.
WMCA	Wesleyan Methodist Connection (or Church) of America.
ZEF	Zion Evangelistic Fellowship.

LIBRARIES

ArStC	Arkansas University, State University.
ArU	University of Arkansas, Fayetteville.
AU	University of Alabama, University.
AzFU	Northern Arizona University, Flagstaff.
CAngP	Pacific Union College, Angwin, Ca.
CAzPC	Azusa Pacific University, Azusa, Ca.
CBGTU	Graduate Theological Union, Berkeley, Ca.
CCC	Claremont Co."eges, Claremont, Ca.
CCmS	Southern California College, Costa Mesa.
CHS	California State University, Hayward.
CLamB	Biola Library, La Mirada, Ca.
CLolC	Loma Linda University, Loma Linda, Ca.
CLSU	University of Southern California, Los Angeles.
CLU	University of California, Los Angeles.
CMlG	Golden Gate Baptist Theological Seminary, Mill Valley, Ca.
CoD	Denver Public Library, Denver.
CoDI	Iliff School of Theology, Denver.
CPFT	Fuller Theological Seminary, Pasadena, Ca.
CSbC	California State College, San Bernardino.
CSdP	Point Loma Nazarene College, San Diego, Ca.
CSfSt	San Francisco State University, San Francisco.
CSt	Stanford University, Stanford, Ca.
CtWeharU	University of Hartford, West Hartford, Ct.
CtY	Yale University, New Haven, Ct.
CtY-D	Yale University, New Haven, Ct. Divinity School.
CU	University of California, Berkeley.
CU-S	University of California, San Diego.
DAU	American University, Washington.
DCU	Catholic University of America, Washington.
DeU	University of Delaware, Newark.
DHU	Howard University, Washington.
DHUD	United States Department of Housing and Urban Development, Washington.
DLC	Library of Congress, Washington.
F	Florida State Library, Tallahassee.
FJ	Jacksonville Public Library, Jacksonville, Fl.
FTaSU	Florida State University, Tallahassee.
FU	University of Florida, Gainesville.
GASU	Georgia State University, Atlanta.
GAU	Atlanta University, Atlanta.
GAUC	Atlanta University Center, Atlanta.
GEU	Emory University, Atlanta.
GEU-T	Emory University, Atlanta. Pitts Theological Library.
GU	University of Georgia, Athens.
IAurC	Aurora College, Aurora, Il.
ICarbS	Southern Illinois University, Carbondale.
ICN	Newberry Library, Chicago.

ICT	Chicago Theological Seminary, Chicago.
ICU	University of Chicago, Chicago.
IDeKN	Northern Illinois University, De Kalb.
IEE	National College of Education, Evanston, Il.
IEG	Garrett-Evangelical Theological Seminary, Evanston, Il.
IEN	Northwestern University, Evanston, Il.
IGreviC	Greenville College, Greenville, Il.
IKON	Olivet Nazarene College, Kankakee, Il.
InAndC	Anderson College, Anderson, In.
InAndC-T	Anderson College, Anderson, In. Graduate School of Theology.
InElkB	Associated Mennonite Bible Seminary, Elkhart, In.
InGoM	Mennonite Historical Library, Goshen, In.
InHi	Indiana Historical Society, Indianapolis.
InIB	Butler University, Indianapolis.
InIT	Christian Theological Seminary, Indianapolis.
InMarC	Marion College, Marion, In.
InMu	Muncie Public Library, Muncie, In.
InRE	Earlham College, Richmond, In.
InU	Indiana University, Bloomington.
InUpT	Taylor University, Upland, In.
IU	University of Illinois, Urbana.
KMK	Kansas State University, Manhattan.
KU	University of Kansas, Lawrence.
KyLoS	Southern Baptist Theological Seminary, Louisville, Ky.
KyLxCB	Lexington Theological Seminary, Lexington, Ky.
KyWAT	Asbury Theological Seminary, Wilmore, Ky.
LNT	Tulane University, New Orleans.
MB	Boston Public Library, Boston.
MBU	Boston University, Boston.
MBU-T	Boston University, Boston. School of Theology.
MCE	Episcopal Divinity School, Cambridge, Ma.
MdBE	Enoch Pratt Free Library, Baltimore.
MdBMC	Morgan State College, Baltimore.
MH	Harvard University, Cambridge, Ma.
MH-AH	Harvard University, Cambridge, Ma. Andover-Harvard Theological Library.
MiBsA	Andrews University, Berrien Springs, Mi.
MiEM	Michigan State University, East Lansing.
MiGrC	Calvin College and Seminary, Grand Rapids, Mi.
MiRochOU	Oakland University, Rochester, Mi.
MiU	University of Michigan, Ann Arbor.
MnHi	Minnesota Historical Society, St. Paul
MnU	University of Minnesota, Minneapolis.
Mo	Missouri State Library, Jefferson City.
MoKN	Nazarene Theological Seminary, Kansas City, Mo.
MoS	St. Louis Public Library, St. Louis.
MoSCEx	Christ Seminary--Seminex, St. Louis.
MoSpA	Assemblies of God Theological Seminary, Springfield, Mo.

MoSpCB	Central Bible College, Springfield, Mo.
MoStcL	Lindenwood College, St. Charles, Mo.
MoSW	Washington University, St. Louis.
MsCliM	Mississippi College, Clinton.
MSohG	Gordon-Conwell Theological Seminary, South Hamilton, Ma.
N	New York State Library, Albany.
NBC	Brooklyn College, Brooklyn.
NBiSU	State University of New York at Binghamton, Binghamton.
NbOU	University of Nebraska at Omaha, Omaha.
NcD	Duke University, Durham, N.C.
NcU	University of North Carolina, Chapel Hill.
NFredU	State University of New York, College at Fredonia, Fredonia.
NIC	Cornell University, Ithaca, N.Y.
NjMD	Drew University, Madison, N.J.
NjNbS	New Brunswick Theological Seminary, New Brunswick, N.J.
NjPT	Princeton Theological Seminary, Princeton, N.J.
NjR	Rutgers University, New Brunswick, N.J.
NjTS	Trenton State College, Trenton, N.J.
NN	New York Public Library, New York.
NNC	Columbia University, New York.
NNerC	College of New Rochelle, New Rochelle, N.Y.
NNR	City College of the City University of New York, New York.
NNUT	Union Theological Seminary, New York.
NRCR	Colgate Rochester Divinity School, Rochester, N.Y.
NRU	University of Rochester, Rochester, N.Y.
NSyU	Syracuse University, Syracuse, N.Y.
OBgU	Bowling Green State University, Bowling Green, Oh.
OC	Public Library of Cincinnati and Hamilton County, Cincinnati.
OCB	Cincinnati Bible Seminary, Cincinnati.
OCedC	Cedarville College, Cedarville, Oh.
OCl	Cleveland Public Library, Cleveland.
OClU	Cleveland State University, Cleveland.
OClW	Western Reserve University, Cleveland.
OCU	University of Cincinnati, Cincinnati.
ODa	Dayton and Montgomery County Public Library, Dayton, Oh.
ODaTS	United Theological Seminary, Dayton, Oh.
ODaU	University of Dayton, Dayton, Oh.
ODaWU	Wright State University, Dayton, Oh.
Ok	Oklahoma Department of Libraries, Oklahoma City.
OkBetC	Bethany Nazarene College, Bethany, Ok.
OkEdT	Central State University, Edmond, Ok.
OkEG	Phillips University, Enid, Ok. Graduate Seminary.
OKentU	Kent State University, Kent, Oh.
OkT	Tulsa City-County Library System, Tulsa.

OkTOR	Oral Roberts University, Tulsa.
OkU	University of Oklahoma, Norman.
OMtvN	Mount Vernon Nazarene College, Mount Vernon, Oh.
ONcM	Muskingum College, New Concord, Oh.
OO	Oberlin College, Oberlin, Oh.
OrU	University of Oregon, Eugene.
OSW	Wittenberg University, Springfield, Oh.
OU	Ohio State University, Columbus.
OWibfC	Central State University, Wilberforce, Oh.
OWibfU	Wilberforce University, Wilberforce, Oh.
PBfG	Geneva College, Beaver Falls, Pa.
PGC	Gettysburg College, Gettysburg, Pa.
PP	Free Library of Philadlephia, Philadelphia.
PPiPT	Pittsburgh Theological Seminary, Pittsburgh.
PPiU	University of Pittsburgh, Pittsburgh.
PPT	Temple University, Philadelphia.
PU	University of Pennsylvania, Philadelphia.
RPB	Brown University, Providence, R.I.
ScCoB	Columbia Bible College, Columbia, S.C.
ScU	University of South Carolina, Columbia.
SdSifB	North American Baptist Seminary, Sioux Falls, S.D.
TCleL	Lee College, Cleveland, Tn.
TM	Memphis and Shelby County Public Library and Information Center, Memphis, Tn.
TMM	Memphis State University, Memphis, Tn.
TNF	Fisk University, Nashville, Tn.
TNJ	Joint University Libraries, Nashville, Tn.
TNJ-R	Joint University Libraries, Nashville, Tn. School of Religion.
TNL	David Lipscomb College, Nashville, Tn.
TNTN	Trevecca Nazarene College, Nashville, Tn.
TxDa	Dallas Public Library, Dallas.
TxDaM	Southern Methodist University, Dallas.
TxDaTS	Dallas Theological Seminary, Dallas.
TxFS	Southwestern Baptist Theological Seminary, Fort Worth.
TxLT	Texas Tech University, Lubbock.
TxShA	Austin College, Sherman, Tx.
TxU	University of Texas, Austin.
TxU-Da	University of Texas at Dallas, Richardson.
TxU-L	University of Texas, Austin. Law Library.
TxWaS	Southwestern Assemblies of God College, Waxahachie, Tx.
TxWB	Baylor University, Waco, Tx.
Uk	British Library, London.
UkBU	Birmingham University, Birmingham.
UU	University of Utah, Salt Lake City.
ViFGM	George Mason University, Fairfax, Va.
ViPetS	Virginia State University, Petersburg.
ViRCU	Virginia Commonwealth University, Richmond.
ViRUT	Union Theological Seminary, Richmond, Va.

ViRVU	Virginia Union University, Richmond.
ViU	University of Virginia, Charlottesville.
Wa	Washington State Library, Olympia.
WaS	Seattle Public Library, Seattle.
WaU	University of Washington, Seattle.
WHi	State Historical Society of Wisconsin, Madison.
WU	University of Wisconsin, Madison.

PLACES

Al.	Alabama	Mn.	Minnesota
Ar.	Arkansas	Mo.	Missouri
Az.	Arizona	Ms.	Mississippi
Ca.	California	N.C.	North Carolina
Co.	Colorado	Ne.	Nebraska
Ct.	Connecticut	N.J.	New Jersey
D.C.	District of Columbia	N.Y.	New York
De.	Delaware	Oh.	Ohio
Fl.	Florida	Ok.	Oklahoma
Ga.	Georgia	Ont.	Ontario
Ia.	Iowa	Or.	Oregon
Il.	Illinois	Pa.	Pennsylvania
In.	Indiana	R.I.	Rhode Island
I.T.	Indian Territory	S.C.	South Carolina
Ks.	Kansas	Tn.	Tennessee
Ky.	Kentucky	Tvl.	Transvaal
La.	Louisiana	Tx.	Texas
Lanarks.	Lanarkshire	Va.	Virginia
Ma.	Massachusetts	Wa.	Washington
Man.	Manitoba	W.I.	West Indies
Md.	Maryland	Wi.	Wisconsin
Mi.	Michigan	W.Va.	West Virginia
Middx.	Middlesex		

PART I. BLACK HOLINESS

In the black context, holiness has taken on a wide range of connotations. For Wesleyan perfectionist believers, it implies commitment to the doctrine and experience of entire sanctification or perfect love. For a much larger group (including Wesleyans), the holiness label often is used to indicate church-sanctioned ethical, behavioral, and dress standards which separate Holy Spirit-centered believers from those in other Christian traditions. Holiness also singles out those who in decades past were called "Holy Rollers." Exuberant worship and stress on faith healing are frequent characteristics. Materials are listed here without reference to the race or denominational affiliation of the author. Works placed here purport to speak for or about movements subsumed by the term "black holiness."

01 Armbruster, Robert J.
   What about a black Pentecost? [By] Robert Armbruster. In National Courier, 2 (Aug. 5, 1977), 3, 22. Interview with James S. Tinney.

02 Bland, Edward
   The black church in conflict, [by] Edward Bland, Jr. New York, 197-. 156 1.

03 Franklin, Robert Michael
   The black male exodus from the church: a diagnostic study, [by] Robert M. Franklin. Cambridge, Ma., 19--. 35 1. Student paper--Harvard Divinity School.

04 Garlington, Paul L.
   Integration is possible in the renewal, [by] Paul L. Garlington. In Logos Journal, 10 (May/June 1980), 22-23.

05 Hollenweger, Walter Jacob, 1927-
   Christen ohne Schriften: Fünf Fallstudien zur Sozialethik mundlicher Religion, [von] Walter J. Hollenweger. Erlanger, Verlag der Ev.-Luth. Mission, c1977. 144 p. (Erlanger Taschenbücher, 35) Translation of Pentecost between black and white. MiBsA

1

06 Hollenweger, Walter Jacob, 1927–
        Pentecost between black and white: five case studies on
    Pentecost and politics, [by] Walter J. Hollenweger. Belfast,
    Christian Journals Ltd., 1974. 143 p. DLC, KyWAT, MCE

07 Hollenweger, Walter Jacob, 1927–
        Pentecostalism and the third world, [by] Walter J. Hollen-
    weger. In Dialog, 9 (Spring 1970), 122–129.

08 Homrighausen, Elmer George, 1900–
        Pentecostalism in the third world, [by] E. G. Homrighausen.
    In Theology Today, 26 (Jan. 1970), 446–448.

09 Tinney, James Steven, 1942–
        Black Pentecostals: the difference is more than color, [by]
    James S. Tinney. In Logos Journal, 10 (1980), 16–19.

10 Tinney, James Steven, 1942–
        The blackness of Pentecostalism, [by] James S. Tinney. In
    Spirit, 3:2 (1979), 27–36.

11 Tinney, James Steven, 1942–
        Pentecostalism in three worlds, [by] James S. Tinney.
    [Washington, 197–]. 38 l.

12 Tinney, James Steven, 1942–
        Pentecostals celebrate their world flame, [by] James S. Tin-
    ney. In Christianity Today, 15 (Dec. 4, 1970), 36.

13 Tinney, James Steven, 1942–
        Prospects of black Pentecostalism: an emerging third world
    religion, [by] James S. Tinney. In Jones, D. J., ed. The
    black church: a community resource. Washington, c1977, 134–
    156. IU

14 Van Dusen, Henry Pitney, 1897–1975.
        The challenge of the "sects." In Christianity and Crisis, 18
    (July 21, 1958), 103–106. Excerpts from The third force in
    Christendom.

15 Van Dusen, Henry Pitney, 1897–1975.
        The third force in Christendom. In Life, 44 (June 9, 1958),
    113–122, 124.

16 Wilmore, Gayraud Stephen, 1921–
        Black religion and black radicalism, [by] Gayraud S. Wilmore.
    Garden City, N.Y., Doubleday, 1972. xiii, 344 p. (C. Eric
    Lincoln series on black religion) On Pentecostal churches: p.
    210–215. DLC

--BIBLIOGRAPHY

17 Harrison, Ira Enell
     A selected annotated bibliography on store-front churches,
     and other religious writings, [by] Ira E. Harrison. Syracuse,
     Syracuse University, Youth Development Center, 1962. 29 l.
     NFredU

18 Hollenweger, Walter Jacob, 1927-
     Handbuch der Pfingstbewegung, [von] Walter J. Hollenweger.
     Zürich, 1966. 3 v. in 10. Inaug.-Diss.--Zürich. Microfilm
     (positive). 3 reels. 35 mm. Reproduced for the American
     Theological Library Association Microtext Project by Department
     of Photoduplication, University of Chicago, 1968. IEG, MH-AH,
     NjMD

19 Tinney, James Steven, 1942-
     Black Pentecostalism: an annotated bibliography, [by] James
     S. Tinney. In Spirit, 3:1 (1979), 1-64.   *

--BIOGRAPHY

20 Jones, Pearl (Williams)
     A minority report: black Pentecostal women. In Spirit, 1:2
     (1977), 31-44.

21 White, Joyce
     Women in the ministry, [by] Joyce White. In Essence, 7
     (Nov. 1976), 62-63, 104, 107, 109.

--FICTIONAL LITERATURE

22 Baldwin, James, 1924-
     Gá och förkunna det på bergen. Stockholm, Wahlström &
     Widstrand, 1955. 252 p. Translation of Go tell it on the moun-
     tain. TxU

23 Baldwin, James, 1924-
     Go tell it on the mountain. New York, Knopf, 1953. 303 p.
     DLC, InU

24 Baldwin, James, 1924-
     Go tell it on the mountain. London, Michael Joseph, 1954.
     256 p. OWibfU, Uk

25 Baldwin, James, 1924-
     Go tell it on the mountain. With commentary, notes and ex-
     ercises by E. N. Obiechina. London, Longmans, 1966. 310 p.
     (Heritage of literature series, sec. B, no. 90) ICarbS, Uk

26   Mais, Roger, 1905-1955.
     Brother man, [by] Roger Mais. With drawings by the au-
     thor. London, Cape, 1954. 191 p. DLC, InU, NRU

27   Mais, Roger, 1905-1955.
     Brother man, [by] Roger Mais. Introduction by Edward
     Brathwaite, with drawings by the author. London, Neinemann,
     1974. xxii, 191 p. (Caribbean writers series, 10) CtWeharU,
     DLC

28   Mais, Roger, 1905-1955.
     The hills were joyful together, [by] Roger Mais. London,
     Cape, 1953. 288 p. ScU

29   Mais, Roger, 1905-1955.
     The hills were joyful together, [by] Roger Mais. Introduc-
     tion by Daphne Morris. London, Heinemann, 1981. xxii, 288 p.
     (Caribbean writers series, 23) DLC

30   Mais, Roger, 1905-1955.
     Las montanas jubilosas, [por] Roger Mais. Traducción Ester
     Muniz. La Habana, Casa de las Americas, 1978. xvi, 392 p.
     (Colección Literatura latinoamericana) Translation of The hills
     were joyful together. OkU

31   Mais, Roger, 1905-1955.
     Sie nannten ihn Bruder Mensch, [von] Roger Mais. Uber-
     setzung aus dem Englischen und Nachwort von Janheinz Jahn.
     Freiburg, Basel, Wein, Herder, 1967. 222 p. Translation of
     Brother man. MdBE

32   Williams, Chancellor, 1905-
     Have you been to the river? A novel. New York, Exposition
     Press, 1952. 256 p. AU, DLC, InU, IU, NcD, NjR, ViU, WaU

          --HISTORY

33   Anderson, Robert Mapes, 1929-
     A social history of the early twentieth century Pentecostal
     movement. New York, 1969. 368 l. Thesis (Ph.D.)--Columbia
     University. NNC

34   Brumback, Carl, 1917-
     A sound from heaven. Springfield, Mo., Gospel Publishing
     House, c1977. iii, 153 p. First published in 1961 as the pro-
     logue and part one of the author's Suddenly from heaven. DLC

35   Clark, Max A. X.
     Latter rain and holy fire: the beginnings of the Pentecostal
     movement, by Max A. X. Clark. n.p., 19--. 47 p.

36 Fidler, R. L.
      Pentecostal history lends important role to blacks, [by]
      R. L. Fidler. In International Outlook (4th quarter, 1971)

37 Hollenweger, Walter Jacob, 1927-
      Enthusiastisches Christentum. Die Pfingstbewegung in
      Geschichte und Gegenwart. [Von] Walter J. Hollenweger.
      Wuppertal, Theologischer Verlag Brockhaus; Zürich, Zwingli-
      Verlag, 1969. xxiii, 640 p. DLC, MCE

38 Hollenweger, Walter Jacob, 1927-
      El Pentecostalismo: historia y doctrinas, [por] Walter J.
      Hollenweger. Buenos Aires, La Aurora, 1976. 530 p. (Bib-
      lioteca de estudios teológicos) Translation of Enthusiastisches
      Christentum.

39 Hollenweger, Walter Jacob, 1927-
      The Pentecostals, [by] W. J. Hollenweger. London, S. C. M.
      Press, 1972. xx, 572 p. "First British edition." Translation
      of Enthusiastisches Christentum. DLC, MH-AH, MSohG

40 Hollenweger, Walter Jacob, 1927-
      The Pentecostals: the charismatic movement in the churches,
      [by] W. J. Hollenweger. Minneapolis, Augsburg Publishing
      House, 1972. xx, 572 p. "First United States edition."
      Translation of Enthusiastisches Christentum. DLC, MH-AH,
      TxWaS

41 Kendrick, Klaude, 1917-
      The history of the modern Pentecostal movement. Austin,
      1959. 388 l. Thesis (Ph.D.)--University of Texas. TxU

42 Kendrick, Klaude, 1917-
      The promise fulfilled; a history of the modern Pentecostal
      movement. Springfield, Mo., Gospel Publishing House, 1961.
      viii, 237 p. Based on thesis (Ph.D.)--University of Texas,
      1959. DLC, MSohG, TxDaTS, TxWaS

43 Kenyon, Howard Nelson, 1955-
      An analysis of racial separation within the early Pentecostal
      movement. Waco, Tx., 1978. ix, 163 l. Thesis (M.A.)--
      Baylor University. TxWB

44 Lovett, Leonard, 1939-
      Black origins of the Pentecostal movement. In Synan, H. V.,
      ed. Aspects of Pentecostal-charismatic origins. Plainfield,
      N.J., 1975, 123-141.

45 Lovett, Leonard, 1939-
      Perspective on the black origins of the contemporary Pente-
      costal movement. In Journal of the Interdenominational Theo-
      logical Center, 1 (Fall 1973), 36-49.

46   Nichol, John Thomas, 1928-
       Pentecostalism. New York, Harper & Row, 1966. xvi, 264 p.
     Based on thesis (Ph.D.)--Boston University. DLC, MCE, MH,
     MSohG

47   Nichol, John Thomas, 1928-
       Pentecostalism. Plainfield, N.J., Logos International, 1971,
     c1966. xvi, 264 p. Cover title: The Pentecostals. Reprint
     of 1966 ed. Based on thesis (Ph.D.)--Boston University.

48   Nichol, John Thomas, 1928-
       Pentecostalism; a descriptive history of the origin, growth,
     and message of a twentieth century religious movement. Boston,
     1965. 526 l. Thesis (Ph.D.)--Boston University. MBU

49   Tinney, James Steven, 1942-
       Black origins of the Pentecostal movement, [by] James S.
     Tinney. In Christianity Today, 16 (Oct. 8, 1971), 4-6.

                --HISTORY AND STUDY OF DOCTRINES

50   Beckmann, David Milton, 1948-
       Trance: from Africa to Pentecostalism, [by] David M. Beck-
     mann. In CTM, 45 (Jan. 1974), 11-26.

51   Daughtry, Herbert Daniel, 1931-
       A theology of black liberation from a Pentecostal perspective,
     [by] Herbert Daughtry. In Spirit, 3:2 (1979), 6-14.

52   Faison, Thurman Lawrence, 1938-
       The effects of Christian television, [by] Thurman L. Faison.
     Evanston, Il., 1981. 48 l. Thesis (M.S.)--National College of
     Education. IEE

53   Forbes, James Alexander, 1935-
       A Pentecostal approach to empowerment for black liberation,
     [by] James A. Forbes, Jr. Rochester, N.Y., 1975. [139] l.
     Thesis (D.Min.)--Colgate Rochester Divinity School. NRCR

54   Forbes, James Alexander, 1935-
       Shall we call this dream progressive Pentecostalism? [By]
     James A. Forbes, Jr. In Spirit, 1:1 (1977), 12-15.

54a Gerloff, Roswith Ingeborg Hildegard, 1933-
       Theory and practice of the Holy Spirit, [by] Roswith Gerloff.
     In Quaker Religious Thought, 16 (Summer 1975), 2-17.

55   Goodwin, Bennie Eugene, 1933-
       Social implications of Pentecostal power, [by] Bennie Goodwin.
     In Spirit, 1:1 (1977), 31-35.

56 Haskins, James, 1941-
    Witchcraft, mysticism, and magic in the black world, [by]
    James Haskins. Garden City, N.Y., Doubleday, 1974. 156 p.
    DLC

57 Haskins, James, 1941-
    Witchcraft, mysticism and magic in the black world, [by]
    James Haskins. New York, Dell, 1976, c1974. 143 p. (Laurel-
    leaf library) NNerC

58 Hollenweger, Walter Jacob, 1927-
    Black Pentecostal concept: interpretations and variations,
    [by] Walter J. Hollenweger. Genèva, World Council of
    Churches, 1970. 70 p. (Concept, 30) Cover title. GAUC

59 Hollenweger, Walter Jacob, 1927-
    Creator spiritus: the challenge of Pentecostal experience
    and Pentecostal theology, [by] W. J. Hollenweger. In Theology,
    81 (Jan. 1978), 32-40.

60 Lewis, Ioan Myrddin, 1930-
    Ecstatic religion: an anthropological study of spirit posses-
    sion and shamanism, [by] I. M. Lewis. Harmondsworth,
    Middx., Penguin Books, 1971. 221 p. OkEG

61 Lovett, Leonard, 1939-
    Conditional liberation: an emergent Pentecostal perspective,
    [by] Leonard Lovett. In Spirit, 1:2 (1977), 24-30.

62 Palmer, Gary Bradford, 1942-
    Trance and dissociation: a cross-cultural study in psycho-
    physiology, [by] Gary Palmer. Minneapolis, 1966. v, 158 l.
    Paper (M.S.)--University of Minnesota.

63 Saunders, Monroe Randolph, 1948-
    Perspectives on the philosophy of Christian education in
    Pentecostalism: the Assemblies of God [and] the Pentecostal
    Assemblies of the World, [by] Monroe R. Saunders, Jr. Wash-
    ington, 1975. v, 74 l. Thesis (M.A.)--Howard University.
    DHU

64 Saunders, Monroe Randolph, 192 -
    Some historical Pentecostal perspectives for a contemporary
    developmental Pentecost, [by] Monroe R. Saunders, Sr. Wash-
    ington, 1974. 146 l. Thesis (D.Min.)--Howard University.
    DHU

65 Tinney, James Steven, 1942-
    Competing strains of hidden and manifest theologies in black
    Pentecostalism, [by] James S. Tinney. [Washington], 1980.
    20 [8] l.

66 Tinney, James Steven, 1942-
      Doctrinal differences between black and white Pentecostals,
      [by] James S. Tinney. In Spirit, 1:1 (1977), 36-45.

67 Tinney, James Steven, 1942-
      Exclusivist tendencies in Pentecostal self-definition: a cri-
      tique from black theology, [by] James S. Tinney. In Journal
      of Religious Thought, 36 (Spring/Summer 1979), 32-39.

68 Tinney, James Steven, 1942-
      A theoretical and historical comparison of black political and
      religious movements, [by] James S. Tinney. Washington, 1978.
      vii, 312 l. Thesis (Ph.D.)--Howard University. DHU

69 Williams, Emanuel L.
      Black Pentecostalism: a doctrine of empowerment, [by]
      Emanuel L. Williams. Atlanta, 1984. [iii], 127 l. Thesis
      (M.Div.)--Emory University. GEU-T

      --MISSIONS

70 Pomerville, Paul Anthony, 1937-
      An audience profile model of the third world for the develop-
      ment of an intercultural curriculum; [by] Paul A. Pomerville.
      Springfield, Mo., 1976. 226 l. Thesis (M.A.)--Assemblies of
      God Graduate School. MoSpA

71 Pomerville, Paul Anthony, 1937-
      Pentecostalism and missions: distortion or correction?
      Pasadena, Ca., 1982. viii, 381 l. Thesis (Ph.D.)--Fuller
      Theological Seminary. CPFT

      --MUSIC

72 Heilbut, Anthony Otto, 1941-
      The gospel sound: good news and bad times, [by] Tony
      Heilbut. New York, Simon and Schuster, 1971. 350 p. "The
      holiness church": p. 199-278. DLC, Ok

73 Heilbut, Anthony Otto, 1941-
      The gospel sound: good news and bad times, [by] Tony
      Heilbut. Garden City, N.Y., Anchor Press/Doubleday, 1975,
      c1971. xxxv, 364 p. (Anchor books) "The holiness church":
      p. 171-251.

74 Hollenweger, Walter Jacob, 1927-
      Spirituals, [by] W. J. Hollenweger. In Davies, J. G., ed.
      A dictionary of liturgy and worship. New York, 1972, 349-350.

75 Jones, Pearl (Williams)
      The musical quality of black religious folk ritual. In Spirit ,
    1:1 (1977), 21-30.

76 Marks, Morton, 1918-
      Uncovering ritual structures in Afro-American music. In
    Zaretsky, I. I., ed. Religious movements in contemporary
    America. Princeton, N.J., c1974, 60-134.

77 Singer swings same songs in church and night club.
      In Life, 7 (Aug. 28, 1939), 37.

78 Szwed, John F., 1936-
      Negro music: urban renewal, [by] John F. Szwed. In
    Coffin, T. P., ed. Our living traditions; an introduction to
    American folklore. New York, 1968, 272-282. TMM

79 Tinney, James Stephen
      Singing from the soul: our Afro-American heritage, [by]
    James S. Tinney. In Christianity Today, 23 (May 4, 1979),
    16-19.

80 Whalum, Wendell
      The folk stream. In Smyth, M. M., ed. The black American
    reference book. Englewood Cliffs, N.J., c1976, 791-808. "Gos-
    pel music": p. 805-808.

            --PERIODICALS

81 Gospelrama news. 1- 1980-
      Washington. LNT

82 Lifted banner. 1- 19 -
      Omaha.

83 Prayer tower. 1- 19 -
      New Orleans.

84 Spirit. 1-3, no. 2, 1977-1979.
      Washington. DLC

            --SERMONS, TRACTS, ADDRESSES, ESSAYS

85 Bhengu, Nicholas Bhekinkosi Hepworth, 1909-
      Christ is the only answer, [by] Nicholas Bhengu. In Pente-
    costal World Conference, 5th, Toronto, 1958. Pentecostal World
    Conference messages. Toronto, c1958, 89-96.

86 Blake, Junious A.
      The undying flame of Pentecost, [by] J. A. Blake. In

World Pentecost, 2:1 (1972), 8-9, 11. Sermon delivered at the
ninth Pentecostal World Conference in Dallas.

87 Forbes, James Alexander, 1935-
    How to be black and a Christian too, [by] James A. Forbes.
    In Warren, M. A. Black preaching: truth and soul. Washing-
    ton, c1977, 79-96.

88 Goodwin, Bennie Eugene, 1933-
    Beside still waters, [by] Bennie Goodwin. Jersey City,
    N.J., Goodpatrick Publishers, 1973.

89 Heroo, Leonard W.
    The religion of form and the religion of force, [by] Leonard
    Heroo. In Pentecostal World Conference, 5th, Toronto, 1958.
    Pentecostal World Conference messages. Toronto, c1958, 37-42.

90 Jones, Ozro Thruston, 1890-1972.
    Our Pentecostal opportunity in this hour of religious crisis,
    [by] Ozro T. Jones. In Pentecostal World Conference, 5th,
    Toronto, 1958. Pentecostal World Conference messages. Tor-
    onto, c1958, 149-160.

91 Williams, Lawrence
    First century Pentecost, [by] Lawrence Williams. In Pente-
    costal World Conference, 6th, Jerusalem, 1961. Addresses.
    Toronto, c1961, 45-50. OkTOR

        --STATISTICS

91a Barrett, David B.
    World Christian encyclopedia: a comparative study of
    churches and religions in the modern world, AD 1900-2000.
    Edited by David B. Barrett. Nairobi, Oxford University
    Press, 1982. xii, 1010 p. DLC, Uk

        --WORSHIP

92 Boggs, Beverly J.
    Some aspects of worship in a Holiness church, [by] Beverly
    Boggs. In New York Folklore, 3 (Summer/Winter 1977), 29-44.

93 Jones, Pearl (Williams)
    The musical quality of black religious folk ritual. In Spirit,
    1:1 (1977), 21-30.

94 Tinney, James Steven, 1942-
    The blackness of Pentecostalism, by James S. Tinney. In
    Spirit, 3:2 (1979), 27-36. "Black rituals": p. 31-32.

95 Tinney, James Steven, 1942-
    The "miracle" of black preaching, [by] James S. Tinney.
    In Christianity Today, 20 (Jan. 30, 1976), 14-16.

    --AFRICA

96 Barrett, David B.
    African initiatives in religion: 21 studies from eastern and
    central Africa. David B. Barrett, editor. Nairobi, East Africa
    Publishing House, 1971. xviii, 288 p. Papers presented at the
    Workshop in Religious Research, 1967-1968, University College,
    Nairobi. DLC

97 Barrett, David B.
    Schism and renewal in Africa; an analysis of six thousand
    contemporary religious movements, [by] David B. Barrett.
    Nairobi, Oxford University Press, 1968. xx, 363 p. DLC

98 Barrett, Leonard Emanuel, 1920-
    African roots in Jamaican indigenous religion, [by] Leonard
    E. Barrett. In Journal of Religious Thought, 35 (Spring/
    Summer 1978), 7-26.

99 Beckmann, David Milton, 1948-
    Trance: from Africa to Pentecostalism, [by] David M.
    Beckmann. In CTM, 45 (Jan. 1974), 11-26.

100 Benz, Ernst, 1907-
    Messianische Kirchen, Sekten und Bewegungen im heutigen
    Afrika. Unter Mitarbeit von Ernst Dammann; Katesa Schlosser,
    O. F. Raum [u. a.] Hrsg. von Ernst Benz. Leiden, E. J.
    Brill, 1965. 127 p. DLC, OClW

101 Bhengu, Nicholas Bhekinkosi Hepworth, 1909-
    Evangelism in Africa, [by] Nicholas B. H. Bhengu. In
    World Congress on Evangelism, 1st, Berlin, 1966. One race,
    one gospel, one task; official reference volumes: papers and
    reports. Minneapolis, 1967, I, 178-181.

102 Hollenweger, Walter Jacob, 1927-
    The Pentecostals: the charismatic movement in the churches ,
    [by] W. J. Hollenweger. Minneapolis, Augsburg Publishing
    House, 1972. xx, 572 p. "First United States edition."
    Translation of Enthusiastisches Christentum. "uMoya: the
    Spirit in the independent African churches": p. 149-175.
    DLC, MH-AH, TxWaS

103 Jules-Rosette, Bennetta (Washington)
    Ceremonial trance behavior in an African church: private
    experience and public expression. In Journal for the Scien-
    tific Study of Religion, 19 (Mar. 1980), 1-16.

104   Jules-Rosette, Bennetta (Washington)
      The new religions of Africa. Bennetta Jules-Rosette, editor.
      Norwood, N.J., Ablex Publishing Corp., c1979. xxii, 248 p.
      (Modern sociology) DLC, OkEdT

105   Mitchell, Henry Heywood, 1919-
      Black belief: folk beliefs of blacks in America and West
      Africa, [by] Henry H. Mitchell. New York, Harper & Row,
      1975. xiii, 171 p. DLC

106   Oosthuizen, Gerhardus Cornelis, 1922-
      The misunderstanding of the Holy Spirit in the independent
      movements in Africa, [by] G. C. Oosthuizen. n.p., 196-.
      172-197 p. Cover title. "Reprinted from Christusprediking
      in de wereld." CtY-D

107   Rasmussen, Marie B.
      De Afrikanske HelligSandskirkers Teologi, [av] Marie B.
      Rasmussen. In Norsk Teologisk Tidsskrift, 40:2 (1977), 101-
      119.

108   Strøm, Erling
      Blant svarte og hvite i Afrika. Oslo, Filadelfiaforlaget,
      1952. 152 p. DLC

109   Walker, Sheila Suzanne
      Ceremonial spirit possession in Africa and Afro-America:
      forms, meanings, and functional significance for individuals
      and social groups, [by] Sheila S. Walker. Leiden, Brill, 1972,
      [1973]. xii, 179 p. (Dissertationes ad historiam religionum
      pertinentes, 4. Supplementa ad Numen, Altera series) DLC

110   Westgarth, J. W.
      The Holy Spirit and the primitive mind; a remarkable ac-
      count of a spiritual awakening in darkest Africa, [by] J. W.
      Westgarth. London, Victory Press, 1946. 64 p. Uk

111   Zaretsky, Irving I.
      Spirit possession and spirit medianship in Africa and Afro-
      America: an annotated bibliograhy, [by] Irving I. Zaretsky
      [and] Cynthia Shambaugh. New York, Garland Publishing,
      1978. xxii, 443 p. (Garland reference library of social sci-
      ence, 56) First ed. published in 1966 under title: Bibliogra-
      phy on spirit possession and spirit medianship. DLC

            -- --ETHIOPIA

112   Rayner, DeCourcy H.
      Persecution in Ethiopia, [by] DeCourcy H. Rayner. In
      Christianity Today, 17 (Nov. 10, 1972), 54-55.

-- --GHANA

113 Anquandah, James
Can the church be renewed? Experiences of an African in-
dependent church, [by] James Anquandah. In Ecumenical
Review, 31 (July 1979), 252-260.

114 Wyllie, Robert W.
Pioneers of Ghanian Pentecostalism: Peter Anim and James
McKeown, [by] Robert W. Wyllie. In Journal of Religion in
Africa, 6:2 (1974), 109-122.

-- --KENYA

115 Charsley, S. R.
Dreams in an independent African church, [by] S. R.
Charsley. In Africa, 43 (July 1971), 244-257.

116 Raatikainen, Alma, 1916-
Itkevä musta kukka. Pohjois-Kenian karua arkipäivää.
Tikkurila, Ristin Voitto, c1972. 219 p. DLC, NNUT

117 Welbourn, Frederick Burkewood, 1912-
A place to feel at home: a study of two independent
churches in western Kenya, [by] F. B. Welbourn [and] B. A.
Ogot. London, Nairobi, Oxford University Press, 1966. xv,
157 p. DLC

-- --NIGERIA

118 Mbagwu, John R.
A living testimony, [by] John R. Mbagwu. Dayton, Oh.,
c1978. 98 p. DLC

119 Turner, Harold Walter, 1911-
History of an African independent church, [by] H. W. Turner. Oxford, Clarendon Press, 1967. 2 v. DLC

120 Turner, Harold Walter, 1911-
Profile through preaching; a study of the sermon texts
used in a West African independent church, [by] Harold W.
Turner. London, Published for the World Council of Churches,
Commission on World Mission and Evangelism by Edinburgh
House Press, 1965. 86 p. (C.W.M.E. research pamphlets,
13) On label: Distributed by Friendship Press, New York,
N.Y. DLC

-- --SOUTH AFRICA

121 Kiernan, J. P.
Old wine in new wineskins: a critical appreciation of Sund-
kler's leadership types in the light of further research, [by]
J. P. Kiernan. In African Studies, 34:3 (1975), 193-201.

122 Kiernan, J. P.
       Where Zionists draw the line: a study of religious exclusive-
     ness in an African township, [by] J. P. Kiernan. In African
     Studies, 33:2 (1974), 79-90.

123 Martin, Marie-Louise, 1912-
       The Biblical concept of Messianism and Messianism in South-
     ern Africa, [by] Marie-Louise Martin. Morija, Morija Sesuto
     Book Depot, 1964. 207 p. A revision and expansion of the
     author's thesis (D.D.)--University of South Africa. CLU,
     CtY-D, ICU, IEG, IEN, InU, MH-AH, NcD, NjPT, PPiPT

124 Sundkler, Bengt Gustaf Malcolm, 1909-
       Bantu prophets in South Africa. 2d ed. New York, Pub-
     lished for the International African Institute by the Oxford
     University Press, c1981. 381 p.

       (Cape Province, East London)

125 Dubb, Allie A.
       Community of the saved: an African revivalist church in
     the East Cape, [by] Allie A. Dubb. Johannesburg, Witwaters-
     rand University Press for African Studies Institute, 1976.
     xvii, 175 p. DLC, MH-AH

126 Moennich, Martha
       God at work in South Africa. In Evangelical Christian, 54
     (Aug. 1958), 368.

       (Transvaal Province)

127 Tyler, Philip
       Pattern of Christian belief in Sekhukuniland. In Church
     Quarterly Review, 167 (Apr./June 1966), 225-236; 167 (July/
     Sept. 1966), 335-347. On Pentecostal churches: p. 338-346.

         -- --SWAZILAND

128 Sundkler, Bengt Gustaf Malcolm, 1909-
       Zulu Zion and some Swazi Zionists, [by] Bengt Sundkler.
     London, New York, Oxford University Press, 1976. 337 p.
     (Oxford studies in African affairs) DLC, KyWAT, MH-AH

         -- --TANZANIA

129 Lutahoire, Sebastian K.
       An analysis of revival group meetings in East Africa, with
     particular emphasis on the West Lake Region, Tanzania, [by]
     Sebastian K. Lutahoire. In Africa Theological Journal, 7:2
     (1978), 34-52.

-- --ZAIRE

130 Andersson, Efraim
     Messianic popular movements in the Lower Congo. Uppsala,
     Almqvist & Wiksells boktr., 1958. xiii, 287 p. (Studia ethno-
     graphica Upsaliensia, 14) CLU, CtY-D, FU, MH, MiU, MnU,
     N, NIC, NjPT, NN, OClW, OCU, TxDaM

131 Bena-Silu.
     The message of expectation from indigenous Christian move-
     ments: a reaction by Bena-Silu. In International Review of
     Mission, 66 (Jan. 1977), 71-74; discussion, 66 (Jan. 1977),
     75-80.

132 Janzen, John Marvin, 1937-
     An anthology of Kongo religion: primary texts from lower
     Zaire, [by] John M. Janzen [and] Wyatt MacGaffey. Lawrence,
     University of Kansas, 1974. 163 p. (University of Kansas
     publications in anthropology, 5) DLC

133 Janzen, John Marvin, 1937-
     Deep thought structure and intention in Kongo prophetism,
     1910-1921, [by] John M. Janzen. In Social Research, 46
     (Spring 1979), 106-139.

134 MacGaffey, Wyatt, 1932-
     Modern Kongo prophets: religion in a plural society, [by]
     Wyatt MacGaffey. Bloomington, Indiana University Press,
     c1983. xiii, 285 p. DLC

135 Raymaekers, Paul
     L'administration et le sacré: discours religieux et parcours
     politiques en Afrique centrale (1921-1957), [par] Paul Ray-
     maekers [et] Henri Desroche. Bruxelles, Académie royale des
     sciences d'outre-mer, 1983. 399 p. (Mémoires in-80. Acad-
     émie royale des sciences d'outremer, Classe des sciences mor-
     ales et politiques, nouv. sér., t. 47, fasc. 1)

136 Ryckmans, André
     Les mouvements prophétiques Konge en 1958: contribution
     à l'etude de l'étude de l'histoire du Congo. Kinshasa, Uni-
     versité Lovanium, Bureau d'organisation des programmes
     ruraux, 1970. 55 p. DeU

-- --ZIMBABWE

137 Daneel, M. L.
     Old and new in southern Shona independent churches, [by]
     M. L. Daneel. The Hague, Mouton, 1971-1974. 2 v.

138 Daneel, M. L.
     Zionism and faith-healing in Rhodesia; aspects of African

independent churches, [by] M. L. Daneel. Translated from
the Dutch by V. A. February. Afrika-Studiecentrum, Leiden.
's-Gravenhage, Mouton, 1970. 64 p., 8 p. of plates (Com-
munications, 2) DLC, MCE

--NORTH AND CENTRAL AMERICA

-- --BELIZE

139 Birdwell-Pheasant, Donna B.
     Cycles of power: social organization in a Belizean village,
[by] Donna B. Birdwell. Dallas, 1979. vii, 383 l. Thesis
(Ph.D.)--Southern Methodist University. TxDaM

140 Birdwell-Pheasant, Donna B.
     The power of Pentecostalism in a Belizean village, [by] Donna
Birdwell-Pheasant. In Glazier, S. D. Perspectives on Pente-
costalism: case studies from the Caribbean and Latin America.
Washington, c1980, 95-109.

-- --BERMUDA

141 Manning, Frank Edward, 1944-
     The rediscovery of religious play: a Pentecostal case, [by]
Frank E. Manning. In Lancy, D. F., ed. The anthropolical
study of play: problems and prospects. Cornwall, N.Y.,
197-, 23-30. DLC

142 Manning, Frank Edward, 1944-
     The rediscovery of religious play: a Pentecostal case, [by]
Frank E. Manning. In Lancy, D. F., ed. The study of play:
problems and prospects. West Point, N.Y., c1977, 151-158.
DLC, OkU

143 Manning, Frank Edward, 1944-
     The salvation of a drunk, [by] Frnk E. Manning. In Amer-
ican Ethnologist, 4 (Aug. 1977), 397-412.

-- --UNITED STATES

144 Alland, Alexander, 1931-
     "Possession" in a revivalistic Negro church. In Journal
for the Scientific Study of Religion, 1 (Spring 1962), 204-213;
abridged in Knudten, R. D., ed. The sociology of religion:
an anthology. New York, c1967, 83-92.

145 Anderson, Robert Mapes, 1929-
     A social history of the early twentieth century Pentecostal
movement. New York, 1969. 368 l. Thesis (Ph.D.)--Columbia
University. NNC

146 Anderson, Robert Mapes, 1929–
  Vision of the disinherited: the making of American Pente-
  costalism. New York, Oxford University Press, 1979. 334 p.
  Based on thesis (Ph.D.)--Columbia University, 1969. DLC,
  TxDaTS

147 Andrews, Sherry
  Black Pentecostals: who are they? [By] Sherry Andrews.
  In Charisma, 4 (Sept. 1978), 52–55.

148 Banks, William Love, 1928–
  The black church in the U.S.: its origin, growth, contrib-
  utions, and outlook, [by] William L. Banks. Chicago, Moody
  Press, 1972. 160 p. "The Apostolics": p. 55–58. DLC

149 Banks, William Love, 1928–
  The black church in the U.S.: its origin, growth, contributions, and outlook, [by] William L. Banks. Rev. ed.
  Shelbyville, Tn., Bible and Literature Missionary Foundation,
  1983, c1979. 160 p. "The Apostolics": p. 55–58.

150 Beckmann, David Milton, 1948–
  Trance: from Africa to Pentecostalism, [by] David M. Beckmann. In CTM, 45 (Jan. 1974), 11–26.

151 Bentley, William H.
  Bible believers in the black community, [by] William H.
  Bentley. In Wells, D. F., ed. The Evangelicals: what they
  believe, who they are, where they are changing. Nashville,
  c1975, 108–121. "Black Holiness and Pentecostals": p. 115–
  116.

152 Benz, Ernst, 1907–
  Der heilige Geist in Amerika. Düsseldorf, Köln. Diederichs,
  1970. 229 p. DLC

153 Clark, Elmer Talmage, 1886–1966.
  The small sects in America, [by] Elmer T. Clark. Nashville, Cokesbury Press, 1937. 311 p. "Negro sects": p.
  142–161. DLC, OkBetC

154 Clark, Elmer Talmage, 1886–1961.
  The small sects in America, [by] Elmer T. Clark. Rev. ed.
  New York, Abingdon-Cokesbury Press, 1949. 256 p. "Negro
  charismatic sects": p. 116–130. DLC, RPB

155 Copeland, Richard A.
  Black Pentecostalism: the influence of the black church
  on the Pentecostalism movement in America, [by] Richard A.
  Copeland. n.p., 198–. iii, 21 p. Cover title. ScCoB

156 Elinson, Howard
     The implications of Pentecostal religion for intellectualism,
     politics, and race relations. In American Journal of Sociology,
     70 (Jan. 1965), 403-415.

157 Fisher, Miles Mark, 1899-1970.
     Organized religion and the cults. In Crisis, 44 (Jan. 1937),
     8-10, 29-30.

158 Frazier, Edward Franklin, 1894-1962.
     The Negro church in America. New York, Schocken Books,
     1964, c1963. xii, 92 p. (Studies in sociology) On storefront
     churches: p. 53-67. DLC

159 Frazier, Edward Franklin, 1894-1962.
     The Negro church in America, [by] E. Franklin Frazier.
     Liverpool, Liverpool University Press, 1964. xii, 90 p.
     (Studies in sociology) On storefront churches: p. 53-67.
     Uk, ViPetS

160 Gerlach, Luther Paul, 1930-
     Pentecostalism: revolution or counter-revolution? [By]
     Luther P. Gerlach. In Zaretsky, I. I., ed. Religious move-
     ments in contemporary America. Princeton, N.J., c1974, 669-
     699. DLC

161 Gerlach, Luther Paul, 1930-
     People, power, change: movements of social transformation,
     [by] Luther P. Gerlach and Virginia H. Hine. Indianapolis,
     Bobbs-Merrill, 1970. xxiii, 257 p. DLC, MCE, MH

162 Harrell, David Edwin, 1930-
     All things are possible: the healing & charismatic revivals
     in modern America, [by] David Edwin Harrell, Jr. Blooming-
     ton, Indiana University Press, 1975. xi, 304 p. On black
     participation: p. 47, 66-67, 69, 155, 198, 213-214. DLC

163 Harrison, Ira Enell
     Diverse doubts, observations and conversations among store-
     front churches, [by] Ira E. Harrison. Syracuse, Syracuse
     University, Youth Development Center, 1962.

164 Harrison, Ira Enell
     Participant observations in store front churches, [by] Ira
     E. Harrison. Syracuse, Syracuse University, Youth Develop-
     ment Center, 1962

165 Harrison, Robert Emanuel, 1928-
     This is my country, [by] Bob Harrison. In Logos Journal,
     7 (May/June 1977), 60-62.

166 Hollenweger, Walter Jacob, 1927–
     Black Pentecostal concept: interpretations and variations,
     [by] Walter J. Hollenweger. Geneva, World Council of
     Churches, 1970. 70 p. (Concept, 30) Cover title. GAUC

167 Hollenweger, Walter Jacob, 1927–
     Pentecost between black and white: five case studies on
     Pentecost and politics, [by] Walter J. Hollenweger. Belfast,
     Christian Journals Ltd., 1974. 143 p. "A kite flies against
     the wind": p. 13-32, 119-121. DLC, KyWAT, MCE

168 Hollenweger, Walter Jacob, 1927–
     Pentecostalism and black power, [by] Walter J. Hollenweger.
     In Theology Today, 30 (Oct. 1973), 228-238.

169 Hurd, Joseph Kindall, 1938–
     Religious experience and trance phenomenon in Negro
     Pentecostal churches, [by] Joseph Kindall Hurd, Jr. Cam-
     bridge, Ma., 1960. Thesis (B.A.)--Harvard University.

170 In U.S., Pentecostal church leading in new membership.
     In Jet, 64 (July 18, 1983), 38.

171 Johnson, Guy Benton, 1928–
     Do holiness sects socialize in dominant values? [By] Benton
     Johnson. In Social Forces, 39 (May 1961), 309-316.

172 Jones, Lawrence Neale, 1921–
     The black Pentecostals. In Hamilton, M. P., ed. The
     charismatic movement. Grand Rapids, Mi., 1975, 145-158.

173 Jones, Raymond Julius, 1910–
     A comparative study of religious cult behavior among Ne-
     groes, with special reference to emotional group conditioning
     factors. Washington, Published by the Graduate School for the
     Division of Social Sciences, Howard University, 1939. v, 125
     p. (Howard University studies in the social sciences, vol. 2,
     no. 2) Cover title. Thesis (M.A.)--Howard University, 1939.
     DHU, DLC, OrU, ScU

174 Kendrick, Klaude, 1917–
     The history of the modern Pentecostal movement. Austin,
     1959. 388 l. Thesis (Ph.D.)--University of Texas. TxU

175 Kendrick, Klause, 1917–
     The promise fulfilled; a history of the modern Pentecostal
     movement. Springfield, Mo., Gospel Publishing house, 1961.
     viii, 237 p. Based on thesis (Ph.D.)--University of Texas,
     1959. DLC, MSohG, TxDaTS, TxWaS

176 Kenyon, Howard Nelson, 1955–
     An analysis of racial separation within the early Pentecostal

movement. Waco, Tx., 1978. ix, 163 l. Thesis (M.A.)--
Baylor University. TxWB

177 Lewis, Elsie Freeman
    Storefront Pentecostal church: an exploratory study of the
    influence of a storefront church on its members. Washington,
    1972. Thesis (M.A.)--Howard University. DHU

178 Lincoln, Charles Eric, 1924-
    The black experience in religion. Edited by C. Eric Lin-
    coln: Garden City, N.Y., Anchor Press, 1974. xii, 369 p.
    (C. Eric Lincoln series on black religion) "Black cults and
    sects: alternatives to tradition": p. 195-236. DLC

179 Lovett, Leonard, 1939-
    Black holiness-Pentecostalism: implications for ethics and
    social transformation. Atlanta, 1978. 3, viii, 183 l. Thesis
    (Ph.D.)--Emory University. GEU

180 Lovett, Leonard, 1939-
    Conditional liberation: an emergent Pentecostal perspective,
    [by] Leonard Lovett. In Spirit, 1:2 (1977), 24-30.

181 Martin, Robert Francis
    The early years of American Pentecostalism, 1900-1940.
    Chapel Hill, 1975. 238 l. Thesis (Ph.D.)--University of North
    Carolina. NcU

182 Mitchell, Henry Heywood, 1919-
    Black belief: folk beliefs of blacks in America and West
    Africa, [by] Henry H. Mitchell. New York, Harper & Row,
    1975. xiii, 171 p. DLC

183 Mitchell, Henry Heywood, 1919-
    Black preaching, [by] Henry H. Mitchell. Philadelphia,
    Lippincott, 1970. 248 p. (C. Eric Lincoln series on black
    religion) DLC

184 Mitchell, Henry Heywood, 1919-
    Black preaching, [by] Henry H. Mitchell. New York, Harper
    & Row, 1979. 256 p. (Harper's ministers paperback library)

185 Moore, Everett Leroy, 1918-
    Handbook of Pentecostal denominations in the United States.
    Pasadena, Ca., 1954. vii, 346 l. Thesis (M.A.)--Pasadena
    College. CSdP

186 Nelsen, Hart Michael, 1938-
    The black church in America. Edited by Hart M. Nelsen,
    Raytha L. Yokley [and] Anne K. Nelsen. New York, Basic
    Books, 1971. vii, 375 p. On storefront churches: p. 240-
    245. DLC

187 Nelson, Douglas J., 1931–
     The black face of church renewal; a brief essay examining
     the meaning of the Pentecostal/Charismatic church renewal
     movement, 1901-1985, [by] Douglas J. Nelson. [Arlington,
     Va.], 1984. 18 l. CCmS

188 Oliver, John Bernard
     Some newer religious groups in the United States: twelve
     case studies. New Haven, Ct., 1946. vi, 502 l. Thesis
     (Ph.D.)--Yale University. CtY

189 Parham, Thomas David, 1920–
     Removing racial and social barriers through charismatic re-
     newal, [by] T. David Parham. In New Covenant, 3 (June 1974),
     14-15; reprinted (Removing racial and social barriers) in Martin,
     R., comp. Sent by the Spirit. New York, c1976, 117-120.

190 Ploski, Harry A.
     The Negro almanac: a reference work on the Afro-American.
     Compiled and edited by Harry A. Ploski [and] James Williams.
     4th ed. New York, Wiley, c1983. xiii, 1550 p. "Other pre-
     dominantly black churches": p. 1271-1274. DLC

191 Reid, Ira
     Storefront churches and cults. In Sherman, R. B., ed.
     The Negro and the city. Englewood Cliffs, N.J., 1970, 104-
     109. DLC

192 Richardson, Harry Van Buren, 1901–
     The Negro in American religious life, [by] Harry V. Rich-
     ardson. In Davis, J. P., ed. The American Negro reference
     book. Englewood Cliffs, N.J., 1966, 396-413. "Store front
     churches": p. 407-408. DLC, ODaWU

193 Richardson, James Collins, 1945–
     Why black and white Pentecostals are separated, [by] James
     C. Richardson, Jr. In Logos Journal, 10 (May/June 1980),
     20-21.

194 Rooth, Richard Arlen
     Social structure in a Pentecostal church. Minneapolis, 1967.
     101 l. Thesis (M.A.)--University of Minnesota. MnU

195 Rosenberg, Bruce Alan, 1934–
     The art of the American folk preacher, [by] Bruce A.
     Rosenberg. New York, Oxford University Press, 1970. x,
     265 p. DLC, FTaSU, KyLxCB

196 Rosenberg, Bruce Alan, 1934–
     The psychology of the spiritual sermon, [by] Bruce A.
     Rosenberg. In Zaretsky, I. I., ed. Religious movements in
     contemporary America. Princeton, N.J., c1974, 135-149.

197   Shopshire, James Maynard, 1942-
        A socio-historical characterization of the black Pentecostal
        movement in America. Evanston, Il., 1975. v, 238 l. Thesis
        (Ph.D.)--Northwestern University. IEN

198   Simpson, George Eaton, 1904-
        Black Pentecostalism in the United States. In Pylon, 35
        (June 1974), 203-211.

199   Smythe, Mabel (Murphy), 1918-
        The black American reference book. Edited by Mabel M.
        Smythe. Sponsored by the Phelphs-Stokes Fund. Englewood
        Cliffs, N.J., Prentice-Hall, c1976. xxviii, 1026 p. "Non-
        establishment black religion": p. 506-514. DLC, Ok

200   Store front church.
        In Our World, 7 (May 1952), 62-65.

201   Stotts, George Raymond, 1929-
        Pentecostal archival material: its nature and availability,
        with emphasis on the Southwest, [by] George R. Stotts.
        n.p., 1974. 19 [1] l. On blacks: . 14, 16-19.

202   Synan, Harold Vinson, 1934-
        The Pentecostal movement in the United States. Athens,
        1967. vi, 296 l. Thesis (Ph.D.)--University of Georgia. "The
        Negro Pentecostals": l. 208-235. GU

203   Tinney, James Steven, 1942-
        Black Pentecostals: the difference is more than color, [by]
        James S. Tinney. In Logos Journal, 10 (May/June 1980), 16-
        19.

204   Tinney, James Steven, 1942-
        The blackness of Pentecostalism, [by] James S. Tinney.
        In Spirit, 3:2 (1979), 27-36.

205   Tinney, James Steven, 1942-
        Exorcism is widespread, [by] James S. Tinney. In Afro-
        American (Washington) (Feb. 9, 1974), 1-2.

206   Tinney, James Steven, 1942-
        Pentecostals refurbish the Upper Room, [by] James S. Tin-
        ney. In Christianity Today, 10 (Apr. 1, 1966), 47-48.

207   Tinney, James Steven, 1942-
        Prospects of black Pentecostalism, [by] James S. Tinney.
        In Jones, D. J., ed. The black church: a community re-
        source. Washington, 1977, 134-156. CLSU

208   Tinney, James Steven, 1942-
        Selected directory of Afro-American religious periodicals,

schools and organizations, [by] James S. Tinney. In Jones,
D. J., ed. The black church: a community resource. Washington, 1977, 158-262. CLSU

209 Tinney, James Steven, 1942-
    A theoretical and historical comparison of black political and
    religious movements, [by] James S. Tinney. Washington, 1978.
    vii, 312 l. Thesis (Ph.D.)--Howard University. DHU

209a Washington, James Melvin
    Pentecostalism as the resurgence of slave religion, [by]
    James M. Washington. Cleveland, Tn., 1983. CCmS, CPFT

210 Washington, Joseph Reed, 1930-
    The black holiness and Pentecostal sects, [by] Joseph R.
    Washington, Jr. In Lincoln, C. E., ed. The black experience
    in religion. Garden City, N.Y., 1974, 198-212.

211 Washington, Joseph Reed, 1930-
    Black religion: the Negro and Christianity in the United
    States, [by] Joseph R. Washington, Jr. Boston, Beacon
    Press, 1964. ix, 308 p. On Holiness and Pentecostal churches:
    p. 114-122. DLC

212 Washington, Joseph Reed, 1930-
    Black religion: the Negro and Christianity in the United
    States, [by] Joseph R. Washington, Jr. With a new preface
    by the author and a review by Martin E. Marty. Boston,
    Beacon Press, 1966, c1964. xvii, 308 p. On Holiness and
    Pentecostal churches: p. 114-122.

213 Washington, Joseph Reed, 1930-
    Black sects and cults, [by] Joseph R. Washington, Jr.
    Garden City, N.Y., Doubleday, 1972. xii, 176 p. (C. Eric
    Lincoln series on black religion) "Holiness and Pentecostal
    blacks: the permanent sects": p. 58-82. DLC

214 Washington, Joseph Reed, 1930-
    Black sects and cults, [by] Joseph R. Washington, Jr.
    Garden City, N. Y., Anchor Books, 1973, c1972. xii, 176 p.
    (C. Eric Lincoln series on black religion) "Holiness and Pente-
    costal blacks: the permanent sects": p. 58-82. TxShA

215 Whiting, Albert Nathaniel, 1917-
    "From saint to shuttler": an analysis of sectarian types,
    [by] Albert N. Whiting. In Quarterly Review of Higher Edu-
    cation among Negroes, 23 (Oct. 1955), 133-140.

216 Williams, Chancellor, 1905-
    The socio-economic significance of the store front church
    movement in the United States since 1920, by Chancellor

Williams. Washington, 1949. 240 l. Thesis (Ph.D.)--American University. DAU

217 Wilmore, Gayraud Stephen, 1921-
     Black religion and black radicalism, [by] Gayraud S. Wilmore. Garden City, N. Y., Doubleday, 1972. xiii, 344 p. (C. Eric Lincoln series on black religion) On Pentecostal churches: p. 210-215. DLC

218 Wilmore, Gayraud Stephen, 1921-
     Black religion and black radicalism, [by] Gayraud S. Wilmore. Garden City, N.Y., Anchor Press, 1973. xiii, 344 p. (C. Eric Lincoln series on black religion) On Pentecostal churches: p. 210-215. OCU

219 Wilmore, Gayraud Stephen, 1921-
     Black religion and black radicalism; an interpretation of the religious history of Afro-American people, [by] Gayraud S. Wilmore. 2d ed., revised and enlarged. Maryknoll, N.Y., Orbis Books, c1983. xv, 288 p. DLC

220 Wright, Nathan, 1923-
     Non-establishment black religion, [by] Nathan Wright, Jr. In Smythe, M. M., ed. The black American reference book. Englewood Cliffs, N.J., c1976, 506-514. DLC

221 Zaretsky, Irving I.
     Spirit possession and spirit mediumship in Africa and Afro-America: an annotated bibliography, [by] Irving I. Zaretsky [and] Cynthia Shambaugh. New York, Garland Publishing, 1978. xxii, 443 p. (Garland reference library of social science, 56. First ed. published in 1966 under title: Bibliography on spirit possession and spirit medianship. DLC

          -- --EASTERN STATES

          (Massachusetts, Boston)

222 Eddy, George Norman, 1906-
     Store-front religion, [by] G. Norman Eddy. In Religion in Life, 28 (Winter 1958/1959), 68-85 [Pentecostal churches: p. 68-74]; abridged in Lee, R., ed. Cities and churches; readings on the urban church. Philadelphia, c1962, 177-194 [Pentecostal churches: p. 178-182].

223 Paris, Arthur Ernest, 1945-
     Black Pentecostalism: Southern religion in an urban world, [by] Arthur E. Paris. Amherst, University of Massachusetts Press, 1982. vii, 183 p. Based on thesis (Ph.D.)--Northwestern University. DLC, OkU

224 Paris, Arthur Ernest, 1945-
     Black Pentecostalism: world view, society and politics.
     Evanston, Il., 1974. vi, 183 [31] l. Thesis (Ph.D.)--
     Northwestern University. IEN

         (New York, New York City)

225 Baldwin, James, 1924-
     Go tell it on the mountain. New York, Knopf, 1953. 303 p.
     A novel about a day in the life of several members of a Pente-
     costal church in Harlem. DLC, InU

226 Haley, Peter
     From saving souls to promoting politics. In Phoenix (July
     13, 1978)

227 Jones, Raymond Julius, 1910-
     A comparative study of religious cult behavior among Ne-
     groes, with special reference to emotional group conditioning
     factors. Washington, Published by the Graduate School for the
     Division of Social Sciences, Howard University, 1939. v, 125 p.
     (Howard University studies in the social sciences, vol. 2, no. 2)
     Cover title. Thesis (M.A.)--Howard University, 1939. Based in
     part on three churches in New York City. DHU, DLC, OrU, ScU

228 Pettiford, Patricia M.
     Harlem's ministry, [by] Patricia M. Pettiford. New York,
     1963. Thesis (M.A.)--College of the City of New York. NNR

229 Rasky, Frank
     Harlem's religious zealots, [by] Frank Rasky. In Tomorrow,
     9 (Nov. 1949), 11-17: abridged in Negro Digest, 8 (Mar.
     1950), 52-62.

230 Wright, William Archer, 1918-
     The Negro store-fronts: churches of the disinherited; a
     study of the store-front churches of East Harlem, New York,
     [by] William A. Wright. New York, 1942. 78 l. Thesis
     (B.D.)--Union Theological Seminary. NNUT

         (New York, Syracuse)

231 Brown, Theodore E.
     The Negro in Syracuse, New York as related to the social
     service program of Dunbar Center, [by] Theodore E. Brown.
     Syracuse, N.Y., 1943. Thesis (M.A.)--Syracuse University.
     NSyU

         (Pennsylvania, Philadelphia)

232 Bare, Paul W.
     The Negro churches in Philadelphia, [by] Paul W. Bare.

Madison, N.J., 1931. Thesis (M.A.)--Drew University.
NjMD

233 Fauset, Arthur Huff, 1899-
     Black gods of the metropolis: Negro religious cults of the
     urban North. Philadelphia, University of Pennsylvania Press;
     London, H. Milford, Oxford University Press, 1944. x, 126 p.
     (Publications of the Philadelphia Anthropological Society, 3;
     Brinton memorial series; [2]) Based on thesis (Ph.D.)--
     University of Pennsylvania. DLC, TxWB

234 Fauset, Arthur Huff, 1899-
     Black gods of the metropolis: Negro religious cults in the
     urban North. New York, Octagon Books, 1970, c1944. ix,
     126 p. (Publications of the Philadelpia Anthropological Society,
     3; Brinton memorial series, [2]) Reprint of 1944 ed. Based
     on thesis (Ph.D.)--University of Pennsylvania. DLC

235 Fauset, Arthur Huff, 1899-
     Negro religious cults in the urban North. Philadelphia,
     1942. 148 l. Thesis (Ph.D.)--University of Pennsylvania.
     PU

236 Keysor, Charles W.
     Journey into joy. Text and photos by Charles W. Keysor.
     In Good News, 12 (May/June 1979), 26-36.

               (Pennsylvania, Pittsburgh)

237 Williams, Melvin Donald, 1933-
     Community in a black Pentecostal church; an anthropological
     study, [by] Melvin D. Williams. Pittsburgh, University of
     Pittsburgh Press, 1974. xii, 202 p. Based on thesis (Ph.D.)
     --University of Pittsburgh. DLC, MSohG

238 Williams, Melvin Donald, 1933-
     Community in a black Pentecostal church; an anthropological
     study, [by] Melvin D. Williams. Prospect Heights, Il., Wave-
     land Press, 1984. xii, 202 p. Based on thesis (Ph.D.)--
     University of Pittsburgh. OO

239 Williams, Melvin Donald, 1933-
     Considerations of a black anthropologist researching Penta-
     costalism, [by] Melvin D. Williams. In Spirit, 3:2 (1979), 20-
     26.

240 Williams, Melvin Donald, 1933-
     Food and animals: behavioral metaphors in a black Penta-
     costal [sic] church in Pittsburgh, [by] Melvin D. Williams.
     In Urban Anthropology, 2 (Spring 1973), 74-79.

241 Williams, Melvin Donald, 1933–
     On the street where I lived, [by] Melvin D. Williams. New
     York, Holt, Rinehart and Winston, c1981. x, 147 p. DLC

242 Williams, Melvin Donald, 1933–
     A Pentecostal congregation in Pittsburgh: a religious com-
     munity in a black ghetto. Pittsburgh, 1973. 328 l. Thesis
     (Ph.D.)--University of Pittsburgh. PPiU

         (Rhode Island, Providence)

242a Splaine, Michael
     They called us Holy Rollers! [By] Michael Splaine. In
     Grass-roots (Providence), 1:14 (Dec. 14-20, 1977), 5.

         --MIDDLE WEST

         (Illinois, Chicago)

243 Brooks, Delores J.
     Preaching the word behind bars, [by] Delores J. Brooks.
     In Ebony, 33 (Aug. 1978), 142.

244 Daniel, Vattel Elbert, 1890–
     Ritual in Chicago's South Side churches for Negroes, [by]
     Vattel E. Daniel. Chicago, 1940 [i.e. 1941] iv, 155 l. ICU

245 Daniel, Vattel Elbert, 1890–
     Ritual stratification in Chicago Negro churches. In American
     Sociological Review, 7 (June 1942), 352-361.

246 Drake, St. Clair
     Black metropolis: a study of Negro life in a northern city,
     [by] St. Clair Drake and Horace R. Cayton. With an intro-
     duction by Richard Wright. New York, Harcourt, Brace, 1945.
     xxxiv, 809 p. On "lower-class" and "storefront" churches:
     p. 412-429, 612-653. DLC, ViRCU

247 Drake, St. Clair
     Black metropolis: a study of Negro life in a northern city,
     [by] Horace R. Cayton and St. Clair Drake. London, J.
     Cape, 1946. xxxiv, 809 p. On "lower-class" and "storefront"
     churches: p. 412-429, 612-653. ODaU, Uk

248 Faith healer.
     In Ebony, 5 (Jan. 1950), 37-39.

249 Neimark, Paul G.
     Can storefront churches meet the black power challenge?
     [By] Paul Neimark. In Sepia, 24 (Nov. 1975), 15-26. Includes
     Pentecostal churches: p. 15-16.

250   Stultz, Bob
        White black man, [by] Bob Stultz [and] Phil Landrum.
        Carol Stream, Il., Creation House, c1972.   172 p.

251   Von Hoffman, Nicholas, 1929–
        Interviewing Negro Pentecostals, [by] Nicholas von Hoffman
        and Sally W. Cassidy. In American Journal of Sociology, 62
        (Sept. 1956), 195–197.

        (Michigan, Detroit)

252   Smith, Vern E.
        The perpetual mission of Mother Waddles, [by] Vern E.
        Smith. In Ebony, 27 (May 1972), 50–52, 54, 56, 58.

        (Minnesota, Minneapolis)

253   Hine, Virginia (Haglin), 1920–
        Personal transformation and social change: the role of com-
        mitment in a modern religious movement. Minneapolis, 1969.
        [iv], 248, 9 l. Thesis (M.A.)--University of Minnesota. MnU

254   Olila, James Howard
        Pentecostalism: the dynamics of recruitment in a modern
        socio-religious movement. Minneapolis, 1968. 57 l. Thesis
        (M.A.)--University of Minnesota. MnU

255   Palmer, Gary Bradford, 1942–
        Trance and dissociation: a cross-cultural study in psycho-
        physiology, [by] Gary Palmer. Minneapolis, 1966. v, 158 l.
        Paper (M.S.)--University of Minnesota. "Possession in the
        third force movement: Negro": l. 51–57.

256   Rooth, Richard Arlen
        Social structure in a Pentecostal church. Minneapolis, 1967.
        101 l. Thesis (M.A.)--University of Minnesota. MnU

        (Nebraska, Omaha)

257   Rowland, Ida Madonna
        An analysis of Negro ritualistic ceremonies as exemplified by
        Negro organizations in Omaha, [by] Ida Madonna Rowland.
        Omaha, 1938. 44 l. Thesis (M.A.)--University of Omaha.
        NbOU

        (Ohio, Cleveland)

258   Blackwell, James Edward, 1925–
        A comparative study of five Negro storefront churches in
        Cleveland. Cleveland, Oh., 1949. viii, 320 l. Thesis (M.A.)
        --Western Reserve University. OClW

(Ohio, Youngstown)

259 I'm saved and I'm proud.
     In Ebony, 30 (June 1975), 84-86, 88, 90, 92.

     -- --SOUTHERN STATES

260 Harrell, David Edwin, 1930-
     White sects and black men in the recent South, [by] David
     Edwin Harrell, Jr. Foreword by Edwin S. Gaustad. Nash-
     ville, Vanderbilt University Press, 1971. xix, 161 p. DLC

261 Washington, Joseph Reed, 1930-
     The peculiar peril and promise of black folk religion, [by]
     Joseph R. Washington, Jr. In Harrell, D. E., ed. Varieties
     of Southern evangelicalism. Macon, Ga., c1981, 59-69. DLC

     (District of Columbia, Washington)

262 Brown, Diane R.
     A directory of black churches in the Washington, D.C.,
     metropolitan area. Compiled by Diane R. Brown. 2d ed.
     Washington, Howard University, Mental Health Research Center,
     c1980. viii, 94 p. ViFGM

263 Cooper, Willia Charlotte.
     A comparative study of religious education in four Pente-
     costal churches in the metropolitan area, D.C. Washington,
     1975. 72 l. Thesis (M.A.)--Howard University. DHU

264 Davis, Arnor S., 1919-
     The Pentecostal movement in black Christianity, [by] Arnor
     S. Davis. In Black Church, 2:1 (1972), 65-88.

265 Hill, Hiley H.
     Negro store-front churches in washington, D.C., [by] Hiley
     H. Hill. Washington, 1947. 107 l. Thesis (M.A.)--Howard
     University. DHU

266 Jones, Raymond Julius, 1910-
     A comparative study of religious cult behavior among Ne-
     groes, with special reference to emotional group conditioning
     factors. Washington, Published by the Graduate School for the
     Division of Social Sciences, Howard University, 1939. v, 125 p.
     (Howard University studies in the social sciences, vol. 2, no.
     2) Cover title. Thesis (M.A.)--Howard University, 1939.
     Based in part on eleven churches in Washington, D.C. DHU,
     DLC, OrU, ScU

266a Moore, Sidney Harrison, 1942-
     Family and social networks in an urban black storefront

church, by Sidney Harrison Moore. Washington, 1975. xi,
318 l. Thesis (Ph.D.)--American University. DAU

267 Weiss, Michael J.
Lord, I cried, Lord, I cried: the sound of the streetsing-
ers, [by] Michael J. Weiss. In Washingtonian, 14 (May 1979),
81, 83.

268 Willoughby, William
Storefront churches: social stabilizers, [by] William Willoughby. In Christianity Today, 13 (May 9, 1969), 44-45.

(Florida, Tallahassee)

269 Benz, Ernst, 1907-
Der heilige Geist in Amerika. Düsseldorf, Köln, Diedericks,
1970. 229 p. DLC

(Georgia, Albany)

270 Bennett, Gerald G.
The black church in American culture: an empirical study
of black church members' perception of the black church in
Albany, Georgia, as a social change agent, [by] Gerald G.
Bennett. Bowling Green, Oh., 1982. xv, 238 l. Thesis
(Ph.D.)--Bowling Green State University. OBgU

(Georgia, Patterson)

271 Davis, Arnor S., 1919-
The Pentecostal movement in black Christianity, [by] Arnor
S. Davis. In Black Church, 2:1 (1972), 65-88.

(North Carolina, Chapel Hill)

272 Brown, Agnes
The Negro churches of Chapel Hill: a community study,
[by] Agnes Brown. Chapel Hill, 1939. viii, 122 l. Thesis
(M.A.)--University of North Carolina. NcU

(North Carolina, Durham)

273 Carter, Luther Clyde
Negro churches in a Southern community. New Haven, Ct.,
1955. 403 l. Thesis (Ph.D.)--Yale University. CtY

274 Tate, Robert Spence
A study of Negro churches in Durham, North Carolina, [by]
Robert Spence Tate, Jr. Durham, N.C., 1939. v, 120 l.
Thesis (B.D.)--Duke University. NcD

274a Walker, Christopher Harlan
    The ritual context of healing by faith, [by] Christopher
    Harlan Walker.   Chapel Hill, 1979.   iv, 54 l.   Thesis (M.A.)--
    University of North Carolina.   NcU

274b Walker, Christopher Harlan
    Three Pentecostal churches, [by] Christopher H. Walker.
    In Perspectives on the American South, 2 (1984), 215-225.

        (Virginia, Richmond)

275 Berlack, Freeman Roosevelt
    A study of religious cults among Negroes in Richmond, Vir-
    ginia, [by] Freeman Roosevelt Berlack.   Richmond, 1940.
    Thesis (B.D.)--Virginia Union University.   ViRVU

        -- --WESTERN STATES

        (California, Los Angeles)

276 Bartleman, Frank, 1871-1935.
    Another wave of revival, [by] Frank Bartleman.   Edited by
    John G. Myers.   Springdale, Pa., Whitaker House, c1982.
    175 p.   Abridgment of How Pentecost came to Los Angeles.
    Reprint with additions and revisions of the 1970 ed. published
    under title: Another wave roles in!

277 Bartleman, Frank, 1871-1935.
    Another wave rolls in!   Formerly What really happened at
    "Azusa Street."   [By] Frank Bartleman.   Edited by John Walk-
    er.   Revised and enlarged ed., edited by John G. Myers.
    Northridge, Ca., Voice Publications, 1970, c1962.   128 p.
    Abridgment of How Pentecost came to Los Angeles.   CCmS,
    TxWaS

278 Bartleman, Frank, 1871-1925.
    Azusa Street, [by] Frank Bartleman.   With foreword by
    Vinson Synan.   Plainfield, N.J., Logos International, c1980.
    xxvi, 184 p.   First published in 1925 under title: How Pente-
    cost came to Los Angeles.   DLC, KyWAT, MSohG

279 Bartleman, Frank, 1871-1935.
    How Pentecost came to Los Angeles: as it was in the begin-
    ning.   2d ed.   Los Angeles, 1925.   167 p.   CPFT

280 Bartleman, Frank, 1871-1935.
    How Pentecost came to Los Angeles: as it was at the begin-
    ning.   3d ed.   Los Angeles, 1925.   167 p.   MoSpA

281 Bartleman, Frank, 1871-1935.
    What really happened at "Azusa Street"?   [By] Frank

Bartleman. Edited by John Walker. Northridge, Ca., Voice
Christian Publications, 1962. 97 p. Abridgment of How Pentecost came to Los Angeles. KyWAT

282 Fidler, R. L.
Historical review of the Pentecostal outpouring in Los Ange-
les at the Azusa Street mission in 1906, [by] R. L. Fidler.
In International Outlook (1st quarter, 1963), 3-14.

283 Frodsham, Stanley Howard, 1882-1969.
With signs following: the story of the Pentecostal revival
of the twentieth century. Rev. [i.e. 3d] ed. Springfield,
Mo., Gospel Publishing House, c1946. 279 p. "Pentecost in
Los Angeles": p. 31-40. MSohG, TxWaS

284 Hollenweger, Walter Jacob, 1927-
The Pentecostals: the charismatic movement in the churches,
[by] W. J. Hollenweger. Minneapolis, Augsburg Publishing
House, 1972. xx, 572 p. "First United States edition."
Translation of Enthusiastisches Christentum. "The Los Angeles
revival": p. 22-24. DLC, MH-AH, TxWaS

285 Jonas, Mack E., 1884-1973.
Let the redeemed of the Lord say so: Mack E. Jonas interview. In Synan, H. V., ed. Aspects of Pentecostal-charismatic
origins. Plainfield, N.J., 131-135. Interview by Leonard
Lovett in Cleveland, Ohio, on October 3, 1971.

286 Lovett, Leonard, 1939-
Perspective on the black origins of the contemporary Pentecostal movement. In Journal of the Interdenominational Theological Center, I (Fall 1973), 36-49.

(California, San Francisco)

287 Price, Thomas Aubrey
Negro storefront churches in San Francisco: a study of
their spatial characteristics in two selected neighborhoods, [by]
Thomas A. Price. San Francisco, 1969. vii, 128 l. Thesis
(M.A.)--San Francisco State College. CSfSt

-- --WEST INDIES

288 Barrett, Leonard Emanuel, 1920-
Soul-force: African heritage in Afro-American religion, [by]
Leonard E. Barrett. Garden City, N.Y., Anchor Press, 1974.
viii, 251 p. (C. Eric Lincoln series on black religion) "Soul
under stress: redemption cults--Caribbean": p. 95-128.
DLC

(Dominican Republic)

289 Platt, Dario
     Nueva esperanza para Santo Domingo. Santo Domingo, Re-
     publica Dominicana, Universidad CETEC, 1981. iv, 168 p.
     (Serie Ensayos, 1) (Coleccion CETEC, 2) Originally presented
     as the author's thesis (M.A.)--Seminario Teologico Fuller, Pasa-
     dena, California, 1975. DLC

     (Haiti)

290 Conway, Frederick James, 1946-
     Pentecostalism in Haiti: healing and hierarchy, [by] Fred-
     erick J. Conway. In Glazier, S. D. Perspectives on Pente-
     costalism: case studies from the Caribbean and Latin America.
     Washington, c1980, 7-26.

291 Conway, Frederick James, 1946-
     Pentecostalism in the context of Haitian religion and health
     practice, [by] Frederick J. Conway. Washington, 1978. vii,
     284 l. Thesis (Ph.D.)--American University. DAU

292 Gerlach, Luther Paul, 1930-
     Five factors crucial to the growth and spread of a modern
     religious movement, [by] Luther P. Gerlach and Virginia H.
     Hine. In Journal for the Scientific Study of Religion, 7
     (Spring 1968), 23-40.

293 Gerlach, Luther Paul, 1930-
     Pentecostalism: revolution or counter-revolution? [By]
     Luther P. Gerlach. In Zaretsky, I. I., ed. Religious move-
     ments in contemporary America. Princeton, N.J., c1974, 686-
     699.

     (Jamaica)

294 Baytop, Adrianne Roberts
     James Baldwin and Roger Mais: the Pentecostal theme. In
     Jamaica Journal, 42 (1978), 14-21.

295 Gerlach, Luther Paul, 1930-
     Five factors crucial to the growth and spread of a modern
     religious movement, [by] Luther P. Gerlach [and] Virginia H.
     Hine. In Journal for the Scientific Study of Religion, 7
     (Spring 1966), 23-40.

296 Hopkin, John Barton
     Music in the Jamaican Pentecostal churches. Cambridge,
     Ma., 1974. 76 l. Thesis (B.A.)--Harvard University. MH

297   Hopkin, John Barton
        Music in the Jamaican Pentecostal churches. In Jamaica
        Journal, 42 (1978), 22-40.

298   Wedenoja, William Andrew, 1948-
        Modernization and the Pentecostal movement in Jamaica, [by]
        William Wedenoja. In Grazier, S. D., ed. Perspectives on
        Pentecostalism: case studies from the Caribbean and Latin
        America. Washington, c1980, 27-48.

299   Wedenoja, William Andrew, 1948-
        Religion and adaptation in rural Jamaica. San Diego, 1978.
        xx, 515 l. Thesis (Ph.D.)--University of California, San
        Diego. CU-S

            (St. Vincent)

300   Goodman, Felicitas Daniels, 1914-
        Glossolalia: speaking in tongues in four cultural settings,
        [by] Felicitas D. Goodman. In Confinia Psychiatrica, 12:2-4
        (1969), 113-129.

301   Goodman, Felicitas Daniels, 1914-
        Phonetic analysis of glossolalia in four cultural settings, [by]
        Felicitas D. Goodman. In Journal for the Scientific Study of
        Religion, 8 (Fall 1969), 227-239.

302   Henney, Jeannette (Hillman), 1918-
        Spirit possession belief and trance behavior in a religious
        group in St. Vincent, British West Indies. Columbus, 1968.
        x, 216 l. Thesis (Ph.D.)--Ohio State University. OU

303   Henney, Jeannette (Hillman), 1918-
        Spirit-possession belief in two fundamentalist groups in St.
        Vincent, [by] Jeannette H. Henney. In Goodman, F. D.
        Trance, healing, and hallucination; three field studies in reli-
        gious experience. New York, 1974.

            (Trinidad)

304   Glazier, Stephen D.
        Pentecostal exorcism and modernization in Trinidad, West
        Indies, [by] Stephen D. Glazier. In Glazier, S. D., ed.
        Perspectives on Pentecostalism: case studies from the Carib-
        bean and Latin America. Washington, c1980, 67-80.

--EUROPE

-- --UNITED KINGDOM

305 Calley, Malcolm John Chalmers
      God's people: West Indian Pentecostal sects in England,
      [by] Malcolm J. C. Calley. London, New York, Oxford Uni-
      versity Press, 1965. xiv, 182 p. "Issued under the auspices
      of the Institute of Race Relations, London." DLC, OCB, Uk

306 Calley, Malcolm John Chalmers
      Pentecostal sects among West Indian migrants, [by] Malcolm
      J. C. Calley. In Race, 3 (May 1962), 55-64.

307 Hill, Clifford S., 1927-
      Black churches: West Indian & African sects in Britain,
      [by] Clifford Hill. London, British Council of Churches, Com-
      munity and Race Relations Unit, 1971. 23 p. (Its Booklet, 1)
      DLC

308 Hill, Clifford S., 1927-
      From church to sect: West Indian religious sect development
      in Britain, [by] Clifford Hill. In Journal for the Scientific
      Study of Religion, 10 (Summer 1971), 114-123.

309 Hill, Clifford S., 1927-
      Immigrant sect development in Britain: a case study of
      status deprivation? [By] Clifford Hill. In Social Compass,
      18:2 (1971), 231-236.

310 Hollenweger, Walter Jacob, 1927-
      The Pentecostals: the charismatic movement in the churches,
      [by] W. J. Hollenweger. Minneapolis, Augsburg Publishing
      House, 1972. xx, 572 p. "First United States edition."
      Translation of Enthusiastisches Christentum. "Crossing the
      race barrier: West Indian Pentecostal": p. 187-190. DLC,
      MH-AH, TxWaS

311 Kiev, Ari, 1933-
      Psychotherapeutic aspects of Pentecostal sects among West
      Indian immigrants to England. In British Journal of Sociology,
      15 (June 1964), 129-138.

312 Ottosson, Krister
      The Pentecostal churches, [by] Krister Ottosson. Exeter,
      Religious Education Press, 1977. 55 p. (Christian denomina-
      tions series) "West Indian Pentecostalism in England": p.
      32-34. OkEG

313 Pearson, David G.
      Race, class and political activism: a study of West Indians

in Britain, [by] David Pearson. Farnborough, Hants., Gower,
c1981. vii, 207 p. DLC

314 Pearson, David G.
     Race, religiosity and political activism: some observations
     on West Indian participation in Britain, [by] David G. Pearson.
     In British Journal of Sociology, 29 (Sept. 1978), 340-357.

315 Pearson, David G.
     West Indians in Easton: a study of their social organization
     with particular reference to participation in formal and informal
     associations, [by] David G. Pearson, Leicester, 1975. Thesis
     (Ph.D.)--Leicester University.

316 Root, John Brereton, 1941-
     Encountering Westindian Pentecostalism: its ministry and
     worship, [by] John Root. Bramcote, Notts., Grove Books,
     1979. 24 p. (Grove booklet on ministry and worship, 88)
     MCE, Uk

          (Birmingham)

317 Gerloff, Roswith Ingebord Hildegard, 1933-
     A plea for British black theologies: the black church move-
     ment in Britain in its transatlantic cultural and theological in-
     teraction, [by] Roswith I. H. Gerloff. Birmingham, 1986.
     2 v. Thesis (Ph.D.)--Birmingham University. UkBU

          (Bristol)

317a Pryce, Ken
     Endless pressures: a study of West Indian life-styles in
     Bristol [by] Ken Pryce. Harmondsworth, Middx., Penguin
     Books, 1979. xiii, 297 p. "Saints": p. 198-218. DLC, Uk

317b Pryce, Ken
     Endless pressure: a study of West Indian life-styles in
     Bristol, [by] Ken Pryce. 2d ed., revised by the author and
     with a new preface by Robin Cohen. Bristol, Bristol Classical,
     1986. [320] p. Uk

          (London)

318 Hill, Clifford S., 1927-
     West Indian migrants and the London churches, [by] Clifford
     S. Hill. London, New York, Oxford University Press, 1963.
     89 p. "Issued under the auspices of the Institute of Race Rela-
     tions, London." "Pentecostals": p. 72-74. FU

PART II. WESLEYAN-ARMINIAN ORIENTATION

Parallel to and sometimes coincident with agitation for abolition of
slavery, there emerged in American Methodism in the 1830s, 1840s,
and 1850s a growing concern for a revival of primitive Wesleyanism,
particularly of the doctrine and experience of Christian perfection.
Promulgated first by Methodist Episcopal bishops and other leaders
gathered by Phoebe Palmer, wife of a homeopathic physician in New
York, the movement became national in scope as well as name through
the agency of the National Camp Meeting Association for the Promotion
of Holiness organized at Vineland, New Jersey, in 1867.

As taught by the Methodist evangelists who represented the
Association, Christian perfection was that sanctity which Christ
coveted for His disciples in the high-priestly prayer recorded in
John 17, and that sanctity for which He "suffered without the gate."
This experience, variously known as perfect love, entire sanctification, personal holiness, and the baptism of the Holy Spirit, marked
the beginning of adulthood in the Christian life and resulted in purity of heart and power for service. A second crisis, entire sanctification represented the completion of the process of sanctification
begun in the confession and forsaking of sins at conversion. The
experience, its proponents taught, released the Christian from his
natural "bent toward sinning," since through grace the carnal na-
ture had been eradicated and he was free perfectly to obey God.
Though process was of necessity involved, entire sanctification was
wrought instantaneously by the Holy Spirit, a crisis of passage from
infancy to adulthood in the spiritual life. The experience was like
a good marriage. Early proponents described the entirely sanctified
believer's focus on the divine will as being analogous to Yahweh's
faithfulness to Israel and adopted Isaiah's term "Beulah" (meaning
married) to describe the relationship. Backsliding, though still a
possibility, was no longer inevitable. "Prone to wander, Lord I feel
it" was no longer the perennial experience of the sanctified.

1. HOLINESS-PERFECTIONIST BODIES

During the 1870s and 1880s with meetings in Knoxville, Baltimore,
Washington, and Augusta, the National Association for the Promotion

of Holiness introduced its message of Wesleyan perfectionism to the
South. There blacks, largely from Baptist backgrounds, accepted
the Methodist perfectionist teaching, creating a "new wine in old
wineskins" situation which by the turn of the century sent most of
the newly sanctified into independency. Typical of the emerging
black leaders were C. P. Jones (a song writer), C. H. Mason, John
A. Jeter, and William and John Christian, all former Missionary Baptists. A similar, less spectacular move characterized the Colored
Methodist Episcopal, the African Methodist Episcopal Zion, and African Methodist Episcopal churches, the chief worker representing
the latter being Amanda Berry Smith. Mrs. Smith, a convert of
John S. Inskip (first president of the National Association and
white), became a popular camp meeting speaker and served as a
"faith" missionary in India and Africa under Bishop William Taylor,
a white National Association evangelist. Smith and Sammy Morris,
member of the Kru tribe and convert of Taylor missionaries in Liberia, became heroes of faith, celebrated in holiness folklore by blacks
and whites alike throughout segregated America. Morris died
while a student at Fort Wayne College. Morris' attendance there
may in part account for the renaming of the school as Taylor University soon thereafter.

--DOCTRINAL AND CONTROVERSIAL WORKS

319 Humphrey, Jerry Miles, 1872-
         The lost soul's first day in eternity, [by] J. M. Humphrey.
     Chicago, Christian Witness Co., c1912. 128 p. InMarC

320 Humphrey, Jerry Miles, 1872-
         The lost soul's first day in eternity, [by] J. M. Humphrey.
     Noblesville, In., Newby Book Room, 197-. 128 p. Reprint of
     1912 ed. KyWAT

321 Humphrey, Jerry Miles, 1872-
         A soul's first day in heaven. Prepared by J. M. Humphrey.
     Lima, Oh., True Gospel Grain Publishing Co., 1917. 86 p.
     DLC, KyWAT

322 Humphrey, Jerry Miles, 1872-
         A vivid description of sin's bypaths for young people, [by]
     J. M. Humphrey. Chicago, Messenger Publishing Co., 1918,
     c1916. 116 p. KyWAT

323 Humphrey, Jerry Miles, 1872-
         A vivid description of sin's bypaths for young people, [by]
     J. M. Humphrey. Salem, Oh., Convention Book Store, 1976.
     112 p. Reprint of 1916 ed. InMarC, KyWAT

324 Humphrey, Jerry Miles, 1872-
         What God hath joined together, [by] J. M. Humphrey.

Phoenix, Az., Don Hughes; printed by Religious Press, Independence, Ks., 197-. 22 p. Cover title. KyWAT

325 Killingsworth, Frank Russell, 1878-
Theologic questions and answers on Christian perfection or sanctification. Philadelphia, Westminister Press, 1949. 93 p.
DLC

326 Kletzing, Henry Frick, 1850-1910.
Progress of a race; or, The remarkable advancement of the American Negro from the bondage of slavery, ignorance, and poverty to the freedom of citizenship, intelligence, affluence, honor, and trust, [by] H. F. Kletzing and W. H. Crogman. With an introd. by Booker T. Washington. Atlanta, J. L. Nichols, 1897. 663 p. DLC, OWibfC

327 Kletzing, Henry Frick, 1850-1910.
Progress of a race; or, The remarkable advancement of the American Negro from the bondage of slavery, ignorance and poverty, to the freedom of citizenship, intelligence, affluence, honor and trust, [by] H. F. Kletzing and W. H. Crogman. With an introd. by Booker T. Washington. Cincinnati, Ferguson, 1900, c1897. 696 p. ONcM

328 Kletzing, Henry Frick, 1850-1910.
Progress of a race; or, The remarkable advancement of the Afro-American from the bondage of slavery, ignorance and poverty, to the freedom of citizenship, intelligence, affluence, honor and trust, [by] H. F. Kletzing and W. H. Crogman. With an introd. by B. T. Washington. Atlanta, J. L. Nichols, 1903. 732 p. WaU

329 Noel, T. H.
Bombing the devil: it is not like you think, [by] T. H. Noel. Oklahoma City, 19--. 1 v. (unpaged) Cover title.

330 Noel, T. H.
Fruit of the vine, [by] T. H. Noel. Oklahoma City, 19--.

--FICTIONAL LITERATURE

331 Humphrey, Jerry Miles, 1872-
Fragments from the King's table, [by] J. M. Humphrey. Lima, Oh., True Gospel Grain Publishing Co., 1915. 213 p.
DLC, KyWAT

332 Humphrey, Jerry Miles, 1872-
Gleanings from Emmanuel's land, [by] J. M. Humphrey. Lima, Oh., True Gospel Grain Publishing Co., 1911. 63 p.
DLC

--HISTORY AND STUDY OF DOCTRINES

333   Clark, William A., 1891-
         Sanctification in Negro religion, [by] William A. Clark. In
      Social Forces, 15 (May 1937), 544-551.

--HYMNS AND SACRED SONGS

334   Harris, Thoro, 1874-1955.
         Blessed hope hymnal. Editor: Thoro Harris. Associate
      editors: Orrin R. Jenks [and] Ross L. Fitch. Chicago, Faith
      Publishing Co. [1910] [126] p. Cover title. With music.
      ICN, PPiPT

335   Harris, Thoro, 1874-1955.
         Blessed hope hymnal. Revised and enlarged. For the Bible
      school, the mid-week meeting, young people's societies and all
      services of the sanctuary. Editor: Thoro Harris. Associate
      editor: C. B. Widmeyer. Chicago, [1911] [160] p. Cover
      title. With music. IAurC, ICN

336   Harris, Thoro, 1874-1955.
         "Christian life" songs, no. 1. Compiled by the board of
      publication of the Union Gospel Press for use in Christian Sun-
      day schools. Thoro Harris, music editor. Cleveland, Union
      Gospel Press, c1926. 1 v. (unpaged) With music. MoSpA

337   Harris, Thoro, 1874-1955.
         Echoes of paradise: a choice collection of Christian hymns
      suitable for sabbath schools and all other departments of reli-
      gious work. [Compiled by] Thoro Harris. Boston, C. H.
      Woodman, c1903. [262] p. With music. ICN, MBU-T, NNUT

338   Harris, Thoro, 1874-1955.
         Eternal praise. Editor: Thoro Harris. Special contributors;
      Will O. Jones [and] S. L. Flowers. For the Bible school, the
      prayer circle, young people's societies and revivals. Chicago,
      Windsor Music Co., [1913] [94] p. Cover title. With music.
      ICN

339   Harris, Thoro, 1874-1955.
         New gospel hymns: for revival meetings, Bible schools,
      prayer meetings, young people's meetings and other services,
      [by] Thoro Harris, John M. Currie [and] Orrin M. Jenks.
      Chicago, Meyer & Brother, [1908]. 1 v. (unpaged) With
      music. IAurC, PPiPT

340   Harris, Thoro, 1874-1955.
         The new hymnal: for church and home. Thoro Harris,
      editor. Chicago, Conference Press, c1925. 352 p. With mu-
      sic. MoStcL

--PASTORAL LITERATURE

341 Humphrey, Jerry Miles, 1872-
    Daily guide for the sanctified, [by] J. M. Humphrey. Chicago, Christian Witness Co., c1917. 147 p. DLC, KyWAT

342 Humphrey, Jerry Miles, 1872-
    Daily guide for the sanctified, [by] J. M. Humphrey.
Salem, Oh., Convention Book Store, 19--. 147 p. Reprint
of 1917 ed. KyWAT

343 Humphrey, Jerry Miles, 1872-
    Dew drops from the rifted clouds, [by] J. M. Humphrey.
Lima, Oh., True Gospel Grain Publishing Co., 1917. 54 p.
DLC

344 Humphrey, Jerry Miles, 1872-
    Echoes from three worlds, [by] J. M. Humphrey. Sacred
poems. 2d ed. Cleveland, Oh., "True Gospel Grain" Publishing Co., c1908. 78 p. ViU

345 Humphrey, Jerry Miles, 1872-
    Select fruits from the highlands of Beulah, [by] J. M.
Humphrey. Lima, Oh., True Gospel Grain Publishing Co.,
1913. 227 p. DLC

346 Humphrey, Jerry Miles, 1872-
    Spiritual lessons from every-day life, [by] J. M. Humphrey.
Lima, Oh., True Gospel Grain Publishing Co., 1914. 210 p.
DLC

--PASTORAL THEOLOGY

347 Humphrey, Jerry Miles, 1872-
    The worker's secret of unction, [by] J. M. Humphrey.
Chicago, Christian Witness Co., c1920. 89 p. DLC, InMarC

348 Massey, James Earl, 1930-
    Designing the sermon: order and movement in preaching,
[by] James Earl Massey. [William D. Thompson, ed.] Nashville, Abingdon Press, c1980. 127 p. (Abingdon preacher's
library) DLC, OkBetC

349 Massey, James Earl, 1930-
    On being a preacher. Louisville, Ky., Southern Baptist
Theological Seminary, 1981. 1 v. (various pagings) (E. Y.
Mullins lectures on preaching, 1980/81) KyLoS

350 Massey, James Earl, 1930-
    The sermon in perspective: a study of communication and

charisma. Grand Rapids, Mi., Baker Book House, c1976.
116 p. Delivered in part as the Mary Claire Gautschi Lectures
at Fuller Theological Seminary, Pasadena, Ca., in 1975, as the
1975 Fall Lectures at Ashland Theological Seminary, Ashland,
Oh., and at Gulf-Coast Bible College, Houston, Tx., in Feb.
1976 during the Fourteenth Annual Ministers' Refresher Institute. DLC

--PERIODICALS

351 Hope. 190 -
       ----, Ar.

--SERMONS, TRACTS, ADDRESSES, ESSAYS

352 Humphrey, Jerry Miles, 1872-
       50 ready-cut sermons, [by] J. M. Humphrey. Chicago,
Christian Witness Co., c1925. 243 p. CLolC, DLC

353 Humphrey, Jerry Miles, 1872-
       Impressive talks, [by] J. M. Humphrey. Lima, Oh., True
Gospel Grain Publishing Co., 1918. 223 p. DLC, SdSifB

354 Humphrey, Jerry Miles, 1872-
       Railroad sermons from railroad stories, [by] J. M. Humph-
rey. Chicago, Messenger Publishing Co., 1917. 84 p. DLC,
KyWAT

355 Humphrey, Jerry Miles, 1872-
       Sermons that never die, [by] J. M. Humphrey. Chicago,
Christian Witness Co., c1913. 174 p. DLC, InMarC

356 Humphrey, Jerry Miles, 1872-
       Seven old time gospel sermons, [by] J. M. Humphrey.
Chicago, 191-. 19 p. Cover title. KyWAT

357 Humphrey, Jerry Miles, 1872-
       X-ray sermons, [by] J. M. Humphrey. Omaha, Ne., "Any-
where Evangelistic Workers" Publishing House, c1924. 247 p.
DLC, SdSifB

358 Humphrey, Jerry Miles, 1872-
       X-ray sermons, [by] J. M. Humphrey. Salem, Oh., Con-
vention Book Store, 1976. 247 p. Reprint of 1924 ed. InMarC

--UNITED STATES

359 Bentley, William H.
       Bible believers in the black community, [by] William H.

Bentley. In Wells, D. F., ed. The Evangelicals: what they believe, who they are, where they are changing. Nashville, c1975, 108-121. "Black Holiness and Pentecostals": p. 115-116.

360 Dayton, Donald Wilber, 1942-
Discovering an evangelical heritage, [by] Donald W. Dayton. New York, Harper & Row, c1976. 147 p. DLC

361 Holt, John Bradshaw
Holiness religion: cultural shock and social reorganization, [by] John B. Holt. In American Sociological Review, 5 (Oct. 1940), 740-747; abridged in Yinger, J. M. Religion, society and the individual. New York, c1957, 463-470.

362 Johnson, Guy Benton, 1928-
Do holiness sects socialize in dominant values? [By] Benton Johnson. In Social Forces, 39 (May 1961), 309-316.

363 Jones, Charles Edwin, 1932-
Perfectionist persuasion: the Holiness movement and American Methodism, 1867-1936. Metuchen, N.J., Scarecrow Press, 1974. xx, 242 p. (ATLA monograph series, 5) Based on thesis (Ph.D.)--University DLC, OkBetC

364 Smith, Timothy Lawrence, 1924-
Revivalism and social reform in mid-nineteenth-century America. Chapters I-XI comprise the Frank S. and Elizabeth D. Brewer Prize Essay for 1955, the American Society of Church History. New York, Abingdon Press, 1957. 253 p. DLC, OkBetC

-- --TEXAS

(Van Alstyne)

364a Jernigan, Charles Brougher, 1863-1930.
From the prairie schooner to a city flat, [by] C. B. Jernigan. Brooklyn, c1926. 140 p. On preaching to blacks in Van Alstyne, Texas: p. 62-65. OkBetC, WHi

ASSOCIATED CHURCHES OF CHRIST (HOLINESS) (1947-)

The mother church, the Bethel Church of Christ of Los Angeles, was organized by Bishop William A. Washington on May 19, 1915, with sixteen members. It obtained a state charter which, following affiliation with the Church of Christ (Holiness) U.S.A. from 1917 to 1947, became the basis for an independent denomination. Doctrine remained identical to the Jackson, Mississippi-based

body and a sense of fraternity continued. When the founder died
in 1949, Bethel Church membership stood at 1,200. By 1973 the
Associated Churches of Christ (Holiness) claimed six churches and
a mission with a combined membership of 2,008, all in the Los
Angeles area.

--GOVERNMENT

365 Associated Churches of Christ (Holiness). Assembly.
     Manual of the history, doctrine, government, and ritual of
     the Associated Churches of Christ (Holiness). Los Angeles,
     1953. 47 p.

*BRETHREN IN CHRIST CHURCH (1863-   )

A branch of the German Baptist Brethren, the Brethren in
Christ Church embraced Wesleyan perfectionism in the late-
nineteenth century. Although only a minute portion of its 9,145
members in 1975 were black, the Brethren in Christ Church remained sensitive to the need for integration. On occasion it has
welcomed black workers, such as J. M. Humphrey, to its pulpits.

--DOCTRINAL AND CONTROVERSIAL WORKS

366 Humphrey, Jerry Miles, 1872-
     A word of warning on divorce-marriage, [by] J. M. Humph-
     rey. Philadelphia, Brethren in Christ Mission Church; printed
     by Gospel Words and music, Philadelphia, 1964. 31 p. Re-
     print of 1907 ed. InGoM

--HISTORY

367 Wittlinger, Carlton Oscar, 1917-
     Quest for piety and obedience: the story of the Brethren
     in Christ, [by] Carlton O. Wittlinger. Nappanee, In., Evangel
     Press, 1978. x, 580 p. "Awakening concern about racism":
     p. 532-536. DLC

CHRISTIAN TABERNACLE UNION (-1934)

On January 22, 1934, the Christian Tabernacle Union merged
into the Kodesh Church of Immanuel. Its headquarters were in
Pittsburgh. Signers of the articles of agreement for the Union were
John Walter Harty, D. H. Barnett, G. W. Turner, Paul J. Wood-
ruff, C. G. Britton, and C. Jefferson.

CHURCH OF CHRIST (HOLINESS) U.S.A. (1900-)
[1900-1906 as Christ's Association of Mississippi of Baptized Believers; 1906-1911 as Churches of God in Christ.]

In 1894 C. P. Jones, a Missionary Baptist pastor in Selma,
Alabama, claimed entire sanctification. The next year he accepted
the pastorate of the Mt. Helm Baptist Church in Jackson, Mississippi,
and in 1897 instituted a series of annual holiness convocations.
Opposition to these by fellow clergy resulted in his expulsion from
the Baptist ministry. At this point Jones and his followers formed
a nondenominational fellowship, Christ's Association of Mississippi
of Baptized Believers. From this emerged a federation of like-
minded congregations, the Churches of God in Christ. (Local affiliates used a variety of names.) Associated with Jones were
C. H. Mason and J. A. Jeter, also former Missionary Baptists. In
1906 Mason and Jeter attended the Azusa Street meeting in Los
Angeles, and Mason returned claiming a third experience, the baptism of the Holy Ghost, which he said had been evidenced by speaking in tongues. Elders Jones and Jeter then disfellowshipped Mason
and reorganized the church, which by 1911 adopted the present
name.
     In 1923 and in 1940 the Church of Christ (Holiness) sent frat-
ernal delegations to general assemblies of the mostly-white Church
of the Nazarene meeting in Kansas City and Oklahoma City. Although the Nazarenes reciprocated by sending a like delegation to
the National Convention in Chicago in 1924, these gestures failed to
lead to union because of lack of positive action by either body. In
1944 the National Convention meeting in Jackson, Mississippi, en-
dorsed an affiliation proposed by the mostly-white Pilgrim Holiness
Church for support of home missions. Projects at Sun, Louisiana,
and in several towns in Mississippi under the direction of F. E.
Williams and H. R. McInnis drew initial support. Williams' death
before the end of the year, however, apparently ended the interest
of the Pilgrim Holiness Church in the arrangement.
     The defection of K. H. Burruss, the Atlanta pastor, in 1920
resulted in formation of the Churches of God, Holiness two years
later. In 1947 separations in Washington, D.C. and Los Angeles resulted in formation of two other splinters: the Evangelical Church
of Christ (Holiness) and the Associated Churches of Christ (Holiness). Personalities rather than doctrines were at issue in each
case. Episcopacy was firmly established under Jones, who led the
movement until his death in 1949. The outstanding achievement of
the founder was in the writing and publishing of gospel songs, a
number of which have enjoyed widespread use in holiness circles,
both black and white.
     Headquarters remain in Jackson although the publishing house
removed to Chicago years ago. In 1965 the Church of Christ (Holiness) reported 9,289 members in 159 congregations spread from Virginia and Michigan to California. Apart from footwashing, which is
practiced in some congregations, doctrinal standards are identical to
most other Wesleyan bodies. The Church of Christ (Holiness)

sponsors the Christ Missionary and Industrial College, Jackson, Mississippi, and supports missionary work in Mexico.

--DOCTRINAL AND CONTROVERSIAL WORKS

368   Jones, Charles Price, 1865-1949.
      The work of the Holy Spirit in the churches, [by] C. P.
      Jones. Jackson, Ms., 1896.

--GOVERNMENT

369   Church of Christ (Holiness) U.S.A.
      Manual of the history, doctrine, government, and ritual of
      the Church of Christ (Holiness) U.S.A., 1926. True holiness.
      Norfolk, Va., Guide Publishing Co., 1928. 83 p. "Published
      by orders of the National Convention of the Church of Christ
      (Holiness) U.S.A., held in Jackson, Miss., August 22-29,
      1926." DLC

370   Church of Christ (Holiness) U.S.A.
      Manual of the history, doctrine, government and ritual of
      the Church of Christ (Holiness) U.S.A., 1926. True holiness.
      3d ed. Jackson, Ms., National Headquarters, Church of
      Christ (Holiness) U.S.A., 1945. 115 p. Reprint with additions
      of 1928 ed. KU

--HISTORY

371   Cobbins, Otho Beale, 1895-
      History of Church of Christ (Holiness) U.S.A., 1895-1965.
      Otho B. Cobbins, editor-in-chief. Chicago, National Publishing
      Board, Church of Christ (Holiness) U.S.A.; printed by Vantage
      Press, New York, c1966. 446 p. DLC, OkEG

--HYMNS AND SACRED SONGS

372   Jones, Charles Price, 1865-1949.
      His fulness: anthems, songs, and hymns; being a collection
      of choice, lovely, lively and powerful anthems for the choir
      with a number of special songs for special occasions--solos,
      duets, quartettes and choruses, with also a happy collection
      of gospel songs for Sunday school or any service, [by]
      Charles P. Jones. Jackson, Ms., Truth Publishing Co., c1913.
      119, 10 p. With music (shape notes) RPB

373   Jones, Charles Price, 1865-1949.
      His fulness; being Sweet selections and His fulness combined

and enlarged. Edited by C. P. Jones, assisted by L. F. Dunn
and Minnie Rhines. Los Angeles, 1928. 154 p. With music.
KyWAT

374 Jones, Charles Price, 1865-1949.
Jesus only, nos. 1 and 2; a blessed collection of songs and
hymns, new and old, for religious services, especially for those
services in which the deepest consecration of life to our Lord
Jesus Christ is emphasized: for such Sunday school services,
camp meetings, holiness meetings, and general worship, [by]
Charles P. Jones. Jackson, Ms., Truth Publishing Co., 19--.
[282] p. With music. NcD

375 Jones, Charles Price, 1865-1949.
Jesus only, songs and hymns; a collection of new and popular songs, hymns and tunes, for praises and prayer meetings,
Sunday schools, camp meetings, holiness assemblies, etc., etc.,
[by] Charles P. Jones. Jackson, Ms., Truth Publishing Co.,
c1901. 1 v. (unpaged) With music. DLC, TxFS

376 Jones, Charles Price, 1865-1949.
Jesus only standard hymnal. Edited by C. P. Jones. Los
Angeles, J. Hart, 196-.

--MUSIC

377 Cobbins, Otto Beale, 1895-
History of Church of Christ (Holiness) U.S.A., 1895-1965.
Otho B. Cobbins, editor-in-chief. Chicago, National Publishing
Board, Church of Christ (Holiness) U.S.A.; printed by Vantage
Press, New York, c1966. 446 p. "The ministry of song":
p. 399-425. DLC, OkEG

--PERIODICALS

378 Truth messenger. 1- 1896-
Jackson, Ms., Chicago, Il. 1896-195- as Truth.

--STATISTICS

379 United States. Bureau of the Census.
Census of religious bodies: 1926. Church of Christ (Holiness). Statistics, denominational history, doctrine, and organization. Washington, Government Printing Office, 1929. 8 p.
DLC

CHURCH OF CHRIST IN GOD (-191_)

In 1906 the Church of Christ in God consisted of nine congregations with 848 members in six Midwestern and Southern states. It had separated a few years earlier from the Church of the Living God, Christian Workers for Friendship because of personal differences of the leaders and a desire to stress education. Before 1916 it returned to the parent body.

CHURCH OF GOD

*CHURCH OF GOD (Anderson, Indiana) (1880-)

In 1880 Daniel Sidney Warner, a minister in the Churches of God (General Eldership), was sanctified as a result of the preaching of National Holiness Association workers. Feeling that sectarianism was antithetical to true Christianity, he broke with the General Eldership and later with the holiness association movement which required church membership as a prerequisite to affiliation as well. The resulting Church of God movement, composed of Warner's followers, regarded itself as a reformation destined to unite all true Christians on the basis of scriptural teaching alone. Blacks were early attracted to the movement, the pioneer worker in South Carolina being Jane Williams, a black woman who in 1886 founded the first congregation in Charleston. Integrated meetings were held even in the South, sometimes in face of great persecution. By 1914 so many blacks were attending the Anderson, Indiana, camp meeting, the principal general gathering, that some whites feared their presence might inhibit whites from continuing to attend, and asked blacks to refrain from massive participation. This action led to the inauguration of a predominantly black meeting at West Middlesex, Pennsylvania, and to the formation of the National Association of the Church of God, an organization of black clergy. In fact a total division of the Church of God reformation movement along racial lines was narrowly averted. A handful of black pastors, including J. D. Smoot, S. P. Dunn, and Raymond S. Jackson, who regularly spoke during the General Ministerial Assembly at Anderson, helped bridge the racial gap.

Since 1933 the Shining Light Survey, a periodical devoted to black interests, has been published in New York. The Bay Ridge Christian College, a predominantly black church-related institution at Kendleton, Texas, dates from 1963. By 1961 the Church of God reported 2,278 United States congregations with 247,461 enrolled in Sunday school. Included were 396 black churches with 20,700 enrolled in Sunday school. In 1971 Marcus H. Morgan, black pastor in Chicago, was elected chairman of the Executive Council of the Church of God. In recent years other blacks, including Edward L. Foggs, Cauthion T. Boyd, Jr., and Thomas J. Sawyer, have served in executive positions, and James Earl Massey has been speaker on the church-sponsored national radio program.

--BIOGRAPHY

379a Massey, James Earl, 1930–
    Three black leaders of the Church of God reformation move-
ment, [by] James Earl Massey and Thomas J. Sawyer. Anderson, In., Center for Pastoral Studies, Anderson School of
Theology, 1981. 65 l.

--CHURCH EXTENSION

380 Foggs, Edward L., 1934–
    With faith we grow! Church growth workbook, Church of
God, Anderson, Ind., [by Edward L. Foggs]. Anderson, In.,
Church of God, Church Growth Strategy and Planning Commit-
tee, [1978]. 95 p. Cover title. InAndC

381 Telfer, David Alden, 1940–
    Red and yellow, black and white and brown: home missions
in the Church of God, [by] David A. Telfer. Anderson, In.,
Warner Press, 1981. vi, 96 p. "The black church in the
United States": p. 42-53, 94-95. InAndC

--DOCTRINAL AND CONTROVERSIAL WORKS

382 Church of God (Anderson, In.). Executive Council.
    The question of race: 1968 resolution on race. In Callen,
B. L., ed. A time to remember. Anderson, In., c1978, 551-
553.

383 Byrum, Enoch Edwin, 1861-1942.
    Color line, [by] E. E. Byrum. In Gospel Trumpet, 18
(Sept. 2, 1897), 2-3.

384 Massey, James Earl, 1930–
    Concerning Christian unity: a study of the relational im-
perative of agape love. Anderson, In., Warner Press, c1979.
141 p. CAzPC

385 Massey, James Earl, 1930–
    These things remain to be done, [by] James Earl Massey.
In Callen, B. L., ed. A time to remember. Anderson, In.,
c1978, 768-772.

386 Massey, James Earl, 1930–
    "When thou prayest": an interpretation of Christian prayer

according to the teachings of Jesus. Anderson, In., Warner
Press, 1960. 64 p. DLC, GAU, InAndC, InMarC, MH-AH

387 Reid, Benjamin Franklin, 1937-
     Priorities for the future, [by] Benjamin F. Reid. In Cal-
     len, B. L., ed. A time to remember: projections. Anderson,
     In., c1978, 89-91. DLC, InAndC

388 Sawyer, Thomas Jason, 1921-
     Racial separation and Christian unity, [by] Thomas J. Saw-
     yer. In Callen, B. L., ed. A time to remember: evaluations.
     Anderson, In., c1978, 110-112. "Excerpted from Colloquium,
     February 1973." DLC

389 Schell, William Gallio, 1869-
     Is the Negro a beast? A reply to Chas. Carroll's book en-
     titled: The Negro a beast, proving that the Negro is human
     from Biblical, scientific, and historical standpoints, [by] Wm.
     G. Schell. Moundsville, W. Va., Gospel Trumpet Publishing
     Co., 1901. 238 p. DLC, TxU-Da, Uk

     --EDUCATION

390 Massey, James Earl, 1930-
     Educating for service: essays presented to Robert H.
     Reardon. Edited by James Earl Massey. Anderson, In.,
     Warner Press, c1984. xii, 244 p. DLC

     --HISTORY

391 Massey, James Earl, 1930-
     An introduction to the Negro churches in the Church of God
     reformation movement, [by] James Earl Massey. With a fore-
     word by Marcus H. Morgan. New York, Shining Light Survey
     Press, c1957. 70 p. InAndC

392 Massey, James Earl, 1930-
     The question of race: an historical overview, [by] James
     E. Massey. In Callen, B. L., ed. A time to remember.
     Anderson, In., c1978, p. 543-553.

393 National Association of the Church of God.
     Commemorative booklet in observance of the centennial cele-
     bration of the Church of God, 1880-1980. Historical Booklet
     Committee: Marcus H. Morgan [et al.]. West Middlesex, Pa.,
     1981. 124 p. InAndC

394 National Association of the Church of God.
     Historical report [of the] National Association of the Church
     of God, 1917-1974. West Middlesex, Pa., 1974. 84 p. InAndC

395 Smith, John William Vernon, 1914-1984
      A brief history of the Church of God reformation movement,
      [by] John W. V. Smith. Rev. ed. Anderson, In., Warner
      Press, c1976. 157 p. First published in 1956 under title:
      Truth marches on. "Among the black people": p. 121-125.
      DLC

396 Smith, John William Vernon, 1914-1984
      The quest for holiness and unity: a centennial history of
      the Church of God (Anderson, Indiana), [by] John W. V.
      Smith. Anderson, In., Warner Press, c1980. 504 p. On
      blacks: p. 162-169, 403-406. DLC

397 Smith, John William Vernon, 1914-1984
      Truth marches on: a brief study of the history of the
      Church of God reformation movement, [by] John W. V. Smith.
      Anderson, In., Gospel Trumpet Co., 1960, c1956. 112 p.
      "Second printing." "Among the Negro people": p. 97-98.

            --PASTORAL LITERATURE

398 Massey, James Earl, 1930-
      The hidden disciplines. Anderson, In., Warner Press, 1972.
      111 p. DLC

399 Massey, James Earl, 1930-
      The soul under siege (a fresh look at Christian experience).
      Anderson, In., Warner Press, 1970. 110 p. DLC

            --PASTORAL THEOLOGY

400 Lewis, Alvin, 1935-
      Family designs for Christian living. Alvin Lewis, consultant
      and editor. Anderson, In., Anderson School of Theology,
      1978. 207 p. InAndC

401 Lewis, Alvin, 1935-
      A study of family life educational programs: resources and
      needs in the Church of God, Anderson, Indiana, [by] Alvin
      Lewis. Manhattan, 1975. viii, 215 l. Thesis (Ph.D.)--Kansas
      State University. KMK

402 Massey, James Earl, 1930-
      Hermeneutics and pulpit work, [by] James Earl Massey. In
      McCown, W., ed. Interpreting God's word for today: an in-
      quiry into hermeneutics from a biblical theological perspective.
      Anderson, In., c1982. DLC, OkBetC

403 Massey, James Earl, 1930-
      The meaning and mission of the local church, [by] James E.

Massey. In Callen, B. L., ed. A time to remember: teachings. Anderson, In., c1978, 154-156. "Excerpted from The
worshiping church." DLC, InAndC

404 Massey, James Earl, 1930-
     The responsible pulpit. Anderson, In., Warner Press,
     1974. 115 p. DLC

405 Massey, James Earl, 1930-
     The sermon in perspective: a study of communication and
     charisma. Grand Rapids, Mi., Baker Book House, c1976.
     116 p. Delivered in part at Gulf-Coast Bible College, Houston,
     Tx., in Feb 1976 during the Fourteenth Annual Ministers'
     Refresher Institute. DLC

406 Telfer, David Alden, 1940-
     Sociological and theological foundations for Church of God
     ministry in ethnic minority communities in the United States.
     Denver, 1975. v, 198 1. Project--(D.Min.)--Iliff School of
     Theology. CoDI

         --PERIODICALS

407 Shining light. 1- 1933-
     New York, Anderson, In. 1934-19-- as Shining Light Sur-
     vey.

         --SERMONS, TRACTS, ADDRESSES, ESSAYS

408 Massey, James Earl, 1930-
     Christian Brotherhood Hour pulpit: notable sermons of W.
     Dale Oldham, R. Eugene Sterner [and] James Earl Massey.
     Edited by Maurice Berquist. Anderson, In., Warner Press,
     1980. iv, 136 p. InAndC

         --WORSHIP

409 Massey, James Earl, 1930-
     The worshiping church: a guide to the experience of wor-
     ship. Anderson, In., Warner Press, 1961. 106 p. DLC,
     TNJ-R

--UNITED STATES

-- --EASTERN STATES

(Pennsylvania, West Middlesex)

409a Cook, Diana Lynn, 1955-
Study of the historical development and current perspectives
of the Inspirational Youth Convention of the National Associa-
tion of the Church of God, West Middlesex, Pennsylvania, [by]
Diana Lynn Cook. Anderson, In., 1981. viii, 137 l. Thesis
(M.R.E.)--Anderson School of Theology. InAndC

410 Davis, Katie R.
Zion's Hill at West Middlesex, [by] Katie R. Davis. Corpus
Christi, Tx., Christian Triumph Press, 1955. 103 p. CMlG,
IndAndC-T

-- --MIDDLE WEST

(Illinois, Chicago)

411 Brown, Charles Ewing, 1883-1971.
When the trumpet sounded: a history of the Church of God
reformation movement. Anderson, In., Warner Press, c1951.
402 p. "S. P. Dunn develops Negro church": p. 201.

412 Telfer, David Alden, 1940-
A study of the relationship between Negro and Caucasian
Church of God congregations in metropolitan Chicago, [by]
David A. Telfer. Chicago, 1968. iii, 97 l. Thesis (M.Th.)--
Chicago Theological Seminary. ICT

(Michigan, Detroit)

413 Brown, Charles Ewing, 1883-1971.
When the trumpet sounded: a history of the Church of God
reformation movement. Anderson, In., Warner Press, c1951.
402 p. "Daniel F. Oden and the colored church in Detroit":
p. 192.

-- --SOUTHERN STATES

414 Brown, Charles Ewing, 1883-1971.
When the trumpet sounded: a history of the Church of God
reformation movement. Anderson, In., Warner Press, c1951.
402 p. "Beginning of colored work in Southeast": p. 266-267.

--WEST INDIES

415 Cumberbatch, Carlton Tertius, 1921-
     The role of leadership training in the development of the
     Church of God in the English-speaking Caribbean. Anderson,
     In., 1976. iv, 110 l. Thesis (M.A.)--Anderson School of
     Theology. InAndC

     -- --JAMAICA

416 Hastings, Raymond Ellis, 1917-
     The Church of God in Jamaica: a critical study of its
     structure and work. Anderson, In., 1958. viii, 152 l. The-
     sis (B.D.)--Anderson School of Theology. InAndC

     CHURCH OF GOD (Gospel Spreading) (1921-   )

     In 1917 Lightfoot Solomon Michaux, recently converted fish-
monger, was impressed while on his way to Camp Lee, Virginia,
to sell his wares that he was to become leader of a new church.
Upon his wife's urging he began attending the Church of Christ
(Holiness) in Newport News, and it was that group which licensed
him to preach and ordained him the next year. The independent
Everybody's Mission which Michaux had established in the interim
then became an affiliate of Elder Jones' group. The mission pros-
pered so that in 1921 when he heard he would be transferred to
another congregation, Michaux told the bishop he would leave the
denomination instead. Although his congregation did not know of
his plan until he returned from the church convention in Jackson,
Mississippi, in June, the pastor had on February 26 incorporated
Gospel Spreading Tabernacle Building Association and in March had
purchased through this organization a building across the street
from the tabernacle where the congregation had been meeting. In
later years Elder Michaux said nothing about his previous church
connection, but his later work was all done on the foundation of
this corporation, later simply called the Gospel Spreading Association. The movement spread as members moved to other communities
in search of work: first to Edenborn, fifty miles northwest of
Pittsburgh, then to Baltimore, Washington, New York, and Philadelphia. These five, together with churches in Hampden and Newport News, constituted the permanent core, and it was upon their
support that Michaux relied for welfare and radio ministries which
he instituted after he moved to Washington in 1928.
     A flamboyant personality, Elder Michaux attracted widespread
attention by conducting mass weddings and baptisms, parachuting
from airplanes to the sites of preaching engagements, and serving
as a self-appointed advisor-prophet to presidents, highlighting each
dramatic event or pronouncement by means of radio. Even after
the broadcasts were discontinued the Washington church continued
to advertise itself as the Radio Church of God. At Michaux's death

in 1968 the movement had approximately 1,200 members. Failure to distinguish the "Happy am I" evangelist's personal finances from those of the church, together with the lack of a recognized successor, has caused the Church of God (Gospel Spreading) to languish in recent years.

--HISTORY

417 Williams, Chancellor, 1905–
     The socio-economic significance of the store front church movement in the United States since 1920, [by] Chancellor Williams. Washington, 1949. 240 l. Thesis (Ph.D.)--American University. DAU

--PASTORAL LITERATURE

418 Michaux, Lightfoot Solomon, 1884–1968.
     Sparks from the anvil of Elder Michaux. Compiled and edited by Pauline Lark. Washington, Happy News Publishing Co., 1950. ix, 139 p. DLC

--PERIODICALS

419 Happy news. 1– 1933–
     Washington.

420 Seven churches. 1– 19 –
     Washington.

--UNITED STATES

-- --EASTERN STATES

(New York, New York City)

421 Rasky, Frank
     Harlem's religious zealots, [by] Frank Rasky. In Tomorrow, 9 (Nov. 1949), 11-17, abridged in Negro Digest, 8 (Mar. 1950), 52-62.

422 Second front in Harlem.
     In Time, 40 (Dec. 21, 1942), 74, 76.

*CHURCH OF GOD (Holiness) (1883–)

At its 1944 General Convention held at Overland Park, Kansas, C. C. Riddle, a white member of the Unity Holiness Commission, reported on an exploratory investigation he had made of the Atlanta-based Churches of God, Holiness, a black body with which the Church of God (Holiness) had a wide area of doctrinal agreement. The convention took no action. Such passivity in relation to race was not new to this old independent holiness church; the attitude had characterized it throughout its history. In 1886 a protest from Alabama concerning the racial implication of an "open to all" statement concerning its infant school at College Mound, Missouri, was met by a clear-cut statement by the sponsors that "no race distinction" would be made in "future administration." Despite such a policy, few if any American black students matriculated at this or later schools sponsored by the group. Ironically, Jamaican blacks have attended without incident over the years. They were housed in integrated dormitories even before the 1954 court ruling. Unwillingness of an American black couple who in 1939 had been placed under missionary appointment to do work among blacks in the United States while awaiting passage to Liberia contributed to a decision by the mission board to cancel their contract. A quite different result obtained from affiliation of a group of independent churches in Jamaica in 1933. A separate convention was established there under an American couple sent to the island following World War II.

By 1975 there were twenty churches and 400 full members in Jamaica. Congregations in London and Birmingham had also been established by Jamaican immigrants in England. The almost totally white United States membership stood at approximately 3,500.

CHURCH OF GOD (Sanctified Church) (1903-   )

In 1903 a group (who under the leadership of Elders John C. Brown and Charlie W. Gray left the Mount Lebanon Baptist Church in Columbia, Tennessee, because of its failure to teach second-crisis sanctification) held its first convention in Nashville. Several like-minded congregations calling themselves Church of God had sprung up in central Tennessee and in order to distinguish themselves from others using the name the assembly added (Sanctified Church). Under Elders John R. Inman and John Ledsay Rucker, the first two chairmen whose combined terms extended to 1946, the movement spread to nine states, the Panama Canal Zone, and Jamaica. This expansion occurred despite unsuccessful merger negotiations with the Church of Christ (Holiness) in 1924, and the withdrawal of Elder Gray and approximately a third of the membership to form the Original Church of God (or Sanctified Church) three years later. Foot washing is practiced in response to Christ's example.

By the early 1970s, the church claimed sixty affiliates with 5,000 members in eight states, and twelve congregations in Jamaica. At that time negotiations were underway looking to reunion with the brethren who had separated under Elder Gray in 1927. Headquarters are in Nashville. Elder Theopolis Dickenson, who succeeded

Elder Rucker as chairman in 1946, died in 1965 and was followed by
Elder Jesse E. Evans.

--DIRECTORIES

423   Church of God (Sanctified Church)
     Yearbook, 1935/36-   . [Nashville], 1935-   . v. [1]-   .
    NN

--GOVERNMENT

424   Church of God (Sanctified Church)
     Manual of the Church of God. Rev. ed. Nashville, Curley
    Printing Co., 1952. .

CHURCHES OF GOD, HOLINESS (1920-)

The Churches of God, Holiness are the outgrowth of a single
congregation in Atlanta established in 1914 with a nucleus of eight.
Until 1920, when the Atlanta church hosted its National Convention,
the group was a local affiliate of the Church of Christ (Holiness)
U.S.A. Under King Hezekiah Burruss, the founder who led until
his death in 1963, the movement expanded to include 32 churches
and 25,600 members. Leadership then passed to his son, Titus
Paul Burruss. Headquarters remain in Atlanta. Footwashing,
though permitted, is not required as an ordinance. The group incorporated as the National Convention of the Churches of God,
Holiness in 1922.

--HISTORY

425   Oliver, John Bernard
     Some newer religious groups in the United States: twelve
    case studies. New Haven, Ct., 1946. vi, 502 l. Thesis
    (Ph.D.)--Yale University. CtY

--PERIODICALS

426   Bethlehem star. 1- 19 -
    Atlanta

--STATISTICS

427   United States. Bureau of the Census.
     Census of religious bodies: 1926. Churches of God,

Holiness. Statistics, denominational history, doctrine, and organization. Washington, Government Printing Office, 1929.
8 p.

ORIGINAL CHURCH OF GOD OR SANCTIFIED CHURCH
(1927-   )

In 1927 Elder Charlie W. Gray, one of the founders of the
Church of God (Sanctified Church), left that body taking about a
third of its members with him, and founded the Original Church of
God or Sanctified Church. At issue was the ordination of women
which Elder Gray frowned upon. The church sees no clear teaching
in the Bible concerning the ordination of women and leaves that decision to local congregations. It does say that a woman who bap-
tizes does it "without Christ's or the apostles' authority." In the
early 1970s Bishop Thomas R. Jeffries of Akron, Ohio, general
chairman, said there were about 85 churches and missions and
4,700 members. Negotiations were then in progress looking toward
reunion with the Church of God (Sanctified Church).

--GOVERNMENT

428 Original Church of God or Sanctified Church.
       The hand book of the Original Church of God or Sanctified
     Church. Nashville, 1945. 25 p.

UNIVERSAL CHURCH OF GOD (1965-   )

In 1965, the largely Jamaican constituency of the Church of
God (Anderson, Indiana) in Britain left the parent body and formed
the Universal Church of God. By 1980 it had a membership of 200
in six congregations. Headquarters are in Ashton under Lyne,
Lancashire.

CHURCH OF THE LIVING GOD

CHURCH OF THE LIVING GOD (1908-1926)

In 1916 the Texas-based Church of the Living God reported
28 churches and 1,743 members. The group, which had been organized eight years earlier, confined its efforts to the state. In
1924 at Athens, Texas, it united with the General Assembly, Church
of the Living God.

CHURCH OF THE LIVING GOD, CHRISTIAN WORKERS FOR
    FELLOWSHIP (1889-   )
[1889-1904 as Church of the Living God, Christian Friendship
    Workers; 1904-1917 as Church of the Living God, Christian
    Workers for Friendship.]

Established by William Christian and his followers of Wrights-
ville, Arkansas, in 1889, the Church of the Living God, Christian
Workers for Fellowship in many ways resembles the Church of God
in Christ. Christian, a former Baptist minister, was in fact an
early associate of C. H. Mason. The Church of the Living God
differs from Mason's group, however, in permitting tongues-
speech in recognizable languages only. It discountenances unin-
telligible utterance and the initial evidence theory as well. It
recognizes three sacraments as being ordained of Christ in the New
Covenant, namely baptism, the Lord's supper, and the washing of
feet. Immersion in the name of Father, Son, and Holy Ghost is, it
teaches, the biblical mode of baptism. Unleavened bread and water
are used in the Lord's supper. Each sacrament is administered only
once. It believes that the Lord's prayer is the only prayer "to be
prayed by all Christians."
    The church affirms the racial pride of its members by asserting
that many biblical saints were black. Like Christian, who was a
Mason, it approves the essentials of Freemasonry. Church buildings
are called temples and are numbered consecutively by date of organization of the congregation. There are twelve administrative
districts, each headed by a bishop. The presiding bishop is addressed as chief. Under Chief Bishop W. E. Crumes headquarters
moved from St. Louis to Cincinnati in 1984. That year a meeting
in Indianapolis of bishops and overseers representing three Church
of the Living God denominations planned a mass convocation of members of all three to be held in Phoenix within three years. The
purpose of this convocation is reunion as one church family as a
step preparatory to organizational union.
    In 1964 the Church of the Living God, Christian Workers for
Fellowship reported 276 congregations and 45,320 members.

--DOCTRINAL AND CONTROVERSIAL WORKS

429   Church of the Living God, Christian Workers for Fellowship.
         Catechism of the Church of the Living God. Motto:
      C.W.F.F. [St. Louis, 197-] 34 p. "The standard primary
      catechism revised."

430   Church of the Living God, Christian Workers for Fellowship.
         The doctrine of the Church of the Living God (C.W.F.F.)
      Christian Workers for Fellowship. [St. Louis, 197-]. folder

431   Church of the Living God, Christian Workers for Fellowship.
         We have a gift for you--free. [St. Louis, 197-]. folder

432   Christian, William, 1856-1928.
        Poor pilgrim's work. Motto: Christian Workers for Fellow-
      ship to unite the people as one in Christ in the name of the
      Father, Son and Holy Ghost, we put our trust. Many impor-
      tant things may be learned by reading this little book.
      Memphis, Tn., 1916; reprinted by Model Printing Co., Del
      City, Ok., 1976. 56 p. Cover title.

433   Noel, T. H.
        Bombing the devil: it is not like you think, [by] T. H.
      Noel. Oklahoma City, 19--. 1 v. (unpaged)

434   Noel, T. H.
        Fruit of the vine, [by] T. H. Noel. Oklahoma City, 19--.

435   Scott, Floyd Claude, 1900-1979.
        The anchor light. Compiled and arranged by F. C. Scott.
      Oklahoma City, 19--. 24 p.

            --GOVERNMENT

436   Church of the Living God, Christian Workers for Fellowship.
        Constitution, general laws, ministerial guide, and manual of
      the Church of the Living God (C.W.F.F.) brotherhood as
      amended: July 15-20, 1930; July 4-9, 1934; July 5-9, 1938;
      July 4-9, 1950; and October 8-13, 1968. Motto: Christian
      Workers for Fellowship. St. Louis, 1970. xvi, 128 p. At
      head of title: Amended articles of agreement.

437   Church of the Living God, Christian Workers for Fellowship.
      National Assembly.
        Minutes. 1st- 1893- . Little Rock, St. Louis, Chicago.
      v. [1]-

            --HISTORY

438   Church of the Living God, Christian Workers for Fellowship.
        Glorious heritage. The golden book. Documentary-
      historical. Church of the Living God. Motto: C.W.F.F.
      Commemorating: diamond jubilee year, 1889-1964 and diamond
      jubilee assembly, 75th annual, 1967. [St. Louis, 1967]
      184 p.

439   Clark, Elmer Talmage, 1886-1966.
        The small sects in America, [by] Elmer T. Clark. Rev. ed.
      New York, Abingdon Press, 1965. 256 p. On Church of the
      Living God, Christian Workers for Fellowship: p. 120-121.
      DLC, RPB

440 Wilmore, Gayraud Stephen, 1921-
        Black religion and black radicalism, [by] Gayraud S. Wil-
     more. Garden City, N.Y., Doubleday, 1972. xiii, 344 p.
     (G. Eric Lincoln series on black religion) On Church of the
     Living God, Christian Workers for Fellowship: p. 211-212.
     DLC

        --PERIODICALS

441 Brotherhood. 1- 1916-
        Memphis

442 Bulletin. 1- 1960-
        Oklahoma City

443 Gospel echo. 1- 1935-
        Louisville

444 Gospel truth. 1- 1981-
        Cincinnati

445 Guiding star of truth. 1- 19 -
        Oklahoma City

446 Reminder. 1- 1929-
        Oklahoma City

447 Torch. 1- 1954-1980.
        Louisville, Wichita. Superseded by Gospel truth.

        --STATISTICS

448 United States. Bureau of the Census.
        Census of religious bodies: 1926. Churches of the Living
     God. Statistics, denominational history, doctrine, and organ-
     ization. Consolidated report: Church of the Living God,
     Christian Workers for Fellowship; Church of the Living God,
     "The Pillar and Ground of Truth." Washington, Government
     Printing Office, 1928. 15 p. DLC, NNUT

449 United States. Bureau of the Census.
        Census of religious bodies: 1936. Churches of the Living
     God. Statistics, denominational history, doctrine, and organ-
     ization. Consolidated report: Church of the Living God,
     Christian Workers for Fellowship; Church of the Living God,
     "The Pillar and Ground of Truth." Washington, Government
     Printing Office, 1940. iv, 12 p. (Bulletin, 41) NNUT

CHURCH OF THE LIVING GOD, GENERAL ASSEMBLY (1902-
1926)
[1902-1908 as Church of the Living God (Apostolic Church)]

The product of a 1902 separation within the Church of the
Living God, Christian Workers for Friendship, the Church of the
Living God (Apostolic Church) existed during its first years as a
loose federation of perhaps fifteen churches, over half of which
were in Arkansas. Under Apostle Charles W. Harris the group in
1908 reorganized as the General Assembly, Church of the Living
God. Most of the Arkansas churches left the movement and the
center then shifted to Texas, where the General Assembly met annually at Waco. In December 1924 at Athens, Texas, it united
with another Texas group also called the Church of the Living God.
These two on January 26, 1926, merged with a third, the Church
of the Living God, the Pillar and Ground of the Truth, taking the
name of the latter. All three had roots in the movement founded
by William Christian in 1889.

CHURCH OF THE LIVING GOD OF EARLSBORO, POTTAWATOMIE
COUNTY, Oklahoma Territory (1899-190-)

On December 4, 1901, the Church of the Living God of Earlsboro, Pottawatomie County, Oklahoma Territory obtained a territorial
charter. Incorporators of the group, which had organized and
elected trustees September 18, 1899, included residents of Earlsboro, Kingfisher, and Guthrie. J. S. Christian of Guthrie was
recognized as founder and chief. The Earlsboro-based group is
one of the foundation stones of the Church of the Living God, the
Pillar and Ground of the Truth of Muskogee, Oklahoma.

CHURCH OF THE LIVING GOD, THE PILLAR AND GROUND OF
THE TRUTH (General Assembly) (1918-   )
[1918-1925 as Church of the Living God, Pillar and the Ground
and the Truth.]

On September 25, 1925, reorganization was perfected of an
Oklahoma City-based group which nearly seven years before had
been incorporated under the leadership of Bishop Arthur Joseph
Hawthorne. The following January E. J. Cain, who had engineered
the recent changes, led the body into union with two other groups
which had withdrawn from the parent organization in the first decade of the century. These groups, both bearing the Church of the
Living God name, had united in 1924 at Athens, Texas. Oklahoma
City, the site of the church-sponsored Booker T. Washington Home
for the aged, became the first headquarters of the united body.
A school and orphans home, the Edmondson Institute, was located
in Athens, Texas. Texas, which had 3,670 of the 4,838 members
reported in 1936, became ever more central as a substantial portion

of the churches and workers (including E. J. Cain) in other states
left the group for the Muskogee, Oklahoma body. As a result
headquarters later were established in Dallas. In 1984 two bishops
of this body met with leaders of its Muskogee- and Cincinnati-based
sister movements, and laid plans for reunion: a mass meeting of
the combined membership of all three to be held in Phoenix, Arizona
within three years as a prelude to organizational unity.

--PERIODICALS

450 Western news review. 1- 192 -
     Oklahoma City

--STATISTICS

451 United States. Bureau of the Census.
        Census of religious bodies: 1926. Church of the Living God.
     Statistics, denominational history, doctrine, and organization.
     Consolidated report: Church of the Living God, Christian
     Workers for Fellowship; Church of the Living God, "The Pillar
     and Ground of Truth." Washington, Government Printing Of-
     fice, 1928. 15 p. DLC, NNUT

452 United States. Bureau of the Census.
        Census of religious bodies: 1936. Churches of the Living
     God. Statistics, denominational history, doctrine, and organ-
     ization. Consolidated report: Church of the Living God,
     Christian Workers for Fellowship; Church of the Living God,
     "The Pillar and Ground of Truth." Washington, Government
     Printing Office, 1940. iv., 12 p. (Bulletin, 41) NNUT

CHURCH OF THE LIVING GOD, THE PILLAR AND GROUND
   OF THE TRUTH OF MUSKOGEE, OKLAHOMA (1915-)

In 1895 in Pine Bluff, Arkansas, William Christian and his
brother John, who six years before had helped establish the Christian Friendship Workers, separated. Competition between them, together with differences concerning prayer, apparently lay behind
the move. The followers of John Christian substituted "the Pillar
and Ground of the Truth" for the original qualifying designation
and split eventually into several groups. The Church of the Living
God, the Pillar and Ground of the Truth of Muskogee, Oklahoma,
incorporated in 1915, is perhaps the most stable of these. Although
the original directors all gave Oklahoma addresses, residential locations in four subsequent versions of the articles of incorporation,
the latest being October 1981, pointed to a widespread constituency:
Oklahoma City, Fort Worth, Houston, and Grand Prairie, Texas;
Indianapolis, Indiana; Decatur, Illinois; and Oakland, Los Angeles,

Fresno, and Stockton, California. The current head is Bishop Herbert Dickerson of Decatur, Illinois. In 1984 he with another bishop and two overseers met with representatives of similarly named Dallas-based body and of the Church of the Living God, Christian Workers for Fellowship and agreed to a mass meeting of the membership of all three in Phoenix within the next three years. The purpose of this convocation is reunion as one church family as a step preparatory to organizational union.

(ORIGINAL) CHURCH OF THE LIVING GOD, THE PILLAR AND GROUND OF THE TRUTH (19 -   )

Frank S. Cherry, the founder, attributed the origin of the congregation in Philadelphia to a vision he had many years ago in a foreign land commanding him to return to America and establish the church. The organization which resulted teaches that black people are the true Israel. It takes Old Testament teachings concerning "graven" images and the sabbath literally and begins its year with the Passover month of April. Passover is substituted for the Lord's supper. Baptism, however, is observed. The church has about 400 members. The founder, who died in 1965, was succeeded by his son, Benjamin Cherry.

*CHURCH OF THE NAZARENE (1908-   )
[1908-1919 as Pentecostal Church of the Nazarene.]

In 1907 and 1908 merger brought together the Brooklyn-based Association of Pentecostal Churches of America, the Los Angeles-based Church of the Nazarene, and the Texas-based Holiness Church of Christ in the Pentecostal Church of the Nazarene, a national body with 10,414 members and 228 congregations. Augmented by additional mergers, membership more than tripled during the next eleven years. The increase included few blacks, however. Although twinges of conscience over lack of concern for U.S. blacks were registered in the official organ by E. C. DeJernett, pioneer preacher in Texas, and Fairy Chism, missionary on furlough from Swaziland, little action resulted. The years 1916 and 1922 witnessed organization of West Indian immigrant churches in Brooklyn in wake of white flight from that early Nazarene center, also formation of the Second Church of Hutchinson, Kansas, another center.

Fraternal delegations sent by the Church of Christ (Holiness) to the 1923 General Assembly in Kansas City and to the 1940 General Assembly in Oklahoma City, though warmly received (and in the first instance reciprocated by a like Nazarene delegation being sent to Chicago in 1924), failed to lead to merger because of lack of positive action by either party. The 1930s witnessed an abortive attempt by Geneva Reese to establish a black work in Kansas City, and the appearance of a few black singing groups, such as those

led by Floyd Lacy and Warren Rogers, on the revival and camp
meeting circuit. Initiative taken by the 1944 General Assembly in
Minneapolis resulted in the calling of the first black workers conference in Meridian, Mississippi three years later. In 1948 the
Nazarene Bible Institute for training black workers opened at Institute, West Virginia. This in turn was followed in 1953 by formation of the Gulf Central District composed of black churches in
the states of the former Confederacy, plus Oklahoma. Edwin E.
Hale and Leon Chambers, white ministers who served as first school
president and district superintendent, were replaced by R. W. Cunningham and Warren Rogers in 1955 and 1958. Given the late start,
growth was impressive. By 1969 when black churches were incorporated into regional districts, Gulf Central reported 26 churches,
798 members and 2,244 enrolled in Sunday school. Six years later
in the United States as a whole, there were 64 predominantly black
churches, and more than 500 congregations with black members or
constituents. The West Virginia school merged with Nazarene Bible
College, a predominantly white institution in Colorado Springs in
1970. Other Nazarene colleges enrolled 129 black students in 1974.
Blacks account for no more than one percent of the 516,020 members
in the United States at the beginning of 1985. Unlike other groups
with work in the Caribbean, no black Nazarene congregations were
established in the United Kingdom as a result of migration there
following World War II. In 1973 the Church of the Nazarene appointed Roger E. Bowman to its headquarters staff in Kansas City
as first ethnic ministries coordinator.

--CHURCH EXTENSION

453 Banks, Melvin Eugene, 1934-
       Ethnic-oriented literature: do we need it? [By] Melvin E.
     Banks. In Hurn, R. W., comp. Black evangelism: which
     way from here? Kansas City, Mo., 1974, 46-55.

454 Black ministers train.
       In Herald of Holiness, 60 (May 26, 1971), 19-22.

455 Bowes, Alpin P.
       Evangelizing the Negro, [by] Alpin P. Bowes. In Herald
     of Holiness, 41 (Feb. 11, 1953), 9.

456 Chalfant, Everette Otis, 1882-1953.
       A great home missionary responsibility, [by] E. O. Chal-
     fant. In Herald of Holiness, 40 (Mar. 5, 1952), 8-9.

457 Chapman, James Blaine, 1884-1947.
       Our colored church project, [by] J. B. Chapman. In
     Herald of Holiness, 36 (June 23, 1947), 5.

458 Ethnic minority churches double.
       In Herald of Holiness, 70 (May 1, 1981), 34.

459   Gish, Carol (Spell)
        Missionary frontiers at home, [by] Carol Gish. Kansas
        City, Mo., Nazarene Publishing House, 1960. 80 p. "Ameri-
        can Negro frontier": p. 33-45. OkBetC

460   Hale, Edwin Erwin, 1894-1976.
        Reaching the Negro for Christ, [by] Edwin E. Hale. In
        Herald of Holiness, 40 (Feb. 27, 1952), 10.

461   Hale, Edwin Erwin, 1894-1976.
        Starting a Negro Sunday school, [by] Edwin E. Hale. In
        Herald of Holiness, 41 (Dec. 3, 1952), 5.

462   Hurn, Raymond Walter, 1921-
        Black evangelism: which way from here? Selected messages
        from the Conference on Urban Ministries, Kansas City, Mo.,
        September 14-15, 1973. Compiled by R. W. Hurn. Kansas
        City, Mo., Nazarene Publishing House, 1974. 70 p.

463   Hurn, Raymond Walter, 1921-
        Bonds of brotherhood, [by] Raymond Hurn. In Herald of
        Holiness, 61 (Feb. 16, 1972), 21-22.

464   Hurn, Raymond Walter, 1921-
        Mission possible: a study of the mission of the Church of
        the Nazarene, [by] R. W. Hurn. Kansas City, Mo., Nazarene
        Publishing House, 1973. 120 p. On black churches: p. 84-
        85. OkBetC

465   Ludwig, Sylvester Theodore, 1903-1964.
        The home mission challenge of the American Negro, [by]
        S. T. Ludwig. In Herald of Holiness, 35 (June 17, 1946),
        12-13.

466   Newest black churches.
        In Herald of Holiness, 60 (May 26, 1971), 28-29.

467   Oster, John C.
        Brotherhood: a human family experience, [by] John C.
        Oster. In Herald of Holiness, 62 (Feb. 14, 1973), 6-7.

468   Rogers, Warren Allen, 1917-
        What the general budget means to our Negro work, [by]
        Warren A. Rogers. In Herald of Holiness, 48 (Mar. 18, 1959),
        11.

469   Serving the colored within our gates.
        In Herald of Holiness, 49 (June 1, 1960), 9.

470   Smee, Roy Francis, 1897-1968.
        Missionary societies pray for U.S., Chinese and Negro work,

[by] Roy F. Smee. In Herald of Holiness, 47 (Aug. 20, 1958), 16-17.

471 Williams, Roy Tilman, 1883-1946.
      Our colored work. In Herald of Holiness, 34 (Oct. 1, 1945), 5, 8.

--DOCTRINAL AND CONTROVERSIAL WORKS

472 Ballard, Sylvester, 1949-
      Where is Samaria? [By] Sylvester Ballard. In Preacher's Magazine, 58 (Dec./Jan./Feb. 1982-1983), 13-14.

473 Barrett, Earl Edward, 1893-
      Holiness is wholeness, [by] E. E. Barrett. In Herald of Holiness, 56 (Nov. 29, 1967), 3-4.

474 Bowman, Roger Eugene
      True soul brothers, [by] Roger E. Bowman. In Herald of Holiness, 63 (Feb. 13, 1974), 3.

474a Chapman, Louise (Robinson), 1892-
      The problem of Africa, [by] Louise R. Chapman. Kansas City, Mo., Beacon Hill Press, 1952. 84 p. CtY-D

475 Chism, Fairy Steele, 1899-1971.
      Waste baskets full of money, [by] Fairy Chism. In Herald of Holiness, 26 (Dec. 4, 1937), 10.

476 Chism, Fairy Steele, 1899-1971.
      What is the matter with us? [By] Fairy Chism. In Herald of Holiness, 26 (July 31, 1937), 6.

477 De Jernett, E. C., 1857-1929.
      Should the church undertake gospel work among American Negroes? [By] E. C. De Jernett. In Herald of Holiness, 13 (Feb. 11, 1925), 7-8.

478 Franco, Sergio
      The challenge of the other Americans, [by] Sergio Franco. Kansas City, Mo., Beacon Hill Press of Kansas City, c1973. 119 p. "One of every ten Americans is black": p. 29-42. OkBetC

479 Franco, Sergio
      Three indispensable words, [by] Sergio Franco. In Hurn, R. W., comp. Black evangelism: which way from here? Kansas City, Mo., 1974, 56-68.

480 Goodman, William
     My duty to my neighbor, [by] William Goodman. In Herald
     of Holiness, 54 (Feb. 24, 1965), 9.

481 Harper, Albert Foster, 1907–
     Toward Christian understanding, [by] A. F. Harper.   In
     Herald of Holiness, 53 (Feb. 3, 1965), 5–6; replies by Mrs.
     A. D. Ellison, Charles E. Roberson and Harold C. Frodge
     (Pro & con), 54 (Apr. 7, 1965), 18.

482 [Haynes, Benjamin Franklin], 1851–1923.
     A problem to be met. In Herald of Holiness, 6 (Sept. 26,
     1917), 2.

483 Hudson, J. Harrison
     In search of real brotherhood, [by] J. Harrison Hudson.
     In Herald of Holiness, 55 (Aug. 17, 1966), 6–7.

484 Kirkland, Robert J.
     The Negro problem, [by] R. J. Kirkland. In Herald of
     Holiness, 8 (May 7, 1919), 6.

484a Murray, D. A., 1876–1962.
     A contemplation of God's works, by D. A. Murray.   In
     Herald of Holiness, 43 (Dec. 29, 1954), 2.

485 Nees, Lawrence Guy, 1916–
     The role of the church in today's social revolution, [by]
     L. Guy Nees. In Herald of Holiness, 52 (Feb. 12, 1964), 5.

486 Oster, John C.
     Which way now? [By] John C. Oster. In Hurn, R. W.,
     comp. Black evangelism: which way from here? Kansas
     City, Mo., 1974, 69.

487 Parr, F. O., 1902–1983.
     Perfect love and race hatred, [by] F. O. Parr. Bour-
     bonnais, Il., 1964. 111 p.

488 Powers, Hardy Carroll, 1900–1972.
     When a nation remembers God in crisis, [by] Hardy C.
     Powers. In Herald of Holiness, 57 (May 1, 1968), 9.

489 Purkiser, Westlake Taylor, 1910–
     The church speaks on current issues, [by] W. T. Pur-
     kiser. In Herald of Holiness, 53 (Aug. 5, 1964), 11–12.

490 Purkiser, Westlake Taylor, 1910–
     Government by anarchy, [by] W. T. Purkiser. In Herald
     of Holiness, 57 (Oct. 9, 1958), 11.

491 Purkiser, Westlake Taylor, 1910–
       Rhetoric or treason? [By] W. T. Purkiser. In Herald of
     Holiness, 58 (July 30, 1969), 10–11.

492 Purkiser, Westlake Taylor, 1910–
       Violence and strife in the city, [by] W. T. Purkiser. In
     Herald of Holiness, 56 (Sept. 20, 1967), 10–11.

493 Roberts, Geren C.
       A neglected field, [by] Geren C. Roberts. In Herald of
     Holiness, 21 (Apr. 27, 1932), 7–8.

494 Sherman, Martha J.
       On racism and civil rights, [by] Martha J. Sherman. In
     Herald of Holiness, 53 (Nov. 4, 1964), 18.

495 Shockley, Jacklyn W.
       Memphis: it can't happen here, [by] Jacklyn W. Shockley.
     In Herald of Holiness, 57 (May 1, 1968), 9.

496 Strait, C. Neil
       The church and race relations, [by] C. Neil Strait. In
     Herald of Holiness, 57 (July 17, 1968), 6–7.

497 Trivitt, G. G.
       Herald and civil rights, [by] G. G. Trivitt. In Herald of
     Holiness, 53 (Feb. 3, 1965), 18.

498 Utter, Robert F.
       You can minister to more than one race in one church, [by]
     Robert F. Utter. In Preacher's Magazine, 56 (June/July/Aug.
     1981), 24–25.

499 Wenger, Fred
       My only regret, [by] Fred Wenger. In Herald of Holiness,
     63 (Jan. 16, 1974), 7.

500 Williamson, Gideon Brooks, 1898–1981.
       Meritocracy. In Herald of Holiness, 53 (July 22, 1964), 2.

         --GOVERNMENT

501 Church of the Nazarene. Districts. Gulf Central.
       Annual assembly journal. 1–17, 1953–1969. Kansas City,
     Mo., Nazarene Publishing House, 1953–1969. 17 v.

         --HISTORY

502 Bowman, Roger Eugene
       Color us Christian: the story of the Church of the

Nazarene among America's blacks, [by] Roger E. Bowman.
Kansas City, Mo., Nazarene Publishing House, 1975. 85 p.
IKON, MoKN, OMtvN, TNTN

503 Hurn, Raymond Walter, 1921–
     The black Nazarenes, [by] R. W. Hurn. In Reza, H. T.
     Missions: both sides of the coin. Kansas City, Mo., 1973,
     113-129. OkBetC

504 Purkiser, Westlake Taylor, 1910–
     Called unto holiness: the second twenty-five years, 1933-
     58, [by] W. T. Purkiser. Kansas City, Mo., Nazarene Pub-
     lishing House, c1983. 356 p. "Among the blacks": p. 197-
     200. DLC

505 Taylor, Mendell Lee, 1913–
     World outreach through home missions, [by] Mendell Taylor.
     Kansas City, Mo., Beacon Hill Press, 1958. 159 p. (Fifty
     years of Nazarene missions, 3) "Work among the colored peo-
     ple (1914-   )": p. 148-156. MoKN, OkBetC

          --HISTORY AND STUDY OF DOCTRINES

506 Purkiser, Westlake Taylor, 1910–
     Called unto holiness: the second twenty-five years, 1933-
     58, [by] W. T. Purkiser. Kansas City, Mo., Nazarene Pub-
     lishing House, c1983. 356 p. "A statement on civil rights":
     p. 89-90. DLC

          --HYMNS AND SACRED SONGS

507 Lacy, Floyd Henry, 1890-1969.
     Hallelujah: unique gospel songs and spirituals. Compiled
     by Lacy Gospel Singers. Music editor: Floyd W. Hawkins.
     Kansas City, Mo., Lillenas Publishing Co., 1958. 1 v. (un-
     paged) With music. OkBetC

          --PERIODICALS

508 Gulf Central informer. 1- 1958-1969.
     Kansas City, Mo.

          --SERMONS, TRACTS, ADDRESSES, ESSAYS

509 Bell, Ralph Shadell, 1934–
     Black evangelism: which way from here? [By] Ralph S.
     Bell. In Hurn, R. W., comp. Black evangelism: which way
     from here? Kansas City, Mo., 1974, 24-36.

510 Bowman, Roger Eugene
     Christ makes men brothers, [by] Roger E. Bowman. In
     Hurn, R. W., comp. Black evangelism: which way from here?
     Kansas City, Mo., 1974, 13-23.

511 Fisher, Charles William, 1916-
     The bridge is love across the color gap, [by] C. William
     Fisher. In Herald of Holiness, 63 (Feb. 13, 1974), 10-11.

         --UNITED STATES

           -- --EASTERN STATES

           (New York, New York City)

512 Jacobs, Clarence
     Personal evangelism in the city, [by] Clarence Jacobs. In
     Hurn, R. W., comp. Black evangelism: which way from here?
     Kansas City, Mo., 1974, 37-45.

           (Pennsylvania, Philadelphia)

513 Luther, Darrell E.
     Partnership with a miracle, [by] Darrell E. Luther. In
     Herald of Holiness, 58 (Nov. 19, 1969), 13-14.

           -- --MIDDLE WEST

           (Illinois, Chicago)

513a Beegle, Nina
     Chicago '86 impact gains momentum with existing ministries:
     what will Nazarenes do with Chicago in 1986? [By] Nina
     Beegle. In Herald of Holiness, 74 (Nov. 1, 1985), 20-21.

514 Furbee, Jack W.
     From church to community, [by] Jack W. Furbee. In
     Herald of Holiness, 62 (Feb. 14, 1973), 3.

           (Illinois, Kankakee)

515 Biracial program begun at Kankakee church.
     In Herald of Holiness, 58 (Jan. 22, 1969), 15-16.

516 Ogden, Ann
     Yes, Lord, yes, [by] Ann Ogden. In Herald of Holiness,
     63 (May 8, 1974), 34.

(Indiana, Indianapolis)

517 Ludwig, Sylvester Theodore, 1903-1964.
     The home mission challenge of the American Negro, [by]
     S. T. Ludwig. In Herald of Holiness, 35 (June 17, 1946),
     12-13.

(Kansas, Hutchinson)

518 Chambers, Herbert Morell, 1871-1928.
     Our church and the American Negro, [by] H. M. Chambers.
     In Herald of Holiness, 11 (Aug. 9, 1922), 9.

(Kansas, Topeka)

519 Beegle, Nina
     A center for hope in Topeka's inner city, [by] Nina Beegle.
     In Herald of Holiness, 71 (Dec. 1, 1982), 11-12.

(Ohio, Warren)

520 Armstrong, Alfred H.
     A Negro church in progress, [by] Alfred H. Armstrong.
     In Herald of Holiness, 35 (June 17, 1946), 12.

521 Ludwig, Sylvester Theodore, 1903-1964.
     The home mission challenge of the American Negro, [by]
     S. T. Ludwig. In Herald of Holiness, 35 (June 17, 1946),
     12-13.

-- --SOUTHERN STATES

522 Edwards, Joe E., 1908-
     When people pray, [by] Joe Edwards. In Herald of Holi-
     ness, 46 (Feb. 12, 1958), 6; note by Alpin P. Bowes, 46
     (Feb. 12, 1958), 6-7.

523 Stowe, Eugene L.
     The Gulf Central District: hail and farewell. In Herald of
     Holiness, 58 (June 11, 1969), 2.

(Arkansas, North Little Rock)

524 Holderfield, Paul
     Brother Paul: the Paul Holderfield story, [by] Paul Holder-
     field [and] Kathy Tharp. Kansas City, Mo., Beacon Hill
     Press of Kansas City, c1981. 108 p. OMtvN

525 Love in action in Little Rock.
     In Herald of Holiness, 62 (Oct. 10, 1973), 32-33.

(Florida, Orlando)

526 National Black Churchman's Conference in Orlando.
In Herald of Holiness, 73 (Aug. 15, 1984), 24-25.

(Louisiana, New Orleans)

527 Ludwig, Sylvester Theodore, 1903-1964.
The home mission challenge of the American Negro, [by]
S. T. Ludwig. In Herald of Holiness, 35 (June 17, 1946),
12-13.

(Mississippi)

528 Wiseman, Neil B.
$44.50 expands brotherhood in Mississippi, [by] Neil B.
Wiseman. In Herald of Holiness, 67 (Sept. 15, 1978), 16-17.

(Mississippi, Meridian)

529 Johnson, Charles, 1939-
Blacks, whites, and the Holy Spirit; an interview with
Charles Johnson, [by Jerry L. Appleby]. In Preacher's
Magazine, 58 (Dec./Jan./Feb. 1982-1983), 26-29.

(Oklahoma, Oklahoma City)

530 Edwards, Joe E., 1908-
When people pray, [by] Joe Edwards. In Herald of Holi-
ness, 46 (Feb. 12, 1958), 6; note by Alpin P. Bowes, 46
(Feb. 12, 1958), 6-7.

(Tennessee, Nashville)

531 Cook, R. Franklin
Nashville conference heralds heritage of urban ministry,
[by] R. Franklin Cook. In Herald of Holiness, 70 (May 15,
1981), 16-17.

(Texas, San Antonio)

531a Adams, Leonard W.
Saying "I love you" in San Antonio, by Leonard W. Adams.
In Preacher's Magazine, 60:4 (Sept./Oct./Nov. 1985), 20-22.

(Virginia, Richmond)

532 Richmond (Va.) Woodville church expands facilities.
In Herald of Holiness, 61 (Feb. 16, 1972), 23.

-- --WESTERN STATES

(California, Sacramento)

533 Oster, John C.
     Sacramento District builds a bridge of fellowship, [by] John
     Oster. In Herald of Holiness, 61 (Feb. 16, 1972), 20.

COOPERATIVE AGENCIES

*ASSOCIATION FOR THE PROMOTION OF SCRIPTURAL HOLI-
NESS IN AFRICA (1942-   )

This trans-denominational organization was composed of British
and American missionary agencies in South Africa. Speakers at its
1942 Conference in Pretoria represented the Church of the Nazarene
and the International Holiness Mission, groups which later merged.

534 Hynd, David, 1895-
     Holiness and race relations, [by] David Hynd. Holiness
     evangelism and the Europeans, [by] H. Kenneth Bedwell.
     Two papers presented to the conference of the Association for
     the Promotion of Scriptural Holiness in Africa, held in St.
     Andrew's Hall, Pretoria, March 3 to 6, 1942. n.p., Associa-
     tion for the Promotion of Scriptural Holiness in Africa; printed
     by Reliance Press, Brakpan, 1942. 13 p.

*HOLINESS ASSOCIATION OF TEXAS (1899-1910)

Formed in November 1899 at Peniel, a new suburb of Greenville, Texas, the Holiness Association of Texas exercised many of
the prerogatives of a church. It attracted members of the Methodist
Episcopal Church, South, the Cumberland Presbyterian Church, and
other denominations who had been ostracized for their holiness testimony. It issued licenses to holiness preachers denied recognition
by old-line denominations. Among the "loyalists" attracted to the
Association were E. C. De Jernett and J. T. Upchurch, men sensitive to the social and racial injustices of the time who later carried
this concern into the Pentecostal Church of the Nazarene with which
most of its members united in 1907 and 1908. The Holiness Association of Texas held its last annual meeting at Peniel in November
1910.

535 De Jernett, E. C., 1857-1929.
     The race problem, [by] E. C. De Jernett, R. L. Averill
     [and] J. T. Upchurch. In Holiness Association of Texas.
     Year book, 1906-7. Peniel, Tx., 1906, 67-69.

EVANGELICAL CHURCH OF CHRIST (HOLINESS) (1947-   )

In 1947 William E., Holman, Los Angeles pastor and bishop of
the Church of Christ (Holiness) for twenty years, left that body
and founded the Evangelical Church of Christ (Holiness). Doctrine
and polity remained identical to the parent body. By the mid-1970s
the Evangelical Church of Christ (Holiness) consisted of four
churches: Washington, Omaha, Denver, and Los Angeles, plus two
missions in the latter place. E. K. McFadden, the senior bishop,
resided in Washington at that time.

FREE CHRISTIAN ZION CHURCH OF CHRIST (1905-   )

On July 10, 1905, E. D. Brown and other ministers who had
withdrawn from the African Methodist Episcopal Zion, African
Methodist Episcopal, Colored Methodist Episcopal, Methodist Episcopal, and Baptist churches, organized the Free Christian Zion
Church of Christ at Redemption, Arkansas. The grievance they
held in common was objection to assessments (which they called
taxes) to support denominational programs. They felt that instead
local churches should use their resources for relief of the poor.
Wesleyan doctrinal positions were maintained and only minor changes
were made in polity. The bishop, who is called chief pastor, ap-
points ministers and other church officials. Principal local church
leaders are pastor and deacon. Headquarters are in Nashville,
Arkansas. In 1956 the denomination reported 22,260 members in
742 churches. Eleven years later a former editor of the church
paper no longer affiliated with the group said there were only five
churches with a combined membership of 100.

--PERIODICALS

536 Zion trumpet. 1- 19 -
     Nashville, Ar.

KODESH CHURCH OF IMMANUEL (1929-   )

Founded at Philadelphia in October 1929, the Kodesh Church
of Immanuel set out to reemphasize the teaching on holiness which
the 120 founding members felt was being lost in the African Methodist
Episcopal Zion Church. The leader, the Reverend Frank Russell
Killingsworth of Washington, D.C., said he received divine inspiration for the name from Isaiah 7:14 and from the Hebrew word
"godêsh," which means pure, sanctified, holy. The movement was
incorporated in 1930.
On January 22, 1934, the Christian Tabernacle Union with

headquarters in Pittsburgh merged into the Kodesh Church of Immanuel. Signers of the articles of agreement for the latter were Frank Russell Killingsworth, A. E. Still, Arthur Taylor, C. H. Payne, Oney Taylor, and M. K. Fuller. In 1936 the church reported nine congregations and 582 members. Forty years later it had only six branches. These, however, claimed a combined membership of 4,000. At that time it had affiliates in Pennsylvania, Ohio, and Virginia. Mission work was in progress in Liberia.

--DOCTRINAL AND CONTROVERSIAL WORKS

537 Killingsworth, Frank Russell, 1878-
     Theologic questions and answers on Christian perfection or
     sanctification. Philadelphia, Westminster Press, 1949. 93 p.
     DLC

--GOVERNMENT

538 Kodesh Church of Immanuel.
     Doctrines and discipline of the Kodesh Church of Immanuel.
     F. R. Killingsworth, comp. Philadelphia, Westminster Press,
     1934. 74 p. DLC

539 Kodesh Church of Immanuel.
     Doctrines and discipline of the Kodesh Church of Immanuel.
     F. R. Killingsworth, comp. Philadelphia, Westminster Press,
     1940. 94 p. DLC

METHODISTS

*FREE METHODIST CHURCH OF NORTH AMERICA (1860-)

     This church, organized on the eve of the Civil War on a platform which included free grace, free worship, free seats and free men, has throughout its history maintained an attitude of openness to blacks, retaining Thoro Harris, a non-member as editor of several song books, and commissioning Emma J. Ray and the much-traveled J. M. Humphrey as evangelists. Concentrated in the "burned-over district" of western New York and in areas settled from it, Free Methodists for most part had little contact with blacks. Until 1943 they prohibited instrumental music, symbolizing an ascetic life style attractive to few black people. Attempts in the 1920s by Free Methodist evangelist E. E. Shelhamer to hold integrated meetings in the South met with such severe opposition that he abandoned the practice. Following his death in 1947, his wife, Julia, and his son-in-law, Gilbert James, persisted in biracial ministry, she in a slum mission in Washington, D.C. and he as head of the church's Department of Interracial Evangelism. Free Methodists continued to sponsor the Olive Branch Mission in Chicago, the institution in which Mrs. Shelhamer had served an apprenticeship in her youth. As pastor in Shreveport, Louisiana, in the 1940s, James founded an interracial day school. Later as professor of pastoral theology at Asbury Theological Seminary, Wilmore, Kentucky, he raised the consciousness of generations of students to the need for urban ministry. Discontinuance of the Department of Interracial Evangelism in 1960 left the Free Methodist Church of North America without an official instrument of outreach across racial barriers. In 1982 Afro-Americans probably accounted for less than one percent of the 70,657 members in the United States.

--DOCTRINAL AND CONTROVERSIAL WORKS

539a McKenna, David Loren, 1929-
        The urban crisis; a symposium on the racial problem in the
    inner city. General editor: David McKenna. Grand Rapids,
    Mi., Zondervan Publishing House, 1969. 146 p. DLC

--HISTORY

540 Marston, Leslie Ray, 1894-
        From age to age a living witness: a historical interpretation
    of Free Methodism's first century, [by] Leslie R. Marston.
    Winona Lake, In., Light and Life Press, c1960. 608 p.
    "Position on racial discrimination": p. 402-403. DLC

541 Smith, David Paul, 1915-
        The growth and development of the interracial movement
    within the Free Methodist Church of North America. Wilmore,
    Ky., 1950. v, 53 l. Student paper--Asbury Theological
    Seminary. KyWAT

--HYMNS AND SACRED SONGS

542 Harris, Thoro, 1874-1955.
        Light and life songs: adapted especially to Sunday schools,
    prayer meetings and other social services. Editors: William
    B. Olmstead [and] Thoro Harris. Associate editor: William J.
    Kirkpatrick. Chicago, W. B. Rose, c1904. [222] p. With
    music. OkBetC

543 Harris, Thoro, 1874-1955.
        Light and life songs, number two: adapted especially to
    Sunday schools, social worship, camp meetings and revival
    services. William B. Olmstead, editor. Thoro Harris, assistant
    editor. Chicago, W. B. Rose, c1914. 224 p. KyWAT, OkBetC

--PASTORAL LITERATURE

544 Humphrey, Jerry Miles, 1872-
     The convert's homeward guide, [by] J. M. Humphrey.
     Chicago, W. B. Rose, 1916. 126 p. DLC

545 Humphrey, Jerry Miles, 1872-
     Crumbs from heaven, [by] J. M. Humphrey. Chicago,
     Light and Life Press, c1927. 144 p. DLC

546 Humphrey, Jerry Miles, 1872-
     Spicy pocket sermons from the alphabet for busy people,
     [by] J. M. Humphrey. Chicago, W. B. Rose, 1917. 96 p.
     KyWAT

--PERIODICALS

547 Interracial news. 1- Feb. 1950-1956.
     Greenville, Il. KyWAT

*WESLEYAN METHODIST CHURCH OF AMERICA (1843-1968)
[1843-1891 as Wesleyan Methodist Connection of America; 1891-
     1947 as Wesleyan Methodist Connection (or Church) of
     America.]

The Wesleyan Methodist Connection of America was born in
protest against the compromise of the Methodist Episcopal Church
with slavery. At the beginning growth was spectacular: from
6,000 to 15,000 members the first year. The years following eman-
cipation, however, witnessed return of nearly a hundred ministers
and thousands of members to the parent body, leaving the Wesleyan
Methodist Connection in 1875 with no larger membership than it had
in 1844. Although post-war evangelism in the South produced some
strength there (particularly in North Carolina), the bulk of the
membership resided in New York and Pennsylvania and in areas
settled from them.
     In 1891 black congregations in Ohio and Tennessee were gath-
ered into annual conferences: South Ohio and West Tennessee.
(The Central Alabama Mission Conference, formed in 1907, later
joined the latter.) In 1957 West Tennessee in turn was merged
into the South Ohio Conference. From 1912 to 1944 the church in
collaboration with the state sponsored the Alabama Mission School
at Brent, Alabama. Numerically, black work proved disappointing.
At its first session in 1894 the South Ohio Conference reported ten
churches. Sixty-four years later it reported the same number.
Under Eugene Ramsey, a black seminary graduate who became conference president in 1957. During the next decade, four additional
churches (including one in Indianapolis) were organized. In 1967,
South Ohio reported a full membership of 365 and 592 enrolled in

Sunday school. The next year the denomination merged with the
Pilgrim Holiness Church. At the time of the union, the Wesleyan
Methodists claimed 1,022 churches, 38,110 full members, and 109,294
enrolled in Sunday school.

--DOCTRINAL AND CONTROVERSIAL WORKS

548 Harper, Albert Foster, 1907-
     Toward Christian understanding, [by] A. F. Harper. In
     Wesleyan Methodist, 123 (Mar. 24, 1965), 8. Reprinted from
     Herald of Holiness, 53 (Feb. 3, 1965).

--GOVERNMENT

549 Wesleyan Methodist Church of America. Conferences. South
     Ohio.
     Minutes. 1-74, 1894-1967. n.p., 1894-1967. 74 v.

--HISTORY

550 McLeister, Ira Ford, 1879-1963.
     Conscience and commitment: the history of the Wesleyan
     Methodist Church of America, [by] Ira Ford McLeister [and]
     Roy Stephen Nicholson. Fourth revised ed., edited by Lee
     M. Haines, Jr. [and] Melvin E. Dieter. Marion, In., Wesley
     Press, 1976. xviii, 693 p. On work among blacks: p. 126,
     283, 357-359, 568, 571-572, 632.

551 McLeister, Ira Ford, 1879-1963.
     History of the Wesleyan Methodist Church of America, [by]
     Ira Ford McLeister. Revised ed. by Roy Stephen Nicholson.
     Marion, In., Wesley Press, 1959. xxvi, 558 p. On work
     among blacks: p. 283, 414, 517-518.

*PILGRIM HOLINESS CHURCH (1897-1968)
[1897-1905 as International Holiness Union and Prayer League; 1905-
   1913 as International Apostolic Holiness Union and Churches;
   1913-1919 as International Apostolic Holiness Church, 1919-1922
   as International Holiness Church.]

     Although its parent stem dated from 1897, the Pilgrim Holiness
Church owed its denominational character in large part to mergers
in 1919 and 1922 with the Indiana-based Holiness Christian Church
and the California-based Pilgrim Church. Although intent from the
start on proclaiming holiness in "slums and jungles" and in "all the
world," the Pilgrim Holiness Church only belatedly sought to enroll

American blacks. In 1941 a promising home mission effort at Car-
uthersville in the "tar heel" of Missouri was aborted by the death
of the pastor, W. S. Small. Two years later a plan to support
F. E. Williams and H. R. McInnis of the Church of Christ (Holiness)
in pioneer efforts in Sun, Louisiana, and several Mississippi communities, was approved by their church body only to be jettisoned
by the Pilgrims following the death of Williams later that year.
Scarcity of qualified workers apparently lay behind the decision of
the secretary of home missions, R. W. Wolfe, to retrench. On the
other hand, Pilgrim success in the Caribbean resulted in the establishment of twelve West Indian churches in the United Kingdom
in the decade before merger with the Wesleyan Methodist Church of
America in 1968. At that time there were 302 full members and 829
enrolled in Sunday school in Britain. The mostly white United States
membership then stood at 32,765.

                         --CHURCH EXTENSION

552 Activities among the Negroes.
        In Pilgrim Holiness Advocate, 23 (Apr. 8, 1943), 12.

                         --HISTORY

553 Thomas, Paul Westphal, 1894-1972.
        The days of our pilgrimage: the history of the Pilgrim
     Holiness Church, [by] Paul Westphal Thomas [and] Paul Wil-
     liam Thomas. Edited by Melvin E. Dieter [and] Lee M.
     Haines, Jr. Marion, In., Wesley Press, 1976. xviii, 382 p.
     "Work among minorities in the United States": p. 180-181.

PILGRIM WESLEYAN HOLINESS CHURCH (1958-   )
[1958-1968 as British Isles District of the Pilgrim Holiness Church.]

     The success of Pilgrim Holiness missions in the Caribbean re-
sulted in establishment of work in the United Kingdom. In March
1958 Dennis Sampson, an immigrant from Antigua, held the first
service in Birmingham in a small room with only nine present. A
decade later he reported that twelve congregations had been established. Full membership stood at 302, Sunday school enrollment at
829. Church locations included Birmingham, London, Leicester,
Bristol, Manchester, Wolverhampton, Nottingham, Leeds, Bedford,
Northampton, and Slough. Following the merger of the Pilgrim
Holiness Church and the Wesleyan Methodist Church of America, the
British churches, though still affiliated with the Wesleyan Church,
adopted the present name: Pilgrim Wesleyan Holiness Church.
     In 1976 there were eighteen churches and 468 members in the

United Kingdom. National headquarters are in Birmingham. The constituency is composed largely of immigrants from Barbados, St. Kitts, Trinidad, and Jamaica.

--HISTORY

554 Thomas, Paul Westphal, 1894-1972.
       The days of our pilgrimage: the history of the Pilgrim Holiness Church, [by] Paul Westphal Thomas [and] Paul William Thomas. Edited by Melvin E. Dieter [and] Lee M. Haines, Jr. Marion, In. Wesley Press, 1976. xviii, 382 p. "The Pilgrim Holiness Church of the British Isles": p. 302-305.

555 Thomas, Paul Westphal, 1894-1972.
       "Send down the gospel rain"; a report of revival work with the Pilgrims in England, [by] P. W. Thomas. In Pilgrim Holiness Advocate, 43 (Nov. 23, 1963), 6-7.

SANCTIFIED CHURCH OF CHRIST (1937-)

     The Sanctified Church of Christ was organized at Columbus, Georgia in July 1937. In both doctrine and prudentials it is a conservative body, enjoining members to refrain from a wide range of practices in dress and amusement. Examples are prohibitions against watching television and women cutting their hair. In the early 1970s the church, which is headed by a bishop, reported seven churches and 1,000 members in six Southern states. Unique among black holiness churches, the Sanctified Church of Christ from 1969 to 1977 maintained a "cooperating" relationship with the Christian Holiness Association.

--GOVERNMENT

556 Sanctified Church of Christ.
       Discipline of Sanctified Church of Christ. Columbus, Ga., 1957. "Second printing."

TRIUMPH THE CHURCH AND KINGDOM OF GOD IN CHRIST (International) (1902-)

     At 12:00 noon on October 20, 1897, Elias Dempsey Smith, a Methodist pastor in Issaquena County, Mississippi, received this church through the revelation and knowledge of God himself. It was not until 1902, however, that the plan was "speeded to the earth," nor until still two years later that it "opened to the world."

Final confirmation came in the form of 225 members in Birmingham
yet eleven years later. Although in 1920 Smith departed for Addis
Ababa and never returned, a remnant of his followers persisted.
In 1936 the entire movement consisted of two churches, both in
Georgia, with a combined membership of 69. Thirty-six years later,
Triumph the Church and Kingdom of God in Christ (International)
reported 475 churches, 54,307 members, and 1,375 clergy of whom
860 were serving parishes. The denomination, which obtained incorporation in the District of Columbia in 1918, has affiliates in 31
states and in Africa and South America. Baton Rouge, Birmingham,
and Atlanta have successively been headquarters.

An elaborate epistemological and eschatological framework covers
a rather conventional Wesleyan doctrinal system. The church's
most noted defector to date is James Francis Marion Jones (commonly
known as Prophet Jones), whom in 1938 it sent from Birmingham to
found a new branch in Detroit. Instead, he established the Church
of Universal Triumph, the Dominion of God, with himself as head.

--CONTROVERSIAL WORKS

557 Mason, Charles Harrison, 1866-1961.
          No dying. In Cornelius, L. J., ed. The pioneer: history
     of the Church of God in Christ. [Memphis], 1975, 61-62.

--DOCTRINAL AND CONTROVERSIAL WORKS

558 Triumph the Church and Kingdom of God in Christ.
          Junior guide and easy lessons (combined) of Triumph the
     Church and Kingdom of God in Christ. [Birmingham, Al.,
     194-]

--HISTORY

559 Harris, D. H.
          Triumph the Church and Kingdom of God in Christ, [by]
     D. H. Harris. In Loetscher, L. A., ed. Twentieth century
     encyclopedia of religious knowledge. Grand Rapids, Mi., 1955,
     II, 1125.

560 Wilmore, Gayraud Stephen, 1921-
          Black religion and black radicalism, [by] Gayraud S. Wil-
     more. Garden City, N.Y., Doubleday, 1972. xiii, 344 p.
     (C. Eric Lincoln series on black religion) On Triumph the
     Church and Kingdom of God in Christ: p. 212. DLC

*WESLEYAN CHURCH (1968-   )

Product of the 1968 union of the Pilgrim Holiness Church and
the Wesleyan Methodist Church of America, the Wesleyan Church
contains a cluster of black churches, known as the South Ohio
District, which had been part of the former Wesleyan Methodist
Church. This unit, which a year before the merger had fourteen
churches and 365 full members, reported one less congregation and
9 fewer members in 1976. The predominantly Caribbean-immigrant
British Isles District (formerly Pilgrim Holiness and known in the
United Kingdom after 1968 as the Pilgrim Wesleyan Holiness Church)
reported twelve churches and 302 members a year before the union.
In 1976 it had eighteen churches and 468 members. In the same
period membership in the United States, Canada and British Isles
for the Wesleyan Church as a whole had risen from 68,985 to
84,550, a rather sharp contrast with the static condition of the
South Ohio churches. Emergence of biracial ministry such as that
undertaken in the Austin neighborhood of Chicago may signal a
change of direction in denominational strategy.

--DOCTRINAL AND CONTROVERSIAL WORKS

561 Ingram, Loana
        Who is my neighbor? [By] Loana Ingram. In Wesleyan Ad-
     vocate, 138 (July 7, 1980, 15-16.

2. HOLINESS-PENTECOSTAL BODIES

The nineteenth-century Wesleyan holiness teachers held that purity
of heart and power for Christian service were the dual accomplish-
ments of the Holy Spirit in entire sanctification. These were, they
said, one nad inseparable. Heavy emphasis, however, was placed
on purity, so heavy in fact that a teaching developed in the 1890s
in the Midwest and South holding that while the second work puri-
fied the vessel, a third, the baptism of fire, was necessary to fill
it. Although the fall in 1900 of its white leader, Benjamin Hardin
Irwin, largely discredited the movement, the baptism of fire teaching opened the way for belief in a third-crisis experience and
pointed out the imbalance between stress on purity and power in
Wesleyan holiness teaching. Tongues-speaking as the initial evidence of the baptism of the Holy Spirit (a doctrine which emerged
from the Topeka, Kansas, revival of 1901 under another white,
Charles Fox Parham) became the centerpiece of the preaching of
William J. Seymour, a black disciple of Parham who led the Azusa

Street revival in Los Angeles five years later. This interracial meeting, which ran around-the-clock for weeks, swept into the third-blessing-empowerment ranks most of the independent holiness leaders of the South, both black and white. Most significant of these for blacks was C. H. Mason, pioneer holiness evangelist and father of the Memphis-based Church of God in Christ. Mason's acceptance of tongues caused a rift between him and C. P. Jones, who was his fellow worker in the emerging black holiness movement in the South, and split the heretofore common work along new doctrinal lines.

In 1908 the remnant of Irwin's fire-baptized movement, having accepted the tongues-centered teaching a year previously, blessed their black brethren in forming a new church, the Colored Fire Baptized Holiness Church, under W. E. Fuller, one of Irwin's early converts. The wrenching brought about first by commitment to second-crisis sanctification and now to a third-crisis Spirit baptism as well, caused many painful separations. Many on both sides knew the turmoil behind "I'm happy with Jesus alone," a much-sung song by C. P. Jones written at the height of the second blessing crusade eleven years earlier.

--DOCTRINAL AND CONTROVERSIAL WORKS

562 Goodwin, Bennie Eugene, 1933-
     Martin Luther King, Jr.: God's messenger of love, justice and hope, [by] Bennie Goodwin. Jersey City, N.J., Goodpatrick, c1976. 89 p. DLC

563 Goodwin, Bennie Eugene, 1933-
     Pray right! Live right! Reflections on the Lord's Prayer, [by] Bennie E. Goodwin. 2d ed. Downers Grove, Il., InterVarsity Press, c1979. [46] p. First published in 1974 under title: Pray and grow rich. PBfG

564 Goodwin, Bennie Eugene, 1933-
     Pray right and grow rich, [by] Bennie Goodwin. Jersey City, N.J., Goodpatrick Publishers, 1974. 46 p.

565 Goodwin, Bennie Eugene, 1933-
     Speak up, black man, [by] Bennie Goodwin. [Jersey City, N.J., Goodpatrick Publishers], 1972. 36 p. PPiPT

566 Lovett, Leonard, 1939-
     What can charismatics learn from black Pentecostals? [By] Leonard Lovett. In Logos Journal, 10 (May/June 1980), 24-26, 28-29.

567 McKinney, George Dallas, 1932-
     The Jehovah's Witnesses, [by] George D. McKinney. San Diego, Ca., Vision Publicaitons, 1975. 130 p. ArStC

568 McKinney, George Dallas, 1932-
     The theology of the Jehovah's witnesses. Grand Rapids,
Mi., Zondervan Publishing House, 1962. 130 p. DLC

569 McKinney, George Dallas, 1932-
     The theology of the Jehovah's Witnesses. London, Marshall,
Morgan & Scott, 1963, c1962. 131 p. InU, Mo, Uk

570 McKinney, George Dallas, 1932-
     The theology of the Jehovah's Witnesses, [by] George D.
McKinney. San Diego, Ca., Production House, c1975. 130 p.
CLamB, KyWAT

571 Tinney, James Steven, 1942-
     Homosexuality as a Pentecostal phenomenon, [by] James S.
Tinney. In Spirit, 1:2 (1977), 45-59.

572 Tinney, James Steven, 1942-
     The prosperity doctrine: perverted economies, [by] James
S. Tinney. In Spirit, 2:1 (1978), 44-53.

573 Turner, William Clair, 1948-
     Is Pentecostalism truly Christian? [By] William C. Turner,
Jr. In Spirit, 2:1 (1978), 29-38.

                    --EDUCATION

574 Goodwin, Bennie Eugene, 1933-
     The effective teacher: a Christian's guide to teaching, [by]
Bennie E. Goodwin II. Downers Grove, Il, InterVarsity Press,
c1985. 48 p. DLC

575 Goodwin, Bennie Eugene, 1933-
     Reflections on education: a Christian scholar looks at King,
Freire and Jesus as social and religious educators, [by] Bennie
E. Goodwin. Jersey City, N.J., Goodpatrick Publishers, 1978.
136 p.

           --HISTORY AND STUDY OF DOCTRINES

576 Clark, William A., 1891-
     Sanctification in Negro religion, [by] William A. Clark. In
Social Forces, 15 (May 1937), 544-551.

577 Clemmons, Ithiel
     Holiness, education, and sexual revolution, [by] Ithiel
Clemmons. In Spirit, 2:1 (1978), 39-43.

578   Forbes, James Alexander, 1935–
         Shall we call this dream progressive Pentecostalism?   [By]
      James A. Forbes, Jr.   In Spirit, 1:1 (1977), 12-15.

579   Lewis, Harvey, –1980.
         A theory of conscience, [by] Harvey Lewis, Jr.   In Spirit,
      3:2 (1979), 15-19.

580   Lovett, Leonard, 1939–
         Black holiness-Pentecostalism: implications for ethics and
      social transformation.   Atlanta, 1978.   3, viii, 183 l.   Thesis
      (Ph.D.)--Emory University.   GEU

         --MUSIC

581   Boggs, Beverly J.
         Some aspects of worship in a Holiness church, [by] Beverly
      Boggs.   In New York Folklore, 3 (Summer/Winter 1977), 29-44.

582   Heilbut, Anthony Otto, 1941–
         The gospel sound: good news and bad times, [by] Tony
      Heilbut.   New York, Simon and Schuster, 1971.   350 p.   "The
      holiness church":   p. 199-278.   DLC, Ok

583   Heilbut, Anthony Otto, 1941–
         The gospel sound: good news and bad times, [by] Tony
      Heilbut.   Garden City, N.Y., Anchor Press/Doubleday, 1975,
      c1971.   xxxv, 364 p.   (Anchor books)   "The holiness church":
      p. 171-251.

         --PASTORAL LITERATURE

584   Goodwin, Bennie Eugene, 1933–
         The effective leader: a basic guide to Christian leadership,
      [by] Bennie E. Goodwin II.   Downers Grove, Il., InterVarsity
      Press, c1981.   61 p.   OCedC

585   McKinney, George Dallas, 1932–
         Christian marriage: an act of faith and commitment, [by]
      George D. McKinney.   San Diego, Ca., Vision Publications,
      1977.   51 p.   ArStC

         --PERIODICALS

586   Last days revival. 1– 1970–
         Kansas City, Mo.

587   Pentecostal Alliance crescendo. 1– Feb./Mar. 1952–
         Chicago.   DLC

--UNITED STATES

588 Synan, Harold Vinson, 1934-
      The Holiness-Pentecostal movement in the United States,
      [by] Vinson Synan. Grand Rapids, Mi., Eerdmans, 1971.
      248 p. Based on thesis (Ph.D.)--University of Georgia. "The
      Negro Pentecostals": p. 165-184. DLC, MBU-T, MH-AH,
      MSohG, TxWaS

ALPHA AND OMEGA PENTECOSTAL CHURCH OF AMERICA (1945-   )
  [Mar.-Apr. 1945 as Alpha and Omega Church of God Tabernacle;
   Apr. 1945-19-- as Alpha and Omega Pentecostal Church.]

    On March 12, 1945, Magdelene Mabe Phillips and eight other
former members of a Baltimore holiness church established the Alpha
and Omega Church of God Tabernacle. The next month they changed
the name to Alpha and Omega Pentecostal Church, "of America" being added upon incorporation sometime later. In 1964 Charles E.
Waters, Sr., Mrs. Phillips' successor, left to found the True Fellowship Pentecostal Church of America, John Mabe, the founder's
brother, became overseer. In the mid-1970s the body consisted of
two churches and a mission, all in Baltimore, with a combined membership of about 400.

AZUSA STREET APOSTOLIC FAITH MISSION OF LOS ANGELES,
    CALIFORNIA (1906-1922)
  [1906-19-- as Pacific Apostolic Faith Movement.]

    In the fall of 1906 Charles Fox Parham, "projector" of the
Apostolic Faith Movement, visited Los Angeles. Parham came at the
invitation of William J. Seymour, pastor of the Azusa Street Apostolic Faith Mission, whom he had assisted in moving from Houston
a few months earlier. The visit was an unfriendly one, to be followed shortly by disclosure of an unnamed indiscretion by the
original leader and his resignation as projector. The October issue
of the official publication listed Parham as projector. Within a month
the mission letterhead had been revised. The heading now read:

              THE PACIFIC APOSTOLIC FAITH MOVEMENT
    W. J. Seymour, Pastor and Manager. Clara Lum, Secretary
              Headquarters: 312 Azusa Street
Hiram Smith, Deacon   G. Cook, Ass't State Manager
Jenny Moore, City Missionary   Florence Crawford, State Director
Phoebe Sargent, City Missionary G. W. Evans, Field Director

The reorganization represented a transparent attempt by Seymour
to wrest control of the movement from Parham. Despite his personal

charisma, Seymour's failure as an organizer and diplomat cost him
dearly. In 1907 Mrs. Crawford (without Seymour's knowledge)
took the non-Los Angeles mailing lists of the official organ and
moved the publication to Portland, Oregon. Two years later a rift
between Seymour and William H. Durham, pioneer proponent of the
"Finished Work of Calvary" teaching, resulted in a dampened spiritual atmosphere and in departure of most whites from the mission.
Although it survived until the pastor's death in 1922, the glory of
the exciting revival days of 1906 and 1907 had departed from the
Azusa Street Mission.

--GOVERNMENT

589   Azusa Street Apostolic Faith Mission of Los Angeles, California.
      The doctrine and discipline of the Azusa Street Apostolic
      Faith Mission of Los Angeles, California. Los Angeles, W. J.
      Seymour, 1915.

--HISTORY

590   Bartleman, Frank, 1871-1935.
      Another wave of revival, [by] Frank Bartleman. Edited by
      John G. Myers. Springdale, Pa., Whitaker House, c1982.
      175 p. Abridgment of How Pentecost came to Los Angeles.
      Reprint with additions and revisions of the 1970 ed. published
      under title: Another wave rolls in!

591   Bartleman, Frank, 1871-1935.
      Another wave rolls in! [By] Frank Bartleman. Edited by
      John Walker. Revised and enlarged ed., edited by John G.
      Myers. Northridge, Ca., Voice Publications, 1970, c1962.
      128 p. First published in 1962 under title: What really hap-
      pened at "Azusa Street"? Abridgment of How Pentecost came
      to Los Angeles. TxWaS

592   Bartleman, Frank, 1871-1925.
      Azusa Street, [by] Frank Bartleman. With foreword by
      Vinson Synan. Plainfield, N.J., Logos International, c1980.
      xxvi, 184 p. First published in 1925 under title: How Pente-
      cost came to Los Angeles. DLC, KyWAT, MSohG

593   Bartleman, Frank, 1871-1935.
      How Pentecost came to Los Angeles; as it was in the begin-
      ning: old Azusa mission from my diary, [by] Frank Bartleman.
      3d ed. Los Angeles, 1925. 166 p.

594   Bartleman, Frank, 1871-1935.
      What really happened at "Azusa Street"? By Frank Bartle-
      man. Edited by John Walker. Northridge, Ca., Voice Christian

Publications, 1962. 97 p. Abridgment of How Pentecost came to Los Angeles. KyWAT

595 Fidler, R. L.
Historical review of the Pentecostal outpouring in Los Angeles at the Azusa Street mission in 1906, [by] R. L. Fidler. In International Outlook (Jan./Mar. 1963), 3-14.

596 Nelson, Douglas J., 1931-
For such a time as this: the story of Bishop William J. Seymour and the Azusa Street revival; a search for Pentecostal/ Charismatic roots, [by] Douglas J. Nelson. Birmingham, 1981. 363 l. Thesis (Ph.D.)--University of Birmingham. UkBU

597 Nickel, Thomas Roy
Azusa Street outpouring, as told to me by those who were there, [by] Thomas R. Nickel. Hanford, Ca., Great Commission International, 1956. 28 [14] p.

598 Parham, Sarah E. (Thistlewaite), 1877-1937.
The life of Charles F. Parham, founder of the Apostolic Faith Movement. Joplin, Mo., Tri-State Printing Co., 1930. 452 p. "Try the spirits": p. 161-170. CoD, MnHi

599 Synan, Harold Vinson, 1934-
The Holiness-Pentecostal movement in the United States, [by] Vinson Synan. Grand Rapids, Mi., Eerdmans, c1971. 248 p. Based on thesis (Ph.D.)--University of Georgia, 1967. "The American Jerusalem--Azusa Street": p. 95-116.

600 Synan, Harold Vinson, 1934-
The Pentecostal movement in the United States. Athens, 1967. vi, 296 l. Thesis (Ph.D.)--University of Georgia. "The American Jerusalem": l. 113-143. GU

601 Valdez, Arthur Clarence, 1896-
Fire on Azusa Street, [by] A. C. Valdez, Sr., with James F. Scheer. Costa Mesa, Ca., Gift Publications, c1980. 139 p.

--PERIODICALS

602 Apostolic faith. 1-15, Sept. 1906-Oct./Nov. 1908.
Los Angeles. Nos. 1-13, Sept. 1906-May 1908 collected by Fred T. Corum and issued under title: Like as of fire (Wilmington, Ma., 1981).

BOUNTIFUL BLESSINGS CHURCHES (197 -)

This body, centered in Memphis, was established in the 1970s under the leadership of Gilbert E. Patterson, nephew of the presiding bishop of the Church of God in Christ from which it had separated.

--PERIODICALS

603   Bountiful blessings.   1-   197 -
      Memphis.

--TENNESSEE

-- --MEMPHIS

604   Memphis blacks dedicate first million-dollar church in over a
      decade.
      In Jet, 55 (Dec. 7, 1978), 19.

CHRIST HOLY SANCTIFIED CHURCH OF AMERICA (19 -)

In the mid-1970s the headquarters of the Christ Holy Sanctified Church of America were in Oakland, California.

--GOVERNMENT

605   Christ Holy Sanctified Church of America.
      Discipline of Christ Holy Sanctified Church of America, Inc.
      [Edited by] Archbishop J. King.   Oakland, Ca., 19--.

--PERIODICALS

606   Gospel voice.   1-   ,   -1967.
      Oakland, Ca.

CHRIST'S SANCTIFIED HOLY CHURCH (Jennings, La.) (1904-)
[1904-1922 as Colored Church South.]

In 1903 Asher Fisher, Charlotte Gray, and Mary Hanson, all followers of Joseph Lynch, held a revival in the Colored Methodist Episcopal Church of West Lake, Louisiana. On April 16 of the next year, converts of this meeting organized the Colored Church South.

In Wichita, Kansas, four years later was established the first congregation of what became the Northern District. By 1910 the name,
Christ's Sanctified Holy Church, had begun to come into use. It
became official in 1922 when headquarters moved from West Lake to
Jennings, Louisiana.

In 1957 the organization reported thirty churches and 600
members. Distinctive teachings include one spiritual (as contrasted
to water) baptism and gradual sanctification. Tongues-speech, it
says, is the initial evidence of the baptism of the Holy Spirit. A
conference meets annually. When the conference is not in session,
the five-member Board No. 1 oversees church affairs.

CHURCH OF GOD

APOSTOLIC FAITH CHURCH OF GOD (1909-)

The Apostolic Faith Church of God, whose present headquarters
are in its Church, no. 1, 5211 A Street, S.E., Washington, D.C.,
dates from 1909. It was founded by Charles W. Lowe of Handsom,
Virginia, during a visit of Elders William J. Seymour and C. H.
Mason. The movement secured a charter in Maryland in 1938, and
in the District of Columbia in 1965. In addition to the District of
Columbia, churches are located in seven states: New York, New
Jersey, Pennsylvania, Maryland, Virginia, and both Carolinas.
Headquarters moved from Baltimore to Washington in 1967. G. B.
White is presiding bishop.

--GOVERNMENT

607 Apostolic Faith Church of God.
     Apostolic faith manual of the Apostolic Faith Church of God,
     Inc. Washington, 1966. ii, 37 p. Cover title. "Authorized
     revision ... by the Constitution Committee. Recompiled by
     Elder Leon Harper, Secretary. Approved by Presiding Bishop
     G. B. White."

--MUSIC

608 Noble, E. Myron
     Introduction to musical instruments of the Bible, [by] Myron
     Noble. Washington, Apostolic Faith Church of God, 1978.
     20 p.

APOSTOLIC FAITH MISSION CHURCH OF GOD (1906-)

The Apostolic Faith Mission Church of God was founded July 10, 1906, in Mobile, Alabama. Perhaps the most noted convert of Bishop F. W. Williams, the founder, was W. T. Phillips, who fathered the Apostolic Overcoming Holy Church of God. In 1982 the Birmingham-based body reported seventeen churches and 1,700 full members. Houston Ward, the current presiding bishop, lives in Cantonment, Florida.

BAPTIST CHURCH OF GOD (1972-)

Composed of Jamaican immigrants to the United Kingdom, the Baptist Church of God, formed in 1972, is the result of acceptance of Pentecostal beliefs by former Free Baptists. Headquarters for the group, which in 1980 consisted of five churches, 130 full members, and 350 constituent members, are in London.

BIBLE CHURCH OF GOD (1964-)

Established in 1964, the Bible Church of God is a British affiliate of the Huntsville, Alabama-based Church of God. Composed of Jamaican immigrants, its three congregations in Nottingham and Birmingham are led by two bishops. In 1980 the Bible Church of God claimed 100 full members and a total community of 300.

CALVARY CHURCH OF GOD IN CHRIST (1952-)

An affiliate of the Memphis-based Church of God in Christ, the Calvary Church of God in Christ was founded in 1952 by Jamaican immigrants to Britain. In 1980 it reported fifty churches, 3,000 members and a total constituency of 5,000. The bishop then lived in London.

*CHURCH OF GOD (Cleveland, Tennessee) (1886-)
[1886-1902 as Christian Union; 1902-1907 as Holiness Church.]

The Cleveland, Tennessee-based Church of God had black members as early as 1909 when its total constituency numbered not much more than a thousand. Although Edmond S. Barr (a black partially responsible for opening the church's work in the Bahamas) was ordained in 1912, no official note of black presence was taken until 1920. Before that date at least nine black congregations had been established in Florida, a state destined to remain a stronghold of black work throughout the country.

In 1922, the year of the confrontation between leading elders and A. J. Tomlinson over direction of the church, black churches

were put under a separate overseer. This arrangement, which
had been abandoned after a two-year trial five years earlier, was
to continue over forty years as was the separate black National
Assembly inaugurated four years later. (Black churches had the
option of representation in both National and General assemblies,
and could remain under state overseers rather than the ethnic
one.) The segregated arrangement resulted in little growth. In
1966 official segregation ended and black churches (except in Florida) were placed under the state overseers. The Executive Committee named a Representative of Black Affairs to coordinate efforts.
    In 1976 about 180 of the 4,615 congregations in the United
States were predominantly black. The 23 black churches and 7,700
black members added in the next two years represented more than
twice the percentage growth of the white work. The New Testament Church of God, the West Indian-immigrant affiliate of the
Church of God (Cleveland, Tennessee) in the United Kingdom, is
perhaps the most viable of the bodies created by transplanted
Caribbeans in that country.

609 Blackwelder, Julia (Kirk)
        Southern white fundamentalists and the civil rights move-
        ment, [by] Julia Kirk Blackwelder. In Phylon, 40 (Winter
        1979), 334-341.

        --CHURCH EXTENSION

610 Elliott, William Winston, 1927-
        Church growth among ethnic groups, [by] Winston Elliott.
     In Church of God Evangel, 68 (May 8, 1978), 20-21.

611 Green, Hollis Lynn, 1933-
        Negro ministers speak about their church and ministry:
        an open group discussion, [by] Thomas E. Chenault, C. C.
        Daniels, Alphonso Menendez, Elisha Parris, Harvey E. Robin-
        son, Asbury R. Sellers. George A. Wallace [and] Randle E.
        Witcher; [moderated by] Hollis L. Green [and] Heinrich C.
        Scherz. In Church of God Evangel, 61 (June 14, 1971), 18-20.

612 Lowery, Thomas Lanier
        Reaching the black community, [by] T. L. Lowery. In
        Church of God Evangel, 67 (Sept. 12, 1977), 12-15.

613 A progress report on ministries to American blacks.
        In Church of God Evangel, 61 (Feb. 28, 1972), 12.

614 Rhea, Homer G.
        Black leadership seminar, [by] Homer G. Rhea, Jr. In
        Church of God Evangel, 68 (May 22, 1978), 3-5. On first
        Church of God Seminar on Black Outreach held in Cleveland,
        Tennessee, March 1-2, 1978.

615   Roberts, J. T.
      The Church of God colored churches march on, [by] J. T.
      Roberts. In Church of God Evangel, 49 (June 29, 1959)

616   Sibley, Wallace Jerome, 1938-
      Hopes of a black minister, [by] Wallace J. Sibley. In
      Church of God Evangel, 61 (Feb. 28, 1972), 13.

      --DOCTRINAL AND CONTROVERSIAL WORKS

617   Tinney, James Steven, 1942-
      Pentecostal view of the ecumenical movement, [by] James
      S. Tinney. In Church of God Evangel, 56 (Oct. 31, 1966),
      8-9, 22.

      --HISTORY

618   Calley, Malcolm John Chalmers
      History of the Church of God. In Calley, M. J. C. God's
      people: West Indian Pentecostal sects in England. London,
      1965, 150-154.

619   Conn, Charles William, 1920-
      Like a mighty army moves the Church of God, 1886-1955,
      [by] Charles W. Conn. Cleveland, Tn., Church of God Pub-
      lishing House, 1955. xxiv, 380 p. On black churches: p.
      132-133, 182, 201-203, 257. DLC, OkBetC, TxWaS

620   Conn, Charles William, 1920-
      Like a mighty army: a history of the Church of God, 1886-
      1976, [by] Charles W. Conn. Rev. ed. Cleveland, Tn.,
      Pathway Press, 1977. xxxi, 477 p. On black churches: p.
      132-133, 180, 199-201, 253, 311-312, 352-353. DLC, TCleL

621   Dirksen, Carolyn
      A history of black churches in the Church of God, [by]
      Carolyn Dirksen. In Church of God Evangel, 61 (Feb. 28,
      1972), 10-12.

      --PERIODICALS

622   Church of God gospel herald. 1- Nov. 1965-
      Cleveland, Tn. TCleL

      --SERMONS, TRACTS, ADDRESSES, ESSAYS

623   Parris, Elisha M.
      Why do the righteous suffer? [By] E. M. Parris. In
      Church of God Evangel, 61 (Feb. 28, 1972), 18-20.

--EASTERN STATES

-- --CONNECTICUT

(Hartford)

624 Barrett, Peter C.
     The West Indian Church of God, [by] Peter C. Barrett.
     In Church of God Evangel, 68 (May 22, 1978), 10-11.

-- --NEW JERSEY

625 Polen, Olly Wayne, 1920-
     New Jersey: another challenging area for the Church of
     God, [by] O. W. Polen. In Church of God Evangel, 68 (May
     22, 1978), 18-26.

-- --NEW YORK

(New York City)

626 Dirksen, Carolyn
     In Harlem's ghetto, [by] C. D. In Church of God Evangel,
     61 (Feb. 28, 1972), 16-17.

627 Jacques, Honore
     Black churches of non-U.S. origin, [by] Honore Jacques.
     In Church of God Evangel, 68 (May 22, 1978), 9-10.

628 Marcelle, Charles E.
     The Jamaican Church of God in New York City, [by]
     Charles E. Marcelle. In Church of God Evangel, 68 (May 22,
     1978), 12-13.

*CHURCH OF GOD (Huntsville, Alabama) (1943-   )
[Also as Church of God, World Headquarters and Church of God,
     U.S.A. Headquarters.]

     After his death, a dispute erupted between the two sons of
A. J. Tomlinson over who should head the Church of God (Tomlinson). Homer, the older son, observed a thirty-day mourning
period, then called an assembly of the whole church to meet in
New York. The resulting organization, the Church of God, World
Headquarters, with Homer as general overseer, consisted of a single
predominantly black congregation in New York and scattered elements
of the Church of God (Tomlinson) that felt Homer was the true successor. Upon Homer Tomlinson's death in 1968, Voy M. Bullen
moved the headquarters from Queens Village, New York, to Huntsville, Alabama, a move which may indicate the declining influence
of blacks in the body.

In 1978 the Church of God (Huntsville, Alabama) reported 2,035 congregations and 75,890 members. West Indian immigrants established the Bible Church of God, its British affiliate, in 1964.

*CHURCH OF GOD (Jerusalem Acres) (1957-   )
[1957-1962 as Church of God of All Nations]

In 1957 Grady R. Kent was excommunicated from the Church of God of Prophecy for claiming a divine commission as leader and prophet, and with 300 followers established the Church of God of All Nations. The church, which dropped "of All Nations" from its name in 1962, consists of about thirty congregations, white and black. Pastors and congregations are matched without concern about race. General assemblies are integrated and blacks serve in high office. In 1966 Chief Bishop Marion W. Hall declared in a sermon that the only difference between blacks and whites is skin color, and urged the churches to support civil rights for all. Headquarters are in Cleveland, Tennessee.

        --DOCTRINAL AND CONTROVERSIAL WORKS

629   Hall, Marion W.
         The shot heard around the world, [by] Marion W. Hall.
      In Vision Speaks, 11 (May 1968), 4.

        --HISTORY

630   Harrell, David Edwin, 1930-
         White sects and black men in the recent South, [by] David
      Edwin Harrell, Jr. Foreword by Edwin S. Gaustad. Nash-
      ville, Vanderbilt University Press, 1971. xix, 161 p. On
      Church of God (Jerusalem Acres): p. 96-98. DLC

      CHURCH OF GOD (United Kingdom) (1958-   )

      Composed of immigrants from Antigua, Barbados, and Jamaica
plus a few whites, the Church of God (United Kingdom) dates from
1958. Its headquarters are in London. In 1980 two bishops were
directing four congregations with 200 members and 300 constituents.

      CHURCH OF GOD BY FAITH (1919-   )

      This body was founded by Elder John Bright at Jacksonville
Heights, Florida, in 1919, and chartered at Alachua in the same
state four years later. It is led by a bishop, an executive secretary, and three ruling elders. A general assembly meets three

times a year. Headquarters are in Jacksonville, and a church-
sponsored academy is in Ocala. The Church of God by faith teaches
that the Word of God is the communion of the body and blood and
makes a determined effort to rid its fellowship of willful sinners.
In 1973 the body reported 105 churches and 4,500 members. Affiliated congregations are scattered from Alabama and Florida to
New York.

--PERIODICALS

631   Spiritual guide. 1- 19 -
        Jacksonville, Fl.

--WORSHIP

632   Church of God by Faith.
        Ritual of the Church of God by Faith. Ocala, Fl., Supreme
        Council of the Church of God by Faith, 1947. 32 p.

CHURCH OF GOD FELLOWSHIP (1967-)

In 1967 the Church of God Fellowship split from the New Testament Church of God. Like its parent, the Church of God Fellowship consists of immigrants to the United Kingdom from Barbados,
Grenada, and Jamaica. The eight churches reported in 1980 had
136 members and 400 constituents. The group is headed by an
overseer.

CHURCH OF GOD FOUNDED BY JESUS CHRIST (19 -)

In 1977 the convocation of the Church of God Founded by Jesus
Christ was racked with controversy over whether six candidates
who did not believe in tongues-speaking as the initial evidence of
the baptism of the Holy Spirit should be ordained. They were,
thus creating a new standard for the church which claimed 37
congregations and nearly a thousand members that year. Headquarters are in Salisbury, North Carolina. Bishop McKinley Smith
resides in Lexington, Kentucky.

--GOVERNMENT

633   Church of God Founded by Jesus Christ.
        Guide of the Church of God Founded by Jesus Christ.
        Lexington, Ky., McKinley Smith, 19--. 40 p.

--PERIODICALS

634   Holy crier inspirational magazine. 1- 19 -
      Lexington, Ky.

CHURCH OF GOD IN CHRIST (1907-)

In 1906 C. H. Mason, D. J. Young, and J. A. Jeter, preachers associated with C. P. Jones of Jackson, Mississippi in a movement then popularly known as the Churches of God in Christ, went
to Los Angeles to check out the revival at Azusa Street. Mason
returned claiming the baptism of the Holy Ghost with tongues as
the initial evidence. While he had been away, Glenn A. Cook had
visited Memphis and convinced many in Mason's congregation of the
new teaching. Jones and Jeter, however, were not won over and
at the convocation of 1907 the group split. Later that year Mason's
faction reorganized as the Church of God in Christ, a name based
on I Thessalonians 2:14, II Thessalonians 1:1, and Galatians 1:22,
which the leader said had been revealed to him ten years earlier
while walking along a Little Rock, Arkansas, street. Mason, who
led the group until his death in 1961, established headquarters in
Memphis and assumed the title and role of senior bishop. At his
death the Church of God in Christ claimed 4,500 congregations and
382,679 members. An extended dispute over succession and litiga-
tion over polity led in 1969 to the departure of fourteen bishops
and the formation of a new body, the Church of God in Christ, International.
      Except for 1911-1913 when a group of future-Assemblies of God
ministers in transit from the Wesleyan to the "Finished work of Calvary" position on sanctification held credentials with it, the
Memphis-based group has been almost entirely black. Until recent
years, segregation and racial prejudice largely isolated it from like-
minded predominantly white North American bodies. In 1948-1949,
for instance, it was not invited to participate in the formation of
the Pentecostal Fellowship of North America. Before the founder's
death, however, Church of God in Christ representatives had appeared on the platform of triennial Pentecostal World conferences.
Under Bishop J. O. Patterson, Mason's son-in-law and successor,
such participation has increased. From 1954 to 1976 it sponsored
the Saints Junior College in Lexington, Mississippi, and in 1970
established the C. H. Mason Theological Seminary as a unit of the
Interdenominational Theological Center in Atlanta.
      In 1982 the Church of God in Christ reported 9,982 congrega-
tions and 3,709,661 members in the United States. It sponsors
mission work in Jamaica, Haiti, and west Africa. The Church of God
in Christ Pentecostal, its affiliate in the United Kingdom, was established in 1948 by American servicemen stationed there. With
the establishment of the Calvary Church of God in Christ by Jamaican immigrants in 1952, the Church of God in Christ Pentecostal
became the First British Jurisdiction of the Memphis-based body.

--CHURCH EXTENSION

635 Moody, Carlis L.
Missions in the local church, [by] Carlis L. Moody.
Memphis, Department of Missions of the Church of God in
Christ, 19--. 12 p.

--DIRECTORIES

636 Church of God in Christ.
International directory, 1975-76. Memphis, Church of God
in Christ Publishing House, 1975. 409 p.

--DOCTRINAL AND CONTROVERSIAL WORKS

637 Church of God in Christ.
The statement of faith. Memphis, Church of God in Christ
Book Store, [198-]. broadside

638 Brooks, P. A.
Understanding Bible doctrine as taught in the Church of
God in Christ, [by] P. A. Brooks and Charles Hawthorne.
Detroit, Church of God in Christ, First Jurisdiction Michigan,
c1981. 40 p.

639 Goodwin, Bennie Eugene, 1933-
Pray right and grow rich, [by] Bennie Goodwin. Jersey
City, N.J., Goodpatrick Publishers, 1974. 46 p.

640 Goodwin, Bennie Eugene, 1933-
Speak up, black man, [by] Bennie Goodwin. [Jersey City,
N.J., Goodpatrick Publishers], 1972. 36 p. PPiPT

641 McKinney, George Dallas, 1932-
The Jehovah's Witnesses, [by] George D. McKinney. San
Diego, Ca., Vision Publications, 1975. 130 p. ArStC

642 McKinney, George Dallas, 1932-
The theology of the Jehovah's Witnesses, [by] George D.
McKinney. San Diego, Ca., Production House, c1975. 130 p.
CLamB, KyWAT

643 Patterson, William Archie, 1898-
From the pen of Bishop W. A. Patterson. Memphis, Deak-
ins Typesetting Service, 1970. xx, 122 p. DLC

--GOVERNMENT

644 Church of God in Christ.
     Charter of incorporation and constitution of the Church of
     God in Christ. Memphis, Church of God in Christ Publishing
     House, 196-. 21 p.

645 Church of God in Christ.
     Manual of the Church of God in Christ. 7th ed. Memphis,
     1957.

646 Church of God in Christ.
     Official manual with the doctrines and discipline of the
     Church of God in Christ, 1973. Written by the authorization
     and approval of the General Assembly. Memphis, Church of
     God in Christ Publishing House, 1973. xl, 256 p. DLC

647 Blake, Charles Edward, 1940-
     The Church of God in Christ: its organizational crisis,
     [by] Charles E. Blake. n.p., c1965. 20 p. GAUC

648 Patterson, James Oglethorpe, 1912-
     Presiding bishop's report: Yesterday, today and tomorrow,
     still building the dream, [by] J. O. Patterson. Memphis,
     Church of God in Christ Publishing House, 1975. 8 p.

     --HISTORY

649 Church celebrates 50th anniversary.
     In Ebony, 13 (Mar. 1958), 54-56, 58-60.

650 Church of God in Christ marks 75th anniversary.
     In Jet, 63 (Nov. 22, 1982), 32.

651 Cornelius, Lucille J.
     The pioneer: history of the Church of God in Christ.
     Compiled and ed. by Lucille J. Cornelius. [Memphis, Church
     of God in Christ], c1975. vii, 103 p. MiRochOU

652 Fastest-growing church.
     In Ebony, 4 (Aug. 1949), 57-60.

653 Garrett, Romeo Benjamin, 1910-
     Famous first facts about Negroes, [by] Romeo B. Garrett.
     New York, Arno Press, 1972. viii, 212 p. "Church of God
     in Christ": p. 26.

654 Kendrick, Klaude, 1917-
     The promise fulfilled: a history of the modern Pentecostal
     movement. Springfield, Mo., Gospel Publishing House, 1961.

viii, 237 p.   "The Church of God in Christ": p. 197-201.
DLC, MSohG, TxDaTS, TxWaS

655 Kenyon, Howard Nelson, 1955-
     An analysis of racial separation within the early Pentecostal
     movement. Waco, Tx., 1978. ix, 163 l. Thesis (M.A.)--
     Baylor University. "The Church of God in Christ": l. 56-57.
     TxWB

656 Largest Pentecostal denomination celebrates diamond anniver-
     sary. In Charisma, 8 (Oct. 1982), 12.

657 Mason, Charles Harrison, 1866-1961.
     The history and life work of Elder C. H. Mason, chief
     apostle, and his co-laborers. Compiled by Prof. Jas. Courts.
     Memphis, Howe Printing Dept., 1920. 97 p. DLC

658 Mason, Charles Harrison, 1866-1961.
     The history and life work of Elder C. H. Mason and his co-
     laborers. Compiled by Mary Esther Mason. [Memphis, Church
     of God in Christ, 1934] [92] p. Cover title.

659 Mason, Charles Harrison, 1866-1961.
     The history and life work of Elder C. H. Mason, chief
     apostle, and his co-laborers from 1893 to 1924. Introduction
     by J. Courts. San Francisco, T. L. Delaney, c1977. 89 p.
     "Recompiled in 1924."

660 Mason, Charles Harrison, 1866-1961.
     History and formative years of the Church of God in Christ,
     with excerpts from the life and works of its founder: Bishop
     C. H. Mason. Reproduced by J. O. Patterson, German R.
     Ross [and] Mrs. Julia Mason Atkins. Memphis, Church of God
     in Christ Publishing House, 1969. 143 p. OSW

661 Moore, Everett Leroy, 1918-
     Handbook of Pentecostal denominations in the United States.
     Pasadena, Ca., 1954. vii, 346 l. Thesis (M.A.)--Pasadena
     College. "Church of God in Christ": l. 174-184. CSdP

662 Nelson, Douglas J., 1931-
     A brief history of the Church of God in Christ, [by] Doug-
     las J. Nelson. [Arlington, Va., 198-] 100 l.

663 Nichol, John Thomas, 1928-
     Pentecostalism. New York, Harper & Row, 1966. xvi,
     264 p. Based on thesis (Ph.D.)--Boston University. "Church
     of God in Christ": p. 102-104. DLC, MCE, MH, MSohG

664 Nichol, John Thomas, 1928-
     Pentecostalism. Plainfield, N.J., Logos International, 1971,
     c1966. xvi, 264 p. Cover title: The Pentecostals. Reprint

of 1966 ed. Based on thesis (Ph.D.)--Boston University.
"Church of God in Christ": p. 102-104.

665 Pleas, Charles H.
       Fifty years achievement, Church of God in Christ, [by]
     Charles M. Pleas. Memphis, Church of God in Christ Publish-
     ing House, 1957.

666 Pleas, Charles H.
       Fifty years achievement, Church of God in Christ, [by]
     Charles H. Pleas. In Cobbins, O. B., ed. History of Church
     of Christ (Holiness) U.S.A., 1895-1965. Chicago, c1966,
     427-433. DLC, OkEG

667 Ritter, Earnestine
       The Holy Ghost fell: the Church of God in Christ. In
     World Pentecost, 1:1 (1971), 8-9.

667a Synan, Harold Vinson, 1934-
       The quiet rise of black Pentecostals, by Vinson Synan. In
     Charisma, 11 (June 1986), 45-48, 50, 55.

       --HISTORY AND STUDY OF DOCTRINES

668 Clark, William A., 1891-
       Sanctification in Negro religion, [by] William A. Clark. In
     Social Forces, 15 (May 1937), 544-551.

669 Kroll-Smith, J. Stephen
       The testimony as performance: the relationship of an ex-
     pressive event to the belief system of a Holiness sect, [by]
     J. Stephen Kroll-Smith. In Journal for the Scientific Study
     of Religion, 19 (Mar. 1980), 16-25.

       --JUVENILE LITERATURE

670 Hall, David A.
       Charles H. Mason; storybook for children, [by] David A.
     Hall. [Memphis], c1983. [31] p. Cover title.

       --MUSIC

671 Boggs, Beverly J.
       Some aspects of worship in a Holiness church, [by] Beverly
     Boggs. In New York Folklore, 3 (Summer/Winter 1977), 29-44.

672 Heilbut, Anthony Otto, 1941-
       The gospel sound: good news and bad times, [by] Tony
     Heilbut. New York, Simon and Schuster, 1971. 350 p. "The
     holiness church": p. 199-278. DLC, Ok

673 Heilbut, Anthony Otto, 1941–
     The gospel sound: good news and bad times, [by] Tony
     Heilbut. Garden City, N.Y., Anchor Press/Doubleday, 1975,
     c1971. xxxv, 364 p. (Anchor books) "The holiness church":
     p. 171-251.

674 Singer swings same songs in church and night club.
     In Life, 7 (Aug. 28, 1939), 37.

675 Szwed, John F., 1936–
     Negro music: urban renewal, [by] John F. Szwed. In
     Coffin, T. P., ed. Our living traditions; an introduction to
     American folklore. New York, 1968, 272-282. TMM

     --PASTORAL LITERATURE

676 McKinney, George Dallas, 1932–
     Christian marriage: an act of faith and commitment, [by]
     George D. McKinney. San Diego, Ca., Vision Publications,
     1977. 51 p. ArStC

677 Rainey, Ross B.
     A book for church members on how to keep the devil from
     getting you down, [by] Ross B. Rainey. Wilmington, De.,
     Mother Church of God in Christ, 1974. 112 p.

678 Ramsey, Jerry R.
     God's answer for afflicted, sick, and dead marriages, [by]
     J. R. Ramsey III. Everett, Wa., 198–. 28 [2] p.

     --PERIODICALS

679 Bible band guide. 1– 19 –
     Memphis

680 Evangelist speaks. 1– 19 –
     Memphis

681 Flame. 1– 1975–
     Kansas City, Mo. .

682 International outlook. 1– 1959–
     Memphis

683 National purity class topic. [1]– 19 –
     Memphis

684 Pentecostal Alliance crescendo. 1– Feb./Mar. 1952–
     Chicago. DLC

685 Prayer and Bible band topics. 1- 19 -
     Memphis

686 Purity guide. 1- 19 -
     Memphis

687 Sunshine band topics. 1- 19 -
     Memphis

688 Voice of missions. 1- 1976-
     Memphis

689 Whole truth. 1- 1907-
     Argenta, Ar.; Memphis, Tn.

690 Y.P.W.W. quarterly. 1- 19 -
     Memphis

691 Y.P.W.W. topics. 1- 19 -
     Memphis

       --SERMONS, TRACTS, ADDRESSES, ESSAYS

692 Goodwin, Bennie Eugene, 1933-
     Beside still waters, [by] Bennie Goodwin. Jersey City,
     N.J., Goodpatrick Publishers, 1973.

       --STATISTICS

693 United States. Bureau of the Census.
     Census of religious bodies: 1926. Church of God in Christ.
     Statistics, denominational history, doctrine, and organization.
     Washington, Government Printing Office, 1929. 10 p. DLC,
     NNUT

694 United States. Bureau of the Census.
     Census of religious bodies: 1936. Church of God in Christ.
     Statistics, denominational history, doctrine, and organization.
     Washington, Government Printing Office, 1940. iv, 8 p.
     NNUT

       --WORK WITH WOMEN

695 Church of God in Christ. Department of Women.
     Women's handbook. Newly revised edition of organization
     and procedure. Memphis, Church of God in Christ Publishing
     House, 1980. 86 p.

--WORSHIP

696 Boggs, Beverly J.
     Some aspects of worship in a Holiness church, [by] Beverly
     Boggs. In New York Folklore, 3 (Summer/Winter 1977), 29-44.

--EASTERN STATES

697 Clemmons, Ithiel
     History, [by] Ithiel and Clara Clemmons. In Church of God
     in Christ, Eastern Jurisdiction. Golden jubilee, 1921-1971.
     New York, 1971.

     -- --MASSACHUSETTS

     (Boston)

698 Latimore, Patricia
     Toward a better understanding of the Holiness church:
     the Church of God in Christ. Cambridge, Ma., 1976. Thesis
     (B.A.)--Harvard University. MH

     -- --NEW YORK

     (Binghamton)

699 Boggs, Beverly J.
     Music and worship in the Mt. Nebo Church of God in
     Christ, Binghamton, New York, [by] Beverly J. Boggs.
     Binghamton, 1975. v, 232 l. Thesis (M.A.)--State Univer-
     sity of New York at Binghamton. NBiSU

700 Boggs, Beverly J.
     Some aspects of worship in a Holiness church, [by] Beverly
     Boggs. In New York Folklore, 3 (Summer/Winter 1977), 29-44.

     (New York City)

701 Blau, Eleanor
     Religious excitement fills air at Pentecostal session here,
     [by] Eleanor Blau. In New York Times, 121 (July 6, 1972),
     24.

702 Singer swings same songs in church and night club.
     In Life, 7 (Aug. 28, 1939), 37.

-- --PENNSYLVANIA

(Philadelphia)

702a Moore, Carey
        Black Pentecostals mount crusade. In Logos Journal, 8
     (Nov./Dec. 1978), 84-86.

(Pittsburgh)

703 Williams, Melvin Donald, 1933-
        Community in a black Pentecostal church; an anthropological
     study, [by] Melvin D. Williams. Pittsburgh, University of
     Pittsburgh Press, 1974. xii, 202 p.   Based on thesis (Ph.D.)
     --University of Pittsburgh. DLC, MSohG

704 Williams, Melvin Donald, 1933-
        Food and animals: behavioral metaphors in a black Penta-
     costal [sic] church in Pittsburgh, [by] Melvin D. Williams.
     In Urban Anthropology, 2 (Spring 1973), 74-79.

705 Williams, Melvin Donald, 1933-
        A Pentecostal congregation in Pittsburgh: a religious com-
     munity in a black ghetto. Pittsburgh, 1973. 328 l. Thesis
     (Ph.D.)--University of Pittsburgh. PPiU

--MIDDLE WEST

-- --ILLINOIS

706 Church of God in Christ. Dioceses. Southeast Missouri and
     Western Illinois.
        50th golden convocation of the Churches of God in Christ
     in session, May 15th through May 25th, 1959, Bishop D.
     Bostick presiding. St. Louis, 1959. 1 v. (unpaged) MoS

-- --KANSAS

(Wichita)

707 Disorderly conduct.
        In Christianity Today, 20 (Apr. 9, 1976), 45.

-- --MISSOURI

708 Church of God in Christ. Dioceses. Southeast Missouri and
     Western Illinois.
        50th golden convocation of the Churches of God in Christ
     in session, May 15th through May 25th, 1959, Bishop D. Bos-
     tick presiding. St. Louis, 1959. 1 v. (unpaged) MoS

(Kansas City)

709 Tinney, James Steven (1942-   )
        COGIC youth congress first here in 1930, [by] James S.
     Tinney. In Kansas City Call (July 5, 1974), 12.

710 Tinney, James Steven (1942-   )
        Dr. Arenia Mallory recalls early days at Barker Temple,
     [by] James S. Tinney. In Kansas City Call (May 5, 1972),
     10.

          -- --OHIO

711 Church of God in Christ. Dioceses. Ohio Northwest.
        50th year jubilee; 6th annual holy convocation, Ohio North-
     west Diocese. Cleveland, 1967. 28 p. Cover title. OCl

        --SOUTHERN STATES

          -- --ARKANSAS

          (Stamps)

712 Angelou, Maya, 1928-
        I know why the caged bird sings. New York, Random
     House, 1970, c1969. 281 p. On tent meeting in Stamps, Ar-
     kansas, sponsored by the Church of God in Christ: p. 118-
     128. DLC, OkEG

          -- --DISTRICT OF COLUMBIA

          (Washington)

713 Davis, Arnor S., 1919-
        The Pentecostal movement in black Christianity, [by] Arnor
     S. Davis. In Black Church, 2:1 (1972), 65-88.

          -- --MISSISSIPPI

          (Drew)

714 Garvin, Philip, 1947-
        Religious America. Photographs by Philip Garvin. Text by
     Philip Garvin and Julia Welch. New York, McGraw-Hill Book
     Co., 1974. 189 p. "Gifts of the Spirit": p. 141-169. DLC

          (Itta Benna)

715 Garvin, Philip, 1947-
        Religious America. Photographs by Philip Garvin. Text by

Philip Garvin and Julia Welch. New York, McGraw-Hill Book
Co., 1974. 189 p. "Gifts of the Spirit": p. 141-169. DLC

(Sunflower)

716 Garvin, Philip, 1947–
      Religious America. Photographs by Philip Garvin. Text by
      Philip Garvin and Julia Welch. New York, McGraw-Hill Book
      Co., 1974. 189 p. "Gifts of the Spirit": p. 141-169. DLC

      -- --TENNESSEE

      (Memphis)

717 Battle, Allen Overton, 1927–
      Status personality in a Negro Holiness sect. Washington,
      1961. v, 114 l. Thesis (Ph.D.)--Catholic University of Amer-
      ica. DCU

718 Church celebrates 50th anniversary.
      In Ebony, 13 (Mar. 1958), 54-56, 58-60.

719 Tinney, James Steven (1942–)
      Black Pentecostals convene, [by] James S. Tinney. In
      Christianity Today, 15 (Dec. 4, 1970), 36.

720 Tinney, James Steven (1942–)
      Black Pentecostals: setting up the kingdom, [by] James S.
      Tinney. In Christianity Today, 20 (Dec. 5, 1975), 42-43.

      -- --TEXAS

      (Jacksonville)

721 [Holland, Ada (Morehead)]
      One-man war on poverty. In Ebony, 20 (Feb. 1965), 77-78,
      80, 82, 84.

722 Sapper, Neil Gary, 1941–
      A survey of the history of the black people of Texas, 1930-
      1954, [by] Neil Gary Sapper. Lubbock, 1972. v, 549 l.
      Thesis (Ph.D.)--Texas Tech University. On White's Temple
      Church of God in Christ, Jacksonville: l. 519-521. TxLT

723 White, Charley C., 1885–
      No quittin' sense, [by] C. C. White [and] Ada Morehead
      Holland. Austin, University of Texas Press, 1969. xi, 216 p.
      DHUD, DLC, ICU, NN

-- --VIRGINIA

(Hampton)

724 Ringle, Ken
Va. Senate rivals attend black church convocation, [by] Ken Ringle. In Washington Post, 101 (Sept. 4, 1978), B8.

--WESTERN STATES

-- --CALIFORNIA

(Los Angeles)

725 Street sermons.
In Human Behavior, 7 (Apr. 1978), 38.

(San Diego)

726 McKinney, George Dallas, 1932-
I will build my church. n.p., 1977. x, 63 p. ArStC, CLamB

CHURCH OF GOD IN CHRIST (Pentecostal) (193 -)

In 1936 the Church of God in Christ (Pentecostal), which had originated a few years earlier, reported nine congregations and 210 members. Churches were located in West Virginia, Michigan, Ohio, Illinois, Tennessee, Alabama, and Texas. At that time the senior bishop resided in Bluefield, West Virginia.

CHURCH OF GOD IN CHRIST, CONGREGATIONAL (1932-)

In 1932 Elder J. Bowe, a founding member of the Church of God in Christ, was forced to leave its fellowship because of his belief that the proper form of church government is congregational, not episcopal. He then established the Church of God in Christ, Congregational. Two years later George Slack, who had been ex-communicated by the parent body for teaching that tithing is not a New Testament doctrine, joined the church. In addition to the convictions of Bowe and Slack, the new body espoused conscientious objection to war. Otherwise its teachings remained identical to the original body, to which Bowe returned in 1945. Headquarters are in East St. Louis, Illinois. In 1971 the Church of God in Christ, Congregational reported 33 affiliates in the United States, six in Mexico, and four in the United Kingdom.

--GOVERNMENT

727   Church of God in Christ, Congregational.
      Manual of the Church of God in Christ, Congregational.
      East St. Louis, Il., 1948.

CHURCH OF GOD IN CHRIST, INTERNATIONAL (1969-   )

     In 1969 fourteen bishops dissatisfied with changes in the
Church of God in Christ following the death of Bishop C. H. Mason,
met in Kansas City, Missouri, and formed the Church of God in
Christ, International. Disagreement over polity, not doctrine, led
to separation. Two years later the new organization reported
1,041 churches and 501,000 members. By 1982, however, it claimed
only 300 churches and 200,000, an indication perhaps of a significant
return to the parent body. Headquarters are in Brooklyn.

--PERIODICALS

728   Holiness call. 1- 19 -
      Memphis, Tn.

729   Message. 1- 19 -
      Hartford, Ct.

CHURCH OF GOD IN CHRIST PENTECOSTAL (1948-   )

     The Church of God in Christ Pentecostal was organized in 1948
by black United States troops stationed in Britain. In 1980 it
claimed eleven churches and 1,500 members, with an inclusive community of 5,000. Headquarters are in Luton where the bishop resides. With the establishment of the Calvary Church of God in
Christ by Jamaican immigrants in 1952, the Luton-based group became the First British Jurisdiction of the Church of God in Christ,
with headquarters in Memphis, Tennessee.

*CHURCH OF GOD OF PROPHECY (1923-   )
[1923-1952 as Tomlinson Church of God.]

     The Church of God of Prophecy is the product of the reorgan-
ization of Tomlinson loyalists following the "disruption" of the Church
of God (Cleveland, Tennessee) in 1923. In that cleavage, blacks
in numbers rallied to the overseer, particularly in the Caribbean.
Placement of blacks in supervisory positions in areas where blacks
predominate, a practice followed by Milton Tomlinson (the present
general overseer), has solidified this loyalty.
     Bahamians and Jamaicans have been particularly active, providing

pastors for work in the United States and the United Kingdom.
By the mid-1970s the British work, begun in 1952, numbered a
hundred churches and 3,200 members. It was unique in bearing
the name of the parent body. A sizeable minority of the 72,877
United States members reported in 1981 were black. Headquarters
are in Cleveland, Tennessee.

--HISTORY

730 Harrell, David Edwin, 1930-
       White sects and black men in the recent South, [by] David
     Edwin Harrell, Jr. Foreword by Edwin S. Gaustad. Nash-
     ville, Vanderbilt University Press, 1971. xix, 161 p. On
     Church of God of Prophecy: p. 94-96. DLC

CHURCH OF GOD PENTECOSTAL (1958-   )

A British branch of the Huntsville, Alabama-based Church of
God, the Church of God Pentecostal consists of immigrants from
Barbados and Jamaica and some native-born British whites. Headquarters are in East Ham, a suburb of London. By 1980 the group
had 1,000 full members and a total constituency of twice that number, and was led by four bishops.

FIRE BAPTIZED HOLINESS CHURCH OF GOD OF THE AMER-
     ICAS (1908-   )
     [1908-1922 as Colored Fire Baptized Holiness Church; 1922-
     1926 as Fire Baptized Holiness Church of God.]

Organized November 24, 1908 at Greer, South Carolina, the
Colored Fire Baptized Holiness Church at first consisted entirely
of black members of the earlier biracial third-blessing movement.
W. E. Fuller, the only black among the 140 founding members of
the Fire Baptized Holiness Association of America ten years earlier,
developed a black membership in the parent body, which ultimately
numbered 925. Difficulty in obtaining facilities for biracial meetings
steadily increased, causing the black brethren to request a separate
convention. Release, including the division of property, was
achieved amicably. Fuller became bishop of the new body, which
during his tenure experienced two name changes. In 1922 Colored
Fire Baptized Holiness Church was changed to Fire Baptized Holiness Church of God, with "of the Americas" being added four years
later, when the General Council met with the Mount Moriah Fire
Baptized Holiness Church of Knoxville, Tennessee.
       Headquarters and the Fuller Press are in Atlanta. The Fuller
Normal and Industrial School, founded in Atlanta in 1912, has been
in Greenville, South Carolina since 1923. The work of the Fire
Baptized Holiness Church of God is concentrated in South Carolina.

In addition, there are scattered congregations in an area bounded
by Connecticut, New York, and Ohio on the north, and by Florida
and Alabama on the south. In 1978 the organization reported 775
churches and missions and 15,450 members. W. E. Fuller, Jr. is
senior bishop.

--GOVERNMENT

731 Fire Baptized Holiness Church of God of the Americas.
     Discipline of the Fire Baptized Holiness Church of God of
     the Americas. Atlanta, Fuller Press, 1966. 162 p.

731a Fire Baptized Holiness Church of God of the Americas.
     Minutes of the district conventions, 1937. [Atlanta, 1937]
     168 p. F

--HISTORY

732 Fire Baptized Holiness Church of God of the Americas.
     [Program]: The twenty-third international quadrennial
     General Council of the Fire Baptized Holiness Church of God
     of the Americas, beginning Tuesday, June 8, 1982, through
     Sunday, June 13, 1982, Fuller Normal and Industrial Institute,
     901 Anderson Road, Greenville, S.C. [Atlanta], Printed by
     Economy Printing Co., Avondale Estates, Ga., 1982. 263 p.
     Cover title.

732a Hogan, Howard B.
     Tongues and the baptism of Holy Spirit: their place in the
     Fire Baptized Holiness Church of God of the Americas, [by]
     Howard B. Hogan. Chicago, 1976. 18 1. Professional paper--
     Chicago Theological Seminary. ICT

733 Synan, Harold Vinson, 1934-
     The old-time power, [by] Vinson Synan. Franklin Springs,
     Ga., Advocate Press, c1973. 296 p. On Fire Baptized Holiness
     Church of God of the Americas: p. 100-101. IEG

--HYMNS AND SACRED SONGS

734 Fire Baptized Holiness Church of God of the Americas.
     Discipline of the Fire Baptized Holiness Church of God of
     the Americas. Atlanta, Fuller Press, 1966. 162 p. "Hymnal
     of the F. B. H. Church of God": p. 100-162.

--PERIODICALS

735 True witness. 1- 1909-
       Atlanta.

--DISTRICT OF COLUMBIA

-- --WASHINGTON

736 Banks, Carolyn
       The fire, [by] Carolyn Banks. Photographs by Margaret
     Thomas. In Potomac (Mar. 10, 1974), 16-17, 30, 32.

FREE CHURCH OF GOD IN CHRIST (1915-1921, 1925-)
[1915-1921 as Church of God in Christ.]

   In 1915 the family of J. H. Morris, a National Baptist pastor
of Enid, Oklahoma, experience the baptism of the Holy Spirit. The
family plus a few others rallied around E. J. Morris, the patriarch's
son, and established a church which they named: the Church of God
in Christ. Union from 1921 to 1925 with the Memphis-based Church
of God in Christ ended in separation after which the Oklahoma congregations became the Free Church of God in Christ. In 1937 the
Enid-based fellowship claimed forty churches and 900 members. Its
only differences with the Memphis-based group were the personalities of leaders and greater stress on divine healing.

--STATISTICS

737 United States. Bureau of the Census.
       Census of religious bodies: 1926. Free Church of God in
     Christ. Statistics, denominational history, doctrine, and or-
     ganization. Washington, Government Printing Office, 1929.
     8 p. DLC

FREE CHURCH OF GOD TRUE HOLINESS (19 -)

   In 1977 the Free Church of God True Holiness held its national
convocation in Kansas City, Kansas. At that time its presiding chief
elect was a woman, the Rev. G. M. Roan.

HEALING CHURCH OF GOD IN CHRIST UNITED KINGDOM
     (1964-)

   Composed of West Indian immigrants, the Healing Church of
God in Christ United Kingdom separated from the Memphis-based

Church of God in Christ in 1964.   Headquarters is in Forest Gate.
In 1980 the movement consisted of two congregations with 70 members
and 150 constituents.

INTERDENOMINATIONAL CHURCH OF GOD (1978-   )

Founded in 1978 by Leon Ralph, former African Methodist
Episcopal California state legislator, the Los Angeles-based Interdenominational Church of God planned prison ministry as a major
concern.   The California lieutenant general, an Episcopal layman,
aided Ralph in securing the first church building.

NEW TESTAMENT CHURCH OF GOD (1955-   )

An affiliate of the Cleveland, Tennessee-based Church of God,
the New Testament Church of God, organized in 1955, is a product
of the migration of Jamaicans to Britain following World War II.
In 1976 the national office moved from Lozells, Birmingham, where
it had been fourteen years, to Bilston, West Midlands, ten miles
west.   The New Testament Church of God reported ninety congregations, 11,000 members and 22,000 constituents in 1980.   Two
years earlier, O. A. Lyseight, who had served as National Overseer from the beginning, was replaced by Jeremiah McIntyre, an
appointee of the Cleveland headquarters.   Worker-training classes
have been offered by the Ebenezer Bible Institute in Birmingham
since 1963, and in London since 1977.

--HISTORY

738   Brooks, Ira V.
          In chains they shall come over, [by] I. V. Brooks.   Birm-
      ingham, 1970.   55 p.

739   Brooks, Ira V.
          Where do we go from here?   [By] Ira V. Brooks.   London,
      1982.   80 p., 8 p. of plates   TCleL

740   Hill, Clifford S., 1927-
          From church to sect: West Indian religious sect development
      in Britain, [by] Clifford Hill.   In Journal for the Scientific
      Study of Religion, 10 (Summer 1971), 114-123.

741   Hill, Clifford S., 1927-
          Immigrant sect development in Britain: a case study of
      status deprivation?   [By] Clifford Hill.   In Social Compass,
      18:2 (1971), 231-236.

742 Lyseight, O. A.
       Tidings from England, [by] O. A. Lyseight. In Church of
God Evangel, 47 (Apr. 8, 1957), 12.

       --PERIODICALS

743 Vision magazine. 1- 19 -
       Birmingham.

       --BERMUDA

744 Manning, Frank Edward, 1944-
       The rediscovery of religious play: a Pentecostal case, [by]
Frank E. Manning. In Lancy, D. F., ed. The anthropological
study of play: problems and prospects. Cornwall, N.Y.,
197-, 23-30. DLC

745 Manning, Frank Edward, 1944-
       The rediscovery of religious play: a Pentecostal case, [by]
Frank E. Manning. In Lancy, D. F., ed. The study of play:
problems and prospects. West Point, N.Y., c1977, 151-158.
DLC, OkU

746 Manning, Frank Edward, 1944-
       The salvation of a drunk, [by] Frank E. Manning. In
American Ethnologist, 4 (Aug. 1977), 397-412.

       PENTECOSTAL CHURCH OF GOD (1956-)

       Initially composed of immigrants from Trinidad and Jamaica, the
Pentecostal Church of God, organized in 1956, is led by two bishops
and supports missionary efforts in Nigeria and India. Headquarters
are in Islington, a borough of London. In 1980 the group had 400
members in eight congregations, and a total community of a thousand.

       SOUGHT OUT CHURCH OF GOD IN CHRIST AND SPIRITUAL
          HOUSE OF PRAYER (1947-)

       In 1947 "Mother" Mozella Cook set in order the Sought Out
Church of God in Christ and Spiritual House of Prayer in a garage
behind her home in Brunswick, Georgia. She had been converted
during a "yard service" in response to her mother's urging and
joined the Baptist church in Brunswick. Later, however, she had
moved to Pittsburgh, Pennsylvania, and affiliated with the Church
of God in Christ. It was there she believed she had received divine
instructions to found a church. Within two years she founded four
congregations. In 1949 they had a combined membership of sixty.

TRIUMPHANT CHURCH OF GOD (1959-   )

In 1959 the Triumphant Church of God split from the British affiliate of the Church of God of Prophecy. Composed of immigrants from Jamaica and Montserrat, the body claimed six churches, 300 members and a total community of 700 in 1980. Headquarters are in West Bromwich, Staffordshire, northwest of Birmingham.

UNITED CHURCH OF GOD (1963-   )

In 1963 some former Jamaicans and Barbadians left the New Testament Church of God, the Church of God (Cleveland, Tennessee) affiliate in the United Kingdom, and formed the United Church of God. The group reported three churches and 104 members and a total constituency of approximately 300 in 1980.

UNITED PENTECOSTAL CHURCH OF GOD (1974-   )

In 1974 the largely Jamaican United Pentecostal Church of God was formed as the result of a split in the Triumphant Church of God, itself the product of independence from the British affiliate of the Church of God of Prophecy. In 1980 it had three churches, 60 members, and a total constituency of about 150. Headquarters are in Birmingham.

VICTORIOUS CHURCH OF GOD (196 -   )

About 1960, the Victorious Church of God separated from the New Testament Church of God, the Church of God (Cleveland, Tennessee) affiliate which serves West Indian immigrants in Britain. By 1980 it claimed a membership of 1,000 and a total constituency of approximately twice that number.

VICTORY WAY FREE CHURCH OF GOD TRUE HOLINESS U.S.A. (19 -   )

At its national convocation in Kansas City, Missouri, in 1977, Bishop C. W. Burchette reported that the Victory Way Free Church of God True Holiness U.S.A. had congregations in six Midwestern states. Although it split from the Free Church of God True Holiness, the Victory Way organization was larger than the original body. At that time it planned to build a retirement home and a new headquarters building.

CHURCH OF THE LIVING GOD

CHURCH OF THE LIVING GOD, THE PILLAR AND GROUND OF THE TRUTH (1903-)

Only distantly related to other groups of the same name, the Church of the Living God, the Pillar and Ground of the Truth is the outgrowth of the evangelistic work of "Mother" M. L. Ester Tate. Assisted by her sons, W. C. Lewis and F. E. Lewis, "Saint Mary Magdalena Tate" founded the group in 1903. Five years later during the first General Assembly at Greenville, Alabama, Mother Tate was ordained first chief overseer and more than a hundred received the baptism with the Holy Ghost and fire. Although the founder's sons became bishops in 1914, they were unable to stem the tide of dissatisfaction and schism which accompanied her death sixteen years later. As a result, in 1931 the church was reorganized into three dominions, which hold their respective conferences in May, June, and July each year. By the 1970s it claimed 500 affiliates and 20,000 members in forty states. It was then supporting missionary work in Jamaica, Spain, and Nassau in the Bahamas. Headquarters are in Nashville.

--GOVERNMENT

747 Church of the Living God, the Pillar and Ground of the Truth.
     The constitution, government, and general decree book of
     the Church of the Living God, the Pillar and Ground of the
     Truth (Incorporated): St. Mary Magdalena, first chief over-
     seer. 2d and rev. ed. Nashville, 1924. 84 p. Publication
     date stamped on t.-p. DLC

--HISTORY

748 Church of the Living God, the Pillar and Ground of the Truth.
     Seventy-fifth anniversary yearbook of the Church of the
     Living God, the Pillar and Ground of the Truth, Inc., 1903-
     1978: Mary Magdalena Tate, revivor and first chief overseer,
     Felix Early Lewis, co-revivor and bishop. [Helen Middleton
     Lewis and Meharry H. Lewis, editors]. Nashville, c1978.
     65 p. DLC

HOUSE OF GOD, THE HOLY CHURCH OF THE LIVING GOD, THE PILLAR AND GROUND OF THE TRUTH, HOUSE OF PRAYER FOR ALL PEOPLE (1914-)

Bishop R. A. R. Johnson, founder and general superintendent of the House of God, the Holy Church of the Living God, the Pillar

and Ground of the Truth, House of Prayer for All People, traced
its origin to Abyssinia. In 1913 Johnson began preaching twenty-
four principles he said had been divinely revealed to him. He organized the body the next year in Washington, D.C. It was incorporated in the District of Columbia in 1918 and soon spread to
other areas, the West Indies, West Africa, and south India. The
body adopted a puritanical code of behavior, observed the Lord's
supper and foot washing together, and took a strong stand in favor
of equality of the races and Christian charity toward the poor, the
hungry, and the displaced. In 1936 the group reported four
churches and 200 members in New York and New Jersey. Editorial
offices of church publications were in Charlottesville, Virginia. At
that time Bishop Johnson was residing in Beaufort, South Carolina.

--DOCTRINAL AND CONTROVERSIAL WORKS

749 House of God, the Holy Church of the Living God, the Pillar
     and Ground of the Truth, House of Prayer for All People.
     Guiding star book. Charlottesville, Va. 193-.

--PERIODICALS

750 Latter day messenger. 1- 193 -
     Charlottesville, Va.

HOUSE OF GOD, WHICH IS THE CHURCH OF THE LIVING
GOD, THE PILLAR AND GROUND OF THE TRUTH (1919-   )

     Formed in 1919, the House of God, Which Is the Church of the
Living God, the Pillar and Ground of the Truth is the product of
a division in the Nashville-based Church of the Living God, the
Pillar and Ground of the Truth. Personalities, rather than doctrinal differences, appear to be the cause of the separation. Headquarters and publishing offices are in Philadelphia. In 1956 the
organization reported 107 churches, 120 clergy, and 2,350 members.
Subordinate jurisdictions operate using various names. Some add
qualifiers to the denominational title, such as: "and Without Controversy" and "Without Controversy in New Jersey." The New York
section has the name Elect Church of the Living God in New York.

--PERIODICALS

751 Spirit of truth magazine. 1- 19 -
     Philadelphia

COOPERATIVE AGENCIES

INTERCOLLEGIATE PENTECOSTAL CONFERENCE INTERNATIONAL (1970-)

The Intercollegiate Pentecostal Conference International, established in 1970, is a transdenominational student organization centered in Howard University, Washington, D.C. Most constituents come from Holiness-Pentecostal backgrounds, but membership is by no means restricted by doctrinal orientation.

INTERNATIONAL EVANGELISTIC ASSOCIATION WORKERS FELLOWSHIP (1959-)

Headquarters of the International Evangelistic Association Workers Fellowship are in Brooklyn.

--PERIODICALS

752 International gospel herald. 1- 19 -
     New York

PENTECOSTAL SINGERS AND MUSICIANS ALLIANCE (1952-)

Many of the members of the Pentecostal Singers and Musicians Alliance, founded in 1952, were affiliated with the Church of God in Christ. It was not designed as a denominational organization, however. Anna Mae Ford of Chicago served as president and editor of the official publication.

--PERIODICALS

753 Pentecostal Alliance crescendo. 1- Feb./Mar. 1952-
     Chicago.

FULL GOSPEL HOLY TEMPLE CHURCHES (197 -)

In 1976 the Full Gospel Holy Temple Churches, Inc. held its annual convocation at 1900 South Ewing, Dallas, Texas. At that time Apostle Lobias Murray was overseer. Although there were affiliates as far away as Chicago, the movement appeared to be concentrated in Texas and Oklahoma.

754   1976 annual convocation of the Full Gospel Holy Temple
      Churches, Inc.
          In Post-Tribune (Dallas), 29:34 (Aug. 21, 1976), 11.   At
      head of title: "Without a vision the people perish."

FULL GOSPEL PENTECOSTAL ASSOCIATION (1969-   )

    The headquarters and publication offices of the Full Gospel
Pentecostal Association, established in 1969, are in Portland, Oregon.

    --PERIODICALS

755   Full gospel news.   1-   1969-
      Portland, Or.

HOUSE OF THE LORD (1925-   )

    In 1936 the House of the Lord was operating in four states:
Michigan, Illinois, Ohio, and Georgia.   A partial report that year
showed a total membership in excess of 300.   The group had been
established eleven years before by Bishop W. H. Johnson.   Headquarters were in Detroit.   The church maintained rigid behavioral
standards.   Members were forbidden to work at jobs involving tobacco, whiskey, beer gardens, or policy rackets.   They were not
to become bell hops nor marry anyone not baptized with the Holy
Ghost.   Similarly, they should refrain from attendance at motion
picture shows, ball games, dances, and horse races and should not
engage in pleasure riding or playing cards.   Membership in secret
societies was forbidden also.   Submission to a discipline, much more
comprehensive than the one summarized above, provided evidence in
addition to speaking in tongues that members had been baptized in
the Holy Ghost.

INTERNATIONAL CITY MISSION (1925-   )
[1925-19-- as City Mission.]

    The organization popularly known as the Kingston City Mission
or City Mission is the result of the evangelistic efforts of W. Raglan
Phillips, an Englishman.   Born in Bristol in 1854, Phillips at age
seventeen migrated to Jamaica, where for a time he worked as an
estate bookkeeper.   Turned down for the Baptist ministry, he in
1887 joined the Salvation Army and applied to General Booth to
send officers to the island.   He commenced work as an evangelist
under Salvation Army auspices, pursuing, however, a rather

independent course. His individualism, plus his tolerance of charismatic manifestations in his meetings, caused repeated rifts with the Army headquarters in London, yet he remained an officer until his death in 1930.

Upon his death, separation from the Salvation Army became final. The City Mission retained a hierarchy of officers headed a "Bishop D.D." Both of Phillips' successors holding this title have been women. The headquarters in Kingston directed work in 1980 in Belize, the United Kingdom, and the United States (New York and California). That year it reported twenty churches and 1,000 full members in Jamaica and more than ten churches and 500 members in other countries.

--HISTORY

756   Calley, Malcolm John Chalmers
        God's people: West Indian Pentecostal sects in England, by
        Malcolm J. C. Calley. London, New York, Oxford University
        Press, 1965. xiv, 182 p. "Issued under the auspices of the
        Institute of Race Relations, London." "History of the City
        Mission": p. 159-160. DLC, OCB, Uk

INTERNATIONAL EVANGELISTIC FELLOWSHIP (1960-   )

Dating from about 1960, the International Evangelistic Fellowship is composed largely of West Indian immigrants to Britain. It has links to the Swedish Pentecostal movement. Headquarters are in London. In 1980 the Fellowship had four churches with 500 members and about 1,000 constituents.

LIFE AND LIGHT FELLOWSHIP (1966-   )

Stressing healing, the Life and Light Fellowship is composed of immigrants from Jamaica and sponsors a mission to the homeland. The group, which is centered in Handsworth, Sheffield, reported two congregations, 103 members, and 250 constituents in 1980. It was founded in 1966.

MOUNT CALVARY HOLY CHURCH OF AMERICA (1929-   )

In 1929 Bishop Bromfield Johnson and 200 followers left the United Holy Church of America and established the Mount Calvary Church. At the founder's death in 1972, the body claimed eighty churches in thirteen states. Headquarters moved from Buffalo to Boston in the 1960s.

--WORK WITH YOUTH

757   Mount Calvary Holy Church of America.
      The Y.P.H.A. manual. Edited by Bromfield Johnson.
      Buffalo, 1962.

      --MASSACHUSETTS

      -- --BOSTON

758   Paris, Arthur Ernest, 1945-
      Black Pentecostalism: Southern religion in an urban world,
      [by] Arthur E. Paris. Amherst, University of Massachusetts
      Press, 1982. vii, 183 p. Based on thesis (Ph.D.)--
      Northwestern University. DLC, OkU

759   Paris, Arthur Ernest, 1945-
      Black Pentecostalism: world view, society and politics.
      Evanston, Il., 1974. vi, 183 [31] l. Thesis (Ph.D.)--
      Northwestern University. IEN

MOUNT SINAI HOLY CHURCH OF AMERICA (1924-   )

      As youthful pastor of the Mount Olive Holy Church in Philadel-
phia, Elder Ida Robinson had a series of dreams and visions in
which she was the head of a large ministry. In these dreams people
from the north, the south, the east, and the west flocked to her
Philadelphia church in search of help. Following a ten-day fast in
1924, she believed the Holy Spirit commanded her to "Come out on
Mount Sinai." As a result, she left the United Holy Church of
America and established the Mount Sinai Holy Church of America
later that year. Women have occupied prominent places in this
church from the beginning. The group embraces a strict code of
personal behavior, eschewing remarriage after divorce in every case
and condemning by name many alleged evidences of worldliness.
Belief in a specific sequence of last things and in baptism as essential to salvation is accepted as dogma. Under Mother Robinson and
her successor, Bishop Elmira Jeffries, the Mount Sinai movement
spread along the Atlantic coast from Massachusetts to Florida, and
leaped across the continent to California. In 1966 there were 92
congregations with an estimated membership of 7,000. Headquarters
remain in Philadelphia.

      --GOVERNMENT

760   Mount Sinai Holy Church of America.
      Manual of Mount Sinai Holy Church of America. Rev. ed.
      Philadelphia, 1947. 48 p.

761 Mount Sinai Holy Church of America.
       Manual of Mount Sinai Holy Church of America, Inc. Phila-
     delphia, 1968. 42 p.

762 Mount Sinai Holy Church of America.
       Requirements for ministers coming before the Board of Ex-
     aminers. [Philadelphia, 19--] leaflet (2 p.)

       --HISTORY

763 Mount Sinai Holy Church of America.
       [Program]: Fiftieth annual convocation of the Mount Sinai
     Holy Church of America, Inc. Philadelphia, 1974. 166 p.

764 Mathison, Richard Randolph, 1919-1980.
       Faiths, cults and sects of America: from atheism to Zen,
     [by] Richard R. Mathison. Indianapolis, Bobbs-Merrill, 1960.
     384 p. On Mount Sinai Holy Church of America: p. 244-245.
     OClU, Ok

765 Mathison, Richard Randolph, 1919-1980.
       God is a millionaire, [by] Richard Mathison. Indianapolis,
     Bobbs-Merrill, 1962, c1960. 384 p. (Charter books, 106)
     First published in 1960 under title: Faiths, cults and sects
     of America. On Mount Sinai Holy Church of America: p.
     244-245. FJ

       --PENNSYLVANIA

       -- --PHILADELPHIA

766 Fauset, Arthur Huff, 1899-
       Black gods of the metropolis: Negro religious cults of the
     urban North. Philadelphia, University of Pennsylvania Press;
     London, H. Milford, Oxford University Press, 1944. x, 126 p.
     (Publications of the Philadelphia Anthropological Society, 3;
     Brinton memorial series, [2]) Based on thesis (Ph.D.)--
     University of Pennsylvania. "Mt. Sinai Holy Church of Amer-
     ica, Inc.": p. 13-21. DLC, TxWB

MOUNT SINAI SAINTS OF GOD HOLY CHURCHES (1946-)

       Founded in 1946, the Mount Sinai Saints of God Holy Churches
is headed by Bishop Mary Maude Pope of Raleigh, North Carolina,
widow of the founder. The alternative name of the organization is
Mount Sinai Churches Worldwide.

NATIONAL FEDERATION OF PENTECOSTAL CHURCHES (19 -   )

The National Federation of Pentecostal Churches is headed by Herbert Daughtry, activist pastor of the House of the Lord Church in Brooklyn.

--HISTORY

767 Haley, Peter
     From saving souls to promoting politics. In Phoenix, 6
     (July 13, 1978)

768 Wright, Nathan, 1923-
     Non-establishment black religion, [by] Nathan Wright, Jr.
     In Smythe, M. M., ed. The black American reference book.
     Englewood Cliffs, N.J., c1976, 506-514. DLC

--PERIODICALS

769 National Federation of Pentecostal Churches newsletter. 1-
     197 -
     New York

770 People's press. 1- 1978-
     New York

771 Victory. 1- 1976-
     New York

NEW REFUGE DELIVERANCE HOLINESS CHURCH (1967-   )

Founded in 1967, the New Refuge Deliverance Holiness Church, Inc. consists of four congregations in Washington and Baltimore. Bishop Naomi C. Durant, the founder, lives in Baltimore.

NEW TESTAMENT ASSEMBLY (England) (1966-   )

The New Testament Assembly (England), organized in 1966, is composed largely of immigrants from Jamaica, Grenada, and Trinidad. In 1980 it consisted of eight churches, 150 members and a total community of 400. Headquarters are in Leyton, a London suburb.

ORIGINAL UNITED HOLY CHURCH INTERNATIONAL (1977-)
[1977-1980 as Original United Holy Church of the World.]

Organized June 29, 1977, during a meeting called for the purpose in the Memorial Auditorium, Raleigh, North Carolina, the
Original United Holy Church owes its existence to a struggle within
the United Holy Church of America between Bishop W. N. Strobhar,
denominational president, and Bishop J. A. Forbes, president of
the Southern District Convocation. The final rift had come during
a denominational meeting in Cleveland, Ohio, a month earlier from
which the Southern District Convocation, though itself parent to the
general organization, was ousted. The new body remains in essential doctrinal agreement with the continuing one, and while protest-
ing its adherence to congregationalism, remains committed to the
polity of the continuing body as well.

Consisting of more than 200 congregations and 15,000 members,
the Original United Holy Church is concentrated on the Atlantic
coast from South Carolina to Connecticut. Additional churches are
located in Kentucky, Texas, and California. Bishop Forbes, its
general president, serves also as pastor and administrator of the
Greater Forbes Temple of Hollis, New York, and as president of the
Southern District Convocation. Headquarters are in Goldsboro,
North Carolina, site of the United Christian College, which the
church sponsors. The denomination supports missionary work in
Liberia. The official organ is printed by Advocate Press, the publishing house of the Pentecostal Holiness Church. On January 24,
1979, in Wilmington, North Carolina, an agreement of affiliation between the Original United Holy Church and the Pentecostal Holiness
Church was signed which envisions a close cooperative relationship
between the two bodies.

--DOCTRINAL AND CONTROVERSIAL WORKS

772 Original United Holy Church of the World. Young People Holy
     Association.
          Quarterly. Clifton E. Buckram, writer and editor. [Golds-
     boro, N.C., 197-]. 24 p. Cover title.

--GOVERNMENT

773 Original United Holy Church of the World.
          1980 minutes [of the] quadrennial session [of the] Original
     United Holy Church of the World, Inc. Goldsboro, N.C.,
     1980. 20 l. Cover title.

774 Original United Holy Church of the World.
          State of the church address, delievered [!] by General
     President Bishop J. A. Forbes to the First General Convocation
     of the Original United Holy Church of the World, Inc., May
     16, 1979. n.p., 1979. 8 l. Cover title.

--PERIODICALS

775   Voice of the world.   1- July 1978-
        Goldsboro, N.C.

*PENTECOSTAL HOLINESS CHURCH (1911-)

        The product of the union January 31, 1911, at Falcon, North
Carolina, of the Fire-Baptized Holiness Church and the Pentecostal
Holiness Church of North Carolina, the Pentecostal Holiness Church
faced the dilemma posed by a biracial constituency by releasing its
black churches to independency. Both bodies had at some time
black minorities. Three years before the merger, the Fire Baptized
group had approved the departure of 27 churches and 925 members
(a third of its constituency) to form under W. E. Fuller the Colored
Fire Baptized Holiness Church. During its first biennium, the
united church organized minority congregations of the former North
Carolina group into a Colored Convention. At the next General
Convention, however, a motion prevailed to drop the unit from the
convention roll, thus ending official work among American blacks.
(Ironically, two years later the church appointed a black West Indian, K. E. M. Spooner, as a missionary to South Africa, who during his twenty-two-year tenure established more than sixty churches
there.) On a local and personal level biracial fraternity continued,
causing the Pentecostal Holiness Church in time to regret its early
decision to segregate. (In 1946 W. E. Fuller attended the funeral
of J. H. King, the white overseer who had officiated at his ordination.)
        In 1949 representatives of the United Holy Church of America
present at the General Conference in Jacksonville requested affiliation with the Pentecostal Holiness Church. Although no action was
then taken, the initiative foreshadowed post-integration ties with
black churches. In 1973 and 1978 the Pentecostal Holiness Church
entered into agreements of affiliation with the Soul Saving Station
for Every Nation and the Original United Holy Church. Also in
recent years communication has been reestablished with the Fire
Baptized Holiness Church of God of the Americas and the Universal
Pentecostal Holiness Church, black bodies with roots in the denomination.

--DOCTRINAL AND CONTROVERSIAL WORKS

776   [Montgomery, Granville Harrison], 1903-1966.
        Christianity, the South, and race relations. In Pentecostal
        Holiness Advocate, 30 (Sept. 5, 1946), 3-5.

777   Tinney, James Steven (1942-)
        A Wesleyan-Pentecostal appraisal of the charismatic movement,

[by] James S. Tinney. In Pentecostal Holiness Advocate, 50 (Jan. 7, 1967), 4-5, 10-11.

--HISTORY

778 Synan, Harold Vinson, 1934-
     The old-time power, [by] Vinson Synan. Franklin Springs, Ga., Advocate Press, 1973. 296 p. On blacks: p. 100-101, 104-105, 107-108, 153-154, 199, 219. IEG

779 Synan, Harold Vinson, 1934-
     Our ministry to black Americans, [by] Vinson Synan. In International Pentecostal Holiness Advocate, 67 (July 1984), 6-7.

--SERMONS, TRACTS, ADDRESSES, ESSAYS

780 Forbes, James Alexander, 1935-
     Release your song, [by] James Forbes, Jr. In International Pentecostal Holiness Advocate, 67 (July 1984), 10, 15, 23.

ST. JUDE DELIVERANCE CENTERS OF AMERICA (1971-)

This organization was established in 1971 by Joseph L. Price, former bishop of the Church of God in Christ. Its headquarters are in Indianapolis.

SOUL SAVING STATION FOR EVERY NATION CHRIST CRUSADERS OF AMERICA (1940-)

Soul Saving Station, a denomination which in 1980 claimed 11,000 members, is the outgrowth of a single congregation in Harlem. In 1932 Billy Roberts, a gangster and drug addict, was converted in Seattle. Later he moved to New York and evangelized in various city churches. There in 1940, with the help of nine young people, Roberts opened the first Soul Saving Station. Branches eventually developed in Buffalo and other Eastern cities. In 1957, when illness forced the founder to step down, Jesse F. Winley left Buffalo to become pastor in New York City and general overseer of the movement. In 1973 the Soul Saving Station entered an agreement of affiliation with the Pentecostal Holiness Church. At Bishop Winley's funeral in June 1980, twenty pastors of Soul Saving affiliates were given opportunity to speak.

--DOCTRINAL AND CONTROVERSIAL WORKS

781 Bland, Edward
       The black church in conflict, [by] Edward Bland, Jr.
     New York, 197-. 156 l.

--HISTORY

782 Winley, Jesse, 1920-1980.
       Jesse, [by] Jesse Winley, with Robert Paul Lamb. Spring-
     dale, Pa., Whitaker House, c1976. 223 p.

TRUE FELLOWSHIP PENTECOSTAL CHURCH OF AMERICA (1964-   )

     In 1964 Charles E. Waters, Sr., overseer of the Alpha and
Omega Pentecostal Church of America, left that body and established
the True Fellowship Pentecostal Church of America. It consists of
two congregations, both in Baltimore. Total membership is about
25.

TRUE VINE PENTECOSTAL HOLINESS CHURCH (19 -   )

     The True Vine Pentecostal Holiness Church was founded by
William Monroe Johnson of Winston-Salem, North Carolina, and
Robert L. Hairston of Martinsville, Virginia. Johnson became pre-
siding bishop and Winston-Salem the headquarters. In 1961 a com-
bination of circumstances--divorce and remarriage, rebaptism in
Jesus' name, and opposition to denominational assessments--caused
Hairston to leave the church. At his father's death, Sylvester D.
Johnson became presiding bishop and pastor of the headquarters
church.

--HISTORY

783 Richardson, James Collins, 1945-
       With water and Spirit, [by] James C. Richardson, Jr.
     Washington, Spirit Press, 1980. 151 p. Based on thesis
     (M.Div.)--Howard University. On True Vine Pentecostal Holi-
     ness Church: p. 87-88. OkTOR

UNITED HOLY CHURCH OF AMERICA (1894-   )
[1894-1900 as Holy Church of North Carolina; 1900-1910 as Holy

Church of North Carolina and Virginia; 1910-1916 as Holy Church
in America.]

In May 1886 a holiness revival broke out among blacks in Meth-
od, a suburb of Raleigh, North Carolina, which during the next decade and a half spread to Durham, Wilmington, and other places in
the piedmont and tidewater sections of North Carolina and Virginia.
This revival resulted in the formation of a new church in several
stages over the next three decades. Convocations in Durham on
October 13, 1894, and October 15, 1900, drew together under one
"banner" the constituencies of the Union Holiness Convention and
the Big Kahara [i.e., Coharie] Holiness Association, the principal
agencies of the revival. The Holy Church in America issued its first
discipline in 1910. The church adopted its present name in 1916
and obtained legal incorporation two years later. In 1920 the "parent" body became the Southern District Convocation following organization of the Northern District Convocation that year, an action of
key importance in the dispute that produced the Original United
Holy Church fifty-seven years later. Headquarters are in Philadelphia. In 1960 the United Holy Church of America reported 470
churches and 28,980 members. The establishment in 1977 of the
Original United Holy Church cost the Philadelphia-based body its
mission field in Liberia, and perhaps a half of its United States
constituency.

--DOCTRINAL AND CONTROVERSIAL WORKS

784 Lawson, Andrew William
       The doctrine of the United Holy Church of America, Inc.
       [Durham, N.C.], 1966. 53 p.

--GOVERNMENT

785 Holy Church in America.
       Standard manual for Holy churches, [by] H. L. Fisher.
       [Durham, N.C.], 1910; Printed by Dalcoe Printing Co., Eden,
       N.C., 1975. 45 p. "Adopted September 1910, by 'The Holy
       Church in America.'" Reprint ed. has introd. by James
       Alexander Forbes.

786 United Holy Church of America.
       Standard manual and constitution and by-laws of the United
       Holy Church of America, Incorporated. Revised 1966. [Phila-
       delphia], Printed by Christian Printing Co., 1966. 124 p.

787 United Holy Church of America.
       1965 year book of the United Holy Church of America (In-
       corporated). Philadelphia, 1965. 220 p.

--HISTORY

788   Fisher, Henry Lee, -1947.
         The history of the United Holy Church of America, Inc.,
      [by] H. L. Fisher. [Durham, N.C., 194-] 55 p.

788a Turner, William Clair, 1948-
         The United Holy Church of America: a study in black
      Holiness-Pentecostalism, [by] William Clair Turner, Jr. Dur-
      ham, N.C., 1984. xii, 221 l. Thesis (Ph.D.)--Duke Univer-
      sity. NcD

      --PERIODICALS

789   Holiness union. 1- 1901-
         Durham, N.C., Philadelphia, Pa.

      --SERMONS, TRACTS, ADDRESSES, ESSAYS

790   Forbes, James Alexander, 1935-
         How to be black and Christian too, [by] James A. Forbes.
      In Warren, M. A. Black preaching: truth and soul. Wash-
      ington, c1977, 79-96.

      --VIRGINIA

      -- --Richmond

791   Forbes, James Alexander, 1935-
         Ministry of hope from a double minority, [by] James A.
      Forbes, Jr. In Theological Education, 9 (Summer 1973,
      suppl.), 305-316.

UNIVERSAL PENTECOSTAL HOLINESS CHURCH (1913-)

   At its 1913 general convention in Toccoa, Georgia, the two-
year-old Pentecostal Holiness Church released its black affiliates to
form a separate convention. Most chose complete independence and
lost contact with one another and with the parent body. An estimated one hundred or more congregations owe their origin to this
source. The Universal Pentecostal Holiness Church, a cluster of
about ten congregations in the vicinity of Anderson, South Carolina,
emerged from this process and in recent years has reestablished
communication with the parent body. In 1984 its leader was Bishop
Ben Cunningham.

WORD OF FAITH FELLOWSHIP (19 -   )

The Word of Faith Fellowship is the result of the ministry of Wendell Wallace. It is based in North Surrey, British Columbia. Wallace, a native of Kansas City and former pastor in the Church of God (Anderson, Indiana), established the Fellowship after acceptance of charismatic beliefs strained his relationship with the church.

--DOCTRINAL AND CONTROVERSIAL WORKS

791a Wallace, Wendell
    The hinds feet of the Spirit-filled that leads to high places. North Surrey, B.C., Word of Faith Fellowship, 19--. 32 p.

PART III. FINISHED WORK OF
CALVARY ORIENTATION

At Azusa Street, William J. Seymour hewed to Wesleyan holiness orthodoxy on the doctrine of entire sanctification, holding that the vessel must be clean before the Holy Spirit will fill it. In short he held that the work of redemption is accomplished in three crises: justification (pardon); entire sanctification (purity); and baptism with the Holy Spirit (power), the initial evidence of which is tongues. At the height of the revival, unity issued from common experience, not from theological or racial bonds. By 1909 converts from non-Wesleyan traditions, particularly whites from Baptist backgrounds, began to challenge the original doctrinal consensus. Although many black converts also had originally been Baptists, most had come to the movement by way of holiness churches and evangelists, and had become Wesleyan thereby. The challengers regarded sanctification as a gradual process, the natural development of gifts and graces necessary for mature Christian living, not a second crisis subsequent to regeneration. To them, second-crisis sanctification was simply not taught in the Bible. In conversion all that was purchased for us by Christ at Calvary is made a free gift to us by faith. This, they declared, is Christ's complete saving work: the finished work of Calvary. Pentecost, called in the latter days the baptism of the Holy Ghost, is divine empowerment for Christian service. The initial physical evidence of having been so empowered, they held, is speaking in other tongues as the Spirit gives "utterance."

A shift also occurred in thinking about baptism. With few exceptions Finished Work advocates, whatever their former tradition, became immersionists, holding that baptism is the sign or testimony of salvation. Neither the baptism of infants nor the baptism of adults by other than immersion, they taught, is any baptism at all.

1. BAPTISTIC-TRINITARIAN BODIES

The pioneer proponent of the Finished Work teaching was the white independent Baptist William H. Durham of Chicago. Durham received the baptism of the Holy Spirit under William J. Seymour in Los

Angeles at the height of the revival and returned home to lead his own flock at the North Street Mission into the movement. In Chicago Durham quickly adjusted his theology to fit his experience and soon returned to Los Angeles to share his findings at Azusa Street. When Seymour (who was out of town at the time) returned and learned of the Finished Work teaching, he locked the Chicagoan out of the mission, thereby forcing Durham and his followers to seek another meeting place. Henceforth, Seymour at Azusa drew mostly blacks; Durham and Elmer Fisher (also white) at the Upper Room Mission a few blocks away, mostly whites. Similarly, most blacks (for the time being) continued to adhere to the Holiness-Pentecostal teaching, testifying to the strength of Seymour as a charismatic leader and accounting in part for the almost totally white character of the Baptistic Trinitarian branch of the movement.

--DOCTRINAL AND CONTROVERSIAL WORKS

792 Price, Frederick Kenneth Cercie, 1932-
      Faith, foolishness, or presumption? [By] Frederick K. C.
      Price. Tulsa, Harrison House, c1979. 148 p. OkTOR

793 Price, Frederick Kenneth Cercie, 1932-
      How faith works, [by] Frederick K. C. Price. Tulsa, Harrison House, c1976. 128 p. OkTOR

794 Price, Frederick Kenneth Cercie, 1932-
      How to obtain strong faith: six principles, [by] Frederick
      K. C. Price. Tulsa, Harrison House, 1978. 128 p. OkTOR

795 Price, Frederick Kenneth Cercie, 1932-
      Is healing for all? [By] Frederick K. C. Price. Tulsa,
      Harrison House, 1976. 127 p. OkTOR

--HYMNS AND SACRED SONGS

796 Harris, Thoro, 1874-1955.
      Gospel quintet songs. [Editor: Thoro Harris]. Chicago,
      193-. 1 v. (unpaged) With music.

797 Harris, Thoro, 1874-1955.
      Gospel songs. [Editor: Thoro Harris]. Chicago, c1931.
      [256] p. DLC

798 Harris, Thoro, 1874-1955.
      Heavenly praises. Compiled by J. O. Olsen [and] Thoro
      Harris for Evangelist John Goben. Chicago, T Harris, 192-.
      [292] p. With music. KyLoS

799 Harris, Thoro, 1874-1955.
        Hymns of hope. [Editor: Thoro Harris]. Chicago, [1922].
     1 v. (unpaged) With music. PPiPT

800 Harris, Thoro, 1874-1955.
        Pentecostal revivalist. Compiled by Thoro Harris. Los
     Angeles, Aimee Semple McPherson, 192-. 1 v. (unpaged)
     With music. CCC

801 Harris, Thoro, 1874-1955.
        Sing His praise. [Editor: Thoro Harris]. Chicago, [1925]
     202 p. Cover title. With music. KyLoS

802 Harris, Thoro, 1874-1955.
        Songs of His coming. [Editor: Thoro Harris]. Chicago,
     [1915]. [188] p. Cover title. With music. KyWAT, RPB

803 Harris, Thoro, 1874-1955.
        Songs of His coming. [Editor: Thoro Harris]. Chicago,
     [1918]. [256] p. Cover title. With music. CAngP, ICN

804 Harris, Thoro, 1874-1955.
        Songs of His coming, no. 2. [Editor: Thoro Harris].
     Chicago, 1919. 1 v. (unpaged) With music. IAurC

805 Harris, Thoro, 1874-1955.
        Songs of praise: Charles A. Shreve campaign special.
     [Editor: Thoro Harris]. Chicago, [1925]. 1 v. (unpaged)
     Cover title. With music. MH-AH

806 Harris, Thoro, 1874-1955.
        Songs of summerland. Prepared in cooperation with Floyd
     Humble, [by] Thoro Harris. Eureka Springs, Ar., T. Harris,
     c1943. [192] p. Cover title. With music. DLC, KyLoS

807 Harris, Thoro, 1874-1955.
        Songs we love. [Editor]: Thoro Harris. Chicago, 1921.
     1 v. (unpaged) Cover title. With music. MH-AH

        --PERIODICALS

808 Deliverance evangel. 1- 19 -
        Philadelphia.

*ASSEMBLIES OF GOD, GENERAL COUNCIL (1914-)

        The past two decades have witnessed the emergence of strong
black preachers, such as Robert Harrison (associate evangelist under

Billy Graham) and Thurman Faison in the Assemblies of God. These years also have seen the first attempt of the denomination at church planting in the black community. From 1911 to 1913 several hundred future Assemblies of God clergy, in transit from the Wesleyan holiness to the Finished Work of Calvary teaching, held ministerial credentials from the predominantly black Church of God in Christ. Remembrance of this caused the new organization for many years to regard itself as the white counterpart of the Memphis-based body, despite the doctrinal gulf which in fact separated the two groups. A reporter at the 1969 General Council session in Dallas said that not one black face was to be seen among the 4,700 clerical and lay delegates present. Only a minute portion of the 9,930 churches and 1,788,394 members reported in 1981 were black. As is true also of other groups, many Assemblies of God church extension pastors are natives of Caribbean islands and Guyana.

809 Blackwelder, Julia (Kirk)
    Southern white fundamentalists and the civil rights movement, [by] Julia Kirk Blackwelder. In Phylon, 40 (Winter 1979), 334-341.

    --CHURCH EXTENSION

810 [Cunningham, Robert Cyril], 1914-
    How can we reach black Americans for Christ? In Pentecostal Evangel, 2920 (Apr. 26, 1970), 6-8, 20. Interview by editor with T. F. Zimmerman, Robert Harrison, Thurman L. Faison, and C. W. H. Scott.

811 Ringness, Curtis Woodrow, 1916-
    Reaching black Americans, [by] Curtis W. Ringness. In Pentecostal Evangel, 2972 (Apr. 25, 1971), 23.

    --DOCTRINAL AND CONTROVERSIAL WORKS

812 Bacon, L. Calvin
    Eyewitness at a funeral, [by] L. Calvin Bacon. In Pentecostal Evangel, 2827 (July 14, 1968), 20-21.

813 Cox, Faye
    Interracial witnessing, [by] Faye Cox. In Pentecostal Evangel, 2855 (Jan. 26, 1969), 5.

814 [Cunningham, Robert Cyril], 1914-
    Watts a year later, [by] R. C. C. In Pentecostal Evangel, 2723 (July 17, 1966), 4.

815 Sanders, D. Leroy
    To serve is still enough, [by] D. Leroy Sanders. In Pentecostal Evangel, 2720 (June 26, 1966), 2-3.

816 Ytterock, David
        Probing our moral identity: a survey on ethical attitudes,
        [by] Dave Ytterock. In Agora, 1:2 (Fall 1977), 6-9.

        --EDUCATION

817 Saunders, Monroe Randolph, 1948-
        Perspectives on the philosophy of Christian education in
        Pentecostalism: the Assemblies of God [and] the Pentecostal
        Assemblies of the World, [by] Monroe R. Saunders, Jr.
        Washington, 1975. v, 74 l. Thesis (M.A.)--Howard Univer-
        sity. DHU

        --HISTORY

818 Kenyon, Howard Nelson, 1955-
        An analysis of racial separation within the early Pentecostal
        movement. Waco, Tx., 1978. ix, 163 l. Thesis (M.A.)--
        Baylor University. "Blacks and the Assemblies of God": l.
        67-69. TxWB

819 Menzies, William Watson, 1931-
        Anointed to serve: the story of the Assemblies of God,
        [by] William W. Menzies. Springfield, Mo., Gospel Publishing
        House, 1971. 436 p. Partially based on thesis (Ph.D.)--
        University of Iowa. "Social concern": p. 369-372.

        --HISTORY AND STUDY OF DOCTRINES

820 Kenyon, Howard Nelson, 1955-
        An analysis of racial separation within the early Pentecostal
        movement. Waco, Tx., 1978. ix, 163 l. Thesis (M.A.)--
        Baylor University. "The sisterhood myth": l. 72-100. TxWB

821 Ytterock, David
        Probing our moral identity: a survey on ethical attitudes,
        [by] Dave Ytterock. In Agora, 1:2 (Fall 1977), 6-9.

        --SERMONS, TRACTS, ADDRESSES, ESSAYS

822 Blake, Junious A.
        The undying flame of Pentecost, [by] Junious A. Blake.
        In Pentecostal Evangel, 2960 (Jan. 31, 1971), 8-10. "A sermon
        delivered at the ninth Pentecostal World Conference in Dallas."

823 Faison, Thurman Lawrence, 1938-
        Climate of change. A convention address [by] Thurman L.

Faison. In Pentecostal Evangel, 2937 (Aug. 23, 1970), 14-15.
Substance of address to the annual convention of the Evangelical Home Missions Convention in Kansas City in April.

824 Harrison, Robert Emanuel, 1928-
These things shall be, [by] Robert E. Harrison.   In
Pentecostal Evangel, 2789 (Oct. 22, 1967), 2-3.   "Sermon
preached at the General Council in Long Beach, California."

--EASTERN STATES

-- --NEW YORK

(New York City)

825 Buchwalter, Paul R.
Revival Center to open in Harlem, [by] Paul R. Buchwalter.
In Pentecostal Evangel, 2766 (May 14, 1967), 10-11.

--MIDDLE WEST

-- --ILLINOIS

(Chicago)

826 New inner-city church thrives in Chicago.
In Pentecostal Evangel, 3002 (Nov. 21, 1971), 20-21.

-- --MINNESOTA

(Minneapolis)

827 Nelson, M. C.
Inner-city church rises in Minneapolis, [by] M. C. Nelson.
In Pentecostal Evangel, 2946 (Oct. 25, 1970), 18-19.

(St. Paul)

828 Olson, Melford A.
Remembering the urban man, [by] Melford A. Olson.   In
Pentecostal Evangel, 3045 (Sept. 17, 1972), 16-17.

-- --MISSOURI

(St. Louis)

829 Southern Missouri opens black church.
In Pentecostal Evangel, 2981 (June 27, 1971), 16-17.

--SOUTHERN STATES

-- --MARYLAND

(Lexington Park)

830   Bonnici, Roberta (Lashley)
        A lesson in love, [by] Roberta Lashley Bonnici.   In Pente-
      costal Evangel, 3075 (Apr. 15, 1973), 8-9.

-- --MISSISSIPPI

(Shelby)

831   Mississippi: a venture in its cotton belt.
        In Pentecostal Evangel, 3077 (Apr. 29, 1973), 10-11.

ASSEMBLIES OF THE FIRST-BORN (1950-)

Organized about 1950, the Assemblies of the First-Born is the
Pentecostal-counterpart of another Jamaican body, the Church of
the First-Born. Headquarters are in Kingston. In 1980 the Assemblies of the First-Born reported twenty churches and 2,000 members in Jamaica and ten churches and 500 members in the United
Kingdom.

BIBLE CHURCH OF CHRIST (1961-)

The Bible Church of Christ was founded on March 1, 1961, by
Bishop Roy Bryant. In 1981 it reported five churches and 2,300
full members. Only 790 were enrolled in Sunday school, however.
Headquarters are in New York.

--PERIODICALS

832   Voice.   1-   196 -
        New York

CHURCH OF GOD

CHURCH OF GOD (Seventh-day) (1963-)

Established by Jamaican immigrants about 1963, this British
branch of the Denver-based Church of God (Seventh-day), a

millenarian and sabbatarian body, has become Pentecostal as well. Its United Kingdom headquarters are in South Norwood in Surrey. In 1980 it had six congregations and 200 members with a total constituency of 500.

CHURCH OF GOD FELLOWSHIP IN GREAT BRITAIN WORLD WIDE (1943-)

Four of the seven congregations reported in 1980 by the Church of God Fellowship in Great Britain World Wide were composed of West Indian immigrants.   Formed in 1943, the group continues the Welsh Latter Rain movement.   There are approximately 200 full members and a total constituency of about 500.

*PENTECOSTAL CHURCH OF GOD OF AMERICA (1919-)
[1919-1922 as Pentecostal Assemblies of the United States of America; 1922-1934 as Pentecostal Church of God.]

The Pentecostal Church of God of America shares common roots and common beliefs with the General Council of the Assemblies of God.   Its founder, Chicago pastor John C. Sinclair, had served in fact as one of the original executive presbyters of the Assemblies. It has shared also the reluctance of its sister-body toward biracial evangelism.   In 1981 it reported 1,118 churches and 34,376 full members, only a minute portion of which were black.   At present headquarters are in Joplin, Missouri.

--DOCTRINAL AND CONTROVERSIAL WORKS

833 Ford, George L.
       Is patriotism sinful? [By] George L. Ford. In Pentecostal Messenger, 36 (July 1962), 3.

-- --MINNESOTA

834 Olila, James Howard
       Pentecostalism: the dynamics of recruitment in a modern socio-religious movement. Minneapolis, 1968. 57 l. Thesis (M.A.)--University of Minnesota. MnU

DELIVERANCE EVANGELISTIC CENTERS (1966-)

Founded in 1966, the Deliverance Evangelistic Centers is one of very few black trinitarian bodies committed to the Finished Work of Calvary view.   Arturo Skinner and Maggie Laura Walker, the original leaders, established a school in connection with the

Newark, New Jersey headquarters. In 1979 Ralph Nichol became
president of the 100-church organization.

--DOCTRINAL AND CONTROVERSIAL WORKS

835 Skinner, Arturo, -1975
         9 gifts of the Spirit. Newark, N.J., Deliverance Evangel-
     istic Centers, c1975. 31 p. OkTOR

--HISTORY

836 Skinner, Arturo, -1975
         Deliverance. Newark, N.J., Deliverance Evangelistic Cen-
     ters, 1969. 52 p.

--PERIODICALS

837 Deliverance voice. 1- 1966-
         Newark, N.J.

*INTERNATIONAL CHURCH OF THE FOURSQUARE GOSPEL (1927-)

     By the 1970s the International Church of the Foursquare Gos-
pel, founded in 1927 by Aimee Semple McPherson, included a small,
significant black minority. Its West Adams Blvd. branch in Los
Angeles claimed lineal descent from the Azusa Street Mission and a
black taught Old Testament in its L.I.F.E. Bible College.

--HYMNS AND SACRED SONGS

838 Harris, Thoro, 1874-1955.
         Foursquare favorites. [Compiled by] Aimee Semple McPher-
     son. Edited by Thoro Harris. Los Angeles, Echo Park Evan-
     gelistic Association, 19--. 212 p. Cover title. With music.
     MBU-T, MoSpCB

--CALIFORNIA

-- --LOS ANGELES

839 West Adams.
         In Foursquare World Advance, 7 (June 1971), 20-21.

*INTERNATIONAL EVANGELICAL CHURCH AND MISSIONARY AS-
   SOCIATION (196 -)

Founded in the 1960s, the International Evangelical Church
and Missionary Association is the amalgamation of more than 400
congregations worldwide. Since 1972 it has been led by John Levin
Meares, white pastor of the predominantly black Evangel Temple
of Washington, D.C. At the 1982 consecration of Meares as first
presiding bishop of the church, black participants included Nicholas
B. H. Bhengu of South Africa and Bishop Benson A. Idahosa of
Nigeria. At that time, the fellowship included seven or eight
congregations in the United States.

840 Gaines-Carter, Patrice
       Celebration for evangelical bishop of bishops, [by] Patrice
     Gaines-Carter. In Washington Post (Nov. 10, 1982)

LATTER HOUSE OF THE LORD FOR ALL PEOPLE AND THE CHURCH
   ON THE MOUNTAIN, APOSTOLIC FAITH (1936-)
[To 19-- as Latter House of the Lord, Apostolic Faith.]

Established in April 1936, the Cincinnati-based House of the
Lord adhered to the teachings of its founder, Bishop L. W. Williams,
former Baptist pastor, who found "enlightenment" while in prayer.
Membership requirements included baptism by immersion and with
the Holy Ghost and fire. The Lord's supper was observed using
water, not wine. The group deplored war and urged noncombattant
service on its members. The year of organization the House of the
Lord reported six small churches. Eleven years later, the bishop
said it had 4,000 members in several states.

        --DOCTRINAL AND CONTROVERSIAL WORKS

841 Latter House of the Lord for All People and the Church on the
     Mountain, Apostolic Faith.
        Decree and doctrine and historical record. Cincinnati,
     194-.

842 Latter House of the Lord for All People and the Church on the
     Mountain, Apostolic Faith.
        Jesus is coming soon. Cincinnati, 194-.

*MIRACLE REVIVAL FELLOWSHIP (1956-1970)

Although the founder claimed it was in "no sense" his organization, the Miracle Revival Fellowship encompassed in fact the

constituency of Evangelist A. A. Allen. Formed in 1956, the Fellowship aimed at providing an instrument for cooperation "without bondage" for independent churches and ministers. The 500-member first ordination class bore visible witness to its role as an agency for issuing ministerial credentials. Allen, who throughout his career had conducted integrated meetings, had a sizeable black following, and about one-fourth of the enrollment of his Miracle Revival Bible Training Center near Hereford, Arizona was black. At its height the Miracle Revival Fellowship claimed 500 affiliated churches with a combined membership of 10,000 in the United States and Canada.

843   Elinson, Howard
      The implications of Pentecostal religion for intellectualism,
      politics, and race relations. In American Journal of Sociology,
      70 (Jan. 1965), 403-415.

      --DOCTRINAL AND CONTROVERSIAL WORKS

844   Allen, Asa Alonson, 1911-1970.
      How God feels about segregation, [by] A. A. Allen. In
      Miracle Magazine, 8 (May 1968), 8.

*MIRACLE TEMPLE CHURCHES (1960-)

     In 1960 Evangelist R. W. Schambach, former associate of A. A.
Allen, struck out on his own. Following a revival that year in
Newark, he established the first of four Miracle Temple Churches
designed to provide support for his itinerant work. Others followed
in Brooklyn, Philadelphia and Chicago. Each had its own pastor,
but the evangelist also made periodic visits. (In 1985 he was listed
as pastor in Chicago.) Like his mentor, Schambach has a large
black following. In 1975 the evangelist's headquarters were in Elwood City, Pennsylvania.

SHILO PENTECOSTAL FELLOWSHIP (United Kingdom) (1965-)

     The Shilo Pentecostal Fellowship (United Kingdom) is composed
of immigrants from Trinidad, Montserrat and Grenada won in their
home islands by workers of the Pentecostal Assemblies of Canada.
Founded in 1965, the London-based group reported 200 members and
eight churches in 1980. The inclusive community consisted of about
500 persons at that time.

2. ONENESS BODIES

Although resistence to William Durham's approach and loyalty to
W. J. Seymour's leadership kept blacks in the Wesleyan holiness
camp temporarily, the appearance in 1913 of the baptism in Jesus'
name teaching altered the ideological alignment considerably.
That year, during the Worldwide Camp Meeting conducted by the
white evangelist Maria Woodworth-Etter at Arroyo Seco near Los
Angeles, John G. Scheppe, a white man inspired by her preaching
on the power of Jesus' name, announced a new revelation. After a
night of prayer, he declared that baptism in the name of Jesus
alone, rather than in the name of the Father, Son and Holy Spirit,
fulfilled the biblical mandate. Rebaptism by the new formula, a
practice which spread the teaching eastward like a prairie fire, left
Finished Work camp in disarray and split the infant General Council of the Assemblies of God. Replacement of the trinitarian formula led to an all out assault on the doctrine of the Trinity as
well. The theophany which emerged was Jesus alone, the Jehovah
of the Old Testament bearing the titles: Father, Son, and Holy
Spirit. Since both trinitarian and the Jesus baptismal formulas
had clear biblical footing, an accommodation of both at first
seemed possible. With the introduction of the Trinity itself, however, an unbridgeable chasm gaped ahead.

The new teaching attracted gifted spokesmen from both races:
G. T. Haywood of Indianapolis and R. C. Lawson of Columbus for
blacks; Frank Ewart of Los Angeles, Glenn Cook of Indianapolis,
and D. C. O. Opperman of Eureka Springs, Arkansas, for whites.
(Haywood, a non-member, led the proponents of the "new issue"
on the floor of the 1916 meeting of the General Council of the Assemblies of God in St. Louis.)

Several factors contributed to the attractiveness of the "Jesus
Only" theology to blacks and wove its adherents into a closely-knit
group. For blacks, perhaps first in importance was insistence on
baptism by immersion in the name of Jesus as an initiatory rite.
Most were former Baptists. Rebaptism built on past commitment
while serving as a "bridge-burning" release from former allegiances.
It also provided an ideology that created an identity beyond race
and experience. Strong leaders, such as Lawson and Haywood,
gave the movement among blacks a nonderivative character not only
in political terms, but in doctrinal teaching and worship practices
as well. Haywood, a theologian and song writer, contributed sig-
nificantly to the musical repertoire of the movement. His "Jesus,
the Son of God" attained widespread use outside the movement as
well.

--BIBLIOGRAPHY

845 Kleinhans, Robert G., 1936-
       The historiography of Oneness or "Jesus Name" Pente-
     costals, [by] Robert G. Kleinhans. In Gill, J. H., comp.
     Papers presented to the first Occasional Symposium on Aspects
     of the Oneness Pentecostal Movement, held at Harvard Divinity
     School, Cambridge, Massachusetts, July 5-7, 1984. Cambridge,
     Ma., 1984, 272-287.

--DOCTRINAL AND CONTROVERSIAL WORKS

846 Bell, Dennis Rayford
       The philosophy of Christ, [by] D. Rayford Bell. Chicago,
     Adams Press, c1980. 104 p. DLC

847 Bell, Dennis Rayford
       The philosophy of Christ, [by] D. Rayford Bell. 2d ed.
     Chicago, Adams Press, c1982. 165 p. MiGrC

848 Bell, Dennis Rayford
       The song book of Israel, [by] D. Rayford Bell. [Editor:
     Norman Mabon]. Chicago, Christ Temple Apostolic Faith Ex-
     tension Ministry, c1983. xv, 303 p. DLC

849 Gerald, William, 1918-
       Coping with and overcoming today's problems. New York,
     Carlton Press, 1973. 63 p.

850 Gerald, William, 1918-
       A panoramic view of the basics of holiness. ----, 19--.

851 Haywood, Garfield Thomas, 1880-1931.
       The birth of the Spirit in the days of the apostles, [by]
     G. T. Haywood. In Seven "Jesus only" tracts. New York,
     1985. DLC

852 Haywood, Garfield Thomas, 1880-1931.
       Divine names and titles of Jehovah, [by] G. T. Haywood.
     In Seven "Jesus only" tracts. New York, 1985. DLC

--HISTORY AND STUDY OF DOCTRINES

853 Gerloff, Roswith Ingeborg Hildegard (1933-   )
       Blackness and Oneness (Apostolic) theology: crosscultural
     aspects of a movement, [by] Roswith I. H. Gerloff. In Gill,
     J. H., comp. Papers presented to the first Occasional Sym-
     posium on Aspects of the Oneness Pentecostal Movement, held
     at Harvard Divinity School, Cambridge, Massachusetts, July
     5-7, 1984. Cambridge, Ma., 1984, 70-100.

854   Kenyon, Howard Nelson, 1955-
         An analysis of racial separation within the early Pentecostal
      movement, Waco, Tx., 1978. ix, 163 l. Thesis (M.A.)--
      Baylor University. "The new issue": 1. 69-71. TxWB

         --HYMNS AND SACRED SONGS

855   Harris, Thoro, 1874-1955, ed.
         Apostolic songs. Eureka Springs, Ar., c1932. 1 v. (un-
      paged) Cover title. With music. TxFS

856   Harris, Thoro, 1874-1955.
         Songs of power. Edited by Thoro Harris. Special con-
      tributors: L. C. Hall and J. O. Olsen. Chicago, T. Harris.
      c1914. [160] p. Cover title. With music (shape notes)
      ICN, RPB

857   Harris, Thoro, 1874-1955.
         Songs of power. Edited by Thoro Harris. Special con-
      tributors: L. C. Hall and J. O. Olsen. Chicago, T. Harris:
      for sale by L. C. Hall; Malvern, Ar., E. N. Bell, c1914.
      1 v. (unpaged) Cover title. With music. OkBetC

858   Harris, Thoro, 1874-1955.
         Songs of power. Revised and enlarged by L. C. Hall.
      Thoro Harris, music editor. Chicago, L. C. Hall, c1914.
      1 v. (unpaged) With music. OkBetC

         --PERIODICALS

859   Apostolic light. 1- 19 -
      Cincinnati

860   Voice in the wilderness. 1- Apr. 1910-1928.
      Indianapolis.

         --SERMONS, TRACTS, ADDRESSES, ESSAYS

861   Haywood, Garfield Thomas, 1880-1931.
         The finest of the wheat, [by] G. T. Haywood. In Seven
      "Jesus only" tracts. New York, 1985. DLC

862   Haywood, Garfield Thomas, 1880-1931.
         The victim of the flaming sword, [by] G. T. Haywood. In
      Seven "Jesus only" tracts. New York, 1985. DLC

--UNITED STATES

863 Anderson, Robert Mapes, 1929–
     Vision of the disinherited: the making of American Pente-
     costalism. New York, Oxford University Press, 1979. 334 p.
     Based on thesis (Ph.D.)--Columbia University, 1969. "Trini-
     tarian controversy and racial separation": p. 176-194. DLC,
     TxDaTS

864 Clanton, Arthur Lee, 1915–
     United we stand: a history of Oneness organizations, [by]
     Arthur L. Clanton. Hazelwood, Mo., Pentecostal Publishing
     House, 1970. 207 p.

865 Ewart, Frank J., 1876–
     The phenomenon of Pentecost: a history of the Latter Rain.
     Frank J. Ewart, author. W. E. Kidson, collaborator. Hous-
     ton, Herald Publishing House, c1947. 111 p. OkEG

866 Ewart, Frank J., 1876–
     The phenomenon of Pentecost: a history of the Latter
     Rain, [by] Frank J. Ewart. St. Louis, Pentecostal Publishing
     House, c1947. 110 p. TxWaS

867 Ewart, Frank J., 1876–
     The phenomenon of Pentecost, [by] Frank J. Ewart. Rev.
     ed. Hazelwood, Mo., Word Aflame Press, 1975, c1947. 207 p.

868 Fester, Fred J.
     Their story: twentieth century Pentecostals, [by] Fred J.
     Foster. Hazelwood, Mo., Word Aflame Press, c1981. 187 p.
     MoSpA

869 Foster, Fred J.
     "Think it not strange"; a history of the Oneness movement,
     [by] Fred J. Foster. St. Louis, Mo., Pentecostal Publishing
     House, 1965. 109 p. ArU

870 Howell, Joseph
     The "New Issue" (1914-1916): the emergence of Oneness
     Pentecostalism in the United States, [by] Joseph Howell.
     Clinton, 1982. iii, 181 l. Thesis (M.A.)--Mississippi College.
     MsCliM

871 Richardson, James Collins, 1945–
     Historical and doctrinal development of the black Pentecostal-
     apostolic churches, 1900 to present, [by] James C. Richardson,
     Jr. Washington, 1974. Thesis (M.Div.)--Howard University.
     DHU

872 Richardson, James Collins, 1945–
     With water and Spirit, [by] James C. Richardson, Jr.

Washington, Spirit Press, 1980.   151 p.   Based on thesis
(M.Div.)--Howard University.   OkTOR

873   Tinney, James Steven (1942-   )
        The significance of race in the rise and development of
   the Apostolic Pentecostal movement, [by] James S. Tinney.
   In Gill, J. H., comp. Papers presented to the first Occasional
   Symposium on Aspects of the Oneness Pentecostal Movement,
   held at Harvard Divinity School, Cambridge, Massachusetts,
   July 5-7, 1984. Cambridge, Ma., 1984, 55-69.

           -- --PENNSYLVANIA

        (Philadelphia)

874   Doub, Robert O., 1924-
        A brief history of the Apostolic Faith Church in Philadelphia,
   Pa., [by R. O. Doub]. In Apostolic Ministers Conference of
   Philadelphia and Vicinity. Program book: "Apostolic Day,"
   June 10th, [1972], being held [at] Blue Horizon, 1314 Broad
   St., Phila., Pa. Philadelphia, 1972, 4.

AFRICAN FAITH TABERNACLE CHURCH (1919-   )

   Established in 1919, the African Faith Tabernacle Church of
Ghana is linked to the Faith Tabernacle Corporation of Churches
based in Portland, Oregon. The group permits the use of medicine.
In the mid-1970s the African Faith Tabernacle Church reported 370
congregations, 40,000 members and a total community of 50,000.
At that time it had missions in three nations.

ANGLO-WEST INDIAN ASSEMBLY (1962-   )

   The Anglo-West Indian Assembly was organized in 1962 by
immigrants from Montserrat, St. Kitts, and Jamaica in the United
Kingdom formerly affiliated with the Pentecostal Assemblies of the
World. Centered in London, the group by 1980 had two churches,
85 full members, and 200 constituents.

APOSTLE CHURCH OF CHRIST IN GOD (1940-   )

   In 1940 five ministers formerly affiliated with the Church of
God (Apostolic) organized the Apostle Church of Christ in God
with headquarters at Winston-Salem, North Carolina. According to
J. C. Richardson, Sr., future presiding bishop, the new body

resulted from dissatisfaction over church administration, not from
doctrinal differences. Despite a number of defections, the Apostle
Church of Christ experienced significant growth. In four decades
it grew from three to thirteen churches. In 1980 it reported 2,150
members. The early-1980s saw reunion with the Macedonia Churches
of Virginia which had separated under Bishop Tilman Carmichael
in 1974. Headquarters which since 1956 had been in Martinsville,
then moved to Gloucester, Virginia. In 1984 the church held membership in the Apostolic World Christian Fellowship.

--DOCTRINAL AND CONTROVERSIAL WORKS

875 Richardson, James Collins, 1910-
       Believer's guide books, [by] James C. Richardson. Mar-
     tinsville, Va., 1973.

--GOVERNMENT

876 Apostle Church of Christ in God.
       Discipline of the Apostle Church of Christ in God. Martins-
     ville, Va., 19--.

--HISTORY

877 Richardson, James Collins, 1945-
       With water and Spirit, [by] James C. Richardson, Jr.
     Washington, Spirit Press, 1980. 151 p. Based on thesis
     (M.Div.)--Howard University. "The Apostle Church of Christ
     in God, 1940": p. 71-76. OkTOR

--PERIODICALS

878 Apostolic journal. 1- 19 -
       Martinsville, Va. To 19-- as Apostolic gazette.

APOSTOLIC ASSEMBLIES OF CHRIST (1970-)

     The Detroit-based Apostolic Assemblies of Christ is a result of
realignments in the Pentecostal Churches of the Apostolic Faith Association in the years following the death of Bishop S. N. Hancock.
G. M. Boone, the presiding bishop, and many other founding clergy
had formerly been affiliated with the Hancock organization. Each
member congregation enjoys complete autonomy. In 1980 the Apostolic Assemblies of Christ had six bishops, more than sixty clergy,
23 churches, and 3,500 members. It holds membership in the Apostolic World Christian Fellowship.

--HISTORY

879 Richardson, James Collins, 1945-
        With water and Spirit, [by] James C. Richardson, Jr.
     Washington, Spirit Press, 1980. 151 p. Based on thesis
     (M.Div.)--Howard University. "The Apostolic Assemblies of
     Christ, Inc., 1970": p. 94-95. OkTOR

APOSTOLIC ASSEMBLY OF OUR LORD AND SAVIOUR JESUS
    CHRIST (19 -)

     The Philadelphia-based Apostolic Assembly takes official stands
against women preachers, military service, self-defense, and pride
in dress or behavior (beauty parlors, straightening of hair, toeless
shoes, earrings, finger rings, television, checkers, football, base-
ball and golf. In the 1960s Bishop W. M. Selby was general overseer.

--DOCTRINAL AND CONTROVERSIAL WORKS

880 Apostolic Assembly of Our Lord and Saviour Jesus Christ.
        Articles of faith. Philadelphia, 19--.   [13] p. Caption
     title.

881 McCoy, Lawrence F.
        The apostolic way of life. Written by Larry F. McCoy.
     Rev. ed. Philadlephia, Apostolic Assembly of Our Lord and
     Saviour Jesus Christ, 1970. 1 v. (unpaged) Cover title.

882 Selby, W. M.
        Apostolic facts: who is this that defies and challenges
     the whole religious world on these subjects? [By] W. M.
     Selby. Philadelphia, Apostolic Assembly of Our Lord and
     Saviour Jesus Christ, 197-. 24 p. Cover title.

APOSTOLIC CHURCH OF CHRIST (1969-)

     On May 12, 1969, Bishop Johnnie Draft and Elder Wallace Snow
organized the Apostolic Church of Christ at Winston-Salem, North
Carolina. Both had been ministers in the Church of God (Apostolic), and Draft had served as pastor of the headquarters church
in Winston-Salem and overseer in North and South Carolina, Pennsylvania, and Virginia. No explanation was offered for the separation. After ten years, the Apostolic Church of Christ reported
one bishop, fifteen clergy, six churches and 300 members.

--HISTORY

883   Richardson, James Collins, 1945-
         With water and Spirit, [by] James C. Richardson, Jr.
      Washington, Spirit Press, 1980. 151 p. Based on thesis
      (M.Div.)--Howard University. "The Apostolic Church of
      Christ, Inc., 1969": p. 94. OkTOR

--PERIODICALS

884   Voice of apostolic churches. 1- 1969-
         Winston-Salem, N.C.

APOSTOLIC CHURCH OF JESUS CHRIST (1960-)

Sixty percent of the members of this West Indian immigrant
church are women. Formed about 1960, the Apostolic Church of
Jesus Christ was by 1980 third largest of the black immigrant
groups in Great Britain. That year it reported twenty congregations, 2,000 members, and 4,000 constituents.

APOSTOLIC FAITH TEMPLE (19 -)

The Apostolic Faith Temple, Inc. holds membership in the
Apostolic World Christian Fellowship. Bishop N. C. Peters, the
head, resides in Chicago.

*ASSEMBLIES OF THE LORD JESUS CHRIST (1952-)

In March 1952 at Memphis, Tennessee, the Assemblies of the
Church of Jesus Christ, the Jesus Only Apostolic Church of God,
and the Church of the Lord Jesus Christ merged into a single,
racially integrated body: the Assemblies of the Lord Jesus Christ.
Distinctive taboos include bearing of arms; membership in any organization which enforces any policy contrary to individual conscience; attendance at shows, dances, or theaters; and the wearing of immodest athletic attire in public schools. Headquarters are
in Memphis. In 1964 the Assemblies of the Lord Jesus Christ had
work in 22 states and four foreign countries. That year it reported
120 churches and 6,300 members.

BAPTISTS

EMMANUEL TABERNACLE BAPTIST CHURCH (APOSTOLIC FAITH) (19 -)

In 1980 headquarters of the Emmanuel Tabernacle Baptist Church (Apostolic Faith) were in Columbus, Ohio.

BETHEL APOSTOLIC CHURCH OF THE PENTECOSTAL MOVEMENT ASSOCIATION (19 -)

In 1984 Bishop D. McCollough was president of the Bethel Apostolic Church of the Pentecostal Movement Association. Headquarters of the church, which holds membership in the Apostolic World Christian Fellowship, are in Chicago.

BIBLE WAY CHURCH OF OUR LORD JESUS CHRIST WORLD WIDE (1957-)

The Bible Way Church of Our Lord Jesus Christ World Wide, established in 1957 during a ministers conference in Washington, D.C., resulted from widespread complaints of authoritarianism in the Church of Our Lord Jesus Christ of the Apostolic Faith. Reform in church government was the principal aim of Elders Smallwood E. Williams, John S. Beane, McKinley Williams, Winfield Showall, and Joseph Moore, and the approximately seventy congregations which followed them. Doctrinal standards of the new group are identical to those of the parent. Members are required to be present each time the Holy Communion is celebrated, and to attend all business meetings. Bible Way churches require tithing, and condemn use of tobacco and alcohol and remarriage of divorced persons while their original partners live. They reject as fanaticism teaching which forbids the straightening and shampooing of hair and the wearing of neckties or shoes without toes or heels. Headquarters offices, a Bible training school, the publishing house, and the residence of Smallwood E. Williams, presiding bishop, are in Washington. In 1970 the denomination reported 350 churches and 30,000 members. At that time it was sponsoring work in Jamaica, Trinidad, Tobago, Liberia, and the United Kingdom. The Bible Way Church holds membership in the Apostolic World Christian Fellowship.

--DOCTRINAL AND CONTROVERSIAL WORKS

885 Gerald, William, 1918–
Coping with and overcoming today's problems. New York,
Carlton Press, 1973.   63 p.

886 Gerald, William, 1918–
A panoramic view of the basics of holiness. ----, 19--.

887 Nichols, James Edward, 1932–
What must I do to be saved. Cleveland, Oh., 1967.

--GOVERNMENT

888 Bible Way Church of Our Lord Jesus Christ World Wide.
Minute book of the General Convocation, Bishops Council,
workers meetings and ministerial record, 1967–68. Washington,
1967.   OkTOR

889 Bible Way Church of Our Lord Jesus Christ World Wide.
Minute book of the General Convocation, Bishops Council.
Workers meetings and ministerial record, 1977–78. Washington,
1977.   77 p.

890 Bible Way Church of Our Lord Jesus Christ World Wide.
Rules and regulations of the Bible Way Church of Our Lord
Jesus Christ World Wide. Washington, Bible Way Church
Press, 1962.

--HISTORY

891 Richardson, James Collins, 1945–
With water and Spirit, [by] James C. Richardson, Jr.
Washington, Spirit Press, 1980.   151 p. Based on thesis
(M.Div.)--Howard University. "Bible Way Church of Our
Lord Jesus Christ World Wide, 1957": p. 79–85. OkTOR

892 Williams, Smallwood Edmond, 1907–
Brief history and doctrine of the Bible Way Churches of
Our Lord Jesus Christ World Wide. Smallwood E. Williams,
ed. Washington, Bible Way Church, 1957. 24 p. Cover title.
MoSCEx

893 Williams, Smallwood Edmond, 1907–
The golden jubilee documentary, [by] Smallwood E. Williams.
Washington, Bible Way Church of Our Lord Jesus Christ World
Wide, 1977.   130 p.

--PERIODICALS

894 Bible Way news voice. 1- 1954-
     Washington. WHi

895 Youth herald. 1- 19 -
     Washington.

--SERMONS, TRACTS, ADDRESSES, ESSAYS

896 Williams, Smallwood Edmond, 1907-
     Significant sermons. Washington, Bible Way Church, c1970.
     164 p. DLC

--DISTRICT OF COLUMBIA

-- --WASHINGTON

897 Bible Way Church holds groundbreaking ceremonies for new
     temple.
     In Capital Spotlight (Sept. 28, 1978), 1, 4, 10.

898 Milloy, Courtland
     A little bit of heaven here on earth, [by] Courtland Milloy.
     In Washington Post, 100 (July 17, 1977), A1, A8.

BIBLE WAY PENTECOSTAL APOSTLE CHURCH (1960-)

     The Virginia-based Bible Way Pentecostal Apostle Church
sprang from the same roots as the Bible Way Church of Our Lord
Jesus Christ World Wide. In 1957 Curtis P. Jones, pastor of the
St. Paul Apostolic Church at Axton, Virginia, left the Church of
Our Lord Jesus Christ of the Apostolic Faith. Rather than joining
the Washington-based group, however, he remained independent.
Three years later Jones organized the Bible Way Pentecostal Apostle
Church with affiliates at Roanoke, Axton, and Rocky Mount. Jones
served as pastor at Roanoke. After his death in 1976, a struggle
for control ensued between Edward Martin and Aaron Moyer, clergy
the founder had recruited from members of the church in Axton.
In 1980 reconciliation appeared imminent.

--HISTORY

899 Richardson, James Collins, 1945-
     With water and Spirit, [by] James C. Richardson, Jr.
     Washington, Spirit Press, 1980. 151 p. Based on thesis

(M.Div.)--Howard University. "The Bible Way Pentecostal
Apostle Church, 1960": p. 85-87. OkTOR

CHRISTIAN MISSION APOSTOLIC CHURCHES (19 -   )

In 1972 W. L. Pye of Philadelphia was bishop of the Northern
Diocese of the Christian Mission Apostolic Churches. At that time
Pye, who was pastor of the Mount Airy Apostolic Temple, held
membership in the Apostolic Ministers Conference of Philadlephia and
Vicinity.

CHURCH OF GOD

APOSTOLIC CHURCH OF GOD (1973-   )

Formed in 1973 by Jamaican immigrants to Great Britain, the
Apostolic Church of God resulted from a split in the Pentecostal
Assemblies of the World. By 1980 its four churches and 100 mem-
bers were affiliated with the Washington-based Highway Christian
Church of Christ.

APOSTOLIC OVERCOMING HOLY CHURCH OF GOD (1917-   )
[1917-1927 as Ethiopian Overcoming Holy Church of God.]

In 1916 W. T. Phillips, a former Methodist who had been won
to the holiness message and ordained by Frank W. Williams three
years earlier in Birmingham, Alabama, set out to work full-time as
an evangelist. In March the next year at Mobile "the Holy Ghost
in a body of elders" set him apart as bishop of the Ethiopian Overcoming Holy Church of God. The body was incorporated in 1920
and renamed Apostolic Overcoming Holy Church of God in 1927. As
pastor of the Greater Adams Holiness Church in Mobile and as bishop, Phillips dominated the church for fifty-seven years. In the
early years outside observers said worship was simply choatic; institutional development, retarded. Distinctive practices include foot
washing as an ordinance. Women are recognized as equal in the
church. Members are forbidden to marry unconverted persons or
to attend services in other churches held at the same hour as those
of the Apostolic Overcoming Holy Church of God. Missionary projects once sponsored in India, Africa, and the Caribbean had all
been abandoned before the founder's death. In 1975, however,
three American workers were sent to Haiti and approximately
$50,000 was raised for work there. Between 1956 and 1980 United
States membership increased from 75,000 to 125,000. It is concentrated in Alabama, Kentucky, Illinois, Oklahoma, and Texas.

Jasper C. Roby, whose daughter Juanita Roby Arrington serves as editor of the official organ, is senior bishop. He lives in Birmingham. Although no tie exists between the two bodies, many statements in the disciplines of the Apostolic Overcoming Holy Church of God and the Church of God (Apostolic) are identical or nearly so.

--GOVERNMENT

900   Apostolic Overcoming Holy Church of God.
      Discipline and doctrine of the Apostolic Overcoming Holy Church of God, Inc. Birmingham, Al., Church Publishing House, 197- . 73 p. Cover title: Book of discipline of the Apostolic Overcoming Holy Church of God, Inc. AU

901   Apostolic Overcoming Holy Church of God.
      Manual of the Apostolic Overcoming Holy Church of God, Inc., founded upon the apostles doctrine: we believe in the one true God, Father, Son and Holy Ghost. All are one. Read it! To know it! Mobile, Al., A. O. H. Church Publishing House, 1962. 56 p. Cover title. MoSCEx

--HISTORY

902   Moore, Everett Leroy, 1918-
      Handbook of Pentecostal denominations in the United States. Pasadena, Ca., 1954. vii, 346 l. Thesis (M.A.)--Pasadena College. "Apostolic Overcoming Holy Church of God": l. 277-281. CSdP

903   Oliver, John Bernard
      Some newer religious groups in the United States. New Haven, Ct., 1946. vi, 502 l. Thesis (Ph.D.)--Yale University. CtY

904   Phillips, William Thomas, 1893-1974.
      Excerpts from the life of the Right Rev. W. T. Phillips and fundamentals of the Apostolic Overcoming Holy Church of God, Inc. Mobile, Al., A. O. H. Church Publishing House, 1967. 14 p.

905   Richardson, James Collins, 1945-
      With water and Spirit, [by] James C. Richardson, Jr. Washington, Spirit Press, 1980. 151 p. Based on thesis (M.Div.)--Howard University. "Apostolic Overcoming Holy Church of God, Incorporated, 1915": p. 53-54. OkTOR

--PERIODICALS

906 People's mouthpiece. 1- 1974-
        Birmingham, Al.

--STATISTICS

907 United States. Bureau of the Census.
        Census of religious bodies: 1926. Apostolic Overcoming
     Holy Church of God. Statistics, denominational history, doc-
     trine, and organization. Washington, Government Printing Of-
     fice, 1929. 7 p. DLC, NNUT

        CHURCH OF GOD (Apostolic) (1897-)
        [1897-1915 as Christian Faith Band.]

     In 1897 Elder Thomas J. Cox organized the Christian Faith
Band in Danville, Kentucky, incorporating the body under that
name four years later. It chose the present "more scriptural" name
in 1915, but delayed applying for incorporation under it four years
because of internal opposition to the change. The church believes
in divine healing, but "does not condemn those who are weak in faith
for using medicine." Instantaneous sanctification, it says, will be
made evident in godly living. The church upholds obedience to the
law, but not "in war, nor going to war." Women are ordained to
the ministry. Five general overseers have served: Thomas J. Cox,
1897-1943; M. Gravely (with Eli Neal), 1943-1945; Eli Neal, 1943-
1964; Love Odom, 1964-1966; David E. Smith, 1966-1974; and
Reuben K. Hash, 1974 to present. All except Bishop Gravely
have died in office. Following the death of Bishop Cox, headquarters moved from Danville, Kentucky, to Beckley, West Virginia.
Several years later it moved to Winston-Salem, North Carolina, its
present location. The residence of the general overseer appears
often to be the determining factor in choosing the headquarters site.
In the early 1970s the Church of God (Apostolic) had approximately
1,000 members. At that time Bishop Smith said that similarities in
the wording of key passages in the disciplines of the Church of God
(Apostolic) and the Apostolic Overcoming Holy Church of God were
coincidental. The Winston-Salem based body holds membership in
the Apostolic World Christian Fellowship.

        --GOVERNMENT

908 Church of God (Apostolic)
        Discipline of the Church of God (Apostolic), Inc. Beckley,
     W. Va., 194-. 40 p.

--HISTORY

909 Richardson, James Collins, 1945-
        With water and Spirit, [by] James C. Richardson, Jr.
     Washington, Spirit Press, 1980. 151 p. Based on thesis
     (M.Div.)--Howard University. "The Church of God (Apostolic),
     1897": p. 41-45. OkTOR

--STATISTICS

910 United States. Bureau of the Census.
        Census of religious bodies: 1926. Church of God (Apos-
     tolic). Statistics, denominational history, doctrine, and or-
     ganization. Washington, Government Printing Office, 1928.
     7 p. DLC

CHURCH OF GOD IN CHRIST (Apostolic) (1945-)

    Established in 1945, the Baltimore-based Church of God in
Christ (Apostolic) was the extension of the work of Randolph Carr,
former elder in the Pentecostal Assemblies of the World. The founder concentrated effort in the eastern cities and in the West Indies,
the United Kingdom and Canada, and within twenty years the organization had more than sixty affiliates in these areas. Carr's
strict standard concerning divorce and remarriage, not always con-
sistently enforced, troubled many within the group, including Monroe Saunders, popular Washington pastor and the founder's chief
assistant. A stand-off developed and Bishop Carr asked Saunders
to leave. The unexpected result of this 1965 action, however, was
the exodus of most of the constituency of the Church of God in
Christ (Apostolic), leaving Carr with a tiny remnant of the heretofore dynamic organization.

CHURCH OF GOD OF THE APOSTOLIC FAITH ASSOCIATION
    (19 -)

    In 1973 the Church of God of the Apostolic Faith Association
held membership in the Apostolic World Christian Fellowship.
B. L. Lumpkins, its presiding bishop, was treasurer of the Fellowship at that time.

GLORIOUS CHURCH OF GOD IN CHRIST APOSTOLIC (1921-)

    Incorporated in 1921 by Bishop C. H. Stokes, the Glorious
Church of God in Christ Apostolic outlawed the remarriage of
divorced persons within its ranks. In 1952, however, its presiding
bishop of twenty-four years, S. C. Bass, married a divorcee. As

a result half of the fifty churches left the denomination, taking the
charter with them, and under Bishop W. O. Howard formed the
Original Glorious Church of God in Christ Apostolic Faith later that
year. In 1980 the continuing body was led by Bishop Perry Lind-
sey. Headquarters are in Roanoke, Virginia.

NEW BETHEL CHURCH OF GOD IN CHRIST (Pentecostal) (1927-)

In 1927, A. D. Bradley was reprimanded by the board of
bishops of the Church of God in Christ for preaching the "Jesus
Only" doctrine. As a result Bradley, his wife, and Lonnie Bates
left the denomination and founded the New Bethel Church of God in
Christ (Pentecostal). Bradley became presiding bishop. Doctrinal
innovations notwithstanding, the new church resembles its parent
in many ways. It regards footwashing as an ordinance. It con-
demns membership in secret societies. And it disapproves school
activities which violate a student's religious convictions. Headquarters are in San Francisco.

911   New Bethel Church of God in Christ (Pentecostal)
        Articles of faith. San Francisco, 19--.

ORIGINAL GLORIOUS CHURCH OF GOD IN CHRIST APOSTOLIC FAITH (1952-)

In 1952 twenty-five of the fifty congregations affiliated with the
Glorious Church of God in Christ Apostolic left the denomination and
under Bishop W. O. Howard reorganized as the Original Glorious
Church of God in Christ Apostolic Faith. The separatists took the
1921 charter with them and included "Original" in the name to indicate allegiance to it. The occasion for the division was the marriage
of the presiding bishop, S. C. Bass, to a divorcee, an act forbidden by church teaching. Two have served as presiding bishop:
W. O. Howard, 1952-1972, and I. W. Hamiter, 1972-1985. Between
1972 and 1980 United States affiliates increased from 40 to 55. In
the latter year the church reported 110 congregations in Haiti,
Jamaica, and India. The world totals were 165 churches, 300 clergy
and 25,000 members. Headquarters are in Columbus, Ohio.

--HISTORY

912   Richardson, James Collins, 1945-
        With water and Spirit, [by] James C. Richardson, Jr.
        Washington, Spirit Press, 1980. 151 p. Based on thesis
        (M.Div.)--Howard University. "Original Glorious Church of
        God in Christ Apostolic Faith, 1921": p. 63-65. OkTOR

CHURCH OF OUR LORD JESUS CHRIST OF THE APOSTOLIC FAITH
   (1919-   )
[1919-1931 as Refuge Churches of Our Lord.]

In 1919 the center of activity of the Refuge Churches of Our
Lord, founded earlier that year in Columbus, Ohio, shifted to New
York. In July of that year Bishop R. C. Lawson, founder of the
denomination, opened the Refuge Church of Christ of the Apostolic
Faith in the heart of Harlem, a center henceforth regarded as the
headquarters church. The group adopted the present name at the
time of incorporation in 1931. It experienced a major setback in
1957 when seventy congregations followed Elder Smallwood E. Williams of Washington, D.C., into the Bible Way Church of Our Lord
Jesus Christ World Wide. Lawson's supposed authoritarianism, not
doctrine, lay behind the dispute. Itself a splinter of the Pentecostal Assemblies of the World, the Church of Our Lord Jesus
Christ of the Apostolic Faith differs in no essential doctrine with
either its parent or any (save one led by J. W. Pernell) of its
offspring. In 1954, three years before the Williams-led defection,
the church reported 155 congregations and 45,000 members. The
founder died in 1961. Successors have been Hubert J. Spencer
and William L. Bonner. Under Bishop Bonner work has been undertaken in Africa, Trinidad, Germany, and the United Kingdom. In
1979 the church raised $176,000 for these projects. At that time it
claimed 450 congregations and approximately 300,000 members.

--CONTROVERSIAL LITERATURE

913   Mason, Charles Harrison, 1866-1961.
          The sonship of Jesus, [by] C. H. Mason. In Mason,
      C. H. History and formative years of the Church of God in
      Christ. Memphis, 1969, 29-31.

914   Williams, Smallwood Edmond, 1907-
          Bishop Lawson's mistakes viewed, [by] S. E. Williams. In
      Bible Way News Voice, 5 (July/Aug. 1958), 5.

--DOCTRINAL AND CONTROVERSIAL WORKS

915   Lawson, Robert Clarence, 1891-1961.
          The anthropology of Jesus Christ, our kinsman, [by]
      R. C. Lawson. Pique, Oh., Ohio Ministries, 1925. 42 p.
      OU

916   Lawson, Robert Clarence, 1891-1961.
          For the defense of the gospel: the writings of Bishop
      R. C. Lawson. Edited by Arthur M. Anderson. New York,
      Church of Christ Publishing Co., 1972.

917 Lawson, Robert Clarence, 1891-1961.
     An open letter upon the burning question of marriage and
     divorce, [by] R. C. Lawson. Columbus, Oh., Contender for
     the Faith, 19--. 40 p.

918 Lawson, Robert Clarence, 1891-1961.
     What is truth, [by] R. C. Lawson. New York, 19--.

919 Long, C. L.
     Showers of blessing, [by] C. L. Long. Washington, Great-
     er Scripture Church of Christ, 1979. 34 p.

     --GOVERNMENT

920 Church of Our Lord Jesus Christ of the Apostolic Faith.
     Discipline book of the Church of Our Lord Jesus Christ of
     the Apostolic Faith. Edited by R. C. Lawson. New York,
     Church of Christ Printing and Publishing, 1955. 129 p.

     --HISTORY

921 Moore, Everett Leroy, 1918-
     Handbook of Pentecostal denominations in the United States.
     Pasadena, Ca., 1954. vii, 346 l. Thesis (M/A.)--Pasadena
     College. "Church of Our Lord Jesus Christ of the Apostolic
     Faith": 1. 289-290. CSdP

922 Richardson, James Collins, 1945-
     With water and Spirit, [by] James C. Richardson, Jr.
     Washington, Spirit Press, 1980. 151 p. Based on thesis
     (M.Div.)--Howard University. "Church of Our Lord Jesus
     Christ of the Apostolic Faith, Inc., 1919": p. 54-63. OkTOR

     --PERIODICALS

923 Apostles' newsletter. 1- 1973-
     New York

924 Contender for the faith. 1- 1919-
     Columbus, Oh., New York

     --NEW YORK

        -- --NEW YORK City

925 New York. Refuge Temple of Christ.
     Souvenir journal of the 27th annual celebration of Refuge

Temple of the Churches of Our Lord Jesus Christ: the
church of all people unfolds her history to the world. [Edited
by] Bishop R. C. Lawson. New York, 1946.

CHURCH OF THE LIVING GOD

CHURCH OF THE LIVING GOD (1962-)

The West-Indian immigrant Church of the Living God resulted
from failure of a founder-pastor in Reading, Berkshire, to obtain
ordination from West Indian bishops of the City Mission. Ultimately
he received ordination from Welsh independent Pentecostals, soon
thereafter becoming convinced of the baptism in Jesus' name teaching and founding his church on this platform. Part of the first
congregation was drawn from the Victorious Church of God. By
1980 there were about 1,000 full members and about twice that many
in the total community.

    --HISTORY

926 Calley, Malcolm John Chalmers
        God's people: West Indian Pentecostal sects in England,
    [by] Malcolm J. C. Calley. London, New York, Oxford Uni-
    versity Press, 1965. xiv, 182 p. "Issued under the auspices
    of the Institute of Race Relations, London." On the Church
    of the Living God: p. 35, 36, 39, 40, 46-47, 49, 54-55, 56,
    85, 90, 97, 130. DLC, OCB, Uk

CHURCH OF THE LIVING GOD, THE PILLAR AND GROUND
    OF THE TRUTH (1898-)

Established in 1898, the Church of the Living God, the Pillar
and Ground of the Truth has been led successively by Bishop F.
Ferguson of Cincinnati, Bishop Hood of Chicago, and Bishop J. W.
Woods of Baton Rouge. Headquarters are in Hammond, Louisiana.
In 1974 the denomination reported 2,000 members. At that time
churches were located in New Orleans, Baton Rouge, and Logans-
port, Louisiana; Gloster, Mississippi; University City, Missouri;
and Cincinnati, Ohio. Distinctive teachings include baptism in the
name of Jesus (according to Acts 2:38) and observance of the
seventh-day sabbath, sunset to sunset.

SEVENTH DAY PENTECOSTAL CHURCH OF THE LIVING GOD
    (194 -)

In the 1940s Charles Gamble, former Roman Catholic and Baptist, founded the mother church of the Seventh Day Pentecostal

Church of the Living God in Washington, D.C. It holds that faithfulness to the scriptures implies keeping Saturday as the sabbath.
In the mid-1970s the movement consisted of four churches and 1,000
members in the District of Columbia and nearby states. At that time
Bishop Theron B. Johnson was general overseer.

CHURCH OF THE LORD JESUS CHRIST OF THE APOSTOLIC FAITH
(1930-   )

In 1930 Bishop S. C. Johnson of Philadelphia withdrew from
Lawson's Church of Our Lord Jesus Christ of the Apostolic Faith
and established the Church of the Lord Jesus Christ of the Apostolic Faith. Personal rivalry and the liberality of the Harlem-based
group on women's dress apparently triggered the break. Substitu-
tion of "the" for "Our" minimized the change in the public mind.
In 1919 Bishop Johnson, a native of Edgecombe County, North Carolina, had begun preaching at 1524 South 17th Street, Philadelphia.
This center became the headquarters church. Of large importance
in attracting followers was the pastor's radio ministry. Indicative
of the increase it generated was the commodious new edifice which
the church occupied on February 28, 1960. Bishop Johnson died
the next year. At that time he was being heard weekly on a network of more than seventy church-owned stations in the United
States and abroad. The founder's teaching, which included con-
demnation of pagan festivals (Christmas, Lent, and Easter), cos-
metics, moving pictures, radio (except his own program), television,
smoking and drinking, is repeated verbatim by his disciple and
much-traveled successor, Bishop S. McDowell Shelton, who is sometimes addressed as "His Excellency" or "His Eminence." Branch
churches have sprung up throughout the United States and in
several foreign countries. At its 30th National and 4th International Convention in 1963, the Church of the Lord Jesus Christ of
the Apostolic Faith claimed 35 affiliates in eighteen states of the
union and seven branches in five foreign areas.

--DOCTRINAL AND CONTROVERSIAL WORKS

927   Johnson, Sherrod C., 1897-1961.
        The Christmas spirit is a false spirit, [by] S. C. Johnson.
      Philadelphia, Church of the Lord Jesus Christ of the Apostolic
      Faith, 19--. folder (6 p.)

928   Johnson, Sherrod C., 1897-1961.
        False Lent and pagan festivals, [by] S. C. Johnson.
      Philadelphia, Church of the Lord Jesus Christ of the Apostolic
      Faith, 19--.

929   Johnson, Sherrod C., 1897-1961.
        Is Jesus Christ the son of God now? Written by S. C.

Johnson, now being delivered by Bishop S. McDowell Shelton. Philadelphia, S. M. Shelton, 19--.   8 p.

930   Johnson, Sherrod C., 1897-1961.
21 burning subjects: who is this that defies and challenges the whole religious world on these subjects?   Written by S. C. Johnson, now being delivered by S. McDowell Shelton. Philadelphia, Church of the Lord Jesus Christ of the Apostolic Faith, 196-.   24 p.   OkTOR

931   Shelton, S. McDowell, 1929-
Let patience have her perfect work, [by] S. McDowell Shelton.   Philadelphia, Church of the Lord Jesus Christ of the Apostolic Faith, 1964.   12 p.

-- --NON-HOLINESS AUTHORS

932   Miller, Luke, 1904-
A review of the "Jesus Only" doctrine.   Austin, Tx., Firm Foundation Publishing House, c1959.   25 p.   Author's argument in debate with S. C. Johnson in Florence, South Carolina.

933   Rudd, Don
Rudd-Johnson debate.   Old Hickory, Tn., Don Rudd Publishing Co., 1960.   xiv, 233 p.   Transcript of debate between Don Rudd and S. C. Johnson "held Philadelphia Pa. 1959." TNL

--HISTORY

934   Church of the Lord Jesus Christ of the Apostolic Faith.
Church yearbook and radio history.   [Edited] by S. C. Johnson.   Philadelphia, 1957.   47 p.

935   Church of the Lord Jesus Christ of the Apostolic Faith.
Pictorial account of 1963.   Philadelphia, 1964.   1 v.   (unpaged)   Cover title.

936   Richardson, James Collins, 1945-
With water and Spirit, [by] James C. Richardson, Jr. Washington, Spirit Press, 1980.   151 p.   Based on thesis (M.Div.)--Howard University.   "Church of the Lord Jesus Christ of the Apostolic Faith, 1930": p. 70-71.   OkTOR

--PERIODICALS

937   B. S. 1, no. 1-5, 196-.
Philadelphia.   Bible study written by Bishop S. McDowell Shelton.

938   Whole truth.   1-   1947-
         Philadelphia.   WiH

COOPERATIVE AGENCIES

APOSTOLIC MINISTERS CONFERENCE OF PHILADELPHIA AND
   VICINITY (1972-   )

Organized in January 1972, the Apostolic Ministers Conference
of Philadelphia and Vicinity was designed to serve as a means of
fellowship for nine or ten black pastors and their congregations.
Beginning in February that year the Conference convened a com-
bined monthly meeting. The place of meeting changed each month.
Bishop Robert O. Doub has served as president from the beginning.
In 1984 the Conference held membership in the Apostolic World
Christian Fellowship.

*APOSTOLIC WORLD CHRISTIAN FELLOWSHIP (1972-   )

Formed in 1972, the Apostolic World Christian Fellowship provides a forum for communication among Oneness organizations. In
1985 the 56 member bodies represented all six continents. Notable
for its absence was the all-white United Pentecostal Church International, whose roots are intertwined with the mostly black Pentecostal Assemblies of the World. Headquarters are in South Bend,
Indiana. An international congress is held each year in May.

--PERIODICALS

939   Clarion.   1-   1979-
         South Bend, In.

*INTERNATIONAL MINISTERIAL ASSOCIATION (1954-   )

Organized under the leadership of W. E. Kidson in 1954, the
International Ministerial Association serves as a credential-issuing
agency with headquarters in Houston. By 1965 independent congregations of Jamaican immigrants served by credentialed members
were being established in the United Kingdom. These in 1980 numbered 15 with 600 members and 900 constituents representing a
significant black minority within a predominantly white organization.

INTERNATIONAL MINISTERIAL COUNCIL OF GREAT BRITAIN
(1974-   )

A nondenominational agency formed in 1974, the International
Ministerial Council of Great Britain claimed eleven affiliated churches
with 700 members and a total constituency of 1,200 in 1980.   It is
composed mostly of immigrants from St. Kitts, Guyana, Jamaica,
and India and has its headquarters in London.

EMMANUEL PENTECOSTAL CHURCH OF OUR LORD, APOSTOLIC
FAITH (19 -   )

In 1984 the Emmanuel Pentecostal Church of Our Lord, Apostolic Faith held membership in the Apostolic World Christian Fellowship.   At that time M. R. Jackson of Detroit was presiding bishop.

EMMANUEL PENTECOSTAL CHURCHES OF THE APOSTOLIC FAITH
(1964-   )

In 1964 Bishop Willie Lee, pastor of the historic Christ Temple
in Indianapolis and presiding bishop of the tension-laden Pentecostal Churches of the Apostolic Faith Association, left the latter
organization and established the Emmanuel Pentecostal Churches of
the Apostolic Faith.   At issue was Lee's belief (identical to that of
Bishop S. N. Hancock) that Jesus was not God, but only the son
of God.   Lee died in 1968 and was succeeded by Bishop James
Stewart of Danville, Illinois.   In 1972 the Executive Board consisted
of Bishop Willie Ivory of St. Clair Shores, Michigan, Bishop Ralph
Harris of Gary, Indiana, and Bishop I. E. Owens of Lemoore, California.   Indianapolis, the site of the national convention that year,
remained the center of the movement.   Bishop Nathaniel Madden,
pastor of the host church there, assisted the presiding bishop
during the convention.

--INDIANA

-- --INDIANAPOLIS

940 Thomas, Willa
     Emmanuel Pentecostal Churches of the Apostolic Faith in
     week-long national Aug. 27-Sept. 3 convention, [by] Willa
     Thomas. In Indianapolis Recorder, 77 (Aug. 26, 1972), 1, 3.

*EMMANUEL'S CHURCH IN JESUS CHRIST (1925-1928)

The Emmanuel's Church in Jesus Christ was organized October 21-23, 1925 during the Trio States Camp Meeting in Houston. It was one of three bodies formed that year as a result of a crisis in the interracial Pentecostal Assemblies of the World. The new body purposed to welcome all without respect to race, color or class into membership. When blacks had sufficient numbers they would be allowed to have their own organization, officers, and headquarters, provided they worked in harmony with the all-white general headquarters. As might be expected, the Emmanuel's Church in Jesus Christ enlisted few if any blacks. In 1927 negotiations began between the Emmanuel's Church and the Apostolic Churches of Jesus Christ, which resulted in union of the two bodies in October the next year.

FAITH TABERNACLE CORPORATION OF CHURCHES (1924-   )
[To 19-- as Faith Tabernacle.]

In 1936 the Faith Tabernacle in Los Angeles, which had been established as a result of a tent revival twelve years earlier, reported 206 members. After World War II branches sprang up in several other West Coast localities making necessary a more comprehensive organization. In 1984 L. W. Osborne of Portland, Oregon, was presiding bishop. Faith Tabernacle Corporation of Churches holds membership in the Apostolic World Christian Fellowship.

FIRST GLORIOUS TEMPLE APOSTOLIC (198 -   )

The First Glorious Temple Apostolic was listed as an affiliate of the Apostolic World Christian Fellowship in 1984. At that time R. L. Davis, the senior bishop, resided in Elgin, Illinois.

FREE GOSPEL CHURCH OF CHRIST (196 -   )

The Free Gospel Church of Christ was established sometime before 1967 by Bishop Ralph E. Green, formerly of the Way of the Cross Church of Christ. The group is based in Coral Hills, Maryland, a suburb of Washington. In 1984 it held membership in the Apostolic World Christian Fellowship.

--PERIODICALS

941 Defense of the gospel. 1- 1978-
     Coral Hills, Md.

FREEDOM CHAPEL PENTECOSTAL ORTHODOX CHURCH OF CHRIST (19 -)

In 1984 the Freedom Chapel Pentecostal Orthodox Church of Christ of Washington, D.C., held membership in the Apostolic World Christian Fellowship. Elder William D. Madison was its representative.

GOD'S HOUSE OF PRAYER FOR ALL NATIONS (1964-)

God's House of Prayer for All Nations is a group of black and interracial churches in Illinois. Several are in the Chicago area. Each congregation is an autonomous unit. Although no coordinating agency exists, a pattern has emerged which may be illustrated by God's House of Prayer for All Nations in Peoria. This congregation was founded under the leadership of Tommie Lawrence in 1964. Although the founder was formerly a minister in the Church of God in Christ, a Trinitarian body, the Peoria churches teaches that baptism should be administered "in the name of Jesus Christ, which is the name of the Father, Son and Holy Ghost." Lawrence refers to himself as "pastor, chief apostle, founder, and senior bishop of God's House of Prayer for All Nations." Reportedly, in the 1970s Lawrence's church and several sister congregations were using materials published by the Miracle Revival Fellowship, an organization founded by the late A. A. Allen.

GOSPEL FAITH MISSION (Ghana) (19 -)

In 1984 N. M. Forson was general overseer and chairman of the Gospel Faith Mission (Ghana). Headquarters of the organization, which holds membership in the Apostolic World Christian Fellowship, are in Kumasi.

GREATER EMMANUEL APOSTOLIC FAITH TABERNACLES (19 -)

The Greater Emanuel Apostolic Faith Tabernacles, based in Columbus, Ohio, are in close fellowship with the Pentecostal Assemblies of the World. Quander L. Wilson is presiding bishop. In

1984 the organization reported 37 congregations. It holds membership in the Apostolic World Christian Fellowship and the National
Association of Evangelicals (with its Trinitarian statement of faith).

HIGHWAY CHRISTIAN CHURCH OF CHRIST (1929-   )

In 1929 James Thomas Morris, formerly an elder of the Pentecostal Assemblies of the World, founded the Highway Christian
Church of Christ in Washington, D.C. Ten years later the group
incorporated. In 1941 Morris was ordained bishop by J. M. Turpin.
The founder died in 1959 and was succeeded by J. V. Lomax, his
nephew and one-time member of Lawson's Refuge Temple in Harlem.
Dress regulations are stringent, black and white being approved
colors. The Highway Church does not ordain women. If ordained
women join, they must surrender their pulpits to men. In 1980 the
thirteen affiliated congregations claimed 3,000 members.

--DOCTRINAL AND CONTROVERSIAL WORKS

942   Highway Christian Church of Christ.
         The path of life through Highway Christian Church of
      Christ. Edited by Carrie Wheeler. n.p., 1968.

--HISTORY

943   Richardson, James Collins, 1945-
         With water and Spirit, [by] James C. Richardson, Jr.
      Washington, Spirit Press, 1980. 151 p. Based on thesis
      (M.Div.)--Howard University. "Highway Christian Church of
      Christ, 1929": p. 69-70. OkTOR

--MARYLAND

-- --T. B.

944   Adams, Donald Conrad
         A comparative study of the social functions of the Highway
      Church of Jesus of the Apostolic Faith of T. B., Maryland,
      and the Grace Methodist Church of Chapel Hill, Maryland.
      Washington, 1966. Thesis (B.D.)--Howard University. DHU

HOLY TEMPLE CHURCH OF CHRIST (1969-   )

In 1969 Elder Joseph Weathers, disappointed that he had not
been called as pastor of the headquarters church, left the Way of

the Cross Church of Christ and founded the Holy Temple Church of Christ. He became presiding bishop and established headquarters in Washington, D.C. In 1984 the Holy Temple Church of Christ held membership in the Apostolic World Christian Fellowship.

JAMAICA WEST INDIES HACKNEY PENTECOSTAL APOSTOLIC CHURCH (1968-)

With headquarters in London, the Jamaica West Indies Hackney Pentecostal Apostolic Church, formed in 1968, consisted of eight churches, 600 members and 1,000 adherents in 1980. There were 22 affiliated congregations in the West Indies.

LIVING WITNESS OF THE APOSTOLIC FAITH (19 -)

Founded by Bishop Charles E. Poole, the Living Witness of the Apostolic Faith is centered in the Bethlehem Healing Temple in Chicago. Of importance in developing the movement was the founder's first wife, Evangelist Mattie B. Poole. Bishop Poole died in 1984. His successor as presiding bishop is A. C. Richards. The Living Witness of the Apostolic Faith holds membership in the Apostolic World Christian Fellowship.

--DOCTRINAL AND CONTROVERSIAL WORKS

945 Poole, Mattie Belle Goldie Ottie Mae (Robinson), 1903-1968.
        Beware of secret sex sins, [by] Mattie B. Poole. Chicago,
        19--.

946 Poole, Mattie Belle Goldie Ottie Mae (Robinson), 1903-1968.
        The book of miracles, [by] Mattie B. Poole. Chicago,
        19--.

947 Poole, Mattie Belle Goldie Ottie Mae (Robinson), 1903-1968.
        God's power in faith, love, happiness, charity, and money
        matters, [by] Mattie B. Poole. Chicago, 19--.

948 Poole, Mattie Belle Goldie Ottie Mae (Robinson), 1903-1968.
        Living witnesses, [by] Mattie B. Poole. Chicago, 19--.

--PERIODICALS

949 Apostolic voice. 1- 194 -
        Chicago

950 God met us in the healing campaigns. 1- 19 -
     Chicago

951 Voice of living witnesses. 1- 19 -
     Chicago

MACEDONIA CHURCHES OF VIRGINIA (1974-198-)

In 1974 Bishop Tilman Carmichael left the Apostle Church of
Christ in God and established the Macedonia Churches of Virginia.
The new body, based in Gloucester, Virginia, held membership in
the Apostolic World Christian Fellowship. In the early 1980s reunion with the parent body was achieved and Carmichael became
presiding bishop.

MESSIAH TABERNACLE CHURCH IN AMERICA (1958-)

In 1972 Bishop H. Moore of the Messiah Tabernacle Church
in America was active in the Apostolic Ministers Conference of
Philadelphia and Vicinity.

MOUNT CARMEL HOLY CHURCH OF THE LORD JESUS (19 -)

In 1980 the Mount Carmel Holy Church of the Lord Jesus held
membership in the Apostolic World Christian Fellowship. For the
training of its clergy it used the branch of the Pentecostal Assemblies of the World-related Aenon Bible College, opened two years
before in Philadelphia. At that time William Payne of Camden, New
Jersey, was general overseer.

MOUNT HEBRON APOSTOLIC TEMPLE OF OUR LORD JESUS OF THE APOSTOLIC FAITH (1963-)

In 1963 Elder G. H. Wiley of Yonkers, New York left the
Apostle Church of Christ in God and founded the Mount Hebron
Temple of Our Lord Jesus of the Apostolic Faith. The reason lay
in the refusal of the official board to make Wiley a bishop. Despite the break, warmth characterizes relations between the two
bodies.

--HISTORY

952 Richardson, James Collins, 1945-
       With water and Spirit, [by] James C. Richardson, Jr.
     Washington, Spirit Press, 1980. 151 p. Based on thesis
     (M.Div.)--Howard University. "Mount Hebron Apostolic Tem-
     ple of Our Lord Jesus of the Apostolic Faith, Inc., 1963":
     p. 90-91. OkTOR

MOUNT OF ZION GOSPEL CHURCH (19 -)

   In 1984, A. U. Eka of Calabar, Nigeria, was president of the
Mount of Zion Gospel Church. At that time the church held membership in the Apostolic World Christian Fellowship.

NEW APOSTOLIC ASSOCIATION OF BALTIMORE, MARYLAND (19 -)

   In 1984 Bishop Morris R. Lane was president of the New Apostolic Association of Baltimore, Maryland. The Association is an
affiliate of the Apostolic World Christian Fellowship.

ORIGINAL APOSTOLIC ASSEMBLY OF OUR LORD AND SAVIOUR JESUS CHRIST FAITH OF 31 A.D. (197 -)

   Formed in the 1970s, the Original Apostolic Assembly of Our
Lord and Saviour Jesus Christ Faith of 31 A.D. is centered in
Chesapeake, Ohio. Bishop Lawrence F. McCoy, its president and
presiding overseer, formerly was affiliated with the Philadelphia-
based Apostolic Assembly of Our Lord and Saviour Jesus Christ.
The body holds membership in the Apostolic World Christian Fellowship.

PENTECOSTAL ASSEMBLIES OF JAMAICA (197 -)

   Organized in the 1970s, the Pentecostal Assemblies of Jamaica
holds membership in the Apostolic World Christian Fellowship.
Bishop O. B. O'Hare, the presiding bishop, resides in Duncans,
Jamaica.

*PENTECOSTAL ASSEMBLIES OF JESUS CHRIST (1931-1945)

The Pentecostal Assemblies of Jesus Christ was the product of merger of the Apostolic Church of Jesus Christ and the Pentecostal Assemblies of the World. The union, consummated November 18, 1931, at Columbus, Ohio, was designed as an instrument for restoring the interracial fellowship which had marked the movement in its early years. This goal was not to be realized. The first blow was struck within weeks of the merger. On March 9-10, 1932, followers of Bishop Samuel Grimes met in Dayton, Ohio, and reorganized the Pentecostal Assemblies of the World under the original charter. Blacks, who remained in the Pentecostal Assemblies of Jesus Christ during the first six years of its existence, constituted about twenty percent of the membership. They, however, occupied half of the seats on the Presbyter Board. Denominational meetings in the first years were always held in the North. A decision in 1936 to allocate seats by race in proportion to membership and to hold the next General Assembly in Tulsa, a city where a riot fifteen years before had claimed the lives of seventy blacks, elicited the resignation of Karl F. Smith as general secretary and the departure of most remaining blacks to the Pentecostal Assemblies of the World. In 1945 the Pentecostal Assemblies of Jesus Christ united with the Pentecostal Church, Incorporated, to form the all-white United Pentecostal Church. At that time it reported 324 churches and 1,028 clergy.

PENTECOSTAL ASSEMBLIES OF THE WORLD (1906-   )

The Pentecostal Assemblies of the World is mother to the black Oneness movement, and most of its spokesmen trace their spiritual lineage to G. T. Haywood. Although it claims 1906 and Los Angeles as the date and place of its birfh, the Pentecostal Assemblies of the World did not hold its first General Assembly until March 25, 1912. At this meeting held in Los Angeles, J. J. Frazee of Portland, Oregon, was chosen general superintendent. The group did not take on its definitive role until it merged with the infant, all-white General Assembly of Apostolic Assemblies at St. Louis, January 22, 1918. Upon incorporation the next year, the body moved its headquarters from Portland to Indianapolis, where Elder G. T. Haywood headed a large congregation then known as the Apostolic Faith Assembly Tabernacle. Most black members lived in the North, and most white members lived in the South. Segregation of public facilities in the South made it necessary to hold denominational meetings in the North. Dissatisfaction surfaced early. In 1922 the white brethren held the Southern Bible Conference in Little Rock. By design or not, this meeting proved to be a first step of a general exodus of whites from the denomination two years later. In 1931 the Pentecostal Assemblies of the World voted to unite with the Apostolic Church of Jesus Christ (a three-year-old body composed

of part of the 1924 exodus) to form a biracial organization: the
Pentecostal Assemblies of Jesus Christ. The next year, however,
followers of Bishop Samuel Grimes met at Dayton, Ohio, and decided to continue the old group under the original charter. Ten-
sions over race again surfaced in the merged group and in 1937
most blacks returned to the original body. Although overwhelming-
ly black, the Pentecostal Assemblies of the World has maintained for
the past eighteen years a practice of rotating the office of presiding
bishop by race. In 1960 it reported 550 churches and 45,000 members in the United States. The denomination holds membership in
the Apostolic World Christian Fellowship. In 1979 it spent $166,233
for work in ten world areas. Overseas fields included Egypt,
Ghana, Liberia, and Nigeria, the Bahamas, Barbados, Montserrat,
and Haiti, and the United Kingdom.

--BIOGRAPHY

953 Golder, Morris Ellis, 1913-
        The bishops of the Pentecostal Assemblies of the World, Inc.,
        [by] Morris E. Golder. Indianapolis, 1980. 69 p. Cover title.

--DOCTRINAL AND CONTROVERSIAL WORKS

954 Golder, Morris Ellis, 1913-
        The confession of sins, [by] Morris E. Golder. Cincinnati,
        Apostolic Light Press, 19--. 40 p. Cover title.

955 Golder, Morris Ellis, 1913-
        A detailed study of the high priest, [by] Morris E. Golder.
        Indianapolis, 1981. 30 p. Cover title: The high priest.

956 Golder, Morris Ellis, 1913-
        The principles of our faith: what we believe, [by] Morris
        E. Golder. Cincinnati, Apostolic Light Press, 19--. 24 p.
        Cover title. OkTOR

957 Haywood, Garfield Thomas, 1880-1931.
        Before the foundation of the world; a revelation of the
        ages, [by] G. T. Haywood. Indianapolis, 1923. 76 p.
        Enlarged and revised edition of A revelation of the ages.
        DLC

958 Haywood, Garfield Thomas, 1880-1931.
        The birth of the Spirit and the mystery of the Godhead,
        [by] G. T. Haywood. Indianapolis. Voice in the Wilderness,
        19--. 16 p. At head of title: Apostolic Bible reading.

959 Haywood, Garfield Thomas, 1880-1931.
        The birth of the Spirit in the days of the apostles, [by]

G. T. Haywood. Indianapolis, Christ Temple Book Store,
19--. 40 p. Cover title. OkTOR

960 [Haywood, Garifield Thomas], 1880-1931.
Christian stewardship: a story of the tenth, [by] G. T.
Haywood. Indianapolis, Christ Temple Book Store, 19--.
16 p. Cover title.

961 Haywood, Garfield Thomas, 1880-1931.
Divine names and titles of Jehovah, [by] G. T. Haywood.
Indianapolis, Voice in the Wilderness, 19--. 19 p.

962 [Haywood, Garfield Thomas], 1880-1931.
Ezekiel's vision; the first chapter of Ezekiel. Indianapolis,
Christ Temple Book Store, 19--. 23 p. (Behold He cometh)
Cover title.

963 Haywood, Garfield Thomas, 1880-1931.
The marriage and divorce question in the church, [by]
G. T. Haywood. Indianapolis, Christ Temple, 19--. 32 p.
Cover title.

964 Haywood, Garfield Thomas, 1880-1931.
The old and new tabernacle compared [by] G. T. Haywood.
Indianapolis, Voice in the Wilderness, 19--. 12 p.

965 Haywood, Garfield Thomas, 1880-1931.
The resurrection of the dead, [by] G. T. Haywood. Indianapolis, Christ Temple Book Store, 19--. 20 p. (Behold He
cometh)

966 Haywood, Garfield Thomas, 1880-1931.
A revelation of the ages, [by] G. T. Haywood. Indianapolis, Voice in the Wilderness, 19--.

967 Moore, Benjamin Thomas, 1927-
A handbook for saints, [by] Benjamin T. Moore. Seattle,
Bethel Christian Ministries, c1974. 67 p.

968 Paddock, Ross Perry, 1907-
The church an organized body, [by] Ross P. Paddock.
Cincinnati, Apostolic Light Press, 19--. 47 p.

969 Paddock, Ross Perry, 1907-
God's financial plan for the church, [by] Ross P. Paddock.
Cincinnati, Apostolic Light Press, 19--. 48 p.

970 Paddock, Ross Perry, 1907-
Marriage and divorce, [by] Ross P. Paddock. Cincinnati,
Apostolic Light Press, 19--. 36 p.

971 Paddock, Ross Perry, 1907–
        Restoration, [by] Ross P. Paddock. Cincinnati, Apostolic
        Light Press, 19--. 24 p. Cover title.

972 Paddock, Ross Perry, 1907–
        Short subjects important to Pentecostals, [by] Ross P. Pad-
        dock. Cincinnati, Apostolic Light Press, 19--. 54 p.

973 Smith, Francis L., 1915–
        What every saint should know, [by] F. L. Smith. East
        Orange, N.J., Lutho Press, 19--. 12 p. Cover title.

974 Smith, Karl Franklin, 1892-1972.
        General outline of the Bible. [Columbus, Oh.], 1941,
        c1947. 175 p.

975 Streitferdt, Thomas, 1929–
        Contending for the faith. New York, 1969.

976 Streitferdt, Thomas, 1929–
        Holiness and the Bible. New York, 1966.

977 Streitferdt, Thomas, 1929–
        The word became flesh. New York, 1958.

978 Tobin, Robert F.,   –1947.
        The principles of the doctrine of Christ, [by] R. F. Tobin.
        Indianapolis, Christ Temple, c1945. 31 p.

979 Wagner, Norman Leonard, 1942–
        Learn to do well, [by] Norman L. Wagner. Cincinnati,
        Apostolic Light Press, 19--. 15 p.

        --EDUCATION

980 Saunders, Monroe Randolph, 1948–
        Perspectives of the philosophy of Christian education in
        Pentecostalism: the Assemblies of God [and] the Pentecostal
        Assemblies of the World, [by] Monroe R. Saunders, Jr. Wash-
        ington, 1975. v, 74 l. Thesis (M.A.)--Howard University.
        DHU

        --GOVERNMENT

981 Pentecostal Assemblies of the World.
        Articles of incorporation of Pentecostal Assemblies of the
        World [1919]. In Golder, M. E. History of the Pentecostal
        Assemblies of the World. Indianapolis, 1973, 56-58.

982   Pentecostal Assemblies of the World.
      Manual of discipline of the Pentecostal Assemblies of the
      World, Inc. New York, Christian Outlook Publishing Co.,
      1945. v, 54 p.

983- Pentecostal Assemblies of the World.
984   Ministerial record, codified rules, and minutes. Indianapo-
      lis, 1952.

985   Pentecostal Assemblies of the World.
      Minute book of the Pentecostal Assemblies of the World.
      Indianapolis, 1963.

986   Pentecostal Assemblies of the World.
      Minute book of the Pentecostal Assemblies of the World.
      Indianapolis, 1964. OkTOR

987   Pentecostal Assemblies of the World.
      Minute book of the Pentecostal Assemblies of the World.
      Indianapolis, 1970. 188 p.

      --HISTORY

988   Pentecostal Assemblies of the World.
      Pictorial directory. Indianapolis, 1974.

989   Clanton, Arthur Lee, 1915-
      United we stand: a history of Oneness organizations, [by]
      Arthur L. Clanton. Hazelwood, Mo., Pentecostal Publishing
      House, 1970. 207 p. "The Pentecostal Assemblies of the
      World": p. 27-34.

990   Foster, Fred J.
      "Think it not strange"; a history of the Oneness movement,
      [by] Fred J. Foster. St. Louis, Mo., Pentecostal Publishing
      House, 1965. 109 p. On Pentecostal Assemblies of the World:
      p. 73-76. ArU

991   Golder, Morris Ellis, 1913-
      History of the Pentecostal Assemblies of the World, [by]
      Morris E. Golder. Indianapolis, 1973. 195 p. CPFT

992   Moore, Everett Leroy, 1918-
      Handbook of Pentecostal denominations in the United States.
      Pasadena, Ca., 1954. vii, 346 l. Thesis (M.A.)--Pasadena
      College. "Pentecostal Assemblies of the World": l. 242-252.
      CSdP

993   Richardson, James Collins, 1945-
      With water and Spirit, [by] James C. Richardson, Jr.

Washington, Spirit Press, 1980. 151 p. Based on thesis
(M.Div.)--Howard University. "The Pentecostal Assemblies
of the World, 1906": p. 45-53. OkTOR

--HISTORY AND STUDY OF DOCTRINES

994 Golder, Morris Ellis, 1913-
     A doctrinal study of the Pentecostal Assemblies of the
     World. Indianapolis, 1959. 76 l. Thesis (M.A.)--Butler
     University. InIB

--HYMNS AND SACRED SONGS

995 The bridegroom songs.
          6th ed., enlarged. Indianapolis, Voice in the Wilderness,
     192-. [80] p. Cover title. With music. KyWAT

996 The bridegroom songs.
          Indianapolis, Christ Temple Bookstore, 19--. 94 p.
     "Christ Temple edition." With music. OkBetC

997 Carradine, Beverly, 1848-1919.
          The best of all complete. [Edited by] B. Carradine,
     C. J. Fowler [and] W. J. Kirkpatrick. Indianapolis, Christ
     Temple, 19--. 288 p. With music.

998 Grimes, Kathleen (Washington), 1880-1960.
          Echoes of Zion, [by] Kathleen Grimes. New York, c1948.

999 Old songs selected.
          Columbus, Oh., Church of Christ, Apostolic Faith, 19--.
     32 p. Cover title. With music (shape notes). OkBetC

--MISSIONS

1000 Pentecostal Assemblies of the World. Foreign Missions De-
      partment.
           We have been there: overseas works of the Pentecostal
      Assemblies of the World, Inc., led by G. T. Haywood, S. J.
      Grimes, Ross P. Paddock [and] F. L. Smith. Indianapolis,
      1977. 101 p. Cover title.

1001 Hopkins, Ellen Miama (Moore), 1921-
           "Don't let the fire go out," [by] Ellen Moore Hopkins.
      Monrovia, Printed by Department of Information and Cultural
      Affairs, Republic of Liberia, c1968. 42, xiv l. DeU

1002 Reeder, Hilda
           A brief history of the Foreign Missionary Department of

the Pentecostal Assemblies of the World. Indianapolis, Foreign Missionary Department, 1951. 76 p. DLC, NNUT

--PASTORAL THEOLOGY

1003 Moore, Willa M. (Lee)
      This is your life, [by] Willa M. Moore. ----, 19--.

1004 Smith, Karl Franklin, 1892-1972.
      The scriptural view of the Christian pastorate. Columbus,
      Oh., 1944. v, 154 p. DLC

1005 Wagner, Norman Leonard, 1942-
      Go ye therefore: an evangelism manual for mass Pente-
      costal crusades, [by] Norman L. Wagner. Youngstown, Oh.,
      Calvary Publications, 197-. 17 p. OkTOR

--PERIODICALS

1006 Christian outlook. 1- 1923-
      Indianapolis, Akron, New York. OkTOR

1007 TIP. 1- 1984-
      Park Forest, Il.

1008 Voice in the wilderness. 1- Apr. 1910-1928.
      Indianapolis.

--SERMONS, TRACTS, ADDRESSES, ESSAYS

1009 Haywood, Garfield Thomas, 1880-1931.
      Before the foundation of the world: a revelation of the
      ages, [by] G. T. Haywood. Indianapolis, 1923. 76 p.
      Enlarged and revised edition of A revelation of the ages.
      DLC

1010 Haywood, Garfield Thomas, 1880-1931.
          Feed my sheep, [by] G. T. Haywood. Indianapolis,
      Christ Temple Book Store, 19--. 62 p. Cover title. OkTOR

1011 Haywood, Garfield Thomas, 1880-1931.
          The finest of the wheat, [by] G. T. Haywood. Indianap-
      olis, Christ Temple Bookstore, 19--. 60 p. OkTOR

1012 Haywood, Garfield Thomas, 1880-1931.
          The victim of the flaming sword, [by] G. T. Haywood.
      Indianapolis, Christ Temple Book Store, 19--. 71 p. Cover
      title. OkTOR

1013   Maynard, Aurora
          The inner guidance. New York, Vantage Press, c1965.
          116 p. InIT, OkTOR

1014   Streitferdt, Thomas, 1929-
          Eight radio messages on water baptism. New York, 1968.

          --STATISTICS

1015   United States. Bureau of the Census.
          Census of religious bodies: 1926. Pentecostal Assemblies
       of the World. Statistics, denominational history, doctrine,
       and organization. Washington, Government Printing Office,
       1929. 9 p. DLC, NNUT

1016   United States. Bureau of the Census.
          Census of religious bodies: 1936. Pentecostal assemblies.
       Statistics, denominational history, doctrine, and organization.
       Consolidated report. Washington, Government Printing Office,
       1940. iv, 49 p. NNUT

          --MIDDLE WEST

          -- --MICHIGAN

          (Detroit)

1017   Apostolic Church of God in Christ Jesus.
          Our heritage. "Upon this rock." Apostolic Church of God
       in Christ Jesus, 1930-1982. Detroit, c1982. [90] p. DLC

          -- --MISSOURI

          (Kansas City)

1018   4,000 Pentecostal youth expected here for national convention.
          In Kansas City Call (Feb. 25, 1977), 1.

1019   Pentecostal convention ends with mass concert.
          In Kansas City Call (Mar. 11, 1977), 12.

1020   Stone, Vickie
          4,000 Pentecostal youth in session at Crown Center, [by]
       Vickie Stone. In Kansas City Call (Mar. 4, 1977), 1.

-- --OHIO

(Youngstown)

1021 I'm saved and I'm proud.
        In Ebony, 30 (June 1975), 84-86, 88, 90, 92.

--SOUTHERN STATES

-- --ARKANSAS

(Little Rock)

1022 Southern Bible Conference, 1st, Little Rock, 1922.
        A call to dust & ashes; a few crumbs that dropped from
     the table which God spread before us during the first South-
     ern Bible Conference at Little Rock, Arkansas, November 3rd
     to 10th inclusive, 1922. Compiled and published by William E.
     Booth-Clibborn. St. Paul, Mn., 1922. 24 p. Cover title.
     OkTOR

-- --TENNESSEE

(Nashville)

1023 Pike, Garnet Elmer, 1937-
        The rise of a black Pentecostal church in a changing city:
     a historical case study. Nashville, 1972. iv, 105 l. Thesis
     (D.Div.)--Vanderbilt University. TNJ

PENTECOSTAL CHURCHES OF THE APOSTOLIC FAITH ASSOCIA-
    TION (1957-)

        Upon the death of G. T. Haywood in 1931, a struggle of
many years duration ensued over the office of presiding bishop in
the Pentecostal Assemblies of the World. The principal contenders
were Bishop S. N. Hancock and Bishop Samuel Grimes. In a runoff
vote between the two during the 1952 General Assembly in Baltimore,
Bishop Grimes won. At issue also was Bishop Hancock's belief that
Jesus is only the son of God, not God himself, and that holiness
standards of conduct were on the decline in the Pentecostal Assemblies of the World. On November 20, 1957, Hancock made good
repeated threats to leave the organization when he, together with
Bishop Heardie Leaston, Bishop Willie Lee, and Elder David Collins,
incorporated the Pentecostal Churches of the Apsotolic Faith Association in Wayne County, Michigan. Three of the four incorporators
were residents of the Detroit metropolitan area, the exception being
Bishop Lee of Indianapolis. Personality and doctrinal conflicts were

present in the new body as in the old one. Bishop Lee, who became presiding bishop upon the founder's death in 1963, served only one year. Lee agreed with Hancock on the sonship of Jesus, but tolerated the older position that Jesus is God. His opponents, led by Bishop Elzie Young of Cincinnati, refused to reciprocate and forced him out. (No issue had been made of the difference during Bishop Hancock's lifetime.) Under Young, a strong financial structure has been built and support of foreign missions substantially increased. Under a system of assessments for the national treasury based on a percentage of local church income, the budget for foreign missions skyrocketed from $3,000 in 1964 to $40,000 in 1980. In the latter year the Pentecostal Churches of the Apostolic Faith Association claimed 380 clergy, 115 churches, and approximately 25,000 members. The Cincinnati-based body is a member of the Apostolic World Christian Fellowship.

--DOCTRINAL AND CONTROVERSIAL WORKS

1024 Bell, Dennis Rayford
       The philosophy of Christ, [by] D. Rayford Bell. Chicago, Adams Press, c1980. 104 p. DLC

1025 Bell, Dennis Rayford
       The philosophy of Christ, [by] D. Rayford Bell. 2d ed. Chicago, Adams Press, c1982. 165 p. MiGrC

1026 Bell, Dennis Rayford
       The song book of Israel, [by] D. Rayford Bell. [Editor: Norman Mabon]. Chicago, Christ Temple Apostolic Faith Extension Ministry, c1983. xv, 303 p. DLC

--GOVERNMENT

1027 Pentecostal Churches of the Apostolic Faith Association.
       The ministerial record: codified rules of the Pentecostal Churches of the Apostolic Faith Association, Inc. Detroit, 1960.

--HISTORY

1028 Richardson, James Collins, 1945-
       With water and Spirit, [by] James C. Collins, Jr. Washington, Spirit Press, 1980. 151 p. Based on thesis (M.Div.) --Howard University. "Pentecostal Churches of Apostolic Faith, 1957": p. 78-79. OkTOR

--INDIANA

-- --MUNCIE

1029 PCAFA meet set at Muncie.
      In Indianapolis Recorder, 75 (Mar. 7, 1970), 3.

POWERHOUSE OF DELIVERANCE CHURCH (19 -)

In 1980 the headquarters of the Powerhouse of Deliverance
Church was Greensboro, North Carolina. J. H. Covington was
presiding bishop.

REDEEMED ASSEMBLY OF JESUS CHRIST, APOSTOLIC (1979-)

In 1979 James Frank Harris of Richmond, Virginia, and Douglas Williams of Washington, D.C., left the HIghway Christian Church
of Christ and established the Redeemed Assembly of Jesus Christ,
Apostolic. At issue was the alleged stranglehold of Bishop J. V.
Lomax and the trustee board of the Washington congregation over
the affairs of the parent denomination. Of the six original churches
in the new body, only three were former affiliates of the Highway
Christian Church of Christ. New York and Richmond each have one
church. The other four are in the Washington metropolitan area.
Harris and Williams are presiding bishop and assistant presiding
bishop. The two bishops together with all other pastors make up
the executive board.

--HISTORY

1030 Richardson, James Collins, 1945-
         With water and Spirit, [by] James C. Richardson, Jr.
      Washington, Spirit Press, 1980. 151 p. Based on thesis
      (M.Div.)--Howard University. "Redeemed Assembly of Jesus
      Christ, Apostolic, 1979": p. 99-100. OkTOR

SHILO UNITED CHURCH OF CHRIST (Apostolic) (1958-)

Founded in 1958, the Shilo United Church of Christ (Apostolic) is linked to the International Ministerial Council of Great Britain. The Shilo group, which in 1980 had five congregations, 165
members and an inclusive community of 400, is composed largely of
immigrants from Jamaica, Trinidad, and Barbados.

SHILOH APOSTOLIC TEMPLE (1954-   )

In 1948 Robert O. Doub, youthful elder in the Apostle Church of Christ in God, set out from Winston-Salem, North Carolina, to establish a pioneer work in Philadelphia. He soon became overseer of a cluster of churches in Pennsylvania and pressed for elevation to the bishopric. When his request was denied, he approached the Baltimore-based Church of God in Christ (Apostolic) and met with similar results; in 1954 he incorporated his own congregation, the Shiloh Apostolic Temple of Philadelphia, as a denomination. Between 1954 and 1980 the organization grew from one to 23 churches, from one to 33 clergy, and from 500 to 4,500 members. At the latter date eight churches were in the United Kingdom, two in Trinidad. Bishop Doub has been president of the Apostolic Ministers Fellowship of Philadelphia and Vicinity since its beginning in 1972.

--HISTORY

1031   Richardson, James Collins, 1945-
       With water and Spirit, [by] James C. Richardson, Jr.
       Washington, Spirit Press, 1980. 151 p. Based on thesis
       (M.Div.)--Howard University. "Shiloh Apostolic Temple, Inc.,
       1953": p. 76-78. OkTOR

--PERIODICALS

1032   Shiloh gospel wave. 1- 19 -
       Philadelphia

TRUE CHURCH OF JESUS (196 -   )

In the confusion which swept over the Pentecostal Churches of the Apostolic Faith Association following the death of Bishop S. N. Hancock, David Collins, his successor as pastor, led the Detroit congregation into the True Church of Jesus.

TRUE VINE PENTECOSTAL CHURCHES OF JESUS (Apostolic Faith)
    (1961-   )

In 1961 R. L. Hairston of Martinsville, Virginia, former vice-bishop of the True Vine Pentecostal Holiness Church, accepted baptism in Jesus name and founded the True Vine Pentecostal Churches of Jesus (Apostolic Faith). Other issues were denominational assessments on small churches and Hairston's recent divorce and remarriage. (The latter matter proved to be barrier to full acceptance

in either Trinitarian or Oneness circles.) A short-lived alliance
with Bishop Willie Giles of Eden, North Carolina, foundered over the
ordination of women, which Bishop Hairston approved. In 1976
Bishop Thomas C. Williams led his followers into the True Vine
Pentecostal Churches of Jesus. At that time Williams became senior
bishop, Hairston the presiding bishop. Four years later the body
reported two bishops, fourteen clergy, ten churches, and 900 members. Headquarters are in Martinsville, Virginia, where the New
Bethel Apostolic Church, the largest congregation, also is located.
The denomination holds membership in the Apostolic World Christian
Fellowship.

--HISTORY

1033 Richardson, James Collins, 1945-
        With water and Spirit, [by] James C. Richardson, Jr.
      Washington, Spirit Press, 1980. 151 p. Based on thesis
      (M.Div.)--Howard University. "True Vine Pentecostal
      Churches of Jesus, 1961": p. 87-90. OkTOR

UNITED CHURCH OF JESUS CHRIST (Apostolic) (1965-)

In 1965 Monroe Saunders, pastor of the Washington church
and chief assistant to the bishop, was asked to leave the Baltimore-
based Church of God in Christ (Apostolic). The cause was Saunders' criticism of inconsistencies in the teaching and practice of
Bishop Randolph Carr on divorce and remarriage. The action, designed to isolate Saunders, had the reverse effect. Most clergy
and their congregations followed the deposed pastor into a new
organization: the First United Church of Jesus Christ (Apostolic).
Headquarters are in Baltimore, where the Institute for Biblical
Studies, the Center for a More Abundant Life, and the Creative
Learning Center (a preparatory school) are operated by the church.
In 1980 the United Church of Jesus Christ reported 52 churches,
150 clergy, and 75,000 members in the United States; and 35
churches and 5,000 adult members in the United Kingdom. Composed largely of immigrants from Jamaica, the British work continues
to use the "First" in the church name. In 1980 the denomination
held membership in the Apostolic World Christian Fellowship.

--GOVERNMENT

1034 United Church of Jesus Christ (Apostolic)
        Book of church order and discipline of the United Church
      of Jesus Christ (Apostolic). Washington, 1965. viii, 83 p.
      "Authorized by the Board of Bishops, September 20, 1965,
      Bishop Monroe R. Saunders, Sr., president."

--HISTORY

1035   Richardson, James Collins, 1945-
         With water and Spirit, [by] James C. Richardson, Jr.
       Washington, Spirit Press, 1980.   151 p.   Based on thesis
       (M.Div.)--Howard University.   "The United Church of Jesus
       Christ (Apostolic), 1965": p. 91-93.   OkTOR

--PERIODICALS

1036   Burning bush.   1-   1976-
       Baltimore

UNITED CHURCHES OF JESUS (Apostolic) (1970-   )

     The United Churches of Jesus (Apostolic), organized in 1970,
is the product of a rather muffled dispute in the Apostle Church of
Christ in God over the divorce and remarriage of its presiding
bishop, J. C. Richardson, Sr.   J. W. Audrey, one of the founders
of the parent body, served as first general bishop.   In the early
1980s he was succeeded by James R. Ziglar of Dudley, North Carolina.   From 1980 to 1984 the United Churches of Jesus (Apostolic)
increased from twenty to 38 congregations.   In 1980 it claimed
2,000 members.   An increase in membership proportionate to that
in churches would indicate approximately 3,800 members in 1984.
The group holds membership in the Apostolic World Christian Fellowship.

--HISTORY

1037   Richardson, James Collins, 1945-
         With water and Spirit, [by] James C. Richardson, Jr.
       Washington, Spirit Press, 1980.   151 p.   Based on thesis
       (M.Div.)--Howard University.   "United Churches of Jesus,
       Apostolic, 1970": p. 96-97.   OkTOR

UNITED WAY OF THE CROSS CHURCHES OF CHRIST OF THE
     APOSTOLIC FAITH (1974-   )

     In 1974 Joseph H. Adams, diocesan bishop in North Carolina,
had a vision in which he was commanded to leave the Way of the
Cross Church of Christ and to establish a new church.   This, together with frustration over having been denied the headquarters
pastorate five years earlier, led to the founding with Elder Harrison
Twyman (formerly of the Bible Way Church) of the United Way of

the Cross Churches of Christ of the Apostolic Faith later that year.
Soon they were joined by Elder Preston Graves, also formerly of
the Bible Way Church, and Elder James Pickard, formerly of the
Apostle Church of Christ in God. By 1980 there were four bishops,
thirty clergy, fourteen churches and about 1,100 members. Amicable
relations have been established with the parent body. The United
Way of the Cross Churches hold membership in the Apostolic World
Christian Fellowship. J. H. Adams, who resides in Axton, Virginia,
continues to serve as presiding bishop. The movement has branches
in five or six states.

                    --HISTORY

1038   Richardson, James Collins, 1945-
            With water and Spirit, [by] James H. Richardson, Jr.
       Washington, Spirit Press, 1980. 151 p. Based on thesis
       (M.Div.)--Howard University. "The United Way of the Cross
       Churches of Christ of the Apostolic Faith, Inc., 1974":
       p. 97-99. OkTOR

VICTORY PENTECOSTAL APOSTOLIC CHURCH (19 -)

     In 1980, R. H. Prince of Landover, Maryland, was presiding
bishop of the Victory Pentecostal Apostolic Church.

WAY OF THE CROSS CHURCH OF CHRIST (1933-)

     In 1933, Elder H. C. Brooks reorganized the constituency of
his Washington church as a denomination: the Way of the Cross
Church of Christ. Brooks, who had established the congregation
six years before, served under Bishop R. C. Lawson from 1928 to
1933. The desire of the New York bishop to merge Brooks' group
with one led by Smallwood Williams sent Brooks into independency
instead. From the founder's death in 1969 to 1978, the Way of the
Cross Church was led by his brother-in-law, J. L. Brooks, who
also served as pastor of the mother church. He in turn was succeeded by the founder's son, Alphonso. Succession has proved
difficult and resulted in several splinter groups. Recent years
have also witnessed expansion. In 1979 thirteen churches and missions in Ghana and Liberia affiliated. The next year the body reported 48 churches and approximately 50,000 members. It holds
membership in the Apostolic World Christian Fellowship. Bishop
Leroy H. Cannady of Baltimore is present chairman.

--GOVERNMENT

1039   Way of the Cross Church of Christ.
         Minutes and church directory of the Way of the Cross
         Church of Christ, 1975. Hartford, Ct., Brooks Chapel
         Press, 1976.

1040   Way of the Cross Church of Christ.
         Minutes and church directory of the Way of the Cross
         Church of Christ, 1978. Hartfort, Ct., Brooks Chapel Press,
         1979.

--HISTORY

1041   Richardson, James Collins, 1945-
         With water and Spirit, [by] James C. Richardson, Jr.
         Washington, Spirit Press, 1980. 151 p. Based on thesis
         (M.Div.)--Howard University. "Way of the Cross Church of
         Christ, 1927": p. 66-69.

WEST INDIAN CANADIAN INTERNATIONAL APOSTOLIC FELLOWSHIP
   (19 -   )

   Since the early 1970s, the West Indian International Apostolic
Fellowship, Inc. has been affiliated with the Apostolic World Chris-
tian Fellowship. The Rev. R. W. Davy, its president, lives in
Mississauga, Ontario, a suburb of Toronto.

PART IV. LEADER-CENTERED ORIENTATION

Unlike the belief-centered bodies in earlier sections, the organizations placed here enjoy little community or status with other groups. In fact, in the past they often received as much or more scorn from other black Holiness churches as from believers in other traditions. Emphasis on emotional experience, faith healing, and puritanical standards of behavior justifies their inclusion here. Several African bodies hold membership in the World Council of Churches, which separates them from all even remotely related North American communions.

AFRICAN APOSTOLIC CHURCH OF JOHANE MARANKE (1932-)

Organized in 1932, the African Apostolic Church of Johane Maranke is the result of an exodus by nationals from the American Methodist mission churches of Southern Rhodesia (Zimbabwe). In succeeding decades the movement spread into neighboring countries. The stronghold remains in Zimbabwe where in the mid-1970s there were 150 churches and 180,000 members. The total community at that time numbered 260,000. Headquarters are on the Maranke Reserve near Umtali.

1042   Bellman, Beryl Larry, 1941-
         A paradigm for looking; cross-cultural research with visual media, [by] Beryl L. Bellman [and] Bennetta Jules-Rosette. Norwood, N.J., Ablex Publishing Corp., c1977. vii, 211 p. DLC

1043   Jules-Rosette, Bennetta (Washington)
         Prophecy and leadership in the Maranke Church: a case study in continuity and change, [by] Bennetta Jules-Rosette. In Bond, G., ed. African Christianity: patterns of religious continuity. New York, c1979, 109-136.

--WORSHIP

1044   Jules-Rosette, Bennetta (Washington)
         African apostles: ritual and conversion in the Church of

188

John Maranke, [by] Bennetta Jules-Rosette.   Ithaca, N.Y.,
Cornell University Press, 1975.   302 p.   (Symbol, myth and
ritual series)   DLC

1045   Jules-Rosette, Bennetta (Washington)
Ceremonial trance, behavior in an African church: private
experience and public expression, [by] Bennetta Jules-Rosette.
In Journal for the Scientific Study of Religion, 19 (Mar.
1980), 1-16.

1046   Jules-Rosette, Bennetta (Washington)
Women as ceremonial leaders in an African church: the
Apostles of John Maranke, [by] Bennetta Jules-Rosetta.   In
Jules-Rosette, B. W., ed.   The new religions of Africa.
Norwood, N.J., c1979, 127-144.   DLC, OkEdT

--ZAIRE

1047   Heimer, Haldor Eugene, 1924-
The Kimbanguists and the Bapostolo: a study of two African independent churches in Luluabourg, Congo, in relation
to similar churches in the context of Lulua traditional culture
and religion.   Hartford, Ct., 1971.   xvii, 478 l.   Thesis
(Ph.D.)--Hartford Seminary Foundation.   KU

--ZAMBIA

1048   Jules-Rosette, Bennetta (Washington)
Symbols of change: urban transition in a Zambian commu-
nity, [by] Bennetta Jules-Rosette.   Norwood, N.J., Ablex
Publishing Corp., c1981.   xiv, 225 p.   DLC, OkEdT

AFRICAN ISRAEL CHURCH NINEVEH (1942-   )

Formed in 1942, the African Israel Church Nineveh is composed of almost equal numbers of two Kenyan peoples: the Luhya
and the Luo.   The founders were formerly part of the Pentecostal
Assemblies of Canada mission.   Headquarters are in the holy city
of Nineveh seventeen miles north of Kisumu.   In the mid-1970s the
African Israel Church Nineveh claimed 274 congregations, 36,904
members, and a total community of 76,200.

1049   Charsley, S. R.
Dreams in an independent African church, [by] S. R.
Charsley.   In Africa, 43 (July 1971), 244-257.

1050   Welbourn, Frederick Burkewood, 1912-
A place to feel at home: a study of two independent

churches in western Kenya, [by] F. B. Welbourn [and]
B. A. Ogot. London, Nairobi, Oxford University Press,
1966. xv, 157 p. DLC

ALADURA INTERNATIONAL CHURCH, UNITED KINGDOM AND OVERSEAS (1970-   )

Ninety-five percent of the Aladura International Church,
United Kingdom and Overseas are students from Nigeria, Ghana,
and the West Indies. The single congregation in London, founded
in 1970, had 300 full and 500 constituent members by 1980.

CHERUBIM AND SERAPHIM (1918-   )

In 1918 West Africa experienced a severe influenza epidemic,
which in the opinion of many Yoruba Christians the mission churches
were powerless to defeat. As a result nationals formed prayer and
healing groups out of which emerged several large indigenous movements. One of these, the Cherubim and Seraphim, mothered over
two hundred distinct bodies among which are some of Nigeria's largest denominations: the Cherubim and Seraphim Church of Zion of
Nigeria, the Eternal Sacred Order of Cherubim and Seraphim, and
the Holy Order of Cherubim and Seraphim. By 1982 these three
alone claimed a combined adult 205,000 members in 1,440 churches.

1050a Omoyajowo, J. Akinyele
       Cherubim and Seraphim: the history of an African inde-
       pendent church, by J. Akinyele Omoyajowo. New York, NOK
       Publishers International, c1982. xvi, 256 p. Revision of
       thesis (Ph.D.)--University of Ibadan. DLC

1050b Omoyajowo, J. Akinyele
       Diversity in unity: the development and expansion of the
       Cherubim & Seraphim church in Nigeria, [by] Akin Omoyajowo.
       Lanham, Md., University Press of America, c1984. xiv,
       106 p. DLC

--UNITED STATES

1051 Larsen, Egon, 1904-
       Strange sects and cults: a study of their origins and in-
       fluence. London, Burker, 1971. 202 p. Includes Cherubim
       and Seraphim. DLC

1052 Larsen, Egon, 1904-
       Strange sects and cults: a study of their origins and

    influence. New York, Hart Publishing Co., 1972, c1971.
    245 p. Includes Cherabim and Seraphim. DLC, OkEG

CHRIST APOSTOLIC CHURCH (1917-)
[1917-1922 as Diamond Society; 1922-1931 as affiliate of Faith Taber-
    nacle, Philadelphia; 1931-1939 as affiliate of Apostolic Church;
    1939-1941 as Nigeria Apostolic Church; 1941-1942 as United
    Apostolic Church.]

    This Nigerian body displays a continuity in leadership scarce-
ly discernible amid changes in name and affiliation. Since 1922,
it has been led (except for forced retirement between 1957 and
1959) by one man: Peter Anim, a national pastor. Headquarters
are in Ibadan. In the mid-1970s the Christ Apostolic Church reported 1,575 churches and 179,029 members in Nigeria, and two
churches and 50 members in the United Kingdom. Since 1931 a
close relationship has been maintained with the Christ Apostolic
Church in Ghana. The 1936 visit of the noted Nigerian revivalist,
Joseph Ayo Babalola, to Ghana was but the first of such visits by
Nigerian leaders to that country which have encouraged the church
there to strengthen its evangelistic efforts.

1053 Anquandah, James
        Can the church be renewed? Experiences of an African
    independent church, [by] James Anquandah. In Ecumenical
    Review, 31 (July 1979), 252-260.

CHRIST REVIVAL CHURCH (1961-1966)

    In 1957 the Church Executive of the Christ Apostolic Church
in Nigeria removed the aging Peter Anim from office as general
superintendent and replaced him with Pastor D. K. Brifo, a younger
man. Anim returned to Boso, his native village, but chafed con-
tinually over his forced retirement. The 1960 meeting of the
Church Executive reversed its earlier decision, removing Brifo and
reinstating Anim as general Superintendent. Although permitted to
continue as pastor, Brifo decided instead to lead a secessionist
movement. In 1961 he founded the Christ Revival Church. The
new organization survived only five years. In 1966, D. K. Brifo
and most of his followers returned to the Christ Apostolic Church.

CHURCH OF THE LORD (Aladura) (1930-)

    The Aladura (a Yoruba word meaning "people who pray")
is an indigenous renewal movement of as many as three million

adherents in five West African nations. In recent decades outposts
have been established in the United Kingdom and the United States.
The Church of the Lord (Aladura) originated in a revival movement
in the Church Missionary Society work in Nigeria about 1930.

--HISTORY

1054   Moede, Gerald F.
            Ecumenical exercise II: the Church of the Lord (Aladura),
       Assemblies of Brethren [and] the African Brotherhood Church.
       Edited by Gerald F. Moede. Geneva, World Council of
       Churches, 1972. 41 p. (Faith and order paper, 61) Re-
       printed from Ecumenical review, 24:2 (Apr. 1972). ODaTS

1055   Peel, John David Yeadon, 1941-
            Aladura: a religious movement among the Yoruba, [by]
       J. D. Y. Peel. London, African Institute by the Oxford Uni-
       versity Press, 1968. xiii, 388 p. Uk

1056   Turner, Harold Walter, 1911-
            History of an African independent church, [by] H. W.
       Turner. Oxford, Clarendon Press, 1967. 2 v. DLC

--HISTORY AND STUDY OF DOCTRINES

1057   Turner, Harold Walter, 1911-
            Profile through preaching; a study of the sermon texts
       used in a West African independent church, [by] Harold W.
       Turner. London, Published for the World Council of
       Churches, Commission on World Mission and Evangelism by
       Edinburgh House Press, 1965. 86 p. (C.W.M.E. research
       pamphlets, 13) On label: Distributed by Friendship Press,
       New York, N.Y. DLC

--WORSHIP

1058   Brown, Kenneth I.
            Worshiping with the African Church of the Lord (Aladura),
       [by] Kenneth I. Brown. In Practical Anthropology, 13
       (Mar. 1966), 59-84.

CHURCH OF THE TWELVE APOSTLES (Nackabah) (1914-)

The Church of the Twelve Apostles was founded in 1914 by

John Nackabah, a disciple of Prophet Harris.   In the mid-1970s,
John Nackabah III was leader.   At that time it reported 107 churches
and 8,983 members in Ghana.

1059   Breidenbach, Paul Stanley, 1939-
        Ritual interrogation and the communication of belief in a
       West African religious movement, [by] Paul Breidenbach.
       In Journal of Religion in Africa, 9:2 (1978), 95-108.

1060   Breidenbach, Paul Stanley, 1939-
        Sunsum edwuma: the limits of classification and the signifi-
       cance of event, [by] Paul S. Breidenbach.   In Social Re-
       search, 46 (Spring 1979), 63-87.

1061a Breidenbach, Paul Stanley, 1939-
        Sunsum edwuma, the spiritual work: forms of symbolic
       action and communication in a Ghanaian healing movement,
       [by] Paul Stanley Breidenbach.   Evanston, Il., 1973.   vi,
       434 l.   Thesis (Ph.D.)--Northwestern University.   IEN

1062   Breidenbach, Paul Stanley, 1939-
        The woman on the beach and the man in the bush: lead-
       ership and adopthood in the Twelve Apostles movement of
       Ghana, [by] Paul Breidenbach.   In Jules-Rosette, B. W.,
       ed.   The new religions of Africa.   Norwood, N.J., c1979,
       99-115.   DLC, OkEdT

CHURCH OF UNIVERSAL TRIUMPH, THE DOMINION OF GOD
   (1938-   )

        In 1938 James Francis Marion Jones, a native of Birmingham,
Alabama, was sent to Detroit by the Triumph the Church and Kingdom of God in Christ to establish a congregation.   Jones quickly
established himself.   Followers showered him with expensive gifts,
which church officials said should be sent to headquarters.   Instead, he left the denomination and founded the Church of Universal Triumph, the Dominion of God.   Radio became the principal
medium of the "all is well" prophet.   He was addressed as, "His
Holiness the Rev. Dr. James F. Jones, D.D., Universal Dominion
Ruler, Internationally known as Prophet Jones," and soon established
churches in most Northern cities.   He acquired a white mink coat, the
the 54-room former residence of a General Motors executive, five
chauffeur-driven Cadillacs, jewelry, and a wardrobe consisting of
nearly 500 ensembles.   Personal conduct of members underwent strict
scrutiny by the ruler.   Vices and most pleasures, including use of

tea and coffee, were forbidden. Women and men both were required
to wear body supporters. And none could befriend non-members,
attend another church, or marry without consent of the ruler.
The church, whose teaching focused on the advent of the Millennium
in the year 2000, met a major setback in 1953, however, when
Prophet Jones was tried for gross indecency. Though acquitted,
he spent the rest of his life under a cloud. His death in 1971 created an institutional crisis out of which his assistant, the Rev.
Lord James Schaffer emerged as Dominion leader. Five thousand
members and clergy attended the funeral of Prophet Jones in Detroit.

1063   Mink-minded prophet dies: successor sought.
          In Jet, 40 (Sept. 2, 1971), 20-23.

1064   The rise and fall of Prophet Jones.
          In Ebony, 11 (Oct. 1956), 63-66.

EDEN REVIVAL CHURCH (1963-   )

      Founded in 1963, the Eden Revival Church is the only inde-
genous body of local origin yet to be admitted to the Christian
Council of Ghana. Its 1971 application for membership in the World
Council of Churches was turned down. Headquarters are in Accra.
In the mid-1970s, the Eden Revival Church reported twenty congregations and 30,000. Its total constituency at that time numbered
50,000.

1065   Beckmann, David Milton, 1948-
          Eden revival: spiritual churches in Ghana, [by] David
       M. Beckmann. Foreword by William J. Dunker. St. Louis,
       Concordia Publishing House, 1975. 144 p. DLC

EGLISE DE JESUS-CHRIST SUR LA TERRE PAR LE PROPHETE
   SIMON KIMBANGU (1921-   )

      In 1921 the Congolese evangelist Simon Kimbangu was impris-
oned after a healing ministry of only six months on a charge of
political subversion. Although innocent, he was to spend his remaining thirty years there. Outlawed, the movement he inspired
spread widely and many underground sects sprang up which,
rightly or wrongly, used his name. In 1957, six years following
the founder's death, the Belgian government lifted its ban. The
Kimbangu family and the core of his followers then formed the
Eglise de Jesus-Christ sur la terre par le prophète Simon Kimbangu,
a body which received official recognition in December 1959. The
Eglise du Christ sur la terre par deux temoins: Simon Kimbangu

et Thomas Ntwalani is representative of many other sects which
were formed. By the 1970s the movement (led by Joseph Diangienda, Kimbangu's youngest son, and centered at Nkamba-Jerusalem,
the founder's birthplace) had spread to ten countries. At its first
celebration of holy communion on April 6, 1971, an estimated
350,000 participated. The communion is now observed three times
a year; Christmas, Easter and the anniversary of Kimbanga's death.
Baptism without the use of water is practiced. In Zaire alone the
Kimbanguist church claims 8,000 churches and 2,000,000 full members. Within the last decade the Eglise par deux temoins and several other separatist bodies have reunited.

1066   Banda-Mwaba, Justin
        Le Kimbanguisme en taut que mouvement prépolitique chez
les Kongo. In Problèmes sociaux congolais, 92-93 (Mar./
June 1971), 3-53.

1067   Béguin, Willy
        Découverte du Kimbanguisme, [par] Willy Béguin [et]
Marie-Louise Martin. In Le monde non-chrétien, 22:89-90
(Jan.-July 1969), 5-37.

1068   Bertsche, James Edwin
        Kimbanguism: a challenge to missionary statesmanship,
[by] James E. Bertsche. In Practical Anthropology, 13:1
(Jan./Feb. 1966), 13-33.

1069   Bertsche, James Edwin
        Kimbanguism: a separatist movement, [by] James Bertsche.
Evanston, Il., 1963. 355 l. Thesis (M.A.)--Northwestern
University. IEN

1070   Crane, William H.
        The Kimbanguist Church and the search for authentic
catholicity, [by] William H. Crane. In Christian Century,
87 (June 3, 1970), 691-695.

1071   Fehderau, Harold Werner, 1932-
        Kimbanguism: prophetic Christianity in Congo, [by] Har-
old W. Fehderau. In Practical Anthropology, 9:4 (July/Aug.
1962), 157-178.

1072   Fehderau, Harold Werner, 1932-
        A report on Kimbanguists: a visit to some Kimbanguists
in the Congo, January 29-February 5, 1967, [by] Harold
Fehderau and Clarence Hiebert. Hillsboro, Ks., 1967. 22,
3, 3 p. InElkB

1073   Handspicker, Meredith B.
        An ecumenical exercise: the Southern Baptist Convention,
the Seventh Day Adventist Church, the Kimbanguist Church

in the Congo, the Pentecostal movement in Europe.   Edited
by M. B. Handspicker and Lukas Vischer.   Geneva, World
Council of Churches, 1967.   46 p.   (Faith and order paper,
49) OkEG

1074 Hollenweger, Walter Jacob, 1927-
      Marxist and Kimbanguist mission: a comparison, [by]
      W. J. Hollenweger.   Birmingham, University of Birmingham,
      1973.   14 p.   Cover title.   DLC

1075 Hollenweger, Walter Jacob, 1927-
      Pentecost between black and white: five case studies on
      Pentecost and politics, [by] Walter J. Hollenweger.   Belfast,
      Christian Journals Ltd., 1974.   143 p.   "Pentecost of
      N'Kamba": p. 55-75, 123-127.   DLC, KyWAT, MCE

1076 Le Kimbanguisme.
      In Courrier Africain (Brussels), 47 (Jan. 8, 1960)

1077 The Kimbanguist church in the Congo.
      In Ecumenical Review, 19:1 (Jan. 1967), 29-36.   An ecu-
      menical exercise, 3.

1078 Krust, Christian Hugo
      Die Kimbanguistenkirche im Kongo, [von] Christian Krust.
      In Heilszeugnisse, 55:10 (Oct. 1, 1970)

1079 Lasserre, Jean
      L'Eglise kimbanguiste du Congo.   In Le monde non-
      chrétien, 79-89 (July/Dec. 1966), 45-52.

1080 Martin, Marie-Louise, 1912-
      Kimbangu: an African prophet and his church, [by]
      Marie-Louise Martin.   With a foreword by Bryan R. Wilson.
      Translated by D. M. Moore.   Oxford, Blackwell, c1975.
      xxiv, 198 p.   Translation of Kirche ohne Weisse.   DLC

1081 Martin, Marie-Louise, 1912-
      Kimbangu: an African prophet and his church, [by]
      Marie-Louise Martin.   With a foreword by Bryan R. Wilson.
      Translated by D. M. Moore.   1st American ed.   Grand
      Rapids, Mi., Eerdmans, 1976.   xxiv, 198 p.   Translation
      of Kirche ohne Weisse.   DLC

1082 Martin, Marie-Louise, 1912-
      Kirche ohne Weisse: Simon Kimbangu und seine Millionen-
      kirche im Kongo.   Basel, Friedrich Reinhardt, 1979.   279 p.
      DLC

1083 Martin, Marie-Louise, 1912-
      Prophetic Christianity in the Congo: the Church of Christ

on Earth through the Prophet Simon Kimbangu. Braamfon-
tein, Christian Institute of Southern Africa, 1968. 40 p.
First three chapters based on a series of articles in Pro
Veritate. DLC

1084 Mwene-Batende, Gaston
       Le phénomène de dissidence des sectes religieuses d'in-
spiration kimbanguiste, [par] Gaston Mwene-Batende. Brux-
elles, Centre d'étude et de documentation africaines, 1971.
37 1. (Les Cahiers du CEDAF, 6/1971: Serie 4. Religion)
Caption title. DLC

1085 Raymaekers, Paul
       L'Eglise de Jésus-Christ sur la terre par le prophete Simon
Kimbangu: contribution a l'étude des mouvements messianiques,
dans le Bas-Kongo. In Zaire, 13:7 (1959), 675-756.

1086 Raymaekers, Paul
       L'Eglise de Jésus-Christ sur la terre par le prophete Simon
Kimbangu: Décembre, 1958-Avril, 1960, contribution a
l'étude des mouvements prophe´tiques dans le Bas-Zahire,
[par] Paul Raymaekers. 2e ed. (rev. et completée). Kin-
shasa, Bureau d'organisation des programmes ruraux, Uni-
versite, 1975. 90 p., [6] leaves of plates. InU

1087 Sinda, Martial, 1935-
       Le messianisme congolais et ses incidences politiques; kim-
banguisme, matsouanisme, autre mouvements. Precede par
Les Christ noirs, de Roger Bastide. Paris, Payot, 1972.
390 p. DLC, NhD

1088 Steiner, Leonhard, 1903-
       Die Kimbanguistenkirche im Kongo. In Wort und Geist,
2:7 (July 1970)

1089 Thomas, George B.
       Kimbanguism: authentically African, authentically Chris-
tian, [by] George B. In Booth, N. S., ed. African religions: a symposium. New York, 1977, 275-296.

1090 Wing, Joseph van
       Le Kibangisme vu par un témoin. In Zaire, 12:6 (1958),
563-618.

       --BIBLIOGRAPHY

1091 Chassard, Paul-Eric
       Essai de bibliographie sur le Kimbanguisme. In Archives
de Sociologie des Religions, 16:31 (1971), 43-49.

--DOCTRINAL AND CONTROVERSIAL WORKS

1092 [Diangienda, Joseph Ku Ntima], 1918-
     The essence of Kimbanguist theology: the Church of
     Jesus Christ on Earth by the Prophet Simon Kimbangu. In
     WCC Exchange, 4 (July 1978) ViRUT

1093 Diangienda, Joseph Ku Ntima, 1918-
     Out of Africa: Kimbanguism, [by] Joseph Diangienda.
     With introductory chapters by Peter Manciom. London,
     Christian Education Movement, 1979. 66 p. (CEM student
     theology series) "The bulk of this present book is a state-
     ment of the theology of the church (...drawn up by the
     spiritual leader, Joseph Diangienda, and approved by the
     church) translated from the original French." InRE

     --EVANGELISTIC WORK

1094 Luntadila Ndala Za Fwa
     Un ray d'espoir: l'evangélisation dans les églises indé-
     pendantes africaines, [par] Luntadila Ndala Za Fwa. Kinshasa,
     CEDI, 1975. 78 p. Cover title: Kimbanguisme. CLU, DLC

     --HISTORY

1095 Desanti, Dominique
     The golden anniversary of Kimbanguism, an African reli-
     gion. In Continent 2000, 19 (Apr. 1971), 7-19.

     --HISTORY AND STUDY OF DOCTRINES

1096 Choffat, Francois
     L'église kimbanguiste africaine et non-violente. In Cahiers
     de la réconciliation, 5-6 (May/June 1966), 3-15.

1097 Droogers, André
     Kimbanguism at the grass roots: beliefs in a local Kim-
     banguist Church, [by] André Droogers. In Journal of Reli-
     gion in Africa, 11:3 (1980), 188-211.

1098 MacGaffey, Wyatt, 1932-
     The beloved city: commentary on a Kimbanguist text. In
     Journal of Religion in Africa, 2:2 (1969), 129-147.

1099 Wainwright, Geoffrey, 1939-
     Theological reflections on "The catechism concerning the
     Prophet Simon Kimbangu" of 1970. In Orita, 6:1 (June 1971)

--MUSIC

1100   Boka, Simon
         250 [i.e., Deux cent cinquante] chants de l'Eglise de
         Jésus-Christ sur la terre par le prophète Simon Kimbangu,
         [par] Simon Boka [et] Paul Raymaekers. [Léopoldville],
         1960- v. [1]- (Universite Lovanium, Léopoldville. Institut
         de recherches economiques et sociales (IRES). Notes & docu-
         ments, 1, no. 3/SC-2. Cover title. DLC

1101   Heintze-Flad, Wilfred
         L'Eglise Kimbanguiste: une église que chante et prie (les
         Chants captés kimbanguistes, expression authentique de la
         foi de l'Afrique), [par] Wilfred Heintze-Flad. Leiden, Inter-
         universitair Instituut voor Missiologie en Oecumenica, 1978.
         ii, 57 p. GEU-T

--LULUABOURG

1102   Heimer, Haldor Eugene, 1924-
         The Kimbanguists and the Bapostolo: a study of two Afri-
         can independent churches in Luluabourg, Congo, in relation
         to similar churches in the context of Lulua traditional culture
         and religion. Hartford, Ct., 1971. xvii, 478 l. Thesis
         (Ph.D.)--Hartford Seminary Foundation. KU

EGLISE DE JESUS-CHRIST SUR LA TERRE PAR LE SAINT-ESPRIT
   (1951-   )

     This group, founded in 1951, is composed largely (85%) of
members of the Luba tribe in Zaire. In the mid-1970s it reported
ninety churches, 32,191 members, and a total community of 110,669.
Its headquarters are in Kinshasa-Kalina.

EGLISE HARRISTE (1913-   )

     The Eglise Harriste consists of followers of William Wadé Har-
ris, a Liberian evangelist who from 1913 to 1915 traversed the Ivory
Coast and Gold Coast preaching spiritual healing and reform (not
abolition) of traditional African practices. His belief that he was
the divinely appointed prophet to West Africa, together with immense
popularity among the people, brought him into conflict with govern-
mental authorities and missionaries alike. The two-year ministry in
the Ivory Coast netted more than 120,000 converts. Although a
sizeable portion became Roman Catholics and Methodists, the major-
ity organized an independent church, which in the mid-1970s

claimed 50,000 full members and a constituency of 150,000. The
secretary general and presiding bishop reside in Abidjan. In 1968
the Eglise Harriste sought membership in the World Council of
Churches.

1103 Bureau, René
        Le prophète Harris et le harrisme (Côte-d'Ivoire). Abid-
        jan, Université d'Abidjan, Institut d'Ethno-sociologie, 1971.
        193 l. MiEM

1104 Walker, Sheila Suzanne
        Christianity African style: the Harrist church of the
        Ivory Coast, [by] Sheila Suzanne Walker. Chicago, 1976.
        vii, 385 l. Thesis (Ph.D.)--University of Chicago. ICU

1105 Walker, Sheila Suzanne
        The message as the medium: the Harrist churches of the
        Ivory Coast and Ghana, [by] Sheila S. Walker. In Bond, G.,
        ed. African Christianity: patterns of religious continuity.
        New York, c1979, 9-64.

1106 Walker, Sheila Suzanne
        The religious revolution in the Ivory Coast: the Prophet
        Harris and the Harrist Church, [by] Sheila S. Walker. Chapel
        Hill, University of North Carolina Press, c1983. xvii, 206 p.
        (Studies in religion) DLC

1107 Walker, Sheila Suzanne
        Witchcraft and healing in an African Christian church, [by]
        Sheila S. Walker. In Journal of Religion in Africa, 10:2
        (1979), 127-138.

1108 Walker, Sheila Suzanne
        Women in the Harrist movement, [by] Sheila S. Walker.
        In Jules-Rosette, B. W., ed. The new religions of Africa.
        Norwood, N.J., c1979, 87-97.

1109 Walker, Sheila Suzanne
        Young men, old men, and devils in aeroplanes: the Har-
        rist Church, the witchcraft complex and social change in the
        Ivory Coast, [by] Sheila S. Walker. In Journal of Religion
        in Africa, 11:2 (1980), 106-123.

FATHER DIVINE PEACE MISSION (1919-   )

        In 1919, George Baker, self-named Father Divine leaped into
public attention when his Sayville, Long Island neighbors took him
to court for creating a public nuisance. Noise created by the
crowds drawn to his house there, they said, disturbed the peace.

(The establishment served as a worship center, commune, employ-
ment agency, and banquet hall.) The trial proceedings brought
forth the fact that followers attributed healing power and divinity
to the leader, characteristics that the leader refused to deny, then
or later. During the next two decades, the movement spread
throughout the United States and to several other countries, New
York and Philadelphia becoming especially strong centers. An as-
cetic ethic (cohabitation was outlawed), communal life centering in
"heavens," and the giving of banquets, during which the providence
of the leader was displayed, characterized the movement. Repeated
investigations of finances proved futile during the life of the founder. Since his death in 1965, the Father Divine Peace Mission has
lapsed into obscurity. At its height, estimates of membership
ranged from a few thousand to millions.

1110   Alexander, Jack
       All Father's chillun got heavens, [by] Jack Alexander. In
       Saturday Evening Post, 212 (Nov. 18, 1939), 8-9, 64, 66,
       69-70, 72, 75.

1111   Angels over Newport.
       In Time, 34 (July 24, 1939), 44.

1112   Bird, Robert S.
       Father Divine's movement expands, [by] Robert S. Bird.
       In New York Times, 88 (July 2, 1939), 10E.

1113   Black elbow.
       In Time, 32 (Aug. 8, 1938), 7-8.

1114   Clark, Elmer Talmage, 1886-1961.
       The small sects in America, [by] Elmer T. Clark. Nash-
       ville, Cokesbury Press, c1937. 311 p. On Father Divine
       Peace Mission: p. 153-161. DLC, OkBetC

1115   Clark, Elmer Talmage, 1886-1961.
       The small sects in America, [by] Elmer T. Clark. Rev.
       ed. New York, Abingdon-Cokesbury Press, 1949. 256 p.
       On Father Divine Peace Mission: p. 124-127. DLC, RPB

1116   Denlinger, Sutherland
       Heaven is in Harlem, [by] Sutherland Denlinger. In Forum
       and Century, 95 (Apr. 1936), 211-218.

1117   Divine ultimatum.
       In Time, 61 (ar. 9, 1953), 72, 74.

1118   Fauset, Arthur Huff, 1899-
       Black gods of the metropolis: Negro religious cults of the
       urban North. Philadelphia, University of Pennsylvania Press;
       London, H. Milford, Oxford University Press, 1944. x, 126 p.

(Publications of the Philadlephia Anthropological Society, 3;
Brinton memorial series, [2]) Based on thesis (Ph.D.)--
University of Pennsylvania. "Father Divine Peace Mission
movement": p. 52-67. DLC, TxWB

1119 Fishburne, Dannette
      The contributions of Father Divine to social welfare, [by]
      Dannette Fishburne. In Spirit, 1:1 (1977), 16-20.

1120 $500,000 (cash) heaven.
      In Newsweek, 34 (Oct. 31, 1949), 20.

1121 Goldsmith, Janet
      Father Divine and the Peace Mission movement, [by] Janet
      Goldsmith. New York, 1977. 86 l. Thesis (M.A.)--City
      College of New York. NNR

1122 Grey, Alan
      God, Inc., gets the ads, [by] Alan Grey. In Canadian
      Forum, 19 (Nov. 1939), 249-250, 252.

1123 Hantman, Sid
      No food shortage for "God," [by] Sid Hantman. In Negro
      Digest, 4 (Oct. 1946), 25-26. Condensed from International
      News Service.

1124 Harkness, Georgia Elma, 1891-1974.
      Father Divine's righteous government, [by] Georgia Hark-
      ness. In Christian Century, 82 (Oct. 13, 1965), 1259-1261.

1125 Heaven-on-the-Hudson.
      In Newsweek, 12 (Aug. 8, 1938), 10-12.

1126 "Heaven": the forces of evil imperil Harlem's dark Divine.
      In News-Week, 9 (May 1, 1937), 11.

1127 Kelley, Hubert
      Heaven incorporated, [by] Hubert Kelley. In American
      Magazine, 121 (Jan. 1936), 40-41, 106-108.

1128 Lahey, Edwin A.
      Peace! It's still wonderful, [by] Edwin A. Lahey. In
      Negro Digest, 2 (May 1944) Condensed from Chicago Daily
      News.

1129 Peace, brother!
      In Time, 54 (Oct. 31, 1949), 15-16.

1130 A religious party.
      In Time, 29 (Apr. 12, 1937), 59-60.

1131 Revolt in "heaven."
      In Newsweek, 15 (Jan. 1, 1940), 29-30.

1132 To Sezar.
      In Time, 30 (Aug. 9, 1937), 30.

1133 Wilmore, Gayraud Stephen, 1921-
      Black religion and black radicalism, [by] Gayraud S. Wil-
      more. Garden City, N.Y., Doubleday, 1972. xiii, 344 p.
      (C. Eric Lincoln series on black religion) On Father Divine
      Peace Mission: p. 215-216. DLC

1134 Wilson, Earl, 1907-
      Hahn'tchuglad? [By] Earl Wilson. In Negro Digest, 2
      (Mar. 1944), 61-63. Condensed from New York Post.

          --CONTROVERSIAL LITERATURE

1135 Gardner, Velmer J.
      "I spent Saturday night in the devil's house": an ex-
      posure [!] of Father Divine, [by] Velmer J. Gardner.
      Springfield, Mo., Velmer Gardner Evangelistic Association,
      c1952. 47 p. OkTOR

          --DOCTRINAL AND CONTROVERSIAL WORKS

1136 Baker, George, self-named Father Divine, 1877-1965.
      The condescension of God as revealed by Father Divine to
      Lewi Pethrus. n.p., c1957. 46 p. "This interview took
      place in one of Father Divine's Manhattan offices during the
      winter of 1936-37." PP

1137 Baker, George, self-named Father Divine, 1877-1965.
      Father Divine and the Peace Mission movement. n.p.,
      197-. portfolio ([19] pieces) PPT

          --PERIODICALS

1138 Der Neue Tag. 1- 1938-
      Zurich. Text in English.

1139 New day. 1- May 21, 1936-
      New York, Philadelphia. CtY, DLC, MB, NN, OCl

1140 Spoken word. 1-3, no. 8, Oct. 20, 1934-July 31, 1937.
      Los Angeles, New York. CtY, DHU, IU, MiU, NN, NNUT,
      TNF

1141   World herald.   I, no. 1-37, Nov. 19, 1936-July 29, 1937.
       New York.   NN

       --SWITZERLAND

       -- --ZURICH

1142   Swiss "heaven."
       In Time, 48 (Oct. 14, 1946), 58.

MOUNT CALVARY ASSEMBLY HALL OF THE PENTECOSTAL FAITH
   CHURCH (1930-   )

     In 1930 Rosa Artimus Horn, a native of Sumter, founded her
first temple in Brooklyn.   A second temple established soon after in
the old Olympia Sport Club in Harlem became the headquarters of a
movement, which by 1949 included branches in Evanston, Illinois,
and Orange and Long Beach, New Jersey.   Mother Horn spread her
influence widely by preaching over the radio, a fact acknowledged
by a neon sign outside the headquarters church: "Church of the
Air.   Jesus Pray for Me."

1143   Fisher, Miles Mark, 1899-1970.
       Organized religion and the cults.   In Crisis, 44 (Jan.
       1937), 3-10, 29-30.

1144   Rasky, Frank
       Harlem's religious zealots, [by] Frank Rasky.   In Tomor-
       row, 9 (Nov. 1949), 11-17.

MUSAMA DISCO CRISTO CHURCH (1922-   )

     The Musama Disco Christo Church (Army of the Cross of
Christ Church) is composed of followers of Joseph Egyanka Appiah.
It grew out of the Faith Society, a prayer group in the Methodist
Church at Gomoa Ogwan in the Winneba district of Ghana.   In 1922
Appiah, who was a minister, and other members of the three-year-
old society were asked to leave the church, whereupon they formed
the present organization.   Sometime later, the founder became known
as Prophet Jemisimihan Jeru-Appiah.   In the mid-1970s the Musama
Disco Christo Church, which is among the oldest indigenous churches
in West Africa, reported 483 churches, 15,472 full members, and an
inclusive community of 55,542.   The general head prophet lives at
Gomoa Eshiem near Agona Swedru.   The body applied for membership
in the World Council of Churches in 1958.

--HISTORY

1145 Goodwin, Mary Ellen
      African Pentecostals: the Army of the Cross of Christ.
      In Spirit, 2:1 (1978), 12-28.

1146 Opoku, Kofi Asare
      Changes within Christianity: the case of the Musama Disco
      Christo Church, [by] Kofi A. Opoku. In Fashole-Luke, E.,
      ed. Christianity in independent Africa. Bloomington, In.,
      c1978, 111-121.

      --PERIODICALS

1147 Mycan. 1- Aug. 1971-
      Mozano

NATIONAL DAVID SPIRITUAL TEMPLE OF CHRIST CHURCH UNION
   (Inc.) U.S.A. (1932-   )
[1932-19-- as Orthodox Christian Spiritual Church.]

     The first David Spiritual Temple of Christ Church was set in
order, December 29, 1932, in Kansas City, Missouri. Three and a
half years later the National Spiritual Temple of Christ Church Union, consisting of eleven churches and 1,880 members in Missouri,
Kansas, Oklahoma, and California, was organized by David William
Short and seven other pastors and lay delegates. Stress was laid
on free exercise of spiritual gifts. The group condemned race dis-
crimination and segregation.
     In 1949 the St. David Orthodox Christian Spiritual Seminary
opened in Des Moines, offering elementary, high school, and cor-
respondence courses. Bishop Short served as first president and
mentor. Although there is a National Annual Assembly, the national
bishop governs in response to divine inspiration, not in reaction to
the desires of the members. In 1959 the National David Spiritual
Temple reported 66 churches and 40,816 members. At that time
headquarters were in Los Angeles. "David" in the names of church
and school refers to the founder, a former Missionary Baptist minister.

      --DOCTRINAL AND CONTROVERSIAL WORKS

1148 Short, David William
      The Orthodox Christian Spiritual Church: canon, creed,
      and doctrines. Los Angeles, 1939. 29 p.

--HISTORY

1149   Moore, Everett Leroy, 1918-
          Handbook of Pentecostal denominations in the United States.
       Pasadena, Ca., 1954. vii, 346 l. Thesis (M.A.)--Pasadena
       College. "National David Spiritual Temple of Christ Church
       Union (Inc.) U.S.A.": 1. 119-126. CSdP

--PERIODICALS

1150   Christian spiritual voice. 1-   193 -
          Kansas City, Mo.

TRUE GRACE MEMORIAL HOUSE OF PRAYER FOR ALL PEOPLE
   (1962-   )

       In 1962 as a result of the court-authorized election of Walter
McCollough as successor to "Sweet Daddy" Grace as bishop of the
United House of Prayer for All People, twelve members of the dis-
satisfied minority in the "mother house" in Washington, D.C. withdrew and established the True Grace Memorial House of Prayer for
All People. They chose Elder Thomas O. Johnson, veteran of
thirty-three years' service in the parent body, as pastor and con-
structed a new "house" on V Street in northwest Washington. The
existence of the new group, which successfully met repeated challenges to its right to use "House of Prayer" in its name, inspired
formation of seven additional congregations. Scattered along the
East coast from New York to Florida, all regard Bishop Grace as
their founder. Local houses share a common name, but have thus
far resisted attempts to organize a single body because of different
worship customs.

UNITED CHRISTIAN EVANGELISTIC ASSOCIATION (1962-   )

       The United Christian Evangelistic Association, founded in
1962, is the corporate vehicle of the Rev. Dr. Frederick J. Eikerenkoetter II, popularly known as Rev. Ike to his listeners on a national radio network of eighty stations and viewers of his regional
television specials. The evangelist's distinctive message of material
prosperity by demand spelled out in his Blessing Plan is regularly
proclaimed to capacity crowds at his 5,000 seat headquarters church
in the Washington Heights section of New York City. The theory of
blessing and healing taught by this Ridgeland, South Carolina native
and taught in his church institute is: "I want my pie now, with ice
cream on top." Never, "Pul-eee-eze, Jeee-sus! If it's your will,
Loord."

1151   That t-bone religion.
      In Time, 100 (Dec. 11, 1972), 97.

--PERIODICALS

1152   Action!   1-   1962-
      Boston

UNITED HOUSE OF PRAYER FOR ALL PEOPLE, CHURCH ON THE
  ROCK OF THE APOSTOLIC FAITH (1926-   )

     In 1903 Charles Emmanuel Grace, nineteen-year-old native of
the Cape Verde Islands, arrived in New Bedford, Massachusetts.
He worked at a variety of jobs: cook, grocer, and patent medicine
salesman.   About 1919 Grace opened the first House of Prayer in a
building he himself had built in West Wareham, Massachusetts.   Later
he secured a job as cook on a Southern railroad and evangelized
as he had opportunity.   In 1927 Grace incorporated the United
House of Prayer for All People, Church on the Rock of the Apostolic
Faith at Washington, D.C.   He concentrated on poverty-scarred
urban areas, taking "rocks" that no one else would use to build
his church.   Venerated as "Sweet Daddy" Grace by the faithful, he
established centers in New Haven, New York, Buffalo, Philadelphia,
Baltimore, Washington, Newport News, Charlotte, Columbia, Savannah, and Augusta.   Each center provides low-rent housing and em-
ployment in church-related enterprises to members.   Ostracized by
sister groups for its near-worship of Grace (By grace are you
saved), the United House of Prayer permits unrestrained emotional-
ism in worship.   Speaking in tongues, dancing, falling into trances,
and jerking are common.   The calendar includes days commemorating
events in the lives of the founder and his successor, Walter McCollough (Sweet Daddy Grace McCollough).   Protest over the elevation
of the latter in 1962 by means of a court-ordered election resulted
in formation of the rival True Grace Memorial House of Prayer, and
left the original body with 137 churches and approximately 27,500
members scattered from coast to coast.

1153   Alland, Alexander, 1931-
      "Possession" in a revivalistic Negro church.   In Journal for
      the Scientific Study of Religion, 1 (Spring 1962), 204-213;
      abridged in Knudten, R. D., ed.   The sociology of religion:
      an anthrology.   New York, c1967, 83-92.

1154   Clark, Elmer Talmage, 1886-1961.
      The small sects in America, [by] Elmer T. Clark.   Nash-
      ville, Cokesbury Press, c1937.   311 p.   On House of Prayer:
      p. 149-152.   DLC, OkBetC

1155   Clark, Elmer Talmage, 1886-1961.
        The small sects in America, [by] Elmer T. Clark. Rev.
        ed. New York, Abingdon-Cokesbury Press, 1949. 256 p.
        On House of Prayer: p. 122-124. DLC, RPB

1156   Court ousts Daddy Grace [!] successor, names lawyer as
        church receiver.
        In Evening Star (Washington), 109 (Aug. 25, 1961), 1A-2A.

1157   Daddy Grace cult joins estate fight.
        In Washington Post, 83 (June 10, 1960), B2.

1158   Eddy, George Norman, 1906-
        Store-front religion, [by] G. Norman Eddy. In Religion
        in Life, 28 (Winter 1958/1959), 68-85 [United House of Prayer
        for All People: p. 74-78]; abridged in Lee, R., ed. Cities
        and churches; readings on the urban church. Philadelphia,
        c1962, 177-194 [United House of Prayer for All People, p.
        182-187].

1159   Eddy, George Norman, 1906-
        The true believers: some impressions of American deviant
        religions, [by] G. Norman Eddy. Boston, 195-. MBU

1160   Fauset, Arthur Huff, 1899-
        Black gods of the metropolis: Negro religious cults of the
        urban North. Philadelphia, University of Pennsylvania Press;
        London, H. Milford, Oxford University Press, 1944. x,
        126 p. (Publications of the Philadelphia Anthropological Society,
        3; Brinton memorial series, [2]) Based on thesis (Ph.D.)--
        University of Pennsylvania. "United House of Prayer for All
        People": p. 22-30. DLC, TxWB

1161   Nichol, John Thomas, 1928-
        Pentecostalism. New York, Harper & Row, 1966. xvi,
        264 p. Based on thesis (Ph.D.)--Boston University. "The
        United House of Prayer for All People": p. 147-151. DLC,
        MCE, MH, MSohG

1162   Robinson, John W.
        A song, a shout, a prayer, [by] John W. Robinson. In
        Lincoln, C. E., ed. The black experience in religion. Garden
        City, N.Y., 213-236.

1163   Whiting, Albert Nathaniel, 1917-
        "From saint to shuttler": an analysis of sectarian types,
        [by] Albert N. Whiting. In Quarterly Review of Higher Edu-
        cation among Negroes, 23 (Oct. 1955), 133-140.

1164   Whiting, Albert Nathaniel, 1917-
        The United House of Prayer for All People; a case study

of a charismatic sect, [by] Albert N. Whiting. Washington,
1952. xi, 319 l. Thesis (Ph.D.)--American University.
DAU

--CONTROVERSIAL LITERATURE

1165 The truth and facts of the United House of Prayer for All
      People and the most honorable Bishop W. McCollough, leader.
      Washington, 1968. viii, 100 p. DLC

--PERIODICALS

1166 Grace magazine. 1- 19 -
      Washington

--EASTERN STATES

    -- --NEW YORK

    (New York City)

1167 Daddy Grace to use fire hose on 300.
      In New York Amsterdam News, 29 (July 28, 1956), 1.

1168 Fire hose baptism.
      In Ebony, 10 (Oct. 1955), 102-104, 106.

1169 Grace to Harlem.
      In Time, 31 (Mar. 7, 1938), 30.

--SOUTHERN STATES

    -- --DISTRICT OF COLUMBIA

    (Washington)

1170 Rhodes, Kathleen G.
      Longtime fire hose baptism tradition fading: United House
      of Prayer to use new pool, [by] Kathleen G. Rhodes. In
      Washington Post, 101 (Sept. 1, 1978), C19.

PART V.   SCHOOLS

Unlike parts II-IV, which consist of summary histories of churches
and associations with related bibliography, Part V combines directory
information and related bibliography.   In this section schools are
listed alphabetically without regard to denominational sponsorship
or affiliation.   Listing is under the most recent name, followed by
former and present locations with dates and former names with
dates.   When appropriate, the sponsoring church or association is
recorded at the end of the entry.   If bibliography is included it
comes immediately after the entry.   Only institutions with substantial
black enrollments are included.

1171   AENON BIBLE COLLEGE.   Est. 1941.
   Columbus, Oh., 1941-1981; Indianapolis, In., 1982- .
1941-1975 as Aenon Bible School.   Pentecostal Assemblies of
the World.

1172   Golder, Morris Ellis, 1913-
   History of the Pentecostal Assemblies of the World, [by]
Morris E. Golder.   Indianapolis, 1973.   195 p.   "Aenon Bible
School":   p. 162.   CPFT

1173   AENON BIBLE COLLEGE.   Est. 197-.
   Los Angeles, Ca.   Pentecostal Assemblies of the World.

1174   AENON BIBLE COLLEGE.   Est. 1978.
   Philadelphia, Pa., 1978- .   Pentecostal Assemblies of the
World.

1175   ALABAMA MISSION SCHOOL.   Est. 1912.
   Brent, Al., 1912-1944.   Wesleyan Methodist Connection (or
Church) of America.

1176   BAY RIDGE CHRISTIAN COLLEGE.   Est. 1961.
   Kendleton, Tx., 1961- .   Church of God (Anderson, Indiana)

1177   BIBLE WAY TRAINING SCHOOL.   Est. 1945.
   Washington, 1945- .   Bible Way Church of Our Lord Jesus
Christ World Wide.

1178   BOYDTON INSTITUTE. Est. 1879.
       Boydton, Va., 1879-1929. Christian and Missionary Alli-
ance, 1911-1923; Church of Christ (Holiness) U.S.A., 1923-
1929.

1179   Cobbins, Otho Beale, 1895-
       History of Church of Christ (Holiness) U.S.A., 1895-1965.
Otho P. Cobbins, editor-in-chief. Chicago, National Publish-
ing Board, Church of Christ (Holiness) U.S.A.; printed by
Vantage Press, New York, c1966. 446 p. "Boydton Institute,
Virginia, gift": p. 328.

1180   C. H. MASON THEOLOGICAL SEMINARY. Est. 1970.
       Atlanta, Ga., 1970- . Church of God in Christ.

1181   C. H. MASON THEOLOGICAL SEMINARY.
       C. H. Mason Theological Seminary building fund campaign.
Atlanta, 197-. 8 p.

1182   CENTRAL FREE METHODIST SCHOOL. Est. 1946.
       Shreveport, La., 1946- . Free Methodist Church of North
America.

1183   CHRIST MISSIONARY AND INDUSTRIAL COLLEGE. Est. 1897.
       Jackson, Ms., 1897- . 1897-1907 as Christ's Holiness
School. Church of Christ (Holiness) U.S.A.

1184   Cobbins, Otho Beale, 1895-
       History of Church of Christ (Holiness) U.S.A., 1895-1965.
Otho B. Cobbins, editor-in-chief. Chicago, National Publish-
ing Board, Church of Christ (Holiness) U.S.A.; printed by
Vantage Press, New York, c1966. 446 p. "C. M. and I.
College": p. 322-345. DLC, OkEG

1185   CHURCH OF CHRIST BIBLE INSTITUTE. Est. 1926.
       New York, 1926- . Church of Our Lord Jesus Christ of
the Apostolic Faith.

1186   DELIVERANCE BIBLE INSTITUTE. Est. 1966.
       Newark, N.J., 1966- . Deliverance Evangelistic Centers.

1187   EBENEZER BIBLE INSTITUTE (London). Est. 1977.
       London, 1977- . New Testament Church of God.

1188   Brooks, Ira V.
       Where do we go from here? [By] Ira V. Brooks. London,
1982. 80 p., 8 p. of plates On Ebenezer Bible Institute
(London): p. 65-67. TCleL

1189   EBENEZER BIBLE INSTITUTE (Midlands). Est. 1963.
       Birmingham, 1963- . 1963-1964 as New Testament Church
of God Bible School. New Testament Church of God.

1190 Brooks, Ira V.
          Where do we go from here? [By] Ira V. Brooks. London,
          1982. 80 p., 8 p. of plates "A brief historical review of
          Ebenezer Bible Institute": p. 65-67. TCleL

1191 EDMONDSON INSTITUTE AND ORPHANAGE. Est. 192-.
          Athens, Tx. Church of the Living God, the Pillar and
          Ground of the Truth (General Assembly)

1192 EMMANUEL BIBLE INSTITUTE. Est. 195-.
          Los Angeles, Ca. Church of God in Christ.

1193 FLORIDA BIBLE INSTITUTE. Est. 1971.
          Jacksonville, Fl., 1971- . Church of God (Cleveland,
          Tennessee)

1194 Hughes, Ray Harrison, 1924-
          Preparing workers for the harvest, [by] Ray H. Hughes.
          In Church of God Evangel, 61 (Feb. 28, 1972), 20-21.

1195 FULLER NORMAL AND INDUSTRIAL INSTITUTE. Est. 1912.
          Atlanta, Ga., 1912-1913; Toccoa, Ga., 1913-1923; Green-
          ville, S.C., 1923- . Colored Fire Baptized Holiness Church,
          1912-1922; Fire Baptized Holiness Church of God, 1922-1926;
          Fire Baptized Holiness Church of God of the Americas, 1926- .

1196 Fire Baptized Holiness Church of God of the Americas.
          [Program]: The twenty-third international quadrennial
          General Council of the Fire Baptized Holiness Church of God
          of the Americas, beginning Tuesday, June 8, 1982, through
          Sunday, June 13, 1982, Fuller Normal and Industrial Institute,
          901 Anderson Road, Greenville, S.C. [Atlanta], Printed by
          Economy Printing Co., Avondale Estates, Ga., 1982. 263 p.
          Cover title. "Fuller Normal and Industrial Institute, organized
          1912": p. 45-47.

1197 FUNDAMENTAL BIBLE SEMINARY AND COLLEGE. Est. 19--.
          ----, Ok.

1198 JACKSON MEMORIAL CHRISTIAN COLLEGE. Est. 197-.
          Topeka, Ks. Church of God in Christ.

1199 MATTHEWS-SCIPPIO ACADEMY. Est. 1963.
          Ocala, Fl., 1963- . Church of God by Faith.

1200 NAZARENE TRAINING COLLEGE. Est. 1948.
          Institute, W. Va., 1948-1970. 1948-1965 as Nazarene Bible
          Institute. Church of the Nazarene.

1201 Bowman, Roger Eugene
          Color us Christian: the story of the Church of the

Nazarene among America's blacks, [by] Roger E. Bowman.
Kansas City, Mo., Nazarene Publishing House, 1975. 85 p.
On Nazarene Training College: p. 51-61. IKON, MoKN,
OMtvN, TNTN

1202   Hale, Edwin Erwin, 1894-1976.
       The Nazarene Bible Institute, [by] Edwin E. Hale. In
       Herald of Holiness, 37 (Sept. 6, 1948), 13.

1203   Rogers, Warren Allen, 1917-
       From sharecropper to goodwill ambassador: the Warren
       Rogers story; the spiritual odyssey of a man in the church,
       [by] Warren A. Rogers [with] Kenneth Vogt. Kansas City,
       Mo., Beacon Hill Press of Kansas City, c1979. 76 p.
       "Nazarene Bible College, West Virginia": p. 30-32, 48-50.
       MoKN, OkBetC

1204   R. C. LAWSON INSTITUTE. Est. 194-.
       Southern Pines, N.C. Church of Our Lord
       Jesus Christ of the Apostolic Faith.

1205   R. F. WILLIAMS COLLEGE. Est. 197-.
       Twinsburg, Oh. Church of God in Christ.

1206   ST. DAVID ORTHODOX SPIRITUAL SEMINARY. Est. 1949.
       Des Moines, Ia., 1949-19--. National David Spiritual
       Temple of Christ Church Union.

1207   SAINTS BIBLE COLLEGE. Est. 197-.
       Sacramento, Ca. Church of God in Christ.

1208   SAINTS JUNIOR COLLEGE. Est. 1918.
       Lexington, Ms., 1918-1976. 1918-1926 as Saints Home
       School; 1926-1954 as Saints Industrial and Literary School.
       Church of God in Christ.

1209   Cornelius, Lucille J.
       The pioneer: history of the Church of God in Christ.
       Compiled and ed. by Lucille J. Cornelius. [Memphis, Church
       of God in Christ], c1975. vii, 103 p. "Lexington school and
       others": p. 45-48. MiRochOU

1210   SAMUEL KELSEY BIBLE INSTITUTE. Est. 197-.
       Washington, D.C. Church of God in Christ.

1211   UNITED CHRISTIAN COLLEGE. Est. 1944.
       Goldsboro, N.C., 1944- . 1944-196- as Bible Training
       Institute. United Holy Church of America, 1944-1977; Original
       United Holy Church of the World, 1977-1980; Original United
       Holy Church International, 1980 .

1212 UNIVERSAL BIBLE COLLEGE.   Est. 19--.
      Alamo, Tn.

1213 WILLIAM J. SEYMOUR PENTECOSTAL FELLOWSHIP OF HOWARD
      UNIVERSITY.
          Washington, D.C., 1965- . 1965-1975 as United Pente-
      costal Association of Howard University.

1214 Lewis, James O.
          The United Pentecostal Association, [by] James O. Lewis.
      In Tinney, J. S. In the tradition of William J. Seymour:
      essays commemorating the dedication of Seymour House at
      Howard University. Washington, 1978, 34-36.

1215 Servance, Sylvester
          The Spirit on campus: a diary, [by] Sylvester Servance.
      In Tinney, J. S. In the tradition of William J. Seymour:
      essays commemorating the dedication of Seymour House at
      Howard University. Washington, 1978, 34-36.

1216 Short, Betty (Lancaster)
          A woman's ministry, [by] Betty Lancaster Short. In
      Tinney, J. S. In the tradition of William J. Seymour: es-
      says commemorating the dedication of Seymour House at How-
      ard University. Washington, 1978, 53-55.

1217 Short, Stephen N.
          The miracle of Seymour House, [by] Stephen N. Short.
      In Tinney, J. S. In the tradition of William J. Seymour:
      essays commemorating the dedication of Seymour House at
      Howard University. Washington, 1978, 47-52.

1218 Short, Stephen N.
          Pentecostal student movement at Howard: 1946-1977, [by]
      Stephen N. Short. In Spirit, 1:2 (1977), 11-23; reprinted in
      Tinney, J. S. In the tradition of William J. Seymour: essays
      commemorating the dedication of Seymour House at Howard
      University. Washington, 1978, 21-33.

1219 Tinney, James Steven, 1942-
          In the tradition of William J. Seymour; essays commemorat-
      ing the dedication of Seymour House at Howard University,
      [by] James S. Tinney [and] Stephen N. Short, editors.
      Washington, Spirit Press, 1978. 81 [23] p.

PART VI. BIOGRAPHY

As in Part V, this section contains directory information and related bibliography. Individuals are listed alphabetically regardless
of their race or denominational affiliation. An asterisk (*) indicates
a white person included because of his or her work among blacks or
because of his or her membership in a predominantly black denomination. The name of the person, with birth and/or death dates, is
followed by a record of church or association affiliation(s), occupa-
tion(s), and date(s) and/or place(s) of birth and/or death.
Brackets ([ ]) imply that church affiliation was assigned by the
compiler on the basis of inductive evidence. If bibliography is included, works written by the subject precede those written about
him or her. For collective biography see "--Biography" as a sub-
division in Parts I-IV.

1220 ADAMS, John Linsy (1906-)
        WWIR (1975-1976), 3.
        PeAW
        Minister, tax accountant
        b. Sept. 1, 1906, Jacksonville, Fl.

1221 ADAMS, Joseph H.
        RWWAS, 67, 97-98.
        WCCChr, UWCCChrAF
        Pastor, bishop

1221a ADAMS, Leonard W.
        CN
        Pastor, author

1222 AKERS, Elmer F.
        GBPAW, 69.
        PeAW
        Pastor, bishop

1223 AKIN, Irene Omalee (1910-)
        MOM (1975), 338.
        CG (T), CGP
        Pastor
        b. Sept. 23, 1910, Royse City, Tx.

215

1224   ALICEA, Benjamin (1952-   )
       CG (C)
       Seminary admin., author

1225   Alicea, Benjamin, 1952-
       Religion and missions in Puerto Rico, [by] Banjamin Alicea.
       New Brunswick, N.J., 1978. iv, 123 1. Thesis (M.A.)--New
       Brunswick Theological Seminary. NjNbS

1226   *ALLEN, Asa Alonso (1911-1970)
           HATAP, 6, 8, 57, 61, 65, 66-75, 79, 85, 87, 88, 89, 97-
       98, 99, 102, 104-105, 113-114, 172, 175, 194-206, 216, 226,
       241, 246, 248-249, 267-268.
           HP, 307, 320, 362, 365-367, 375, 377, 383, 416, 422, 464.
           HWSBM, 36, 104-105, 107, 141, 148.
           MP, 1-53, 83, 240, 249.
           SFH, 42, 54, 64, 71, 78, 79, 87, 89-90, 97, 99, 111, 126,
       133, 150, 155, 178.
           AGGC, I
           Pastor, evangelist, editor, author
           b. Mar. 27, 1911, Sulphur Rock, Ar.
           d. June 11, 1970, San Francisco, Ca.

1227   Allen, Asa Alonso, 1911-1970.
           Born to lose, bound to win; an autobiography, [by] A. A.
       Allen, with Walter Wagner. Garden City, N.Y., Doubleday,
       1970. 202 p. DLC

1228   Allen, Asa Alonso, 1911-1970.
           My cross: the life story of A. A. Allen as told by him-
       self. Miracle Valley, Az., A. A. Allen Revivals, 1957.
       95 p. Cover title. AzFU

1229   Allen, Lexie E.
           God's man of faith and power: the life story of A. A.
       Allen written by his wife, Lexie E. Allen. Hereford, Az.,
       A. A. Allen, c1954. 184 p. MoSpCB

1230   Allen, Lexie E.
           Ein Mann Gottes mit Glauben und Kraft. Übersetzt von
       C. R. Leonberg, Württ., Philadelphia-Verlag, 1960. 104 p.
       Translation of God's man of faith and power.

1231   Elinson, Howard
           The implications of Pentecostal religion for intellectualism,
       politics, and race relations. In American Journal of Sociology,
       70 (Jan. 1965), 403-415.

1232   Getting back double from God.
           In Time, 93 (Mar. 7, 1969), 64, 67.

1233 Hedgepeth, William
        Brother A. A. Allen on the gospel trail: he feels, he
      heals & he turns you on with God. In Look, 33 (Oct. 7,
      1969), 23-31.

1234 ALLEN, Clarence (1901-1974)
        GBPAW, 36.
        GHPAW, 153, 157.
        PeAW
        Pastor, bishop
        b. 1901, Elberton, Ga.
        d. 1974, Hartford, Ct.

1235 ALLEN, Gilbert Lee (1943-   )
        AOHUTR
        PeAW
        Pastor
        b. Jan. 15, 1943, Detroit, Mi.

1236 ALLEN, Lyndon Samuel (1934-   )
        MOM (1975), 222.
        CGP
        Pastor
        b. May 15, 1934, Manchester, Jamaica

1237 ALSTON, Gene
        WJGIG, 79, 97-99.
        FMCNA
        Pastor, school prin.
        b. 194-, Washington, D.C.

1238 ANDERSON, C. L.
        CP, 94. WWIR (1985), 8.
        CGIC
        Pastor, bishop

1239 ANDERSON, Jesse (1911-   )
        CG (C)
        b. 1911, Bahamas

1240 Richardson, Carl Herbert, 1939-
        A black family demonstrates home is where love is, [by]
      Carl H. Richardson. In Church of God Evangel, 61 (Feb. 28,
      1972), 14-16.

1241 ANIM, Peter (1890-   )
        EMIB, FT, AC, CAC
        Pastor, general supt.
        b. Feb. 4, 1890, Boso, Volta region, Ghana

1242 Wyllie, Robert W.
        Pioneers of Ghanian Pentecostalism: Peter Anim and James

McKeown, [by] Robert W. Wyllie. In Journal of Religion in
Africa, 6:2 (1974), 109-122.

1243 APPLEBY, Henry Lloyd (1927-   )
      WWIR (1977), 17.
      CGIC
      Pastor
      b. Aug. 31, 1927, Kingston, Jamaica

1244 ARDREY, J. W.
      RWWAS, 72, 73, 75, 77, 97.
      CG (AP), ACChrG, UCJA
      Pastor, bishop

1245 ARNOLD, Florencia
      RC, M, I
      Evangelist

1246 West, Malcolm R.
      Rev. Florencia Arnold shuns ties of religion, blazes her
      own trails, [by] Malcolm R. West. In Jet, 54 (May 4, 1978),
      44-45.

1247 ARRINGTON, Juanita Roby (1936-   )
      WWIR (1985), 11.
      AOHCG
      Teacher, editor
      b. Dec. 15, 1936, Birmingham, Al.

1248 ARTHUR, Ralph James (1924-   )
      MOM (1975), 222.
      CGP
      Pastor
      b. Apr. 22, 1924, Bahamas

1249 ARTHUR, Rudolph Withfield (1945-   )
      MOM (1975), 223.
      CGP
      Pastor
      b. Feb. 2, 1945, Turks Island, Bahamas

1250 ASH, Michael O. (1955-   )
      MOM (1975), 223.
      CGP
      Evangelist
      b. Aug. 6, 1955, Tallahassee, Fl.

1251 BAILEY, Anne L. (1894-1975)
      CP, 29, 93.
      MHAFY, 85, 136.
      Ba, CGIC

         Missionary (evangelist)
         b. 1894, Temple, Tx.
         d. Dec. 18, 1975, Detroit, Mi.

1252 Church of God in Christ leader, Anne L. Bailey, dies.
         In Jet, 49 (Jan. 8, 1976), 6.

1253 Garner, June (Brown)
         She went to make fun, but now Mother Bailey leads her
         church, by June Brown Garner. In Sunday News Magazine
         (Detroit) (June 20, 1971), 10, 40. At head of title: June
         Brown's Detroit.

1254 BAILEY, John Seth
         CP, 72.
         MBAFY, 75, 76, 77, 88, 138.
         TBPALM, 96. WWIR (1985), 15.
         CGIC
         Evangelist, pastor, bishop

1255 BAILEY, Rubie O. (1909-)
         MOM (1975), 339.
         CG (T), CGP
         Pastor
         b. May 6, 1909, Clayton, N.C.

1256 BAKER, George, self-named Father Divine (1877-1965)
         MHAFY, 61.
         NYT (Sept. 11, 1965), 1:5; (Sept. 12, 1965), 86:8.
         WAB (1975), 54-55.
         FDPM
         Evangelist
         b. 1877, near Savannah, Ga.
         d. Sept. 10, 1965, Gladwyne near Philadelphia, Pa.

1257 Baker, George, self-named Father Divine, 1877-1965.
         Father Divine and the Peace Mission movement. n.p.,
         197-. portfolio ([19] pieces). PPT

1258 Alexander, Jack
         All Father's chillun got heavens, [by] Jack Alexander.
         In Saturday Evening Post, 212 (Nov. 18, 1939), 8-9, 64, 66,
         69-70, 72, 75.

1259 Altitude record.
         In Time, 34 (Dec. 18, 1939), 17.

1260 Angels over Newport.
         In Time, 34 (July 24, 1939), 44.

1261 Bach, Marcus Louis, 1906-
         Strange sects and curious cults, [by] Marcus Bach.

New York, Dodd, Mead, 1961.   viii, 277 p.   "Father Divine":
p. 125-139.   DLC, Ok

1262   Bird, Robert S.
       Father Divine's movement expands, [by] Robert S. Bird.
       In New York Times, 88 (July 2, 1939), 1OE.

1263   Black elbow.
       In Time, 32 (Aug. 8, 1938), 7-8.

1264   Buehrer, Edwin T.
       Father Divine enters politics, [by] Edwin T. Buehrer.   In
       Christian Century, 53 (Oct. 7, 1936), 1334.

1265   Buehrer, Edwin T.
       Harlem's god, [by] Edwin T. Buehrer.   In Christian Cen-
       tury, 52 (Dec. 11, 1935), 1590-1593.

1266   Burnham, Kenneth Edward, 1915-
       Father Divine: a case study of charismatic leadership, [by]
       Kenneth E. Burnham.   Philadelphia, 1963. xvi, 206 l.   Thesis
       (Ph.D.)--University of Pennsylvania.   PU

1266a Burnham, Kenneth Edward, 1915-
       God comes to America: Father Divine and the Peace Mis-
       sion movement, [by] Kenneth E. Burnham.   Boston, Lambeth
       Press, 1979.   167 p.   DLC

1267   Cosmic lubritorium.
       In Time, 62 (Sept. 21, 1953), 79-80.

1268   A deity derepersonifitized.
       In Time, 86 (Sept. 17, 1965), 41.

1269   Denlinger, Sutherland
       Heaven is in Harlem, [by] Sutherland Denlinger.   In
       Forum and Century, 95 (Apr. 1936), 211-218.

1270   Divine babble.
       In Time, 27 (Mar. 16, 1936), 30, 32.   Includes interview
       with Robert Ernest Hume of Union Theological Seminary, New
       York.

1271   Divine dinner.
       In Newsweek, 29 (May 12, 1947), 31-32.

1272   Divine judgment.
       In Literary Digest, 123 (May 1, 1937), 6-7.

1273   Divine ultimatum.
       In Time, 61 (Mar. 9, 1953), 72, 74.

1274 Divine week.
      In Time, 28 (Aug. 31, 1936), 26, 28.

1275 Father Divine.
      In Commonweal, 26 (May 7, 1937), 46.

1276 Father Divine: little black man in great big Rolls Royce.
      In News-Week, 8 (Aug. 29, 1936), 34.

1277 Fishburne, Dannette
      The contributions of Father Divine to social welfare, [by]
      Dannette Fishburne. In Spirit, 1:1 (1977), 16-20.

1278 $500,000 (cash) heaven.
      In Newsweek, 34 (Oct. 31, 1949), 20.

1279 Flynn, John Thomas, 1882-1964.
      Other people's money, [by] John T. Flynn. In New Re-
      public, 91 (May 26, 1937), 73-74.

1280 Gardner, Velmer J.
      "I spent Saturday night in the devil's house": an exposure
      [!] of Father Divine, [by] Velmer J. Gardner. Springfield,
      Mo., Velmer Gardner Evangelistic Association, c1952. 47 p.
      OkTOR

1281 God's income.
      In Time, 28 (Dec. 28, 1936), 18.

1282 Goldsmith, Janet
      Father Divine and the Peace Mission movement, [by] Janet
      Goldsmith. New York, 1977. 86 l. Thesis (M.A.)--City
      College of New York. NNR

1283 Grey, Alan
      God, Inc., gets the ads, [by] Alan Grey. In Canadian
      Forum, 19 (Nov. 1939), 249-250, 252.

1284 Hall, Gordon Langley
      The sawdust trail: the story of American evangelism.
      Philadelphia, Macrae Smith Co., 1964. 249 p. "Father will
      provide": p. 207-218. DLC, IDeKN, Ok

1285 Hantman, Sid
      No food shortage for "God," [by] Sid Hantman. In Negro
      Digest, 4 (Oct. 1946), 25-26. Condensed from International
      News Service.

1286 Harkness, Georgia Elma, 1891-1974.
      Father Divine's righteous government, [by] Georgia Hark-
      ness. In Christian Century, 82 (Oct. 13, 1965), 1259-1261.

1287 Harris, Sara
        Father Divine, holy husband, [by] Sara Harris, with the
        assistance of Harriet Crittenden. Garden City, N.Y., Double-
        day, 1953. 320 p. DLC, OKentU

1288 Harris, Sara
        Father Divine, holy husband, [by] Sara Harris, with the
        assistance of Harriet Crittenden. Garden City, N.Y., Double-
        day, 1954, c1953. 354 p. OClU

1289 Harris, Sara
        Father Divine, [by] Sara Harris, with the assistance of
        Harriet Crittendon [i.e., Crittenden]. Newly rev. and ex-
        panded, and with an introd. by John Henrik Clarke. New
        York, Collier Books, 1971. xxxiv, 377 p. DLC

1290 Heaven-on-the-Hudson.
        In Newsweek, 12 (Aug. 8, 1938), 10-12.

1291 "Heaven": the forces of evil imperil Harlem's dark Divine.
        In News-Week, 9 (May 1, 1937), 11.

1292 Heavenly treasure.
        In Time, 35 (Mar. 18, 1940), 44.

1293 Hoshor, John
        God in a Rolls Royce: the rise of Father Divine: madman,
        menace, or messiah, [by] John Hoshor. New York, Hillman,
        Curl, 1936. 272 p. DLC

1294 Hoshor, John
        God in a Rolls Royce; the rise of Father Divine: madman,
        menace, or messiah, [by] John Hoshor. Freeport, N.Y.,
        Books for Libraries Press, 1971. 272 p. (The black heritage
        library collection) Reprint of 1936 ed. DLC

1295 Kelley, Hubert
        Heaven incorporated, [by] Hubert Kelley. In American
        Magazine, 121 (Jan. 1936), 40-41, 106-108.

1296 Lahey, Edwin A.
        Peace! It's still wonderful, [by] Edwin A. Lahey. In
        Negro Digest, 2 (May 1944) Condensed from Chicago Daily
        News.

1297 Levick, Lionel
        Father Divine is God, [by] Lionel Levick. In Forum and
        Century, 92 (Oct. 1934), 217-221; reply by Oliver G. Powell
        (Divine and lung power), 92 (Nov. 1934), [suppl.] x-xi.

1298 Liebling, Abbott Joseph, 1904-1963.
      The rise of Father Divine, [by] A. J. Liebling. In Satur-
      day Review of Literature, 14 (Oct. 3, 1936), 11.

1299 Life with Father.
      In Newsweek, 66 (Sept. 20, 1965), 28.

1300 McKay, Claude, 1890-1948.
      Father Divine's rebel angel, [by] Claude McKay. In
      American Mercury, 51 (Sept. 1940), 73-80.

1301 McKay, Claude, 1890-1948.
      "There goes God!" The story of Father Divine and his
      angels, [by] Claude McKay. In Nation, 140 (Feb. 6, 1935),
      151-153.

1302 McKelway, St. Clair, 1905-1980.
      Who is this king of glory? [By] St. Clair McKelway and
      A. J. Liebling. In New Yorker, 12 (June 13, 1936), 21-26,
      28; 12 (June 20, 1936), 22-26, 28; 12 (June 27, 1936), 22-26,
      28, 32; abridged in Reader's Digest, 29 (Sept. 1936), 79-84.

1303 Made in heaven.
      In Time, 48 (Aug. 19, 1946), 45.

1304 Malediction.
      In Time, 62 (Nov. 30, 1953), 64-65.

1305 Mathison, Richard Randolph, 1919-1980.
      Faiths, cults and sects of America; from atheism to Zen,
      [by] Richard R. Mathison. Indianapolis, Bobbs-Merrill,, 1960.
      384 p. "Father Divine": p. 235-239. OClU, Ok

1306 Mathison, Richard Randolph, 1919-1980.
      God is a millionaire, [by] Richard Mathison. Indianapolis,
      Bobbs-Merrill, 1962, c1960. 384 p. (Charter books, 106)
      First published in 1960 under title: Faiths, cults and sects
      of America. "Father Divine": p. 235-239. FJ

1307 Mead, Frank Spencer, 1898-1982.
      God in Harlem, [by] Frank S. Mead. In Christian Cen-
      tury, 53 (Aug. 26, 1936), 1133-1135.

1308 Messiah's troubles.
      In Time, 29 (May 3, 1937), 61-63.

1309 Moon, Henry Lee
      Thank you, Father so sweet. In New Republic, 88 (Sept.
      16, 1936), 147-150.

1310 A "mortal" mystery.
      In Newsweek, 49 (June 10, 1957), 35.

1311 Parker, Robert Allerton, 1889-1970.
      The incredible messiah: the deification of Father Divine,
      [by] Robert Allerton Parker. Boston, Little, Brown, 1937.
      xiii, 323 p. DLC, MB, NcD, NN, OCl, OO, OrU, PP, ViU,
      WaS

1312 Peace, brother!
      In Time, 54 (Oct. 31, 1949), 15-16.

1313 People.
      In Review of Reviews, 95 (June 1937), 23-24.

1314 People.
      In Time, 49 (May 12, 1947), 48.

1315 A prophet and a Divine meet.
      In Life, 35 (Sept. 28, 1953), 103-104, 106.

1316 Rasky, Frank
      Harlem's religious zealots, [by] Frank Rasky. In Tomor-
      row, 9 (Nov. 1949), 11-17, abridged in Negro Digest, 8
      (Mar. 1950), 52-62.

1317 A religious party.
      In Time, 29 (Apr. 12, 1937), 59-60.

1318 Revolt in "heaven."
      In Newsweek, 15 (Jan. 1, 1940), 29-30.

1319 Stewart, Ollie
      "Father Divine is God," [by] Ollie Stewart. In Scribner's
      Commentator, 8 (June 1940), 20-26; abridged in Reader's
      Digest, 36 (June 1940), 22-26, under title: Harlem god in
      his heaven.

1320 Streator, George
      Father Divine, [by] George Streator. In Commonweal,
      31 (Dec. 15, 1939), 176-178.

1321 The ten richest Negroes in America.
      In Ebony, 4 (Apr. 1949), 13-18. "Father Divine": p. 13.

1322 Thomason, John W.
      Father Divine's afflatus, [by] John W. Thomason, Jr. In
      American Mercury, 39 (Dec. 1936), 500-505.

1323 Transition.
      In Newsweek, 28 (Aug. 19, 1946), 52.

1324 Weisbrot, Robert
      Father Divine and the struggle for racial equality, [by]
      Robert Weisbrot. Urbana, University of Illinois Press, c1983.
      241 p. (Blacks in the new world) DLC

1325 Weisbrot, Robert
      Father Divine and the struggle for racial equality, [by]
      Robert Weisbrot. Boston, Beacon Press, 1984, c1983. 241 p.
      Reprint of 1983 ed. DLC

1326 Wilson, Earl, 1907-
      Hahn'tchuglad? [By] Earl Wilson. In Negro Digest, 2
      (Mar. 1944), 61-63. Condensed from New York Post.

1327 BAKER, Richard

      Singer, author

1328 Baker, Richard
      I've learned to smile again, [by] Richard Baker as told to
      Marion Collins. In Abundant Life, 25 (Jan. 1971), 19-20.

1329 BALDWIN, James (1924-)
      CA (new rev.), 3

      Writer
      b. Aug. 2, 1924, New York, N.Y.

1330 Baldwin, James, 1924-
      Ga och förkunna det pa bergen. Stockholm, Wahlström &
      Widstrand, 1955. 252 p. Translation of Go tell it on the
      mountain. Autobiographical novel. DLC, InU

1331 Baldwin, James, 1924-
      Go tell it on the mountain. New York, Knopf, 1953.
      303 p. Autobiographical novel. DLC, InU

1332 Baldwin, James, 1924-
      Go tell it on the mountain. London, Michael Joseph, 1954.
      256 p. Autobiographical novel. OWibfU, Uk

1333 Baldwin, James, 1924-
      Go tell it on the mountain. With commentary, notes and
      exercises by E. N. Obiechina. London, Longmans, 1966.
      310 p. (Heritage of literature series, sec. B, no. 90)
      Autobiographical novel. ICarbS, Uk

1334 Baldwin, James, 1924-
      Notes of a native son, [by] James Baldwin. New York,
      Dial Press, 1963, c1955. 158 p. DLC, Ok

1335   Baytop, Adrianne Roberts
       James Baldwin and Roger Mais: the Pentecostal theme. In
       Jamaica Journal, 42 (1978), 14-21.

1336   BALLARD, Sylvester (1949-   )
       CN
       Pastor, author

1337   Beegle, Nina
       A Center for hope in Topeka's inner city, [by] Nina
       Beegle. In Herald of Holiness, 71 (Dec. 1, 1982), 11-12.

1338   BARKER, Virgil M. (1879-1974)
       MHAFY, 66, 102, 103, 135, 139
       TBPALM, 95
       CGIC
       Teacher, pastor, bishop
       b. 1879, Drew County, Ar.
       d. Aug. 30, 1974, Kansas City, Mo.

1339   Bishop V. M. Barker dies at 94 years.
       In Kansas City Call (Aug. 30, 1974), 1, 2.

1340   Blue, Louis
       Large crowd at funeral for Bishop Barker. In Kansas City
       Call (Sept. 6, 1974), 1, 2.

1341   Tinney, James Steven, 1942-
       Bishop Barker retires at 92, Dr. E. H. Moore new bishop,
       [by] James S. Tinney. In Kansas City Call (Jan. 23, 1972),
       1.

1342   Tinney, James Steven, 1942-
       Dr. Arenia Mallory recalls early days at Barker Temple,
       [by] James S. Tinney. In Kansas City Call (May 5, 1972),
       10.

1343   *BARNETT, Harry (1888-1952)
       GBPAW, 9.
       GHPAW, 113.
       J, PeAW
       Evangelist, pastor, bishop
       b. 1888, Indianapolis, In.
       d. 1952, Niles, Mi.

1344   BARNETT, Lorena (1908-   )
       MOM (1975), 340.
       CGP
       Pastor
       b. June 15, 1908, Bakewell, Tn.

1345 BASS, Ralph (1893-1972)
        GBPAW, 28.
        GHPAW, 153, 157.
        PeAW
        Pastor, district elder, bishop
        b. 1893, West Jefferson, Oh.
        d. 1972, Dayton, Oh.

1346 BATTLE, Walter Leroy (1921-   )
        WWABA (1985), 48.
        WWIR (1985), 21.
        CGIC, I
        Barber, editor, pastor, radio preacher
        b. July 1, 1921, Battle, Ms.

1347 BEARDEN, J. E. 91893-   )
        CHCCH, 290-291.
        MBaC, CChr (H)
        Pastor
        b. Mar. 7, 1893, Fayette, Ms.

1348 BELL, Dennis Rayford
        RWWAS, 79.
        PeCAFA
        Pastor, bishop, author

1349 BENJAMIN, Kenneth Michael (1944-   )
        MOM (1975), 229.
        CGP
        Pastor, district overseer
        b. Nov. 26, 1944, Tortola, Virgin Islands

1350 BETTERSON, Emma Lee (1917-   )
        MOM (1975), 340.
        CG (T), CGP
        Evangelist, pastor
        b. June 1, 1917, South Carolina

1351 BEVERLY, Sethard
        CG (A)
        Pastor, denominational admin.

1352 BHENGU, Nicholas Bhekinkosi Hepworth (1909-   )
        ATF, 54, 224, 248-249, 271.
        BSFH, 343.
        DBWS, 1, 104-106.
        HP, 66, 71, 122, 126-139, 164, 173, 174, 307, 481, 517-518.
        KWGHW, 263, 336, 338, 339.
        NP, 172.
        Lu, AGSCA
        Pastor, evangelist, author
        b. 1909, Eshowe, Zululand.

1353 Bhengu, Nicholas Bhekinkosi Hepworth, 1909-
        Revival fire in South Africa, [by] Nicholas B. H. Bhengu.
Philadelphia, Afro-American Missionary Crusade, 1949.   15 p.
Autobiography.

1354 Bhengu, Nicholas Bhekinkosi Hepworth, 1909-
        The soul of South Africa, [by] Nicholas Bhengu. In De-
cision, 15 (Oct. 1974), 4; 15 (Nov. 1974), 10. Autobiography.

1355 Dubb, Allie A.
        Community of the saved: an African revivalist church in
the East Cape, [by] Allie A. Dubb. Johannesburg, Witwaters-
rand University Press for African Studies Institute, 1976.
xvii, 175 p. DLC, MH-AH

1356 Hollenweger, Walter Jacob, 1927-
        The Pentecostals: the charismatic movement in the
churches, [by] W. J. Hollenweger. Minneapolis, Augsburg
Publishing House, 1972. xx, 572 p. "First United States
edition." Translation of Enthusiastisches Christentum.
"Nicholas B. H. Bhengu: a charismatic African prophet":
p. 126-139. DLC, MH-AH, TxWaS

1357 Moennich, Martha
        God at work in South Africa. In Evangelical Christian, 54
(Aug. 1958), 368.

1358 BLACKMAN, H. (1870-1946)
            CHCCH, 45-46.
            AME, CGIC, CChr (H)
            Pastor
            b. 1870
            d. Dec. 25, 1946, Canton, Ms.

1359 BLACKMON, John David (1937-   )
            MOM (1975), 230.
            CGP
            Pastor
            b. Mar. 13, 1937, Mount Pleasant, N.C.

1360 BLADES, Joseph Preston
            RTU, 135-136.
            b. 189-, Barbados, W.I.

1361 Ayres, Burt Wilmot, 1865-
        Honor to whom honor is due; the life story of Joseph
Preston Blades, especially as related to Taylor University,
Upland, Indiana. Upland, In., c1951. iv, 71 p. DLC

1362 BLAKE, Charles Edward (1940-   )
            MHAFY, 137.

WWIR (1975-1976), 54.
CGIC
Pastor, editor, district supt., author
b. Aug. 5, 1940, North Little Rock, Ar.

1363 BLAKE, Junious A.
WWIR (1985), 30.
CGIC
Pastor, bishop, author

1364 BOAZ, Ruth (1902-   )
FDPM, AGGC
Domestic, nurse
b. 1902, Waupaca, Wi.

1365 Boaz, Ruth, 1902-
My thirty years with Father Divine, [by] Ruth Boaz. In
Ebony, 20 (May 1965), 88-90, 92, 94-96, 98.

1366 BONNER, William L.
RWWAS, 60, 61-63. WWIR (1985), 33.
COLJCAF
Pastor, bishop, author

1367 Bonner, William L.
My father in the gospel, [by] William L. Bonner. [New
York, 197-] 54 p. Autobiographical.

1368 BOONE, G. M.
RWWAS, 94-95.
PeCAFA, AAChr
Pastor, bishop

1369 BOSTICK, D. E.
MHAFY, 66, 107.
CGIC
Pastor, state overseer

1370 BOWDAN, Frank Reuben (1910-1976)
GBPAW, 31, 46.
GHPAW, 143, 153, 157, 175.
RWWAS, 52.
PeAW
Pastor, district elder, bishop
b. 1910, Los Angeles, Ca.
d. 1976, Los Angeles, Ca.

1371 BOWE, Justus
MHAFY, 52, 63.
CGIC, CGICC, CGIC
Pastor

1372 BOWERS, Paul A. (1929-)
        GBPAW, 58.
        PeAW
        Pastor, bishop
        b. 1929, Oxford, Pa.

1373 BOWMAN, Clarence
        BCUC, 57-58, 59, 61, 65.
        ChrMA, CN
        Pastor, Bible college prof. and dean, editor

1374 BOWMAN, Roger Eugene
        CN
        Pastor, denominational admin., author

1375 Rev. Roger Bowman to K. C. post.
        In Herald of Holiness, 62 (Feb. 14, 1973), 23.

1376 BOYD, Alfred L. (1914-1978)
        GBPAW, 39.
        GHPAW, 153, 157.
        PeAW
        Pastor, district elder, bishop
        b. 1914, Crofton, Ky.
        d. 1978, Bettendorf, Ia.

1377 BOYD, Cauthion Tilmon (1918-)
        BDNM (1975), 41.
        SBHCGRM, 124.
        WWIR (1977), 70.
        CG (A)
        Pastor, military chaplain, denominational official
        b. Nov. 13, 1918, Spencer, N.C.

1378 BOYD, Mary E. Range (1918-)
        WWABA (1980-1981), 78.
        CG (A)
        Teacher
        B. Aug. 26, 1918, Haddock, Ga.

1379 BRAZIEL, David (1920-)
        GBPAW, 55.
        PeAW
        Pastor, district elder, bishop
        b. 1920, Cedartown, Ga.

1380 BRAZIER, Arthur M. (1921-)
        GBPAW, 59.
        HP, 298-299, 309
        WWABA (1977-1978), 94
        PeAW

Pastor, community organizer, bishop, author
b. July 22, 1921, Chicago, Il.

1381 Brazier, Arthur M., 1921-
Black self-determination; the story of the Woodlawn Organization, [by] Arthur M. Brazier. Grand Rapids, Mi.,
Eerdmans, 1969. 148 p. Self-help neighborhood organization
led by the author, a black Pentecostal pastor. DLC, RPB

1382 Brazier, Arthur M., 1921-
What kind of model cities? [By] Arthur M. Brazier. In
Williams, E. N., ed. Delivery systems for model cities; new
concepts in serving the urban community. Chicago, 1969,
7-13. DLC

1383 BREWER, Madeline
WJGIG, 79.
FMCNA
Teacher and prin.

1384 *BRISBIN, Lawrence Edwin (1915-)
GBPAW, 29.
GHPAW, 153, 157, 158, 179.
RWWAS, 53. WWIR (1985), 39.
PeAW
Pastor, district elder, bishop
b. 1915, Grand Rapids, Mi.

1385 BRONSON, Audrey (1930-)
I
Pastor

1386 White, Joyce
Women in the ministry, [by] Joyce White. In Essence, 7
(Nov. 1976), 62-63, 104, 107, 109.

1387 BROOKS, Alphonzo
RWWAS, 66, 67, 68, 98.
WCCChr
Pastor

1388 BROOKS, George Harold (1898-)
GBPAW, 33.
GHPAW, 153, 157.
PeAW
Pastor, district elder, bishop
b. 1898, Brunswick, Md.

1389 BROOKS, Henry Chauncey (-1967)
GBPAW, 34.
RWWAS, 66-67, 68, 98.

COLJCAF, WCCChr
Pastor, supreme bishop
b. 18--, Franklinton, N.C.
d. 1967, Washington, D.C.

1390 BROOKS, John Luke (1896-)
RWWAS, 67, 68, 69, 98.
WCCChr
Pastor, presiding bishop

1391 BROOKS, Johnie Thomas (1928-)
MOM (1975), 233.
CGP
Pastor
b. Sept. 20, 1928, Pasquotank County, N.C.

1392 BROWN, Chester Eugene (1932-)
WWIR (1977), 81.
PeAW
Pastor
b. Apr. 14, 1932, Canton, Oh.

1393 BROWN, Dexton John (1892-)
MOM (1975), 192.
CG (T), CGP
Pastor, district overseer
b. July 23, 1892, Crooked Island, Bahamas

1394 BROWN, E. D.
AMEZ, FCZCC
Pastor

1395 BROWN, Grace
GPC
Bishop, radio preacher

1396 Browne, J. Zamgba
Bishop Grace Brown, believer in action, [by] J. Zamgba
Browne. In New York Amsterdam News, 67 (Mar. 27, 1976),
B4.

1397 BROWN, John C.
PPIB, III, 38.
Ba, CG (SC)
Pastor
d. 19--, Columbia, Tn.

1398 BROWN, Oscar Patrick Johnson (1923-)
WWIR (1985), 83.
CGIC
Pastor, youth leader
b. Mar. 9, 1923, Mobile, Al.

1399 BRUNSON, Louis J. (-1941)
         CHCCH, 46, 47.
         MBaC, CChr (H)
         Pastor   d. 1941, Jackson, Ms.

1400 BRYANT, Clinton L. (1875-1923)
         CGH, 24.
         CLGCWFF
         Pastor, vice chief bishop
         b. July 12, 1875, Goldsboro, N.C.
         d. Feb. 22, 1923, Denison, Tx.

1401 BRYANT, J. E. (1879-)
         MHAFY, 66, 127-128.
         MBaC, CGIC
         Pastor, state overseer
         b. 1879, Jasper County, Tx.

1402 BRYANT, Marie Carter Pryor (1899-1978)
         CLGCWFF
         b. 1899. d. Dec. 1978, Peoria, Il.

1403 Richard Pryor joins grieving family for grandmother's funeral.
         In Jet, 55 (Jan. 4, 1979), 14-16.

1404 BRYANT, Robert James (1894-)
         CGH, 31-32.
         CLGCWFF
         Pastor, bishop
         b. Dec. 22, 1894, Texarkana, Ar.

1405 BRYANT, Roy (1923-)
         WWIR (1985), 43.
         BCChr
         Pastor, bishop, theological institute pres., radio host,
            editor
         b. July 18, 1923, Armour, N.C.

1406 BURKS, James Titus (1916-)
         WWIR (1985), 46.
         CGIC
         Pastor, training institute dean
         b. Mar. 22, 1916, Samson, Al.

1407 BURREL, William Lee (1927-)
         GBPAW, 60.
         PeAW
         Pastor, district elder, bishop
         b. 1927, Clarksdale, Ms.

1408 *BURROWS, S. R. (1878-1952)
         GBPAW, 17.

       GHPAW, 131.
       PeAW
       Pastor, district elder, bishop
       b. 1878, Gibson County, Tn.
       d. 1952, Bedford, Ky.

1409   BURRUSS, King Hezekiah (-1963)
       CHCCH, 434-435.
       PPIB, III, 18, 19-20.
       CChr (H), CGH
       Pastor, bishop
       d. 1963, Atlanta, Ga.

1410   BURRUSS, Titus Paul
       PPIB, III, 20, 65.
       CGH
       Pastor, bishop

1411   BUTLER, Edward W. (1870-1953)
       CHCCH, 272, 273.
       MBaC, CChr (H)
       Pastor, bishop
       b. 1870, Jackson, Ms.
       d. Aug. 1953, Jackson, Ms.

1412   BUTLER, Henry Alfred (1922-)
       MOM (1975), 194.
       CG (T), CGP
       Pastor
       b. June 23, 1922, Nassau, Bahamas

1413   BUTLER, Ramsey Nathaniel (1906-)
       GBPAW, 34.
       GHPAW, 153, 157.
       PeAW
       Pastor, district elder, bishop
       b. Mar. 3, 1906, Saluda, S.C.

1414   CAIN, Emory J.
       CGH, 11, 12, 25, 64, 96.
       CSSIA (1949), 120.
       PPIB, IV, 109.
       CLGCWFF, CLGPGT
       Pastor, editor
       d. 19--, Wrightsville, Ar.

1415   CALDWELL, John (-1972)
       GBPAW, 21.
       GHPAW, 136.
       PeAW
       Pastor, district elder, bishop

b. 187-, Columbia, Mo.
d. 1972, San Diego, Ca.

1416 CALLAHAN, Samuel Paul (1924-)
      WWIR (1977), 97.
      I
      Dentist, pastor
      b. Apr. 15, 1924, Galax, Va.

1417 CAMPBELL, Bernice

1418 Campbell, Bernice
      To serve God is to serve man: profile of Bernice Camp-
      bell, a 52 karat life. n.p., 19--. 14 p. Autobiography.

1419 CANNADY, Leroy H.
      RWWAS, 69
      WCCChr
      Pastor, bishop

1420 CANNON, Goldie
      CG (C)

1421 Delaware's mother of the year.
      In Church of God Evangel, 67 (Feb. 27, 1978), 14.

1422 CANTY, Charlie

      Mail clerk, author

1423 Canty, Charlie
      A miracle happened and changed everything; now "I know
      no defeat," [by] Charlie Canty, as told to Yvonne Nance.
      In Abundant Life, 23 (Nov. 1969), 14-16.

1424 CANTY, F. C.
      FBHCGA
      Pastor, presiding elder, bishop

1425 CAPRON, Cleophas Leon (1925-)
      MOM (1975), 238.
      CGP
      Pastor
      b. Feb. 18, 1925, Turks Island, Bahamas

1426 CARHEE, C. C.
      CHCCH, 58-59, 279, 280.
      MBaC, CChr (H)
      Laborer, pastor

1427 CARMICHAEL, Tilman
      RWWAS, 40, 75, 129.

          ACChrG, MCV
          Pastor, bishop

1428   CARR, Randolph A.
          RWWAS, 77, 91.
          PeAW, CGIC (A)
          Pastor, bishop

1429   CARTWRIGHT, Jacob C.
          CHCCH, 48.
          CChr (H)
          Pastor

1430   CARTY, Amos W. (1939-   )
          MOM (1975), 90.
          CGP
          Pastor, district overseer
          b. Apr. 30, 1939, Anguilla, W.I.

1431   CAVER, Henry L. (1880-1944)
          CHCCH, 272-274, 328.
          CChr (H)
          Teacher, pastor, bishop
          b. Feb. 14, 1880, Monroe, La.
          d. Mar. 16, 1944, Detroit, Mi.

1432   *CHAMBERS, Leon (1922-   )
          BCUC, 34, 36-41.
          PCUH, 199-200.
          TFYNM, III, 152-156.
          CN
          Pastor, district supt., college prof., evangelist
          b. May 16, 1922, Nauvoo, Al.

1433   CHAMBERS, Singleton Robert (1909-   )
          CGIC
          Pastor, radio preacher

1434   Top radio ministers.
          In Ebony, 4 (July 1949), 56-61. On Singleton Robert
          Chambers: p. 57, 59.

1435   *CHAPMAN, Louise Robinson (1892-   )
          BCUC, 44-45.
          CN
          Missionary, denominational admin., author
          b. Oct. 9, 1892, La Center, Clark County, Wa.

1435a Chapman, Louise (Robinson), 1892-
          Africa, O Africa: twenty years a missionary on the dark
          continent, [by] Louise Robinson Chapman. Kansas City,
          Mo., Beacon Hill Press, 1945. 221 p. KyWAT

1436   CHAPMAN, Robert Lee (1923-   )
         WWABA (1985), 150.
         CGIC
         Pastor
         b. Apr. 13, 1923, Saluda, S.C.

1437   CHENAULT, Thomas E.
         CG (C)
         Pastor

1438   CHOPFIELD, Roland
         BCUC, 7, 34, 48, 49.
         CN
         Pastor

1439   Richmond (Va.) Woodville church expands facilities.
         In Herald of Holiness, 61 (Feb. 16, 1972), 23.

1440   CHRISTIAN, Arthur Russell
         KAC
         Pastor, bishop
         d. 19--, Washington, D.C.

1441   CHRISTIAN, Lillian Waller (1895-1979)
         KAC
         Evangelist
         b. 1895, Gordonsville, Va.
         d. July 25, 1979, Washington, D.C.

1442   The Rev. Lillian Christian, founded mission of King's Apostles
         Church.
         In Washington Post, 102 (June 29, 1979), B4.

1443   CHRISTIAN, William (1856-1928)
         CGH, 7-15, 17, 22, 54, 123.
         PPIB, IV, 109.
         WWICA (1927), 41, pl. xiv
         MBaC, CLGCWFF
         Evangelist, pastor, chief bishop, author
         b. Nov. 10, 1856, Mississippi
         d. Apr. 11, 1928, Memphis, Tn.

1444   Christian, William, 1856-1928.
         Poor pilgrim's work. Motto: Christian Workers for Fellow-
         ship to unite the people as one in Christ in the name of the
         Father, Son and Holy Ghost, we put our trust. Many impor-
         tant things may be learned by reading this little book.
         Memphis, Tn., 1916; reprinted by Model Printing Co., Del
         City, Ok., 1976. 56 p. Cover title. Autobiographical.

1445   CLARK, Alma Lee Williams (1920-   )
         WWIR (1977), 118.

CGIC
Missionary
b. July 13, 1920, Camden, Ar.

1446 *CLARK, Fred L. (1886-1953)
        GBPAW, 12.
        GHPAW, 117, 118, 120-121, 125, 127.
        PeAW
        Pastor, bishop
        b. 1886, Captene, Oh.
        d. 1953, Warren, Oh.

1447 CLEMMONS, Ithniel (1921-)
        MLMR, 35, 139, 148
        CGIC
        Pastor, bishop, author

1448 CLEMON, Tony (1921-)
        BDNM (1975), 92.
        CGIC, CGICI
        Pastor, bishop, businessman
        b. Dec. 2, 1921, Madison, Fl.

1449 COATIE, Charles Everett (1929-)
        WWIR (1985), 65.
        CGIC
        Pastor, district supt.
        b. Apr. 14, 1929, Mound City, Il.

1450 COBBINS, Lee Porter (1866-1913)
        CHCCH, 48.
        CGIC, CChr (H)
        Farmer, pastor
        b. 1866, Holmes County, Ms.
        d. 1913, Carroll County, Ms.

1451 COBBINS, Otho Beale (1895-)
        CHCCH, 7-10, 278.
        CChr (H)
        Teacher and prin., editor, bishop, author
        b. Oct. 21, 1895, near Lexington, Ms.

1452 COBBS, Ira Jean
        CG (C)

1453 Cobbs, Ira Jean
        God is a first-class doctor. In Church of God Evangel,
        61 (June 14, 1971), 6.

1454 COFFEY, Lillian Brooks (1896-1964)
        MHAFY, 68, 118-119.

TBPALM, 95-96.
CGIC
Evangelist, denominational admin.
b. 1896, Memphis, Tn.
d. June 9, 1964, Chicago, Il.

1455 Coffey, Lillian (Brooks), 1896-1964.
Mother Lillian Brooks Coffey story (as told in 1963, the year before her expiration). In Cornelius, L. J., ed. The pioneer: history of the Church of God in Christ. [Memphis], c1975, 25-26.

1456 Calhoun, Lillian (Scott)
Woman on the go for God, [by] Lillian S. Calhoun. In Ebony, 18 (May 1963), 78-81, 84, 86, 88.

1457 COLEMAN, Pharoah H. (1899-)
CGH, 32.
CLGCWFF
Pastor, overseer, bishop
b. 1899, Rural Shade, Tx.

1458 COLLINS, David
RWWAS, 78, 95.
PeAW, PeCAFA, TCJ
Pastor, bishop

1459 COLLINS, I. C. (1899-)
CGH, 28.
CLGCWFF
Pastor, vice chief bishop
b. 1899, Eagletown, I.T.

1460 CONIC, James L. I. (1876-1939)
CHCCH, 270-271, 282.
CChr (H)
Pastor, bishop
b. Oct. 15, 1876, Lexington, Ms.
d. May 1939, Jackson, Ms.

1461 CONIC, Major Rudd (1909-)
CHCCH, 282, 283-285.
WWIR (1977), 129.
CChr (H)
College teacher and pres., pastor, bishop
b. Dec. 22, 1909, Jackson, Ms.

1462 COOK, B. (-1940)
CHCCH, 279, 282.
CChr (H)
Pastor, bishop (adjutant)

1463 COOKE, Wilson C. (1923-)
        I
        Businessman, pastor, author
        b. 1923, Alabama

1464 Cooke, Wilson C., 1923-
        The rungless ladder: a story of how failures led to suc-
        cessful living, [by] W. C. Cooke. New York, Exposition
        Press, 1960. 49 p. MoSW, NNUT

1465 COOPER, Joseph (1926-)
        WWIR (1985), 69.
        Ba, AGGC
        Pastor
        b. Nov. 3, 1926, Raywick, Ky.

1466 COOPER, Mitchell (1903-)
        MOM (1975), 95.
        CG (T), CGP
        Pastor
        b. Apr. 29, 1903, Bahamas

1467 CORNELIUS, Lucille J.
        CGIC
        Evangelist, author

1468 COURTS, James H. (-1926)
        MHAFY, 24, 69, 122.
        CGIC
        Academy teacher and prin.
        d. 1926, Lexington, Ms.

1469 COVINGTON, J. H.
        RWWAS, 40.
        PDC
        Pastor, bishop

1470 COX, Leviticus H. (1928-)
        MOM (1975), 96.
        CGP
        Pastor, radio preacher
        b. July 10, 1928, Nassau, Bahamas

1471 COX, Thomas J. (-1943)
        PPIB, III, 36.
        RWWAS, 41-42.
        ChrFB, CG (AP)
        Pastor, bishop
        d. 1943, Danville, Ky.

1472 CRAWFORD, Ethel Lee (1934-)
        WWIR (1975-1976), 128.

CGIC
Evangelist, radio preacher
b. Aug. 15, 1934, Helena, Ar.

1473 CROSBY, T. J. (1854-)
COLJCAF
Pastor

1474 Powell, Constance
121-year-old pastor refuses to let age slow him down as
he starts to rebuild his church, by Constance Powell. In
National Powell. In National Tattler (May 11, 1975), 6.

1475 CROSSLEY, William (1908-)
GBPAW, 27.
GHPAW, 157, 158.
PeAW
Evangelist, pastor, bishop
b. 1908, Eufaula, Al.

1476 CROUCH, Andrae (1942-)
WWABA (1985), 193.
CGIC
Musician
b. July 1, 1942, Pacoima, Ca.

1477 Crouch, Andrae, 1942-
Andrae Crouch "rocks" the church. [Interview by Richard
Dalrymple]. In Inspiration, 1 (Sept./Oct. 1978), 58-59,
72-73.

1478 Crouch, Andrae, 1942-
Through it all, [by] Andrae Crouch, with Nina Ball.
Waco, Tx., Word Books, 1974. 148 p. Autobiography.
DLC

1479 Banks, Lacy J.
Andrae Crouch: gospel music's international ambassador,
[by] Lacy J. Banks. In Black Stars, 7 (Feb. 1978), 32-36.

1480 Heilbut, Anthony Otto, 1941-
The gospel sound: good news and bad times, [by] Tony
Heilbut. Garden City, N.Y., Anchor Press/Doubleday, 1975.
xxxv, 364 p. (Anchor books) On Andrae Crouch: p. 319-
321.

1481 CROUCH, Samuel M.
CP, 43, 94.
MHAFY, 66, 75, 76, 88, 90, 91, 92, 100, 101, 135, 138.
TBPALM, 96.
CGIC
Evangelist, radio preacher, pastor, bishop

1482   CRUMES, William E. (1914-   )
           CGH, 27, 84-85.
           Ba, CLGCWFF
           Pastor, chief bishop
           b. Mar. 8, 1914, Louisville, Ky.

1483   CULMER, Burk Edward (1939-   )
           MOM (1975), 246.
           CGP
           Pastor
           b. Oct. 29, 1939, Eleuthera Island, Bahamas

1484   Culmer, Dolly I. Cancens (1940-   )
           MOM (1975), 348.
           CGP
           Evangelist, missionary
           b. July 29, 1940, Harbour Island, Bahamas

1485   CUMBERBATCH, Theodosia Francis (1926-   )
           CG (A)
           b. 1926, St. Kitts, W.I.

1486   Cumberbatch, Theodosia (Francis), 1926-
           I was determined! [By] Theodosia F. Cumberbatch. In
       Callen, B. L. A time to remember: testimonies. Anderson,
       In., c1978, 108-111. DLC, InAndC-T

1487   CUNNINGHAM, Raymond W.
           BCUC, 55-57.
           CMA, WMCA, CN
           Pastor, Bible institute teacher and pres., college prof.

1488   CUNNINGHAM, Sara (-1966)
           CMA, WMCA, CN
           d. May 6, 1966, Institute, W. Va.

1489   Mrs. Cunningham dies.
           In Herald of Holiness, 55 (June 22, 1966), 18.

1490   CUNNINGHAM, William A. (1923-   )
           MOM (1975), 196.
           CGP
           Pastor
           b. Apr. 21, 1923, Nassau, Bahamas

1491   CURRY, Eddie (1937-   )
           MOM (1975), 99.
           CGP
           Pastor
           b. Nov. 17, 1937, Shaw, Ms.

1492 CURRY, Marvin S. (1932-)
      MOM (1975), 247.
      CGP
      Pastor
      b. Nov. 12, 1932, Bahamas

1493 CURRY, Mollie B. (1936-)
      MOM (1975), 349.
      CGP
      Pastor
      b. Jan. 22, 1936, Abbeville, Al.

1494 CURTIS, Homer N. (1930-)
      MOM (1975), 247.
      CGP
      Pastor
      b. Mar. 30, 1930, Bahamas

1495 DAMES, Cleveland Wellington (1914-)
      MOM (1975), 248.
      CG (T), CGP
      Pastor, district overseer, evangelist
      b. Mar. 13, 1914, Bahamas

1496 DANIELS, C. C.
      CG (C)
      Pastor

1496a DARKINS, Duane Adrian (1934-)
      WWABA (1985), 203.
      CGIC
      Pastor, asst. bishop
      b. Oct. 31, 1934

1497 DAUGHTRY, Herbert Daniel (1931-)
      WWABA (1985), 203.
      HLC
      Pastor, national presiding minister
      b. Jan. 13, 1931, Savannah, Ga.

1498 Black United Front demands rights.
      In Guardian (Dec. 20, 1978), 6.

1499 Browne, J. Zamgba
      March at city hall draws 3,000: a cry for power, justice,
      [by] J. Zamgba Browne. In New York Amsterdam News, 72
      (Oct. 7, 1978), 1.

1500 Caldwell, Earl
      Rev. Daughtry is fit to be a king, [by] Earl Caldwell.
      In New York Daily News (Nov. 25, 1978), 18.

1501   Clergyman promotes African-black American unity.
       In New York Amsterdam News, 70 (Dec. 3, 1977), B1.

1502   Di Dio, Laura
       What ailing the cops? [By] Laura Di Dio. In Village
       Voice, 23 (July 24, 1978), 19-20.

1503   Fraser, C. Gerald
       Feisty preacher in vanguard of rights issues in Brooklyn,
       [by] C. Gerald Fraser. In New York Times, 127 (Aug. 6,
       1978), 36.

1504   Haley, Peter
       From saving souls to promoting politics. In Phoenix.
       6 (July 13, 1978)

1505   Lang, Perry
       Black United Front a new voice, [by] Perry Lang. In
       New York Amsterdam News, 72 (Nov. 4, 1978), 1.

1506   Moses, Knolly
       Black rage grows in Brooklyn, [by] Knolly Moses. In
       Black Enterprise, 9 (Sept. 1978), 17.

1507   Pentecostal movement rapidly gaining new adherents.
       In New York Times, 118 (Sept. 6, 1969), 31.

1508   Rojas, Don
       Black Christmas in Brooklyn, [by] Don Rojas. In New
       York Amsterdam News, 70 (Dec. 24, 1977), B1.

1509   Rojas, Don
       Citizen protest still mounting, [by] Don Rojas. In New
       York Amsterdam News, 70 (Dec. 17, 1977), B1.

1510   Thomas, Ianthe
       Primal screams, [by] Ianthe Thomas. In Village Voice, 23
       (July 24, 1978), 18-19.

1511   Wilkerson, Lorna
       A talk with the Rev. Herbert Daughtry, [by] Lorna Wilker-
       son. In Black American, 17:31 (1978), 1.

1512   Wood, George
       Profile of an activist, [by] George Wood. In New York
       Amsterdam News, 69 (Apr. 8, 1978), 1.

1513   DAVIS, Gladys Louise
       WWIR (1977), 151.

         CGIC
         Evangelist, radio preacher
         b. July 25, 19--, New York, N.Y.

1514 DAVIS, Herbert John (1892-1959)
         GBPAW, 23.
         GHPAW, 157.
         PeAW
         Pastor, district elder, bishop
         b. 1892, Leavenworth, Ks.
         d. 1959, Leavenworth, Ks.

1515 DAVIS, R. L.
         FGTA
         Pastor, senior bishop

1516 DAVIS, Randolph Birth (1904-)
         MOM (1975), 101.
         (T) CG, CGP
         Pastor
         b. May 9, 1904, San Salvador Island, Bahamas

1517 DAVIS, Rosie Lee Whitney (1930-)
         WWIR (1977), 152.
         CGIC
         Evangelist
         b. Sept. 16, 1930, Tralake, Ms.

1518 DAVIS, William Henry (1899-1974)
         GBPAW, 44.
         GHPAW, 157.
         PeAW
         Pastor, district elder, bishop
         b. Sept. 11, 1899, Greenville County, S.C.
         d. 1974, Inman, S.C.

1519 DAWKINS, David
         GBPAW, 61.
         PeAW
         Pastor, bishop
         b. 19--, Bahamas

1520 DAXON, David (1883-)
         MOM (1975), 249.
         CG (T), CGP
         Pastor
         b. May 1, 1883, Bahamas

1521 DEAN, Ivis Gertrude (1919-)
         MOM (1975), 351.
         CG (T), CGP

Pastor
b. Nov. 15, 1919, Long Island, Bahamas

1522 *DE JERNETT, E. C. (1857-1929)
      MES, HAT, PeCN, CN
      Pastor, evangelist, author
      b. Jan. 18, 1857, Gainesville, Al.
      d. Sept. 1, 1929, Greenville, Tx.

1523 Another pioneer gone to his reward.
      In Herald of Holiness, 18 (Oct. 9, 1929), 17.

1524 DELEVEAUX, Wilbur Marrel (1897-)
      MOM (1975), 101.
      CG (T), CGP
      Pastor
      b. Sept. 2, 1897, Crooked Island, Bahamas

1525 DERRICKSON, Donald Lee (1929-)
      WWIR (1985), 86.
      CGIC
      Pastor, denominational admin.
      b. Jan. 25, 1929, Nashville, Tn.

1526 DE VEAUX, Maurice E. (1938-)
      MOM (1975), 250.
      CGP
      Pastor
      b. Oct. 16, 1938, Miami, Fl.

1527 DICKERSON, Eugene Ellis (1920-)
      WWIR (1985), 87.
      CGIC
      Pastor
      b. May 26, 1920, near Bells, Tn.

1528 DILL, William Boyd (1941-)
      MOM (1975), 250.
      CGP
      Pastor
      b. Nov. 28, 1941. Bermuda

1528a DIXON, Gabriel P. (1908-)
      CG (A)
      Pastor

1528b Willowby, RIchard L.
      The bigness of God: an interview with Gabriel P. Dixon,
      [by] Richard L. Willowby. In Vital Christianity, 106 (Feb.
      16, 1986), 11-13.

1529 DIXON, Lewis H.
        CGH, 29.
        CLGCWFF
        Pastor, bishop
        b. 189-, Arkansas

1530 DIXON, W. Nah (1932-   )
        GBPAW, 62.
        PeAW
        Pastor, district elder, bishop
        b. 1932, Monrovia, Liberia

1531 DORSETT, Ewing I. O. (1943-   )
        MOM (1975), 42.
        CGP
        Evangelist, pastor, overseer
        b. Apr. 17, 1943, English Harbour, Antigua

1532 DOUB, Robert O. (1924-   )
        RWWAS, 73, 77-78.
        ACChrG, SAT
        Pastor, state overseer, bishop, author

1533 DOUGLAS, Floyd Ignatius (1887-1951)
        GBPAW, 7.
        RC, PeAW
        Pastor, bishop
        b. 1887, Nelson County, Ky.
        d. 1951, Los Angeles, Ca.

1534 DRAFT, Johnnie
        RWWAS, 94.
        CG (AP), ACChr
        Pastor, bishop

1535 DREHER, Lucille G. (1910-   )
        WWABA (1985), 235.
        Social worker
        b. June 24, 1910, Greenville, S.C.

1536 A Bronx activist proves catalyst for many projects in commu-
        nity.
          In New York Times, 126 (Aug. 14, 1977), 46.

1537 Morehouse, Ward
          Lucille Dreher: slum fighter, [by] Ward Morehouse III.
        In Christian Science Monitor (Eastern ed.), 71 (Feb. 6, 1979),
        B8-B9.

1538 DREW, Cyrus Alfredo (1932-   )
        MOM (1975), 42.

CGP
Pastor, overseer
b. Oct. 29, 1932, Jessups Village, Nevis

1539 DRIVER, E. R.
CP, 68.
MHAFY, 63, 66, 130.
CGIC
Pastor, state overseer, editor

1540 DRIVER, Louie M. (1924-)
MHAFY, 91.
WWABA (1985), 236.
CGIC
Pastor, district supt., bishop
b. Mar. 18, 1924, Los Angeles, Ca.

1541 DRUMMOND, David L. (1918-)
WWABA (1985), 237.
CGIC, CGICI
Pastor, bishop
b. Jan. 30, 1918, Hastings, Fl.

1542 DUKES, Dorothy Dixon (1926-)
WWIR (1985), 96.
CGIC
Hairdresser, Sunday school leader
b. Jan. 24, 1926, Birmingham, Al.

1543 DUNN, Leonidas Francis (1890-1964)
CHCCH, 347, 348, 362-364.
CChr (H)
Teacher, postal clerk, editor, minister
b. Dec. 24, 1890, Monroe, La.
d. Apr. 6, 1964, Chicago, Il.

1544 DUNN, Sethard P. (1881-)
BWTS, 201, 283.
CTTR, 509, 547-548.
SBHCGRM, 124.
MBaC, CG (A)
Pastor
b. 1881, Louisiana
d. 19--, Chicago, Il.

1545 DUNN, William Hudson (1879-1942)
CHCCH, 205, 274, 282.
MBaC, CChr (H)
Pastor, bishop
b. Apr. 28, 1879, Monroe, La.
d. Oct. 29, 1942, Norfolk, Va.

1546 DU PREE, Sherry Ann Sherrod (1946-)
       MBaC, CGIC
       Librarian
       b. Nov. 25, 1946, Raleigh, N.C.

1547 Ludwig, Harriet
       Black Pentecostals: S[anta] F[e] C[ommunity] C[ollege]
       librarian researches history of widespread movement, [by]
       Harriet Ludwig. In Gainesville (Fl.) Sun (Nov. 3, 1984), B.

1548 DURANT, Naomi C. (1938-)
       WWABA (1977-1978), 257.
       NRDHC
       Pastor, radio host, bishop
       b. June 23, 1938, Baltimore, Md.

1549 DURHAM, Christine (1914-)
       MOM (1975), 351.
       CGP
       Evangelist, pastor
       b. July 29, 1914, Rocky Point, N.C.

1550 EDDINGS, A. C. (1907-)
       GBPAW, 57.
       PeAW
       Pastor, district elder, bishop
       b. 1907, Atlanta, Tx.

1551 EDWARDS, Joe E. (1908-)
       BCUC, 34.
       Ba, PrCUSA, CN
       Railroad switchman, evangelist, pastor, singer, author
       b. Feb. 11, 1908, Birmingham, Al.

1552 EGGLESTON, Harry C. (1912-1984)
       RWWAS, 69.
       WCCChr
       Pastor, presiding bishop
       b. Apr. 29, 1912, Henry County, Va.
       d. 1984, Martinsville, Va.

1553 EIKERENKOETTER, Frederick J. (1935-)
       HATAP, 234-235.
       MP, 168-185.
       WWABA (1985), 251.   WWIR (1985), 103.
       Ba, I
       Evangelist, radio preacher, editor
       b. June 1, 1935, Ridgeland, S.C.

1554 *EUDALEY, Emily Leota (1893-1964)
       CN

          b. Nov. 8, 1893, Lamar, Ar.
          d. Aug. 27, 1964, Freeport, Tx.

1555 Cotton, R. Earl
          Another approach, [by] R. Earl Cotton. In Herald of
      Holiness, 53 (Nov. 4, 1964), 18.

1556 EVANS, Jesse E. (1903-)
          PPIB, III, 38, 68.
          CG (SC)
          Pastor, denominational chairman

1557 FAISON, Thurman Lawrence (1938-)
          MATS, 238, 371, 372
          WWABA (1980-1981), 250.
          AGGC
          Pastor, denominational admin., author
          b. Feb. 17, 1938, Texarkana, Tx.

1558 Buchwalter, Paul R.
          Revival Center to open in Harlem, [by] Paul R. Buchwalter.
      In Pentecostal Evangel, 2766 (May 14, 1967), 10-11.

1559 FELTUS, Henry (1877-)
          CP, 77.
          MHAFY, 123-124.
          Ba, CGIC
          Pastor, state overseer
          b. Dec. 15, 1877, near Centerville, Ms.

1560 FELTUS, James (18 -)
          MHAFY, 66, 103, 107.
          CGIC
          Pastor, state overseer

1561 FELTUS, James (1921-)
          BDNM (1975), 159.
          WWABA (1985), 268.
          CGIC
          Pastor, teacher, overseer
          b. Apr. 16, 1921, Gloster, Ms.

1562 FERGUSON, Alfred Evans (1901-)
          MOM (1975), 108.
          CG (T), CGP
          Pastor, district overseer
          b. July 19, 1901, Crooked Island, Bahamas

1563 FERGUSON, Cephas (1926-)
          MOM (1975), 257.
          CGP

Pastor, district overseer, prison chaplain
b. Feb. 22, 1926, Crooked Island, Bahamas

1564 *FIDLER, R. L.
      CGIC
      Pastor, bishop, denominational admin., author

1565 FIELDS, Melvin B.
      CG (C)

1566 Fields, Melvin B.
      Thankful for Pentecost, [by] Melvin B. Fields. In Church
      of God Evangel, 61 (June 14, 1971), 15.

1567 FINLAYSON, Rufus Benny (1931-)
      MOM (1975), 44.
      CGP
      Evangelist, pastor, overseer
      b. Dec. 23, 1931, Miami, Fl.

1568 FINLEY, James Edward (1933-)
      WWIR (1985), 112.
      AOHCG
      Pastor
      b. Dec. 20, 1933, Mobile, Al.

1569 FISHBURNE, Dannette
      CG (C)
      Minister, college instructor, author

1570 FISHER, Edward Guy (1932-)
      AMD (1973), I, 309; II, 1832.
      DMS (1977-1978), II, 2840.
      WWABA 91980-1981), 257-258.
      CGIC
      Physician
      b. Apr. 22, 1932, Kingston, Jamaica

1571 FISHER, Henry Lee (-1947)
      HCIA, UHCA
      Pastor, evangelist, bishop, author
      d. 1947, Henderson, N.C.

1572 FLAGLER, William March (1951-)
      CG (C)
      b. May 4, 1951, Florence, S.C.

1573 Flagler, William March, 1951-
      A black youth finds his way to Christ: "If you want me
      Jesus, I want you," [by] Willie Flagler as told to Steve In-
      gram. In Church of God Evangel, 62 (Aug. 14, 1972), 12-14.

1574   FLUKER, Samuel Anthony (1937-   )
          WWIR (1977), 207-208.
          CGIC
          Pastor
          b. May 11, 1937, Greenwood, Ms.

1575   FOGGS, Edward L. (1934-   )
          SBHCGRM, 124-125.
          WWABA (1985), 276.
          CG (A)
          Pastor, college prof., denominational admin., author
          b. July 11, 1934, Kansas City, Ks.

1576   FONVILLE, Cephus E.
          CGH, 30, 80.
          CLGCWFF
          Pastor, overseer, bishop
          b. 189-, Calhoun, Al.

1577   FOOTE, Julia A. J. (1823-   )
          AME
          Evangelist

1578   Foote, Julia A. J., 1823-
          A brand plucked from the fire: an autobiographical
          sketch, [by] Mrs. Julia A. J. Foote. Cleveland, Printed for
          the author by W. F. Schneider, 1879. 124 p. DLC, OCl,
          OU, WHi

1579   Foote, Julia A. J., 1823-
          A brand plucked from the fire; an autobiographical sketch,
          [by] Mrs. Julia A. J. Foote. New York, G. Hughes & Co.,
          1879. 124 p.

1580   Foote, Julia A. J., 1823-
          A brand plucked from the fire: an autobiographical
          sketch, [by] Mrs. Julia A. J. Foote. Cleveland, Printed for
          the author by Lauer & Yost, 1881. 124 p. IU

1581   FORBES, James Alexander (1914-   )
          UHCA, OUHCW, OUHCI
          Pastor, bishop
          b. Mar. 19, 1914, Greenville, N.C.

1582   FORBES, James Alexander (1935-   )
          MLMR, 109, 200.
          UHCA, OUHCW, OUHCI
          Pastor, college and seminary prof., author
          b. Sept. 6, 1935, Burgaw, N.C.

1583   Forbes, James Alexander, 1935-
          Ministry of hope from a double minority, [by] James A.

Forbes, Jr. In Theological Education, 9 (Summer 1973, suppl.), 305-316. Autobiographical.

1584 FORD, Anna Mae (1916-   )
      WWIR (1985), 116.
      CGIC
      Singer, composer, editor, evangelist
      b. Aug. 15, 1916, Lexington, Ms.

1585 FORD, Eddye Betty Chambers (1911-   )
      WWIR (1985), 116.
      CGIC
      Missionary
      b. Aug. 7, 1911, Greenwood, Ms.

1586 FRANCIS, Silburn B. (1932-   )
      MOM (1975), 261.
      CGP
      Pastor
      b. Mar. 29, 1932, Jamaica

1587 FRASER, Wilhelmina (1904-   )
      CTTR, 228, 230-231.
      CG (A)
      Missionary, author

1588 Fraser, Wilhelmina, 1904-
      Memoirs of Wilhelmina Fraser. Rev. ed. New York, Shining Light Survey Press, 1977. 75 p. InAndC-T

1589 *FRAZEE, J. J.
      CUWS, 27.
      FTINS, 73-74.
      RWWAS, 45.
      PeAW
      Pastor, general supt.

1590 FREEMAN, Mary Jayne Hill (1918-   )
      WWIR (1977), 216.
      PeAW
      Evangelist, counselor, Bible college instructor and admin.
      b. Dec. 20, 1918, Columbus, Oh.

1591 FULLER, William Edward (1875-1958)
      MHPD, 221.
      NP, 129.
      SAOPCO, 138.
      SHPM, 65-66, 174.
      SOTP, 100-101, 153, 219.
      WBWF, 17-18.
      M, FBHAA, FBHC, CFBHC, FBHCG, FBHCGA

Evangelist, pastor, general overseer
b. Jan. 29, 1875, Mountville, S.C.
d. Jan. 20, 1958

1592 FULLER, William Edward (1921-)
ERIS, 253.
FBHCG, FBHCGA
Pastor, bishop, school pres.
b. 1921, Atlanta, Ga.

1593 GARY, General Grant (1917-)
WWIR (1977), 227.
CGIC
Evangelist, pastor
b. Jan. 5, 1917, Tublow, Ar.

1594 GASERY, John L.
CG (C)
Air force officer, pastor, author

1595 Gasery, John L.
John L. Gasery: air force officer and preacher, [by]
John L. Gasery, Jr. In Church of God Evangel, 61 (Feb.
18, 1972), 13.

1596 GEORGES, Reginald C. (1921-)
MOM (1975), 264.
CG (T), CGP
Pastor, evangelist, district overseer
b. Sept. 17, 1921, Virgin Islands

1597 GERALD, William (1918-)
WWABA (1985), 305.
WWIR (1977), 231.
BWCOLJCWW
Pastor, district elder, musician, author
b. Dec. 15, 1918, Irwin County, Ga.

1598 GIBSON, Wilbur Albert (1909-)
MOM (1975), 264.
CGP
Pastor
b. Jan. 1, 1909, Bahamas

1599 GIBSON, William Taylor (1927-)
WWIR (1977), 233.
PeAW
Evangelist, pastor
b. Apr. 11, 1927, Indianapolis, In.

1600 GILLEMS, Flanders (1914-)
WWIR (1977), 235.

CGIC
Pastor, district supt.
b. Aug. 7, 1914, Little Rock, Ar.

1601 GILLIAM, Edith Griffin (1924-   )
WWIR (1977), 235.
CGIC
Evangelist
b. Feb. 14, 1924, Norfolk, Va.

1602 GODFREY, William Nelson (1911-   )
WWIR (1985), 132.
CGIC
Pastor, district supt.
b. Oct. 12, 1911, Wallisville, Tx.

1603 GOLDER, Morris Ellis (1913-   )
GBPAW, 50.
GHPAW, 153, 157, 160, 171, 172, 175, 195.
PeAW
Pastor, denominational official, bishop, editor, author
b. 1913, Indianapolis, In.

1604 *GOLTA, Sudkey Saleeb (1930-   )
GBPAW, 63.
PeAW
Pastor, bishop
b. 1930, Sohag, Egypt

1605 GOODLOE, Clifton
CHCCH, 283, 289, 290.
CChr (H)
Pastor, bishop

1606 GOODSON, John Douglas Daniel (1901-1938)
AOHUTR
PeAW
Pastor
b. Apr. 28, 1901, Groveton, Tx.
d. Sept. 17, 1938, Detroit, Mi.

1607 GOODWIN, Bennie Eugene (1933-   )
CA, 112.
CGIC
Pastor, teacher, seminary prof. and admin., author
b. Aug. 27, 1933, Chicago, Il.

1608 Goodwin, Bennie Eugene, 1933-
The emergence of black colleges; an introduction to the
origins of black institutions of higher learning in the United
States, [by] Bennie E. Goodwin. With original drawings by

Oplenell Rockamore. Jersey City, N.J., Goodpatrick Publishers, 1974. xii, 47 p. PPiU

1609 Goodwin, Bennie Eugene, 1933-
       Martin Luther King, Jr.: American social educator.
       Pittsburgh, 1974. 270 l. Thesis (Ph.D.)--University of
       Pittsburgh. PPiU

1610 GOODWIN, Ed

       Publisher
       b. 190-, Mississippi

1611 Nance, Yvonne
       "God, I'm in your hands": the Ed Goodwin story, [by]
       Yvonne Nance. In Abundant Life, 24 (Apr. 1970), 19-23.

1612 GOODWIN, Mary Ellen
       MCHCA
       Writer, missionary society executive

1613 GRACE, Charles Emmanuel (1881-1960)
       BDARB (1977), 179-180.
       NP, 147-150.
       NYT (Jan. 13, 1960), 47:3; (Jan. 23, 1960), 19:5.
       UHOPFAP
       Cook, salesman, grocer, pastor, bishop
       b. Jan. 25, 1881, Brava, Cape Verde Islands
       d. Jan. 12, 1960, Los Angeles, Ca.; buried New Bedford,
       Ma.

1613a America's richest Negro minister.
       In Ebony, 7 (Jan. 1952), 17-20, 23.

1614 Casey, Phil
       Banks in area hold over $1 million of Daddy Grace's money,
       [by] Phil Casey. In Washington Post, 83 (Mar. 11, 1960),
       B1, B12.

1614a Casey, Phil
       Daddy Grace came a long way from early days in New Bedford, [by] Phil Casey. In Washington Post, 83 (Mar. 7,
       1960), 81.

1615 Casey, Phil
       Daddy's outstanding miracle: hold on flock, [by] Phil
       Casey. In Washington Post, 83 (Mar. 22, 1960), E1.

1616 Casey, Phil
       Friends say Daddy Grace didn't need money, he had everything, [by] Phil Casey. In Washington Post, 83 (Mar. 10,
       1960), A26.

1617 Casey, Phil
        Many setbacks failed to deter Daddy Grace, [by] Phil
      Casey. In Washington Post, 83 (Mar. 8, 1960), B1, B4.

1618 Casey, Phil
        Parable served Daddy Grace to evade direct reply, [by]
      Phil Casey. In Washington Post, 83 (Mar. 9, 1960), B1, B12.

1619 D. C. eyes taxes, claims Daddy Grace lived here.
        In Evening Star (Washington), 108 (Apr. 14, 1960), C4.

1620 Daddy Grace.
        In Life, 19 (Oct. 1, 1945), 51-56, 58.

1621 Daddy Grace: millionaire with a Bible.
        In Our World, 8 (Oct. 1953), 50-53.

1622 Daddy Grace to use fire hose on 300.
        In New York Amsterdam News, 29 (July 28, 1956), 1.

1623 Daddy Grace's Cuban paradise.
        In Ebony, 9 (Nov. 1953), 86-88.

1624 Eddy, George Norman, 1906-
        Store-front religion, [by] G. Norman Eddy. In Religion in
      Life, 28 (Winter 1958/1959), 68-85 [Daddy Grace: p. 74-78];
      abridged in Lee, R., ed. Cities and churches; readings on
      the urban church. Philadelphia, c1962, 177-194 [Daddy Grace:
      182-187].

1625 The enigma of Daddy Grace: did he play God?
        In Washington Post, 83 (Mar. 6, 1960), E1.

1626 Fire hose baptism.
        In Ebony, 10 (Oct. 1955), 102-104, 106.

1627 Fisher, Miles Mark, 1899-1970.
        Organized religion and the cults. In Crisis, 44 (Jan.
      1937), 8-10, 29-30.

1628 Grace to Harlem.
        In Time, 31 (Mar. 7, 1938), 30.

1629 Hall, Gordon Langley
        The sawdust trail: the story of American evangelism.
      Philadelphia, Macrae Smith Co., 1964. 249 p. "Prophet in
      a long fur coat": p. 163-170. DLC, IDeKN, Ok

1630 La Farge, John, 1880-1963.
        The incredible Daddy Grace. In America, 103 (Apr. 2,
      1960), 5.

1631 Levick, Lionel
          Father Divine is God, [by] Lionel Levick. In Forum and
      Century, 92 (Oct. 1934), 217-221; reply by Oliver G. Powell
      (Divine and lung power), 92 (Nov. 1934), [suppl.] x-xi.

1632 Mathison, Richard Randolph, 1919-1980.
          Faiths, cults and sects of America; from atheism to Zen,
      [by] Richard R. Mathison. Indianapolis, Bobbs-Merrill, 1960.
      384 p. "Sweet Daddy Grace": p. 240-243. OClU, Ok

1633 Mathison, Richard Randolph, 1919-1980.
          God is a millionaire, [by] Richard Mathison. Indianapolis,
      Bobbs-Merrill, 1962, c1960. 384 p. (Charter books, 106)
      First published in 1960 under title: Faiths, cults and sects
      of America. "Sweet Daddy Grace": p. 240-243. FJ

1634 A "mortal" mystery.
          In Newsweek. 49 (June 10, 1957), 35.

1635 Poinsett, Alexander Ceasar, 1926-
          Farewell to Daddy Grace, [by] Alex Poinsett. In Ebony,
      15 (Apr. 1960), 25-28, 30, 32, 34.

1636 Sweet Daddy's sugar.
          In Newsweek, 55 (Feb. 15, 1960), 32.

1637 GRAHAM, Lesmon R. (1936-)
          MOM (1975), 113.
          CGP
          Pastor
          b. Sept. 4, 1936, Clarendon, Jamaica

1638 GRAHAM, Robert L.
          AGGC
          Barber, pastor

1639 Olson, Melford A.
          Remembering the urban man, [by] Melford A. Olson. In
      Pentecostal Evangel, 3045 (Sept. 17, 1972), 16-17.

1640 GRANNUM, Clarence Milton (1941-)
          WWIR (1977), 247.
          CG (A)
          Pastor
          b. Nov. 28, 1941, Guyana

1641 GRANT, Simon Tenyen (1904-)
          GBPAW, 64.
          PeAW
          Pastor, bishop
          b. 1904, Cape Palmas, Liberia

1642 GRAVELY, M.
          RWWAS, 42.
          CG (AP), I
          Pastor, bishop
          d. 197-, Beckley, W. Va.

1643 GRAVES, Marvin Eugene (1940-   )
          WWIR (1975-1976), 219.
          PeAW
          Pastor, postal clerk
          b. July 10, 1940, Springfield, Oh.

1644 GRAVES, Preston
          RWWAS, 98.
          BWCOLJCWW, UWCCCHrAF
          Pastor, bishop

1645 GRAY, Charlie W. (1861-1945)
          PPIB, III, 38, 39, 40.
          Ba, CG (SC), OCGSC
          Pastor, denominational chairman
          b. 1861
          d. 1945, Columbia, Tn.

1646 GREEN, R. S. (-1964)
          CN
          Pastor
          d. Aug. 1964, Columbus, Tx.

1647 GREEN, Ralph E.
          RWWAS, 40, 67, 68.
          WCCChr, FGCChr
          Pastor, bishop, editor

1648 GREEN, Samuel L.
          MLMR, 80, 83, 148.
          CGIC
          Pastor, bishop

1648a GREER, Hester (1880-   )
          CG (A)
          Missionary, author

1648b Greer, Hester, 1880-
          Life and work of Hester Greer: a personal autobiography.
      n.p., 19--. 93 p. InAndC

1649 GRIMES, Kathleen Washington (1880-1960)
          CMA, PeAW
          Missionary, author
          b. 1880, Collingwood, Ont.
          d. Mar. 1960, New York, N.Y.

1650 Grimes, Kathleen (Washington), 1880-1960.
        Four years in the land of Ham, [by] Kathleen Grimes.
      New York, 19--.

1651 Hopkins, Ellen Miama (Moore), 1921-
        "Don't let the fire go out," [by] Ellen Moore Hopkins.
      Monrovia, Printed by Department of Information and Cultural
      Affairs, Republic of Liberia, c1968. 42, xiv 1. DeU

1652 GRIMES, Samuel Joshua (1884-1967)
        CUWS, 89.
        GBPAW, 8.
        GHPAW, 140, 171.
        RWWAS, 49, 51, 52.
        CMA, PeAW
        Missionary, presiding bishop, editor
        b. Jan. 3, 1884, Barbados, W.I.
        d. June 13, 1967, New York, N.Y.

1653 Grimes, Kathleen (Washington), 1880-1960.
        Four years in the land of Ham, [by] Kathleen Grimes.
      New York, 19--.

1654 Hopkins, Ellen Miama (Moore), 1921-
        "Don't let the fire go out," [by] Ellen Moore Hopkins.
      Monrovia, Printed by Department of Information and Cultural
      Affairs, Republic of Liberia, c1968. 42, xiv 1. DeU

1655 GWEBU, Petros Johannes (1902-)
        MOM (1975), 45.
        CGP
        Pastor, overseer
        b. Mar. 22, 1902, Caroline, Tvl.

1656 HACKETT, Paul
        ICFG
        Pastor, Bible college prof.

1657 HADDEN, Lillie J. (1893-)
        MOM (1975), 357.
        CG (T), CGP
        Pastor
        b. Jan. 21, 1893, Oklahoma

1658 HAINES, Lula (-1966)
        CN
        d. Aug. 14, 1966, Concord, N.C.

1659 HAIRSTON, Robert Leonard
        RWWAS, 87-90.
        TVPeHC, TVPeCJ
        Pastor, bishop

1660 HAIRSTON, Roland Eugene (1944-)
        WWIR (1977), 263.
        PeAW
        Pastor
        b. July 27, 1944, Wilmington, De.

1661 *HALE, Edwin Erwin (1894-1976)
        BCUC, 10, 52, 53, 54-55.
        CN
        Pastor, district supt., military chaplain, evangelist, Bible
        institute pres., author
        b. Dec. 4, 1894, Altus, Ar.
        d. Mar. 30, 1976, Houston, Tx.

1662 Hale, Edwin Erwin, 1894-1976.
        Autobiographical notes, [by] Edwin E. Hale. (Pasadena,
        Ca., 197-]. [114] l.

1663 HALL, Joseph Sylvester (1910-)
        WWIR (1977), 264.
        CGIC
        Pastor, bishop
        b. Aug. 22, 1910, Omaha, Ne.

1664 HALL, Ollie V. (1895-1955)
        CGH, 23.
        Ba, CLGCWFF
        Pastor, chief bishop
        b. Aug. 22, 1895, Fulshear, Fort Bend County, Tx.
        d. Dec. 22, 1955, Los Angeles, Ca.

1665 HAMILTON, Albert (1903-1962)
        CHCCH, 278-279, 283.
        CChr (H)
        Pastor, bishop
        b. Sept. 22, 1903, Pocahontas, Ms.
        d. June 18, 1962, Los Angeles, Ca.

1666 HAMITER, I. W. (1919-1985)
        RWWAS, 63, 64, 65.
        GCGIC, OGCGIC
        Pastor, presiding bishop
        b. Apr. 17, 1919, Cincinnati, Oh.
        d. Jan. 1, 1985, Columbus, Oh.

1667 HANCOCK, Samuel Nathan (1883-1963)
        CUWS, 68.
        GBPAW, 6, 27, 40.
        GHPAW, 88, 90, 125, 126, 128, 135, 139, 140, 141, 142.
        RWWAS, 48, 49-50, 78, 79.
        PeAW, PeAJC, PeAW, PeCAFA

Pastor, bishop
b. 1883, Adair, Ky.
d. 1963, Detroit, Mi.

1668   HANNA, Gertrude Elizabeth (1909-   )
       MOM (1975), 358.
       CG (T), CGP
       Pastor
       b. Dec. 20, 1909, Acklins Island, Bahamas

1669   HANNAH, Frederick Marvin (1938-   )
       WWIR (1977), 270.
       CGIC
       Musician, theological institute instructor, medical college
       admin.
       b. June 24, 1938, Richmond, In.

1670   HARPER, Leon
       AFCG
       Pastor

1671   HARRIS, D. H.
       WWIR (1977), 275.
       TCKGIC
       Pastor, archbishop, author

1672   HARRIS, James Frank
       RWWAS, 99-100.
       HChrCChr, RAJCA
       Pastor, bishop

1673   HARRIS, Robert L.
       WWIAP (1977-1978), 427.
       CGIC
       Pastor, politician

1674   HARRIS, Thoro (1874-1955)
       BSFH, 154.
       GHPAW, 39.
       KMIE (1959), 197-198.
       LMGSS, 38-39.
       MAWCSM, 359.
       I
       Song writer, music editor, publisher
       b. Mar. 31, 1874, Washington, D.C.
       d. Mar. 29, 1955, Eureka Springs, Ar.

1675   HARRIS, William Wadé (1865-1929)
       NCDCWM, 243-244.
       MEL, PECL, I
       Teacher, prophet

        b. 1865, Liberia
        d. 1929

1676 Bureau, René
        Le prophète Harris et le harrisme (Côte-d'Ivoire). Abid-
    jan, Université d'Abidjan, Institut d'Ethno-sociologie, 1971.
    193 l. MiEM

1677 Haliburton, Gordon MacKay
        The prophet Harris: a study of an African prophet and
    his mass-movement in the Ivory Coast and the Gold Coast,
    1913-1915. London, Longman, 1971. xix, 250 p. DLC, Uk

1678 Haliburton, Gordon MacKay
        The prophet Harris: a study of an African prophet and
    his mass-movement in Ivory Coast and the Gold Coast, 1913-
    1915. New York, Oxford University Press, 1973. xv, 155 p.
    DLC

1679 Hayford, Casely
        William Waddy Harris, the West African reformer: the man
    and his message. London, C. M. Phillips, 1915. 19 p. NN

1680 Musson, Margaret
        Prophet Harris: the amazing story of Old Pa Union Jack,
    [by] Margaret Musson. Wallington, Surrey, Religious Educa-
    tion Press, 1950. 111 p. (Pioneer series) NjMD

1681 Platt, William James, 1893-
        An African prophet: the Ivory Coast movement and what
    came of it, [by] W. J. Platt. London, Student Christian
    Movement Press, 1934. 157 p. CtY, CU, DLC, IEN

1682 Walker, Sheila Suzanne
        The religious revolution in the Ivory Coast: the Prophet
    Harris and the Harrist Church, [by] Sheila S. Walker. Chapel
    Hill, University of North Carolina Press, c1983. xvii, 206 p.
    (Studies in religion) DLC

1683 HARRISON, Robert Emanuel (1928-   )
        BDNM (1975), 214-215.
        MATS, 371, 372.
        I, AGGC
        Pastor, evangelist, singer, missionary, author
        b. 1928, San Francisco, Ca.

1684 Harrison, Robert Emanuel, 1928-
        When God was black, [by] Bob Harrison, with Jim Mont-
    gomery. Grand Rapids, Mi., Zondervan Publishing House,
    c1971. 160 p. Autobiography. DLC, OkBetC

1685   Bob Harrison named consultant on inner city evangelism.
        In Pentecostal Evangel, 3060 (Dec. 31, 1972), 28.

1686   HART, R. E.
            CHCCH, 433.
            MHAYF, 24, 63.
            AME, CGIC
            Pastor, lawyer

1687   HASH, Reuben K.
            RWWAS, 43, 44.
            CG (AP)
            Pastor, bishop, general overseer

1688   HAY, J. Gordon (-1946)
            CHCCH, 43, 277-278, 282.
            CChr (H)
            Pastor, bishop
            d. 1946, Chicago, Il.

1689   HAYWOOD, Garfield Thomas (1880-1931)
            ATF, 60
            AVOD, 177, 178, 181, 182, 187, 189-190
            BSFH, 154, 193, 197, 201, 208
            CUWS, 15, 16, 18, 27-28, 188-189
            EPOP (1975), 202-203
            FTINS, 54.
            GBPAW, 1, 2, 3, 6, 11, 16, 42, 69.
            KWGHW, 115
            SAOPCO, 95, 150
            SHPM, 155, 158, 170-172
            I, PeAW
            Pastor, evangelist, presiding bishop, editor, song writer.
            b. July 15, 1880, Greencastle, In.
            d. Apr. 12, 1931, Indianapolis, In.

1690   Haywood, Garfield Thomas, 1880-1931.
            The life and writings of Elder G. T. Haywood. Compiled
        by Paul D. Dugas. Stockton, Ca., Apostolic Press, 1968.
        28, 19, 39, 71, 60 p. (Oneness Pentecostal pioneer series:
        tongues of fire for Jesus). OkTOR

1691   Golder, Morris Ellis, 1913-
            The life and works of Bishop Garfield Thomas Haywood
        (1880-1931), [by] Morris E. Golder. [Indianapolis], c1977.
        71 p. InHi

1691a Hall, Thomas Floyd
            Bishop Garfield T. Haywood, black Pentecostal pioneer,
        and Christ Temple of Indianapolis, by Thomas Floyd Hall, Jr.
        Muncie, In., 1980. 29 l.   Student paper--Ball State Uni-
        versity. InHi

1692 Tyson, James L.
    Before I sleep, [by] James L. Tyson. Indianapolis,
    Pentecostal Publications, c1976. 108 p. OkTOR

1693 HAYWOOD, Jacob M.
    CHCCH, 277, 282.
    CGIC, CChr (H)
    Pastor, bishop

1694 HENDRICKS, Allen (1941-)
    AGGC
    Pastor
    b. 1941, Guyana

1695 Adams, James S.
    A missionary to inner city, [by] James S. Adams. In St.
    Louis Post Dispatch, 93 (July 23, 1971), 12A.

1696 Southern Missouri opens black church.
    In Pentecostal Evangel, 2981 (June 27, 1971), 16-17.

1697 HEPBURN, Steve A. (1934-)
    MOM (1975), 274.
    CGP
    Pastor
    b. Jan. 23, 1934, Cat Island, Bahamas

1698 HERNE, Jacques Vital (1901-)
    MOM (1975), 48.
    CG (T), CGP
    Pastor, overseer
    b. Aug. 16, 1901, Cayes, Haiti

1699 HEROO, Leonard W.
    KWGHW, 338.
    ZEF, I
    Pastor, Bible institute pres., author

1700 HICKS, Woodrow Wilson (1918-)
    WWIR (1985), 163.
    CGIC
    Pastor
    b. July 14, 1918, Lexington, Ms.

1701 HIGGS, Franklyn Victor (1922-)
    MOM (1975), 274.
    CGP
    Pastor
    b. Nov. 13, 1922, Bahamas

1702 HINES, Mary
    AGGC

1703 Bonnici, Roberta (Lashley)
        A lesson in love, [by] Roberta Lashley Bonnici. In
      Pentecostal Evangel, 3075 (Apr. 15, 1973), 8-9.

1704 HINES, Samuel G.
        WWIR (1985), 164.
        CG (A)
        Pastor, denominational chairperson

1705 HINES, Thynoise
        AGGC
        Serviceman

1706 Bonnici, Roberta (Lashley)
        A lesson in love, [by] Roberta Lashley Bonnici. In
      Pentecostal Evangel, 3075 (Apr. 15, 1973), 8-9.

1707 HINKSON, Frank G.
        CG (C)
        Pastor, overseer

1708 Neal, Nancy
        Overseer of Barbados is honored, [by] Nancy Neal. In
      Church of God Evangel, 68 (June 26, 1978), 14.

1708a HOGAN, Howard B.
        FBHCGA
        Pastor, author
        b. 19--, Mount Holly, N.C.

1709 HOLDER, William Maud (1893-   )
        GBPAW, 42. GJPAW, 153, 157.
        PeAW
        Pastor, bishop
        b. 1893, Indianapolis, In.

1710 *HOLDERFIELD, Paul
        BCUC, 22-24.
        CN
        Firefighter, pastor
        b. 19--, Scott, Ar.

1711 Holderfield, Paul
        Brother Paul: the Paul Holderfield story, [by] Paul
      Holderfield [and] Kathy Tharp. Kansas City, Mo., Beacon
      Hill Press of Kansas City, c1981. 108 p. OMtvN

1712 Love in action in Little Rock.
        In Herald of Holiness, 62 (Oct. 10, 1973), 32-33.

1713 HOLLY, John Silas (1900-1979)
        GBPAW, 22, 48.

GHPAW, 128, 153, 157.
PeAW
Pastor, district elder, bishop
b. Aug. 12, 1900, Monroe, La.
d. Oct. 16, 1979, Chicago, Il.

1714 HOLMAN, William E.
CHCCH, 276-277, 282.
PPIB, III, 19, 20.
CChr (H), ECChr (H)
Pastor, bishop

1715 HOPKINS, Easter Richard (-1971)
CBPAW, 65.
GHPAW, 179.
PeAW
Pastor, bishop, carpenter, mason, engineer
b. 19--, Baltimore, Md.
d. 1971, Katata, Liberia

1716 HOPKINS, Ellen Miama Moore (1921-)
GBPAW, 8, 65.
GHPAW, 179, 182.
PeAW
Missionary, nurse, author
b. 1921, Talla, Cape Mount County, Liberia

1717 Hopkins, Ellen Miama (Moore), 1921-
"Don't let the fire go out," [by] Ellen Moore Hopkins.
Monrovia, Printed by Department of Information and Cultural
Affairs, Republic of Liberia, c1968. 42, xiv l. DeU

1718 Hopkins, Ellen Miama (Moore), 1921-
Liberian baby care, [by] Ellen Moore Hopkins. Katata,
Liberia, 19--.

1719 Hopkins, Ellen Miama (Moore), 1921-
A short story of my life, [by] Ellen Miama Moore. [Co-
lumbus, Oh., 1944] folder ([8] p.) ViU

1720 Brock, Henrietta
A short sketch of the life of Ellen Moore, R.N. ... Samuel
Grimes Maternal and Child Welfare Center ... Liberia. Los
Angeles, H. E. Grimes, 194-. 15 p. NNUT

1721 Furnas, Joseph Chamberlain, 1905-
The house that saves lives, [by] J. C. Furnas. In
Saturday Evening Post, 225 (May 16, 1953), 22-23, 102-103.

1722 Lady with the lamp.
In Ebony, 6 (Aug. 1951), 46-48, 50.

1723   HOPKINS, Ivy Anne Rucker (1940-   )
          WWIR (1977), 306.
          [HGW] CLG [PGT]
          Pastor
          b. Oct. 18, 1940, Steelton, Pa.

1724   HORN, Rosa Artimus
          MCAHPFC
          Dressmaker, evangelist, radio preacher
          b. 18--, Sumter, S.C.

1725   Baldwin, James, 1924-
          Go tell it on the mountain. New York, Knopf, 1953.   303
          p. Autobiographical novel. The woman preacher is reputably
          Mother Horn. DLC, InU

1726   Rasky, Frank
          Harlem's religious zealots, [by] Frank Rasky. In Tomor-
          row, 9 (Nov. 1949), 11-17; abridged in Negro Digest, 8
          (Mar. 1950), 52-62.

1727   HOWARD, Sherman Scott (1926-   )
          WWIR (1977), 309.
          CGIC
          Pastor, district supt.
          b. Dec. 12, 1926, Roanoke, Va.

1728   HUMPHREY, Jerry Miles (1872-   )
          FMCNA
          Evangelist, author
          b. June 30, 1872, near Memphis, Tn.
          d. 19--, California

1729   Humphrey, Jerry Miles, 1872-
          What God hath joined together, [by] J. M. Humphrey.
          Phoenix, Az., Don Hughes; printed by Religious Press,
          Independence, Ks., 197-. 22 p. Cover title. Autobiograph-
          ical. KyWAT

1730   HUSBANDS, John
          AGGC
          Pastor
          b. 19--, Guyana

1731   Mississippi: a venture in its cotton belt.
          In Pentecostal Evangel, 3077 (Apr. 29, 1973), 10-11.

1732   INMAN, John R. (1848-1917)
          PPIB, III, 38.
          CG (SC)
          Pastor, denominational chairman

    b. 1848
    d. 1917, Lebanon, Tn.

1733 JACKSON, Jannie (1916-   )
    MOM (1975), 362.
    CG (T), CGP
    Pastor
    b. June 12, 1916, Camden, S.C.

1734 JACKSON, John Edward (1950-   )
    WWIR (1985), 179.
    CGIC
    Pastor, youth leader, evangelist
    b. July 23, 1950, Troy, Al.

1735 JACKSON, M. R.
    EPeCOLAF
    Pastor, presiding bishop

1736 JACKSON, Madeline Manning (1948-   )
    WWABA (1977-1978), 461.

    Athlete, teacher, evangelist, singer, author
    b. Jan. 11, 1948, Columbus, Oh.

1737 Jackson, Madeline (Manning), 1948-
    Running for Jesus, [by] Madeline Manning Jackson as told
    to Jerry B. Jenkins. Waco, Tx., Word Books, c1977. 192 p.
    Autobiographical. DLC

1738 From Innsbruck to Montreal, Tim, Kornelia, Sheila and Vasli
    are best bets for Olympic gold.
    In People Weekly, 4 (Dec. 29, 1975), 103-105. On Madeline
    Manning Jackson: p. 104.

1739 Gilbert, Bil
    See how they run, [by] Bil Gilbert. In Saturday Evening
    Post, 241 (Oct. 19, 1968), 34-39, 82, 84, 86-87, 90. "The
    beautiful half-miler: Madeline Manning": p. 84, 86-87.

1740 Thompson, Al
    Madeline Manning Jackson: praise the Lord and pass the
    other runners, [by] Al Thompson. In People Weekly, 4 (Sept.
    15, 1975), 33-35.

1741 JACKSON, Milton Paul (1923-   )
    BDNM (1975), 257-258.
    CGIC
    Pastor, district supt.
    b. July 24, 1923, Denver, Co.

1742 JACKSON, Raymond Samuel (1892-1983)
      BWTS, 190, 192, 361.
      CTTR, 165-167, 547, 551.
      SBHCGRM, 124.
      CG (A)
      Pastor
      b. Mar. 20, 1892, Cass County, Mi.
      d. Jan. 1983, Detroit, Mi.

1743 Elder statesman dies.
      In Vital Christianity, 103 (Apr. 3, 1983), 23.

1744 Massey, James Earl, 1930-
      I found my true home, [by] James Earl Massey. In Callen,
      B. L., ed. A time to remember: testimonies. Anderson,
      In., c1978, 45-47. DLC

1745 Massey, James Earl, 1930-
      Raymond S. Jackson: a portrait, [by] James Earl Massey.
      With a foreword by Charles E. Brown. Anderson, In., Warner
      Press, 1967. 96 p. DLC

1746 JACKSON, Samuel Charles (1929-)
      WWIA (1978-1979), I, 1628.
      WWIAP (1977-1978), 495.
      CGIC
      Lawyer, government official, author
      b. May 8, 1929, Kansas City, Ks.

1747 Jackson, Samuel Charles, 1929-
      Plant location, a corporate social responsibility, [by] Sam-
      uel C. Jackson. In Suburban Action Institute. Open or
      closed suburbs: corporate location and the urban crisis.
      White Plains, N.Y., 1971. N

1748 Jackson, Samuel Charles, 1929-
      Using the law to attack discrimination in employment, [by]
      Samuel C. Jackson. In Washburn Law Journal, 8 (Winter
      1969).

1749 JACOBS, Clarence
      BCUC, 14-15.
      SA, FrC, CN
      Pastor, author
      b. 19--, Guyana

1750 JACQUES, Honore
      CG (C)
      Pastor, author
      b. 19--, Haiti

1751 *JAMES, Gilbert Morris (1915-1982)
       WJGIG, 73-74, 78-79, 80, 84, 93-94, 96, 113.
       UBIC, FMCNA
       Pastor, denominational admin., editor, seminary prof., au-
thor
       b. Nov. 5, 1915, Brazil, In.
       d. Jan. 21, 1982, Wilmore, Ky.

1752 James, Gilbert Morris, 1915-1982.
       Seminars in the slums, [by] Gilbert M. James. In Chris-
tian Life, 29 (June 1967), 34-35, 39-41.

1753 JEFFERSON, Illie L.
       WWIR (1977), 327.
       CGIC, CGICI
       Pastor, bishop

1754 JEFFERSON, Ralph Livingston (1932-)
       WWIR (1985), 182.
       CGIC
       Pastor
       b. Nov. 6, 1932, Southampton, N.Y.

1755 JEFFRIES, Elmira (-1964)
       PPIB, III, 99.
       MSHCA
       Pastor, bishop
       d. 1964, Philadelphia, Pa.

1756 JETER, John A. (1854-1945)
       CHCCH, 27, 118, 119, 276, 416, 429, 431, 432, 444.
       MHAFY, 16, 55
       MBaC, CGIC, CChr (H)
       Pastor, bishop
       b. 1854, Nottoway County, Va.
       d. Sept. 15, 1945, Little Rock, Ar.

1757 JOHN, Sarah P. (1923-)
       MOM (1975), 363.
       CG (T), CGP
       Pastor
       b. June 20, 1923, Montserrat, W.I.

1758 JOHNSON, Aaron
       I
       Evangelist, author

1759 Johnson, Aaron
       The end of Youngblood Johnson, [by] Aaron (Youngblood)
       Johnson, as told to Jamie Buckingham. New York, Chosen
       Books; distributed by F. H. Revell Co., Old Tappan, N.J.,
       1973. 190 p. Autobiography. DLC

1760 Johnson, Aaron
      The end of Youngblood Johnson, [by] Aaron (Youngblood)
      Johnson, as told to Jamie Buckingham. Old Tappan, N.J.,
      F. H. Revell Co., c1973. 205 p. (Spire books) Autbiogra-
      phy. DLC, TxDa

1761 JOHNSON, Bromfield (1901-1972)
      Ba, UHCA, MCHCA
      Pastor, evangelist, bishop, author
      b. 1901, Charlotte, N.C.
      d. 1972, Boston, Ma.

1762 Paris, Arthur Ernest, 1945-
      Black Pentecostalism: Southern religion in an urban world,
      [by] Arthur E. Paris. Amherst, University of Massachusetts
      Press, 1982. vii, 183 p. Based on thesis (Ph.D.)--North-
      western University. On Bishop Bromfield Johnson: p. 32-36.
      DLC, OkU

1763 JOHNSON, Buford C.
      CN
      Pastor

1764 Chambers, Herbert Morell, 1871-1928.
      Our church and the American Negro, [by] H. M. Chambers.
      In Herald of Holiness, 11 (Aug. 9, 1922), 9.

1765 JOHNSON, Charles (1939-)
      RFSTGA, 52.
      CN
      Pastor, denominational admin., author

1766 Johnson, Charles, 1939-
      Blacks, whites, and the Holy Spirit; an interview with
      Charles Johnson, [by Jerry L. Appleby]. In Preacher's
      Magazine, 58 (Dec./Jan./Feb. 1982-1983), 26-29.

1767 Appleby, Polly
      "What color is God's skin?" Stories of ethnic leaders in
      America, by Polly Appleby. Kansas City, Mo., Beacon Hill
      Press of Kansas City, c1984. 87 p. "Charles Johnson:
      American black/Mississippi District": p. 28-42. OMtvN

1768 Tharp, Kathy (Talmadge)
      Another title for Charles Johnson: black consultant, [by]
      Kathy Tharp. In Herald of Holiness, 72 (Aug. 1, 1983),
      5-6.

1769 Wiseman, Neil B.
      $44.50 expands brotherhood in Mississippi, [by] Neil B.
      Wiseman. In Herald of Holiness, 67 (Sept. 15, 1978), 16-17.

1770 JOHNSON, Charles C. (-1964)
          BCUC, 38, 50.
          CN
          Evangelist, pastor
          d. July 17, 1964, Columbus, Ms.

1771 *JOHNSON, David (1893-1971)
          GBPAW, 24.
          GHPAW, 157.
          PeAW
          Pastor, district elder, bishop
          b. June 1893
          d. 1971, Superior, Wi.

1772 JOHNSON, Gordon
          SBWL, 251, 280.
          SGDIM, 12.
          FMCNA
          Pastor, evangelist
          b. 19--, Windsor, Ont.

1773 JOHNSON, James Archie (1924-)
          GBPAW, 46.
          GHPAW, 153, 157.
          PeAW
          Pastor, bishop
          b. 1924, Flint, Mi.

1774 JOHNSON, James Edward (1926-)
          WWIAP (1973-1974), 539
          Ba
          Insurance agent, politician, government executive, author
          b. Mar. 3, 1926, Madison, Il.

1775 Johnson, James Edward, 1926-
          Beyond defeat, [by] James E. Johnson, with David W.
          Balsiger. Introduction by Charles W. Colson. Garden City,
          N.Y., Doubleday, 1978. ix, 274 p. DLC

1776 Johnson, James Edward, 1926-
          Broad stripes and bright stars, [by] James Johnson. In
          Full Gospel Business Men's Voice, 23 (July 1975), 2-6.

1777 JOHNSON, James Ezra (1936-)
          WWABA (1980-1981), 430.
          AMAF
          Pastor, senior bishop
          b. May 2, 1936, Birmingham, Al.

1778 JOHNSON, Samuel Malachi (1924-)
          MOM (1975), 280.

CG (T), CGP
Pastor
b. June 16, 1924, Eleuthera Island, Bahamas

1779 JOHNSON, Sarah E. (1936-)
MOM (1975), 363.
CGP
Pastor
b. Feb. 28, 1936, West Columbia, Tx.

1780 JOHNSON, Sherrod C. (1897-1961)
HP, 393, 398, 541
NYT (Feb. 26, 1961), 93:1
COLJCAF, CLJCAF
Pastor, bishop, radio preacher, author
b. 1897, Pine Tree Quarter, Edgecomb County, N.C.
d. Feb. 22, 1961, Kingston, Jamaica

1781 Top radio ministers.
In Ebony, 4 (July 1949), 56-61. On Sherrod C. Johnson:
p. 56.

1782 JOHNSON, Sylvester D.
RWWAS, 87.
TVPeHC
Pastor, bishop

1783 JOHNSON, Thomas F. (1924-)
WWIR (1977), 334.
CGIC
Pastor
b. Nov. 14, 1924, Waller, Tx.

1784 JOHNSON, Uhijah (1913-)
MOM (1975), 280.
CG (T), CGP
Pastor
b. Jan. 20, 1913, Acklins Island, Bahamas

1785 JOHNSON, William Monroe
RWWAS, 87, 88.
TVPeHC
Pastor, bishop

1786 JONAS, Mack E. (1884-1973)
MHAFY, 127, 139.
SAOPCO, 131-135.
CGIC
Pastor, bishop
b. Oct. 30, 1884, Edwardville, Al.
d. Feb. 26, 1973, Cleveland, Oh.

1787 Jonas, Mack E., 1884-1973.
      Let the redeemed of the Lord say so: Mack E. Jonas in-
      terview. In Synan, H. V., ed. Aspects of Pentecostal-
      charismatic origins. Plainfield, N.J., 131-135. Interview by
      Leonard Lovett in Cleveland, Ohio, on October 3, 1971.

1788 Bishop Mack E. Jonas dead.
      In Call and Post (Cleveland), 60 (Mar. 3, 1973), 1A, 4A.

1789 Ward, Alvin
      Final rites held for Bishop Mack E. Jonas, [by] Alvin Ward.
      In Call and Post (Cleveland), 60 (Mar. 10, 1973), 6A.

1790 JONES, Booker T. (1902-   )
      GBPAW, 35.
      GHPAW, 153, 157.
      PeAW
      Pastor, district elder, bishop
      b. Mar. 26, 1902, Independence, Va.

1791 JONES, Charles Price (1865-1949)
      AVOD, 143.
      CHCCH, 17-35, 44, 117, 118, 128-129, 269, 427, 429, 430,
      431, 434, 435-436, 446.
      FTINS, 47.
      MHAFY, 16, 63.
      PPIB, III, 18, 110.
      RFSTGA, 49.
      MBaC, CGIC, CChr (H)
      Pastor, song writer, senior bishop, author
      b. Dec. 9, 1865, near Rome, Ga.
      d. Jan. 19, 1949, Los Angeles, Ca.

1792 Jones, Charles Price, 1865-1949.
      Autobiographical sketch of Charles Price Jones, founder of
      the Church of Christ (Holiness) U.S.A. [1935] In Cobbins,
      O. B., ed. History of Church of Christ (Holiness) U.S.A.,
      1895-1965. Chicago, c1966, 21-30. DLC, OkEG

1793 Cooley, Steven, 1954-
      The legacy of Bishop C. P. Jones, [by] Steve Cooley.
      In Herald of Holiness, 74 (May 15, 1985), 9. Nazarene roots.

1794 Jones, Cornelius J. (1915-   )
      WWIR (1985), 187.
      CGIC
      Teacher, pastor, district supt.
      b. Mar. 15, 1915, Dallas, Tx.

1795 JONES, Curtis (1932-   )
      WWIR (1977), 336.
      CGIC

Elder, Bible college dean
b. July 6, 1932, Minden, La.

1796 JONES, Curtis P. (-1976)
RWWAS, 86-87.
CG (AP), BWPeAC
Pastor, bishop

1797 *JONES, David

Evangelist

1798 Brisbane, Arthur S.
Faith healer draws flocks of believers, [by] Arthur S.
Brisbane. In Kansas City Star, 99 (May 5, 1979), 1, 6.

1799 JONES, Edward L. (1928-)
MOM (1975), 53.
CGP
Pastor, state overseer, denominational admin.
b. Apr. 15, 1928, High Point, N.C.

1800 JONES, James Francis Marion (1907-1971)
TCKGIC, CUTDG
Evangelist, pastor, radio preacher
b. 1907, Birmingham, Al.
d. Aug. 12, 1971, Detroit, Mi.

1801 All is well?
In Newsweek, 47 (Mar. 5, 1956), 82.

1802 Brean, Herbert, 1907-1973.
A Life reporter visits Prophet Jones in church and at
home, [by] Herbert Brean. In Life, 17 (Nov. 27, 1944), 58.

1803 Cartwright, Marguerite
Observations on community life, [by] Marguerite Cartwright. In Negro History Bulletin, 18 (Dec. 1954), 66-67;
18 (Jan. 1955), 88-89; 18 (Feb. 1955), 109-111. "I visit
Prophet Jones": p. 88-89.

1804 Cosmic lubritorium.
In Time, 62 (Sept. 21, 1953), 79-80.

1805 Detroit's Prophet Jones, 63; colorful preacher of the '50s.
In Evening Star (Washington), 119 (Aug. 13, 1971), B5.

1806 Diamonds on the left.
In Time, 64 (Sept. 20, 1954), 68.

1807 Kobler, John, 1910-
Prophet Jones: messiah in mink, [by] John Kobler.

In Saturday Evening Post, 227 (Mar. 5, 1955), 20-21, 74, 76-77.

1808 Mink-minded prophet dies: successor sought.
          In Jet, 40 (Sept. 2, 1971), 20-23.

1809 Preview for the prophet.
          In Time, 61 (Mar. 2, 1953), 17.

1810 A prophet and a Divine meet.
          In Life, 35 (Sept. 28, 1953), 103-104, 106.

1811 Prophet Jones.
          In Ebony, 5 (Apr. 1950), 67-72.

1812 The Prophet Jones.
          In Newsweek, 41 (Jan. 12, 1953), 73.

1813 The prophet threatened?
          In Newsweek, 47 (Feb. 13, 1956), 90-91.

1814 Prophet's mink.
          In Life, 34 (Mar. 30, 1953), 64-66, 69.

1815 The rise and fall of Prophet Jones.
          In Ebony, 11 (Oct. 1956), 63-66.

1816 Thompson, Era Bell, 1905-
          Black astrologers predict the future, [by] Era Bell Thompson. In Ebony, 24 (Apr. 1969), 62-64, 66-68, 70. "Prophet Jones": p. 66-67.

1817 JONES, John Albert (1929-)
          WWIR (1985), 187.
          CGIC
          Pastor, district supt.

1818 JONES, Marcelene N. (1901-)
          MOM (1975), 282.
          CG (T), CGP
          Pastor
          b. July 23, 1901, Turks Island, Bahamas

1818a JONES, Miriam McGregor
          MHAFY, 85, 103, 106, 143.
          CGIC
          Teacher, author

1819 JONES, Ozro Thurston (1890-1972)
          AVOD, 268, 293.
          KPF, 198

        MHAFY, 66, 67, 75, 76, 77, 78, 100, 102.
        Ba, CGIC
        Pastor, bishop, author
        b. Mar. 26, 1890, Fort Smith, Ar.
        d. Sept. 23, 1972, Philadelphia, Pa.

1819a Pentecostal minister dies in Philadelphia.
        In Jet, 43 (Oct. 19, 1972), 18.

1820 JONES, Ozro Thurston (192 -)
        AVOD, 268.
        BDNM (1975), 286.
        MHAFY, 78, 85.
        WWABA (1985), 469.
        CGIC
        Pastor, missionary, editor, bishop, denominational admin.,
        author
        b. 192-, Fort Smith, Ar.

1821 Jones, Ozro Thurston, 192 -
        The meaning of the "moment" in the existential encounter
        according to Kierkegaard, [by] Ozro T. Jones, Jr. Philadel-
        phia, 1962. 185 l. Thesis (S.T.D.)--Temple University.
        PPT

1822 JONES, Pearl Williams
        HGS, xiii.
        BWCOLJCWW
        Musician, university prof., author
        b. 19--, Washington, D.C.

1823 Grace concert to feature Mrs. Pearl W. Jones Sun[day].
        In Indianapolis Recorder, 75 (June 6, 1970), 7.

1824 JONES, Randy
        UM
        Pastor

1825 Keysor, Charles W.
        Journey into joy. Text and photos [by] Charles W. Key-
        sor. In Good News, 12 (May/June 1979), 26-36.

1826 JONES, Walt (1933-)
        RC, MenC
        Legal assistant, author
        b. 1933, New York, N.Y.

1827 Jones, Walt, 1933-
        A revolutionary change, [by] Walt Jones. In New Cove-
        nant, 7 (May 1978), 31-33.

1828 JONES, William Virgil (1926-   )
      AMD (1982)
      CP, 97.
      CGIC
      Physician
      b. 1926, Philadelphia, Pa.

1829 JULES-ROSETTE, Bennetta
      ACJM
      University prof., author

1830 Jules-Rosette, Bennetta
      African apostles: ritual and conversion in the Church of
      John Maranke. Ithaca, N.Y., Cornell University Press, 1975.
      302 p. DLC

1831 KELLY, Henry Franklin (1924-   )
      WWIR (1977), 348.
      CGIC
      Pastor, district supt., Bible college instructor
      b. Mar. 10, 1924, Ripley, Ca.

1832 KELLY, Otha M.
      MHAFY, 88, 90, 91, 106, 109, 135, 137, 139
      CGIC
      Pastor, bishop, author

1833 Kelly, Otha M.
      Profile of a churchman, [by] Otha M. Kelly. New York,
      K & C Publishers, 1976. 144 p.

1834 KELSEY, Samuel
      BDNM (1975), 293.
      MHAFY, 139.
      CGIC
      Pastor, bishop
      b. 19--, Sandville, Ga.

1835 Davis, Arnor S., 1919-
      The Pentecostal movement in black Christianity, [by] Arnor
      S. Davis. In Black Church, 2:1 (1972), 65-88. On Samuel
      Kelsey: p. 84, 87.

1836 He never has left me alone.
      In Washington Afro-American (Jan. 12, 1974), 12.

1837 KILLINGSWORTH, Frank Russell (1878-   )
      PPIB, III, 46.
      WWIR (1977), 353.
      AMEZ, KCI
      Pastor, supervising elder, author

1838 KIMBANGU, Simon (1889-1951)
       HP, 167, 175, 443.
       NCDCWM, 324-325.
       Ba, EJCTPSK
       Farmer, prophet
       b. Sept. 24, 1889, Nkamba, Belgian Congo
       d. Oct. 10, 1951, Elisabethville, Congo (now Lubumbashi,
       Zaire)

1839 Chomé, Jules
       La passion de Simon Kimbangu, 1921-1951. Bruxelles,
       Les Amis de Présence africaine, 1959. 131 p. DLC

1840 Chomé, Jules
       La passion de Simon Kimbangu, 1921-1951. 2. éd. Brux-
       elles, Les Amis de Présence africaine, 1960. 134 p. FU, WU

1841 Gilis, Charles André
       Kimbangu, fondateur d'église. Bruxelles, Librairie ency-
       clopédique, 1960. 123 p. DLC, PPT

1842 Martin, Marie-Louise, 1912-
       Kimbangu: an African prophet and his church, [by]
       Marie-Louise Martin. With a foreword by Bryan R. Wilson.
       Translated by D. M. Moore. Oxford, Blackwell, c1975.
       xxiv, 198 p. Translation of Kirche ohne Weisse. DLC

1843 Martin, Marie-Louise, 1912-
       Kimbangu: an African prophet and his church, [by]
       Marie-Louise Martin. With a foreword by Bryan R. Wilson.
       Translated by D. M. Moore. 1st American ed. Grand Rapids,
       Mi., Eerdmans, 1976. xxiv, 198 p. Translation of Kirche
       ohne Weisse. DLC

1844 Martin, Marie-Louise, 1912-
       Kirche ohne Weisse: Simon Kimbangu und seine Millionen
       im Kongo. Basel, Friedrich Reinhardt, 1979. 279 p. DLC

1845 Nfinangani.
       Histoire de Simon Kimbangu, prophète, d'après les écrivains
       Nfinangani et Nzungu, 1921: contribution à l'etude de l'his-
       toire du Congo. [Texte introduit et annoté par] Paul Ray-
       maekers. Préf. d'Henri Desroche. Kinshasa, Bureau d'or-
       ganisation des programmes ruraux, Université, 1971. 55 p.
       Caption title: Histoire de l'apparition du prophete Simon Kim-
       bangu. Translated from the Congo language. DLC

1846 Sinda, Martial, 1935-
       Simon Kimbangu, prophète et martyr zahirois, [par] Martial
       Sinda. Paris, A.B.C. [Afrique biblio-club]; Dakar, Abidjan,
       N.E.A. [Nouvelles editions africaines], 1977. 111 p. (Grandes
       figures africaines, 0338-0882) CtY-D, DLC

1847 Ustorf, Werner, 1945-
      Afrikanische Initiative: das aktive Leiden des Propheten
      Simon Kimbangu, [von] Werner Ustorf. Bern, Herbert Lang;
      Frankfurt/M., Peter Lang, 1975. 457 p. (Studien zur inter-
      kulturellen Geschichte des Christentums, 5) Originally pre-
      sented as the author's thesis, Hamburg. DLC

1848 KIRKLAND, Pauline Janette Sneed (1915-)
         WWIR (1977), 357.
         CG (A)
         Pastor, teacher, national asso. officer
         b. July 15, 1915, Nashville, Tn.

1849 KNOWLES, Charlie A. (1902-)
         MOM (1975), 130.
         CG (T), CGP
         Pastor, district overseer, evangelist
         b. July 2, 1902, Bahamas

1850 KNOWLES, George H. (1929-)
         MOM (1975), 130.
         CGP
         Pastor, district overseer
         b. Apr. 19, 1929, Hallandale, Fl.

1851 LACY, Floyd Henry (1890-1969)
         BCUC, 14.
         CN
         Singer
         d. Sept. 29, 1969, Duarte, Ca.

1852 LANE, Morris R.
         RWWAS, 41.
         NAAB
         Pastor, bishop

1853 LANG, Emanuel (1940-)
         WWIR (1985), 212.
         CGIC
         Evangelist, pastor, Bible college dean
         b. Mar. 21, 1940, Newton, Ms.

1854 LANTON, Wade (-1978)
         CG (C)
         d. May 4, 1978, Cleveland, Tn.

1855 Polen, Olly Wayne, 1920-
         Sonny, [by] O. W. Polen. In Church of God Evangel, 68
      (July 10, 1978), 31.

1856 LARSON, Jeane

1857 Larson, Jeane
        Sovreign intervention, [by] Jeane Larson. In New Cove-
        nant, 8 (July 1978), 32-33. Autobiographical.

1858 LATTA, William
        BWCOLJCWW
        Pastor, Bible college admin., bishop

1859 LAWRENCE, Benjamin J. (1930-)
        MOM (1975), 27.
        CGP
        Pastor, district overseer
        b. Nov. 22, 1930, High Point, N.C.

1860 LAWSON, Andrew William
        UHCA
        Bishop, college pres., author

1861 LAWSON, Robert Clarence (1891-1961)
        AVOD, 132.
        CPH (1963), 35.
        NYT (July 4, 1961), 19:3.
        RWWAS, 37, 45-46, 54-59, 60, 62
        WWICA (1950), 333.
        PeAW, COLJCAF
        Pastor, bishop, author
        b. May 5, 1891, New Iberia, La.
        d. June 30, 1961, New York, N.Y.

1862 Lawson, Robert Clarence, 1891-1961.
        For the defense of the gospel: the writings of Bishop
        R. C. Lawson. Edited by Arthur M. Anderson. New York,
        Church of Christ Publishing Co., 1972.

1863 Bonner, William L.
        My father in the gospel, [by] William L. Bonner. [New
        York, 197-] 54 p.

1864 Top radio ministers.
        In Ebony, 4 (July 1949), 56-61. On Robert C. Lawson:
        p. 57.

1865 Williams, Smallwood Edmond, 1907-
        Bishop Lawson's mistakes viewed, [by] S. E. Williams.
        In Bible Way News Voice, 5 (July/Aug. 1958), 5.

1866 LAYNE, Austin Augustus (1891-1967)
        GBPAW, 18.
        GHPAW, 132.
        PeAW
        Pastor, district elder, bishop

   b. Apr. 2, 1891, Barbados, W.I.
   d. 1967, St. Louis, Mo.

1867 LEASTON, Heardie J. (1895-1972)
      AOHUTR
      GHPAW, 141.
      PeAW, PeCAFA
      Pastor, bishop
      d. 1972, Ferndale, Mi.

1868 LEE, Clester Richard (1896-)
      GBPAW, 43.
      GHPAW, 153, 157.
      PeAW
      Pastor, district elder, bishop
      b. 1896, Kentucky

1869 LEE, Willie (-1968)
      RWWAS, 78-79, 95.
      PeAW, PeCAFA, EPeCAF
      Pastor, bishop
      d. 1968, Indianapolis, In.

1870 LEWIS, Alvin (1935-)
      WWABA (1985), 514.
      CG (A)
      Pastor, university prof., counselor, denominational official
      b. Oct. 1, 1935, Chicago, Il.

1871 *LEWIS, Arthur William (1896-1973)
      GBPAW, 5.
      Lu, PeAW
      Pastor, bishop
      b. 1896, Pennsylvania
      d. 1973, Santa Ana, Ca.

1872 LEWIS, Essie B. (1913-)
      MOM (1975), 366.
      CG (T), CGP
      Pastor
      b. Dec. 7, 1913, Randolph County, N.C.

1873 LEWIS, Harvey (-1980)
      CGIC
      Minister, musician, author
      d. Jan. 9, 1980, Washington, D.C.

1873a LEWIS, Helen Middleton (1905-)
      WWABA (1985), 516.
      Pastor, bishop, chief overseer
      b. Apr. 25, 1905, Crystal River, Fl.

1874   LEWIS, Meharry Hubbard (1936-   )
       WWABA (1977-1978), 555.
       CLGPGT
       College prof. and dean, denominational official
       b. Aug. 2, 1936, Nashville, Tn.

1875   LITTLE, Robert L.
       RWWAS, 79.
       PeCAFA
       Pastor, bishop

1876   LOMAX, J. V.
       RWWAS, 69-70, 99, 100.
       COLJCAF, HChrCChr
       Pastor, bishop

1877   LONG, C. L.
       COLJCAF
       Pastor, bishop, television preacher, author

1878   Swanson, Tonya D.
       Preaching fire and brimstone via television, [by] Tonya D.
       Swanson. In Washington Star, 127 (Feb. 11, 1979), F5.

1879   LOPEZ, Charles G. (1902-   )
       MOM (1975), 290.
       CG (T), CGP
       Pastor, district overseer
       b. Dec. 2, 1902, Long Island, Bahamas

1880   LOTT, James Junior (1944-   )
       MOM (1975), 290.
       CGP
       Pastor
       b. July 31, 1944, Shelby, N.C.

1881   LOVETT, Leonard (1939-   )
       SAOPCO, 123-124.
       TBPALM, 150.
       WWABA (1985), 530.
       CGIC
       Pastor, seminary prof. and admin., author
       b. Dec. 5, 1939, Pompano Beach, Fl.

1882   LOWE, Charles W.
       AFCG
       Pastor

1883   LUCAS, Calvin (1951-   )

       Prison chaplain

1884 Brooks, Delores J.
          Preaching the word behind bars, [by] Delores J. Brooks.
      In Ebony, 33 (Aug. 1978), 142.

1885 LUCAS, Mary (1952-)

          Teacher, prison chaplain

1886 Brooks, Delores J.
          Preaching the word behind bars, [by] Delores J. Brooks.
      In Ebony, 33 (Aug. 1978), 142.

1887 LUMPKINS, B. L.
          CGAFA
          Pastor, bishop

1888 LUMPKINS, Julius Smith (1895-)
          WWIR (1985), 229.
          CGIC
          Pastor, jurisdictional supt.
          b. Oct. 3, 1895, White Oak, S.C.

1889 LUNDY, Eugene
          AMD (1982)
          PeAW
          Physician

1890 LYSEIGHT, O. A.
          CLMA (1977), 296-297, 375.
          CWSHT, 252-253.
          CG (C), NTCG
          Pastor, overseer
          b. 19--, Jamaica

1891 MABE, John
          PPIB, III, 149.
          AOPeCA
          Pastor, overseer

1892 McCOLLOUGH, D.
          BACPeMA
          Pastor, bishop

1893 McCOLLOUGH, Walter (1915-)
          NP, 150-151.
          UHOPFAP
          Pastor, bishop
          b. May 22, 1915

1894 Court ousts Daddy Grace [!] successor, names lawyer as
      church receiver.

In Evening Star (Washington), 109 (Aug. 25, 1961), 1A-2A.

1895 Milloy, Courtland
      City politicians wait for bishop's word, [by] Courtland
      Milloy. In Washington Post, 101 (Sept. 5, 1978), A1, A4.

1896 The truth and facts of the United House of Prayer for All
      People and the most honorable Bishop W. McCollough, leader.
      Washington, 1968. viii, 100 p. DLC

1897 McCOY, Andrew (1910-   )
      WWIR (1985), 246.
      CGIC
      Pastor, district supt.
      b. Dec. 15, 1910, Sibley, La.

1898 McCOY, Lawrence F.
      AAOLSJC, OAAOLSJC
      Pastor, bishop, author

1899 McCRACKEN, Abraham Lincoln (1907-1981)
      FBHCGA
      Pastor, district elder, bishop
      d. 1981, Evanston, Il.

1900 McCRACKEN, James (1911-   )
      WWIR (1977), 432.
      CGIC
      Pastor, evangelist
      b. Aug. 24, 1911, Newberry, S.C.

1901 MacDONALD, William H.
      CGIC
      Pastor, bishop

1902 Ross, Marie
      Crowd hears COGIC leader at installation of Kansas bishop,
      [by] Marie Ross. In Kansas City Call (Feb. 6, 1976)

1903 McEWEN, A. B.
      MHAFY, 77, 78, 88, 90, 91, 92, 100, 101, 132, 135, 140
      TBPALM, 149.
      CGIC
      Pastor, bishop

1904 McGEE, Welton (1924-   )
      WWIR (1977), 436.
      CGIC
      Pastor, radio program host, district supt.
      b. Nov. 1, 1924, Fairfield, Tx.

1905 McGHEE, Theopolis Dickenson (1882-1965)
       PPIB, III, 38.
       CG (SC)
       Pastor, denominational chairman
       b. 1882
       d. 1965, Detroit, Mi.

1906 McINNIS, Henry R. (-1956)
       CHCCH, 51, 52, 192, 233.
       TDOOP, 180.
       ME, CChr (H), PHC, CChr (H)
       Pastor
       b. 18--, Capiah County, Ms.
       d. Dec. 6, 1956, Utica, Ms.

1907 McINNIS, Obadiah Wesley (1909-)
       CHCCH, 187, 282, 285-287.
       CChr (H)
       Teacher, pastor, bishop, editor
       b. Dec. 24, 1909, Myles, Ms.

1908 McIVER, Minnie (1904-)
       MOM (1975), 369.
       CG (T), CGP
       Pastor
       b. May 10, 1904, Seagrove, N.C.

1909 *McKEOWN, James (1900-)
       EEB, AC, GCAC, CP
       Pastor, missionary, denominational leader
       b. Sept. 12, 1900, Glenboig, Lanarks.

1910 Wyllie, Robert W.
       Pioneers of Ghanian Pentecostalism: Peter Anim and James
       McKeown, [by] Robert W. Wyllie. In Journal of Religion in
       Africa, 6:2 (1974), 109-122.

1911 MACKEY, Charles Irwin (1915-)
       MOM (1975), 138.
       CG (T), CGP
       Pastor, district overseer
       b. Nov. 5, 1915, Eleuthera Island, Bahamas

1912 McKINNEY, George Dallas (1932-)
       CA (1st rev.), 5/8, 765.
       WWABA (1985), 573.
       CGIC
       Pastor, author
       b. Aug. 9, 1932, Jonesboro, Ar.

1913 McKinney, George Dallas, 1932-
       A descriptive study of the new world society of Jehovah's

Witnesses. Oberlin, Oh., 1956. ix, 174 1. Thesis (M.A.)--
Oberlin College. OO

1914 McKINNEY, George Dallas, 1932-
           I will build my church. n.p., 1977. x, 63 p. Autobio-
           graphical. ArStC, CLamB

1915 McLEOD, Maria B. (1913-)
           MOM (1975), 370.
           CG (T), CGP
           Pastor
           b. Dec. 12, 1913, Manchester, Jamaica

1916 McMURRAY, Robert William (1926-)
           GBPAW, 52.
           GHPAW, 157, 177.
           PeAW
           Pastor, district elder, bishop
           b. 1926, Cincinnati, Oh.

1917 Christmas, Faith C.
           Officials seek mediation in police-clergy dispute, [by] Faith
           C. Christmas. In Los Angeles Sentinel, 43 (Aug. 21, 1975),
           A1, C11.

1918 Christmas, Faith C.
           Pastor's arrest triggers outrage, [by] Faith C. Christmas.
           In Los Angeles Sentinel, 43 (Aug. 14, 1975), A1, C12.

1919 McNEILL, Bobby Earl (1934-)
           WWIR (1985), 251.
           CGIC
           Pastor
           b. July 2, 1934, Fayetteville, N.C.

1920 McPHERSON, David P.
           CHCCH, 282, 287-288.
           CChr (H)
           Pastor, bishop

1921 MADISON, Charlie (1912-1977)
           I
           Building contractor
           b. Mar. 12, 1912, near Glenwood, Ga.
           d. Mar. 22, 1977, New Brunswick, N.J.

1922 Worrell, William
           That couple with all those kids, [by] William Worrell. In
           Logos Journal, 8 (Sept./Oct. 1978), 44-45, 50-51.

1923 MAIS, Roger (1905-1955)

Writer
b. Aug. 11, 1905, Kingston, Jamaica
d. June 21, 1955

1924 Baytop, Adrianne Roberts
James Baldwin and Roger Mais: the Pentecostal theme. In
Jamaica Journal, 42 (1978), 14-21.

1925 Vanouse, Evelyn (Hawthorne)
Roger Mais: the romantic voice and the nationalist image,
[by] Evelyn Hawthorne Vanouse. Minneapolis, 1982. 141 l.
Thesis (Ph.D.)--University of Minnesota. MnU

1926 MALLORY, Arenia Conelia (1905-1977)
MHAFY, 69, 89, 137.
WWIACUA (1970-1971), 327.
WWISS (1973-1974), 463.
WWOAW (1977-1978), 563.
CGIC
College teacher and pres.
b. Dec. 28, 1905, Jacksonville, Il.
d. May 1977

1927 Herbers, John N., 1923-
Negro officials score Nixon plan, [by] John Herbers. In
New York Times, 118 (Sept. 13, 1969), 28. "Brutality start-
ing again": p. 28.

1928 Mississippi dignitaries pay tribute to black educator.
In Jet, 46 (May 30, 1974), 28.

1929 Powell gets plaque: woman college head honored also by Utility
Club.
In New York Times, 105 (June 3, 1956), 79.

1930 Tinney, James Steven, 1942-
Dr. Arenia Mallory recalls early days at Barker Temple,
[by] James S. Tinney. In Kansas City Call (May 5, 1972),
10.

1931 MAQUILING, Leonard (-1971)
CG (C)
Air force officer
d. Oct. 24, 1971, Vietnam; buried Honolulu.

1932 Fisher, Robert Elwood, 1931-
Joy in the midst of mourning, [by] Robert E. Fisher. In
Church of God Evangel, 62 (Mar. 27, 1972), 14.

1933 MARSHALL, Evans Bromley (1903-)
BWTS, 248.

SBHCGRM, 125.
WWIR (1975-1976), 362.
CG (A)
Pastor, editor
b. July 16, 1903, Barbados, W.I.

1934 *MARTIN, William
          GBPAW, 69.
          GHPAW, 118.
          PeAW
          Pastor, bishop

1935 MASON, Charles Harrison (1866-1961)
          ATF, 30, 61, 91.
          AVOD, 71, 102, 106, 143, 167, 174, 189.
          BDARB, 293-294.
          BSFH, 83-84, 154.
          CHCCH, 27, 50-52, 429-432.
          DBWS, 83
          FTINS, 47.
          HP, 43, 482
          KPF, 79-80, 197-198
          MATS, 56, 64
          NP, 37, 102
          SAOPCO, 93, 133, 138-139
          SHPM, 79-80, 92, 135-137, 138, 150, 167-168, 221
          SOTP, 139
          TBPALM, 88-100, 148-149, 154.
          WWWA (1961-1968), 618
          WWWCH (1968)
          MBaC, CGIC
          Pastor, evangelist, bishop, author
          b. Sept. 9, 1866, Bartlett, Tn.
          d. Nov. 17, 1961, Memphis, Tn.

1936 Mason, Charles Harrison, 1866-1961.
          C. H. Mason, a man greatly used of God. [Memphis],
      Women's Dept., Churches of God in Christ, 1967. 86 p.
      "Collected and recompiled by Elnora L. Lee." GAUC

1937 Mason, Charles Harrison, 1866-1961.
          History and formative years of the Church of God in
      Christ, with excerpts from the life and works of its founder:
      Bishop C. H. Mason. Reproduced by J. O. Patterson, Ger-
      man R. Ross [and] Mrs. Julia Mason Atkins. Memphis,
      Church of God in Christ Publishing House, 1969. 143 p.
      OSW

1938 Mason, Charles Harrison, 1866-1961.
          The history and life work of Elder C. H. Mason, chief
      apostle, and his co-laborers. Compiled by Prof. Jas. Courts.
      Memphis, Howe Printing Dept., 1920. 97 p. DLC

1939 Mason, Charles Harrison, 1866-1961.
        The history and life work of Elder C. H. Mason and his
        co-laborers. Compiled by Mary Esther Mason. [Memphis,
        Church of God in Christ, 1934] [92] p. Cover title.

1940 Mason, Charles Harrison, 1866-1961.
        The history and life work of Elder C. H. Mason, chief
        apostle, and his co-laborers from 1893 to 1924. Introduction
        by J. Courts. San Francisco, T. L. Delaney, c1977. 89 p.
        "Recompiled in 1924." TM

1941 Battle, Allen Overton, 1927-
        Status personality in a Negro Holiness sect. Washington,
        1961. v, 114 1. Thesis (Ph.D.)--Catholic University of
        America. DCU

1942 Church celebrates 50th anniversary.
        In Ebony, 13 (Mar. 1958), 54-56, 58-60.

1943 Coffey, Lillian Brooks, 1896-1964.
        A tribute to the memory of our founder, Bishop Charles
        H. Mason. In Cornelius, L. J., ed. The pioneer: history
        of the Church of God in Christ. [Memphis], c1975, 25-26.

1944 Fastest-growing church.
        In Ebony, 4 (Aug. 1949), 57-60.

1945 Hall, David A.
        Charles H. Mason; storybook for children, [by] David A.
        Hall. [Memphis], c1983. [31] p. Cover title.

1946 Tinney, James Steven, 1942-
        Black Pentecostals: setting up the kingdom, [by] James
        S. Tinney. In Christianity Today, 20 (Dec. 5, 1975), 42-43.

1947 MASON, J. B.
        CGH, 31.
        Ba, CLGCWFF
        Pastor, evangelist, overseer, bishop, nursing home supt.
        b. 189-, Alabama

1948 MASSEY, James Earl (1930-   )
        BDNM (1975), 346.
        CA (new rev.), 12:306.
        SBHCGRM, 122.
        WWABA (1985), 551.
        WWIR (1985), 240.
        CG (A)
        Pastor, seminary prof. and pres., radio preacher, author
        b. Jan. 4, 1930, Ferndale, Mi.

1949   MATTHEWS, Willie W.
          WWIR (1985), 241.
          CGBF
          Pastor, bishop

1949a MAY, James S. (1880-1955)
          CG (A)
          Pastor, evangelist
          b. Apr. 15, 1880, Washington County, Ga.
          d. Feb. 2, 1955, Dublin, Ga.

1949b [Sawyer, Thomas Jason], 1921-
          James S. May, 1880-1955. In Massey, J. E. Three black
       leaders of the Church of God reformation movement. Ander-
       son, In., c1981, 31-65.

1950   MAYFIELD, Charles B. (1935-)
          WWIR (1977), 427.
          CGIC
          Pastor, realtor
          b. Aug. 21, 1935, Memphis, Tn.

1951   MAYNARD, Aurora
          PeAW
          Pastor, author
          b. 19--, Nevis, B. W. I.

1952   Maynard, Aurora
          The inner guidance. New York, Vantage Press, c1965.
          116 p. InIT, OkTOR

1953   MBAGWU, John R.

1954   Mbagwu, John R.
          A living testimony, [by] John R. Mbagwu. Dayton, Oh.,
          c1978. 98 p. DLC

1955   MELENDEZ-NIEVES, Jose
          CG (C)
          Pastor, evangelist, soldier, author

1956   Melendez-Nieves, Jose
          From crime to Christ, [by] Jose Melendez-Nieves. In
       Church of God Evangel, 69 (Mar. 26, 1979), 19. Autobio-
       graphical.

1957   MELVIN, Pecolia Headen (1910-)
          MOM (1975), 370.

CG (T), CGP
Pastor
b. Nov. 15, 1910, Liberty, N.C.

1958 MENENDEZ, Alphonso
CG (C)
Pastor

1959 MICHAUX, Lightfoot Solomon (1884-1968)
NYT (Oct. 21, 1968), 47:2.
CChr (H), CG (GS)
Fishmonger, pastor, evangelist, editor, radio preacher
b. Nov. 7, 1884, Newport News, Va.
d. Oct. 20, 1968, Washington, D.C.; buried Newport News,
Va.

1960 Michaux, Lightfoot Solomon, 1884-1968.
Sparks from the anvil of Elder Michaux. Compiled and
edited by Pauline Lark. Washington, Happy News Publishing
Co., 1950. ix, 139 p. DLC

1961 Elder Michaux.
In Our World, 2 (Jan. 1950), 46.

1962 Elder Solomon Michaux dies; cult leader aided Roosevelt.
In New York Times (Oct. 21, 1968), 47.

1963 Garnett, Bernard, 1940-
Most unbelievable black businessman in history. In Jet,
35 (Apr. 24, 1969), 20-24.

1964 Milestones.
In Time, 92 (Nov. 1, 1968), 98.

1965 Rasky, Frank
Harlem's religious zealots, [by] Frank Rasky. In Tomorrow,
9 (Nov. 1949), 11-17; abridged in Negro Digest, 8 (Mar. 1950),
52-62.

1966 Second front in Harlem.
In Time, 40 (Dec. 21, 1942), 74, 76.

1967 Webb, Lillian (Ashcraft)
About my father's business: the life of Elder Michaux, [by]
Lillian Ashcraft Webb. Foreword by Henry H. Mitchell. West-
port, Ct., Greenwood Press, 1981. xix, 210 p. (Contributions
in Afro-American and African studies, 61) DLC

1968 MILES, Floyd Alexander (1928-)

1969 Miles, Floyd Alexander, 1928-
         Black tracks: nineteen years on the mainline, by Floyd
      Miles, Jr., as told to Irene Burk Harrell. Plainfield, N.J.,
      Logos International, c1972. vi, 115 p. DLC

1970 MILES, Levy Moses (1888-1967)
         AOHUTR
         PeAW
         Pastor
         b. July 31, 1888, Moultrie, Ga.
         d. 1967, Detroit, Mi.

1971 MINOR, J. B. W.
         CGH, 30.
         CLGCWFF
         Pastor, bishop
         b. 189-, St. Louis, Mo.

1972 MISSICK, Hilton Charles (1915-)
         MOM (1975), 294.
         CGP
         Evangelist
         b. Feb. 26, 1915, Turks Island, Bahamas

1973 MITCHELL, Harry B.
         CTTR, 548.
         CG (A)
         Pastor

1974 MITCHELL, O. L.
         CHCCH, 276, 282.
         CChr (H)
         Pastor, bishop

1975 MITCHELL, William (1874-1951)
         CHCCH, 274-276, 282.
         CChr (H)
         Pastor, bishop
         b. Feb. 20, 1874, La Pine, Al.
         d. Feb. 21, 1951, St. Louis, Mo.

1976 MOORE, Benjamin Thomas (1927-)
         GBPAW, 32.
         GHPAW, 153, 157.
         PeAW
         Pastor, bishop, author
         b. 1927, Toledo, Oh.

1977 MOORE, Willa M. Lee
         GBPAW, 32.
         PeAW
         b. 19--, Mansfield, Oh.

1977a MORGAN, Fabor (1921-1985)
  CJC
  Pastor, presiding bishop
  b. July 30, 1921, Parsons, Ks.
  d. Aug. 6, 1985, Parsons, Ks.

1978 MORGAN, Marcus Harold (1920-)
  SBHCGRM, 124.
  WWIR (1977), 462.
  CG (A)
  Pastor, denominational official, author
  b. Oct. 18, 1920, Pittsburgh, Pa.

1979 MORRIS, Ernest Carl (1933-)
  WWIR (1977), 463.
  CGIC
  Pastor
  b. Feb. 23, 1933, Philadelphia, Pa.

1980 MORRIS, Frederick C. (1931-)
  MOM (1975), 297.
  CGP
  Pastor
  b. Dec. 23, 1931, Antigua, W.I.

1981 MORRIS, James Thomas (-1959)
  RWWAS, 69.
  PeAW, HChrCChr
  Pastor, bishop
  d. Apr. 23, 1959

1982 MORRIS, Samuel (1872-1893)
  ME
  b. 1872, Liberia
  d. May 12, 1893, Fort Wayne, In.

1983 Baldwin, Lindley J., 1862-
  African prince: the true story of Samuel Morris (Prince
  Kaboo). Ilorin, Nigeria, United Missionary Society, 1958.
  47 p. "Adapted from The march of faith, by Lindley J. Baldwin." InUpT

1984 Baldwin, Lindley J., 1862-
  The ebony saint: Samuel Morris's miraculous journey of
  faith, by Lindley J. Baldwin. Evesham, Worcs., James, 1967.
  125 p. DLC

1985 Baldwin, Lindley J., 1862-
  The march of faith: the challenge of Samuel Morris to
  undying life and leadership, [by] Lindley J. Baldwin. Chicago, National Institute of Applied Religion, 1941. 94 p.
  KyWAT

1986   Baldwin, Lindley J., 1862-
       The march of faith: the challenge of Samuel Morris to un-
       dying life and leadership, [by] Lindley J. Baldwin. New
       York, c1944. 92 p. MoSpCB

1987   Baldwin, Lindley J., 1862-
       The march of faith: the challenge of Samuel Morris to un-
       dying life and leadership, [by] Lindley J. Baldwin. Victory
       Center ed. New York, Distributed by Christian Business
       Men's Committee, Inc., of N.Y., 1944. 94 p. DLC

1988   Baldwin, Lindley J., 1862-
       The march of faith: the challenge of Samuel Morris to un-
       dying life and leadership, [by] Lindley Baldwin. Chicago,
       Mary E. Baldwin, c1947. 92 p. InMarC

1989   Baldwin, Lindley J., 1862-
       Samuel Morris: the march of faith, [by] Lindley Baldwin.
       Minneapolis, Bethany Fellowship, 1971, c1942. 95 p. (Dimen-
       sion books) "29th printing."

1990   Masa, Jorge O.
       The angel in ebony; or, The life and message of Sammy
       Morris, [by] Jorge O. Masa. Published by class of 1928 of
       Taylor University. Upland, In., Taylor University Press,
       c1928. 131 p. DLC, OC, UU

1991   Merritt, Stephen, 1843-1917.
       En time med Sammy Morris, [av] Stephen Merritt [og]
       T. C. Reade. Oslo, Filadelfia-forlaget, 194-. 32 p. (Time
       biblioteket, 2) IU

1992   Merritt, Stephen, 1843-1917.
       Samuel Morris, a true story. Colorado Springs, Co., Gos-
       pel Stationery & Tract House, 19--. folder ([6] p.)

1993   Reade, Thaddeus Constantine, 1846-1902.
       Biografi af Samuel Morris, Prins Kaboo. Minneapolis,
       G. A. Törnkvist, 189-. 20 p. Cover title. Translation of
       Sketch of the life of Samuel Morris (Prince Kaboo). MnHi

1994   Reade, Thaddeus Constantine, 1846-1902.
       Samuel Morris: Prince Kaboo of the Kru tribe, seamen of
       Africa, [by] Thaddeus C. Reade. Berne, In., Golden Rule
       Book Shop, 19--. 30 p. IEG

1995   Reade, Thaddeus Constantine, 1846-1902.
       Sketch of the life of Samuel Morris (Prince Kaboo). Up-
       land, In., 1896. 19 p. Cover title. DHU, DLC, MiU

1996   Reade, Thaddeus Constantine, 1846-1902.
       Sketch of the life of Samuel Morris (Prince Kaboo), [by]

T. C. Reade. Toledo, M. C. Reade, 190-, c1896. 23 p.
Cover title. PGC

1997 Reade, Thaddeus Constantine, 1846-1902.
Sketch of the life of Samuel Morris (Prince Kaboo). Cincinnati, Mrs. M. W. Knapp, 19--, c1896. 23 p. Cover title.
WHi

1998 Ringenberg, William Carey, 1939-
Taylor University: the first 125 years, [by] William C.
Ringenberg. Grand Rapids, Mi., Eerdmans, c1973. 184 p.
"A new emphasis": p. 70-75. DLC

1999 Samuel Morris, Prince Kaboo: the case and the course; a
treatise on black studies. London, Committee on Black Studies,
1973. 37 p. Cover title. DLC, Uk

2000 Wengatz, John Christian, 1880-
Samuel Morris: Spirit-filled life, [by] John C. Wengatz.
Upland, In., Taylor University, c1954. 67 p. CSt, GU, IU

2001 MORRIS, Usril Alexander (1945-)
MOM (1975), 297.
CGP
Evangelist, pastor, district overseer
b. Jan. 15, 1945, Turks Islands

2002 MORRISON, Francine Reese (1935-)
WWIR (1985), 265.
IDC
Singer, minister
b. Aug. 16, 1935, Paris, Tx.

2003 MORRISON, John F. (-1935)
CHCCH, 270, 282.
CChr (H)
Pastor, evangelist, bishop

2004 MOSS, Alvin S. (1898-)
MOM (1975), 28.
CG (T), CGP
Pastor, overseer
b. Mar. 13, 1898, Crooked Island, Bahamas

2005 MOSS, B. J.
CGH, 34.
CLGCWFF
Pastor, overseer
b. 189-, Texas

2006 MOSS, Cecilia (1914-)
MOM (1975), 371.

        CG (T), CGP
        Pastor
        b. Mar. 7, 1914, Bahamas

2007 MOSS, Clayton A. (1941-)
        MOM (1975), 298.
        CGP
        Pastor
        b. Dec. 16, 1941, Crooked Island, Bahamas

2008 MOUKANGOE, Buller (-1972)
        PeHC
        Evangelist
        d. 1972, Mafeking, Cape Province

2009 List, W. S.
        Tribute to Buller Moukangoe, [by] W. S. List. In Worldo-
        rama, 6 (Winter 1972), 7.

2010 MUNZ, Anita (-1974)
        CLJCAF
        d. Sept. 1974

2011 White, Maurice F.
        Maceo Shelton, Anita Munz, buried; died in plane crash,
        [by] Maurice F. White. In Philadelphia Tribune (Sept. 28,
        1974), 1, 16.

2012 MURPHY, Willie (1933-)

        Singer, minister, author

2013 Murphy, Willie, 1933-
        Black and trying. Harrison, Ar., New Leaf Press, c1976.
        165 p. Written by W. Murphy and C. Dudley. DLC

2014 MURRAY, D. A. (1876-1962)
        BCUC, 34, 37-38.
        CChr (H), CN
        Pastor
        b. 1876
        d. Feb. 13, 1962, Winnsboro, La.

2015 MURRAY, Lobias
        CGIC, FGHTC
        Pastor, overseer

2016 MUSGROVE, Leo M. (1898-)
        CGH, 29-30, 88.
        CLGCWFF
        Pastor, bishop
        b. Mar. 19, 1898, Austin, Tx.

2017   NEAL, Eli N. (-1964)
         RWWAS, 42-43.
         CG (AP)
         Pastor, bishop
         d. 1964, Winston-Salem, N.C.

2018   NEAL, Wiley Cleven (1929-)
         WWIR (1985), 270.
         CGIC
         Pastor, district supt.
         b. Nov. 4, 1929, Dothan, Al.

2019   *NELSON, Bennie (1895-1971)
         GBPAW, 10.
         PeAW
         Evangelist, pastor, bishop
         b. 1895, Sweden
         d. 1971, Red Wing, Mn.

2020   NICHOLS, James Edward (1932-)
         WWIR (1977), 480.
         BWCOLJCWW
         Pastor, author
         b. Oct. 21, 1932, Portsmouth, Oh.

2021   NOEL, T. H.
         CGH, 90.
         CLGCWFF
         Pastor, author

2022   NORWOOD, Dorothy
         HGS (1975), 181, 209, 210, 244, 326, 344.

         Singer

2023   Norwood, Dorothy
         My testimony, [by] Dorothy Norwood. In Miracle Magazine,
         15 (Dec. 1970), 5.

2024   NORWOOD, James Madison (1948-)
         WWIR (1977), 485.
         PeAW
         Minister, musician
         b. Oct. 30, 1948, Salina, Ks.

2025   NUBIN, Katie Bell (1880-1969)
         HGS (1975), 189-190, 194.
         CGIC
         Evangelist, singer
         b. 1880
         d. 1969, Philadelphia, Pa.

2026 NUNES, Winston I.
        BSIAM, 161.
        MIS, 152, 215-216.
        EMA, EF
        Pastor, evangelist
        b. 19--, Trinidad

2027 O'BRYANT, L. D. (1942-)
        WWIR (1985), 278.
        CGIC
        Pastor
        b. Apr. 2, 1942, Grenada, Ms.

2028 ODEN, Daniel Felix (1871-1931)
        BWTS, 192, 266-267, 269.
        CTTR, 547.
        SBHCGRM, 122.
        CG (A)
        Pastor
        b. June 23, 1871, Maplesville, Al.
        d. Dec. 17, 1931, Detroit, Mi.

2029 Brown, Charles Ewing, 1883-1971.
        When the trumpet sounded: a history of the Church of God
        reformation movement. Anderson, In., Warner Press, c1951.
        402 p. "Daniel F. Oden and the colored church in Detroit":
        p. 192.

2029a [Massey, James Earl], 1930-
        Daniel Felix Oden, 1871-1931. In Massey, J. E. Three
        black leaders of the Church of God reformation movement.
        Anderson, In., c1981, 6-30.

2030 ODOM, Love (-1966)
        RWWAS, 43.
        CG (AP)
        Pastor, bishop
        d. 1966, Tipton, Ga.

2031 ODOM, William Byron (1897-)
        MHAFY, 136, 140.
        WWIR (1975-1976), 419.
        CGIC
        Pastor, bishop, denominational admin.
        b. June 26, 1897, Paris, Tx.

2032 O'HARE, Oscar B.
        PeAJ
        Pastor, presiding bishop

2033 O'NEAL, Ernest Joe (1924-)
        WWIR (1985), 282.

CGIC
Pastor, district supt., realtor
b. Jan. 10, 1924, Raleigh, N.C.

2033a O'NEIL, Henry
Evangelist
b. 18--, Liberia

2033b Jolley, Jennie (Arnold), 1881-1967.
As an angel of light; or, Bible tongues and holiness and
their counterfeits, [by] Jennie A. Jolley. New York, Vantage
Press, c1964. 112 p. "Henry O'Neil": p. 26. KyWAT

2034 OSBORNE, L. W.
RWWAS, 40.
FT
Pastor, bishop

2035 OVERTON, Henry Martin (1884-)
CGH, 28.
CLGCWFF
Pastor, bishop
b. Oct. 14, 1884, Tennessee

2036 OWENS, Jesse (1913-1980)
CA, 97/100, 417.
WWIA (1978-1979), II, 2476.
Ba
Athlete, business executive, author
b. Sept. 12, 1913, Danville, Al.
d. Mar. 31, 1980, Tucson, Az.

2037 Owens, Jesse, 1913-1980.
Jesse, a spiritual autobiography, [by] Jesse Owens, with
Paul Neimark. Plainfield, N.J., Logos International, c1978.
206 p. DLC

2038 *PACE, Noble (1896-1968)
GBPAW, 26
GHPAW, 145, 157.
PeAW
Pastor, district elder, denominational admin., bishop
b. 1896, Bedford, In.
d. 1968, Hartford City, In.

2039 *PADDOCK, Ross Perry (1907-)
GBPAW, 20.
GHPAW, 133, 135, 136, 138, 143.
RWWAS, 52.
PeAW
Pastor, denominational admin., bishop, author
b. Mar. 9, 1907, South Haven, Mi.

2040 PAGE, E. M. (1871-1944)
        MHAFY, 63, 64, 67, 97, 124-126.
        NH (1946-1947), 284.
        TBPALM, 96.
        AME, CGIC
        Evangelist, bishop
        b. May 19, 1871, Yazoo County, Ms.
        d. Jan. 4, 1944, Dallas, Tx.

2041 PAIGE, Grace
        I
        Evangelist
        b. 193-

2042 Cohen, Richard
        Sister Paige's circle inside the barbed wire, [by] Richard
        Cohen. In Washington Post, 101 (Dec. 3, 1978), B1, B9.

2043 PARCHIA, Earl (1927-)
        GBPAW, 48.
        GHPAW, 157, 179, 181.
        PeAW
        Pastor, district elder, bishop, denominational admin.
        b. 1927, Stephens, Ar.

2044 PARHAM, Thomas David (1920-)
        BDNM (1975), 391.
        FVOM, 30-32.
        MSBS, 187.
        WWABA (1980-1981), 613.
        UPrCUSA
        Pastor, naval chaplain, author
        b. Mar. 21, 1920, Newport News, Va.

2045 Parham, Thomas David, 1920-
        Removing racial and social barriers through charismatic re-
        newal, [by] T. David Parham. In New Covenant, 3 (June
        1974), 14-15; reprinted (Removing racial and social barriers)
        in Martin, R., comp. Sent by the Spirit. New York, c1976,
        117-120. Autobiographical.

2046 PARRIS, Elisha M.
        CG (C)
        Pastor, author

2047 PATTERSON, Deborah Mason
        CGIC

2048 Church's first lady has grave responsibilities.
        In Chicago Daily defender (Nov. 8, 1975), 12.

2049 PATTERSON, Gilbert E.
        CGIC, BBC
        Pastor

2050 Memphis blacks dedicate first million-dollar church in over a
        decade.
        In Jet, 55 (Dec. 7, 1978), 19.

2051 PATTERSON, James Oglethorpe (1912-   )
        HP, 494, 537.
        KPF, 199, 200.
        MHAFY, 75, 76, 77, 83, 88, 89, 90, 91, 92, 135, 140.
        MLMR, 137, 139, 140, 148.
        TBPALM, 148-151.
        WWABA (1985), 653.
        WWIR (1985), 290.
        CGIC
        Pastor, publishing house manager, presiding bishop
        b. July 21, 1912, Derma, Ms.

2052 Harris, Ron
        The turning point that changed their lives, [by] Ron Har-
        ris. In Ebony, 34 (Jan. 1979), 75-76, 78, 80, 82. Includes
        Bishop J. O. Patterson.

2053 Kelley, Frances Burnett
        Here am I; the dramatic story of Presiding Bishop J. O.
        Patterson, challenging and bold leader of the Church of God
        in Christ. Memphis, Church of God in Christ Publishing House,
        1970. 133 p. OSW

2054 Moore, Carey
        Black Pentecostals mount crusade. In Logos Journal, 8
        (Nov./Dec. 1978), 84-86.

2055 Patterson raps dress, divisiveness.
        In Commercial Appeal (Memphis) (Nov. 10, 1975), 15.

2056 Tinney, James Steven, 1942-
        Black Pentecostals: setting up the kingdom, [by] James
        S. Tinney. In Christianity Today, 20 (Dec. 5, 1975), 42-43.

2057 PATTERSON, James Oglethorpe (1935-   )
        WWIAP (1983-1984), 1306.
        CGIC
        Lawyer, bishop, legislator
        b. May 28, 1935, Memphis, Tn.

2058 O'Neal, Kelly
        J. O. Patterson, Jr., [by] Kelly O'Neal. In Black Family,
        3 (Nov./Dec. 1983), 46-49.

2059 PATTERSON, William Archie (1898-   )
        MHAFY, 90, 91, 135.
        CGIC
        Pastor, bishop, author

2060 PAULCEUS, Joseph (1893-   )
        GBPAW, 66.
        CGIC, PeAW
        Pastor, district elder, bishop
        b. Apr. 3, 1893

2061 PEPPERS, Sam
        CGIC
        Teacher, printer, purchasing agent, author
        b. 19--, Mississippi

2061a Peppers, Sam
        Sam Peppers. In Manney, J., ed. Come and see what
        God has done for parents, kids, women, men, clerics, Catho-
        lics, Protestants, Orthodox, blacks, whites, Asians, Euro-
        peans, Americans, Africans, and others in the charismatic re-
        newal. Ann Arbor, Mi., c1976, 152-154. Autobiogrpahical.
        DLC, InNd

2062 *PETTIFORD, Otho (1894-1973)
        GBPAW, 30. GHPAW, 153, 157.
        PeAW
        Pastor, district elder, bishop
        b. 1894, Marion, In.
        d. 1973, Albuquerque, N.M.

2063 *PETTIS, Robert G.
        GBPAW, 69. GHPAW, 93, 157.
        PeAW
        Pastor, bishop

2064 PHILLIPS, Magdelene Mabe (1905-   )
        PPIB, III, 149.
        AOCGT, AOPeC, AOPeCA
        Pastor, overseer
        b. 1905; d. 19--, Baltimore, Md.

2065 PHILLIPS, William Thomas (1893-1974)
        CSSIA (1949), 122
        PPIB, III, 200-201
        ME, AFMCG, EAOHCG, AOHCG
        Pastor, evangelist, bishop, author
        b. 1893
        d. 1974, Mobile, Al.

2066 Phillips, William Thomas, 1893-1974.
        Excerpts from the life of the Right Rev. W. T. Phillips

and fundamentals of the Apostolic Overcoming Holy Church of
God, Inc. Mobile, Al., A. O. H. Church Publishing House,
1967. 14 p.

2067 PICKARD, James
         RWWAS, 98.
         ACChrG, UWCCChrAF
         Pastor

2068 PITT, Benjamin Augustus (1916-)
         GBPAW, 67.
         PeAW
         Pastor, bishop
         b. 1916, Jamaica

2069 PITTS, Percy James (-1971)
         AOHUTR
         PeAW
         Evangelist, pastor
         d. May 26, 1971, Detroit, Mi.

2070 PLEAS, Charles H.
         MHAFY, 105, 106.
         CGIC
         Pastor, state overseer, author

2071 PLEASANT, Walter S. (1853-1935)
         CHCCH, 27, 51, 52, 429, 430.
         MHAFY, 16.
         MBaC, CGIC, CChr (H)
         Pastor
         B. Oct. 24, 1853, Utica, Ms.
         d. Feb. 7, 1935

2072 POE, Artie Monroe (1924-)
         WWIR (1977), 525.
         CGIC
         Pastor, radio preacher, Bible college instructor
         b. Nov. 16, 1924, Kennedy, Al.

2073 PONDER, Alonzo L. (1930-)
         CGH, 98.
         MBaC, CLGCWFF
         Pastor, overseeing elder, bishop
         b. Jan. 27, 1930, Seminole, Ok.

2074 POOLE, Charles Edward (1898-1984)
         RWWAS, 41.
         PeAW, LWAF
         Pastor, bishop
         b. May 10, 1898, Gillesville, Ga.
         d. Jan. 14, 1984, Chicago, Il.

2075 POOLE, Mattie Belle Goldie Ottie Mae Robinson (1903-1968)
      PeAW, LWAF
      Evangelist, pastor, author
      b. June 13, 1903, Memphis, Tn.
      d. Sept. 13, 1968, Chicago, Il.

2076 Poole, Mattie Belle Goldie Ottie Mae (Robinson), 1903-1968.
      Evang. Mattie B. Poole, late assistant pastor of Bethlehem
      Healing Temple. [Compiled by Jeffie M. Chamblis]. Chicago,
      1968. 95 p. Cover title.

2077 POPE, Mary Maude (1916-)
      WWABA (1985), 676.
      MSSGHC
      Pastor, bishop
      b. Jan. 27, 1916, Wake County, N.C.

2078 PORTER, Charlie E. (1920-)
      CGH, 33.
      CLGCWFF
      Pastor, overseer, denominational official
      b. Apr. 27, 1920, Beaumont, Tx.

2079 PORTER, Elizabeth (-1924)
      GLWBGTH, 49, 52.
      PeAW
      Missionary
      d. Feb. 11, 1924, Liberia

2080 PRICE, Frederick Kenneth Cercie (1932-)
      WWIR (1985), 306.
      NBaC, AME, ChrMA, I
      Pastor, evangelist, author
      b. Jan. 3, 1932, San Francisco, Ca.

2081 Price, Frederick Kenneth Cercie, 1932-
      The Holy Spirit--the missing ingredient: my personal
      testimony, [by] Frederick K. C. Price. Tulsa, Harrison
      House, c1978. 31 p. OkTOR

2082 PRICE, Joseph L. (1931-)
      WWABA (1985), 684.
      CGIC, I
      Pastor, evangelist, district supt., bishop, businessman,
      realtor
      b. Dec. 25, 1931, Gary, In.

2083 PRICE, Theophilus Augustus (1934-)
      WWIR (1977), 534.
      PeAW
      Pastor
      b. Nov. 10, 1934, Uniontown, Al.

2084 PROCTOR, Boyd L. (-1962)
      CChr (H), CN
      Pastor
      d. Nov. 13, 1962, Richmond, Va.

2085 RALPH, Leon Douglas (1932-)
      WWIAP (1975-1976), 761-762.
      AME, ICG
      Politician, legislator, pastor, author
      b. Aug. 20, 1932, Richmond, Va.

2086 Ralph, Leon Douglas, 1932-
      Report on the education of children in the ghetto school:
      a legislative program for reform by Assemblyman Leon D.
      Ralph. Sacramento, California Legislature, 1970.   131 p.
      CHS, CSbC, NBC, TxU-L

2087 RAMSEY, Eugene (1930-)
      MCAC, 359, 571, 572.
      WMCA, WC
      Pastor, district supt.
      b. Oct. 1, 1930, Sharpsburg, Oh.

2088 Ramsey, Eugene (1930-)
      Canaanite religion and its impact upon Israel before the
      monarchy divided, [by] Eugene Ramsey. Kansas City, Mo.,
      1956.   92 l.   Thesis (B.D.)--Nazarene Theological Seminary.
      MoKN

2089 RANGER, R. E. (1899-)
      MHAFY, 78.
      CGIC
      Pastor, Radio preacher

2090 Top radio ministers.
      In Ebony, 4 (July 1949), 56-61. On R. E. Ranger: p. 60.

2091 RATLIFF, Caleb D.
      CHCCH, 51, 53.
      CChr (H)
      Pastor

2092 RAY, Emma J. Smith (1859-1930)
      AME, FMNA
      Evangelist, author
      b. Jan. 7, 1859, Springfield, Mo.

2093 Ray, Emma J. (Smith), 1859-1930.
      Twice sold, twice ransomed; autobiography of Mr. and
      Mrs. L. P. Ray. Introduction by C. E. McReynolds. Chi-
      cago, Free Methodist Publishing House, c1926.   320 p.
      DLC, IEG, PP, Wa

2093a Ray, Emma J. (Smith), 1859-1930.
         Twice sold, twice ransomed: autobiography of Mr. and
         Mrs. L. P. Ray. Introduction by C. E. McRaynolds. Free-
         port, N.Y., Books for Libraries Press, 1971. 320 p. (Black
         heritage library collection) Reprint of 1926 ed. DLC

2094   RAY, Lloyd P. (1860-)
         AME, FMNA
         Evangelist
         b. Feb. 8, 1860, Kentucky Town, Tx.

2095   RAYL, J. A.
         GBPAW, 13.
         GHPAW, 74, 88, 123, 125.
         PeAW
         Pastor, bishop

2096   REESE, Geneva Nadine (1890-1980)
         CN
         Minister (elder)
         b. Jan. 10, 1894, Nebraska
         d. June 13, 1980, Kansas City, Mo.

2097   REID, Benjamin Franklin (1937-)
         CTTR, 807-809.
         WWABA (1985), 701.
         WWIR (1985), 315.
         CG (A)
         Pastor, police chaplain, author
         b. Oct. 5, 1937, New York, N.Y.

2098   RENNICK, Roosevelt Sims (1904-1976)
         GBPAW, 54.
         PeAW
         Pastor, district elder, bishop
         b. 1904, Newberry, S.C.
         d. 1976, Winston-Salem, N.C.

2099   REYNOLDS, Beatrice (1932-)
         WWIR (1985), 318.
         CGIC
         Missionary, evangelist, social worker
         b. Nov. 19, 1932, Sherrells, Ar.

2100   RICHARDSON, James Collins (1910-)
         RWWAS, i, 71, 72, 73-76, 96.
         CG (AP), ACChrG
         Pastor, bishop, editor
         b. 1910, South Carolina

2101   RICHARDSON, James Collins (1945-)
         BDNM (1975), 428.

WWABA (1977-1978), 755
ACChrG
Pastor, author
b. May 25, 1945, Martinsville, Va.

2102 RICKS, James R. (1931-   )
MOM (1975), 311.
CGP
Pastor
b. Sept. 22, 1931, High Point, N.C.

2103 RICKS, Sophia S. (1910-   )
MOM (1975), 377.
CGP
Pastor
b. Oct. 2, 1910, Kershaw, S.C.

2104 RITCHINGS, Edna Rose, re-named Mother Divine (1924-   )
FDPM
b. 1924, Vancouver, B.C.

2105 [Ritchings, Edna Rose, re-named Mother Divine], 1924-
Life with Father, [by] Mother Divine. In Ebony, 6 (Dec.
1950), 52-54, 56-60.

2106 Divine dinner.
In Newsweek, 29 (May 12, 1947), 31-32.

2107 Life with "God."
In Newsweek, 36 (Dec. 4, 1950), 72.

2108 Made in heaven.
In Time, 48 (Aug. 19, 1946), 45.

2109 New Mrs. Divine.
In Life, 21 (Aug. 19, 1946), 38.

2110 People.
In Time, 49 (May 12, 1947), 48.

2111 Transition.
In Newsweek, 28 (Aug. 19, 1946), 52.

2112 ROACHE, Obadiah (1922-   )
MOM (1975), 312.
CG (T), CGP
Pastor
b. May 1, 1922, Bahamas

2113 ROBERSON, Orzealyea

Minister, social worker

2114 Rehabilitation pioneer leaves Iowa.
      In Iowa Bystander (Nov. 29, 1973), 1, 6.

2115 ROBERTS, Billy (1900-1962)
          WJ, 54-55, 63-65, 73-74, 84-86, 123-124, 126, 131-136,
      146-152.
          SSS
          Evangelist, pastor, general overseer
          b. July 26, 1900, Cincinnati, Oh.
          d. Jan. 17, 1962, New York, N.Y.

2116 Roberts, Billy, 1900-1962.
          Out of crime into Christ.   Saratoga Springs, N.Y., 196-.
      32 p. Autobiography.

2117 ROBERTS, Nebo
          CGIC
          Pastor

2118 ROBINSON, Carl
          CP, 96.
          CGIC
          Pastor, bishop

2119 ROBINSON, Harvey E.
          CG (C)
          Pastor

2120 ROBINSON, Ida (-1946)
          CSSIA (1965), 104.
          PPIB, III, 99.
          UHCA, MSHCA
          Pastor, bishop
          b. 189-, Florida
          d. 1946, Philadelphia, Pa.

2121 ROBINSON, James L.
          PeAW
          Pastor, Bible school instructor and dean

2122 ROBINSON, Lizzie (1860-1945)
          MHAFY, 67, 68, 116-118, 121, 126-127.
          MBaC, CGIC
          College matron, evangelist, denominational official
          b. Apr. 5, 1860, Phillips County, Ar.
          d. Nov. 1945, Memphis, Tn.

2123 Church of God in Christ. Department of Women.
          The history of our women's organizational structure.   In
      Church of God in Christ. Department of Women. Women's
      handbook. Memphis, 1980, 66-70.

2124 Jones, Miriam (McGregor)
        A slave becomes an organizer. In Lifted Banner (Omaha)
        (Spring 1944)

2125 ROBINSON, Raymon Laverne (1912-1978)
        GBPAW, 25.
        GHPAW, 130, 138, 157.
        PeAW
        Pastor, district elder, denominational admin., bishop
        b. 1912, Newcastle, Ky.
        d. 1978, Akron, Oh.

2126 ROBINSON, Wallace Peter (1907-)
        I
        Pastor, radio preacher

2127 Top radio ministers.
        In Ebony, 4 (July 1949), 56-61. On Wallace Peter Robin-
        son: p. 58.

2128 ROBY, Jasper (1912-)
        WWIR (1985), 325.
        AOHCG
        Pastor, presiding elder, bishop, radio preacher
        b. Apr. 19, 1912, Brookville, Ms.

2129 RODGERS, Charles (1941-)
        WWABA (1985), 723.
        WWIR (1977), 567.
        CGIC
        Pastor, evangelist, asst. district elder
        b. July 28, 1941, Memphis, Tn.

2130 ROGERS, Warren Allen (1917-)
        BCUC, 10, 41, 42-44, 45, 48, 49, 50, 52, 65.
        MBaC, CN
        Pastor, evangelist, district supt., singer, author
        b. 1917, Woodland, La.

2131 Rogers, Warren Allen, 1917-
        From sharecropper to goodwill ambassador: the Warren
        Rogers story; the spiritual odyssey of a man in the church,
        [by] Warren A. Rogers with Kenneth Vogt. Kansas City,
        Mo., Beacon Hill Press of Kansas City, c1979. 76 p. MoKN,
        OkBetC

2132 ROSS, German Reed
        MHAFY, v, 137.
        WWIR (1985), 329.
        CGIC
        Clerk, pastor, bishop, denominational admin.
        b. 19--, Mart, Tx.

2133   ROSS, Marcellus (-1960)
           CGH, 24, 78.
           CLGCWFF
           Pastor, bishop
           b. 18--, Henderson, Tn.
           d. 1960, Cincinnati, Oh.

2134   *ROWE, Glen Beecher (1890-1963)
           GBPAW, 2.
           PeAW
           Pastor, evangelist, bishop
           b. 1890, Noble County, In.
           d. 1963, Mishawaka, In.

2135   RUCKER, A. T.
           CHCCH, 117, 154, 396.
           CChr (H)
           Pastor

2136   RUCKER, John Ledsay (1872-1946)
           PPIB, III, 38.
           CG (SC)
           Pastor, denominational chairman
           b. 1872
           d. 1946, Knoxville, Tn.

2137   RYMER, Samuel Reuben (1931-   )
           MOM (1975), 65.
           CGP
           Pastor, state overseer, evangelist
           b. Sept. 15, 1931, Virgin Islands

2138   SAMPSON, Dennis
           TDOOP, 300, 302-304.
           PHC, WC
           Pastor, district supt.
           b. 19--, Antigua, W.I.

2139   SAMUELS, Wesley Eddie (1931-   )
           WWIR (1985), 336.
           PeCGA
           Hospital clerk, denominational official
           b. Apr. 6, 1931, Columbia, S.C.

2140   SANDERS, Marion (1932-   )
           WWIR (1977), 583.
           PeCJC, FT, PeAW
           Pastor
           b. June 5, 1932, Haskell, Ok.

2141   SANDERS, Oscar Haywood (1892-1972)
           GBPAW, 16, 170.

PeAW, PeCAFA
Pastor, evangelist, bishop
b. Dec. 2, 1892, Lonoke, Ar.
d. Oct. 15, 1972, Muncie, In.

2142 Fairley, David L.
Moved by such a man, [by] David L. Fairley. Muncie,
In., Townsends Printing, c1980. x, 128 p. InMu

2143 SANDLIN, Gerald W. (1944-)
MOM (1975), 314.
CGP
Soldier, pastor
b. June 15, 1944, Cullman, Al.

2144 SANDS, John Manwell (1927-)
MOM (1975), 66.
CGP
Pastor, overseer
b. May 19, 1927, Miami, Fl.

2145 SAPP, Beatrice
BWTS, 269.
SBHCGRM, 122.
CG (A)
Evangelist

2146 SAUNDERS, Elijah (1934-)
WWABA (1980-1981), 704.
CGIC (A), UCJC (A)
Physician
b. Dec. 9, 1934, Baltimore, Md.

2147 SAUNDERS, Monroe Randolph (192 -)
RWWAS, 77, 91-93.
CGIC (A), UCJC (A)
Pastor, bishop, author
b. 192-, Baltimore, Md.

2148 SAUNDERS, Monroe Randolph (1948-)
UCJC (A)
Pastor, author
b. 1948, Baltimore, Md.

2149 SAVAGE, Beatrice Mary Colbreath (1899-)
WWIR (1977), 586.
[HGW] CLG [PGT]
Pastor, bishop
b. Jan. 1, 1899, Windsor, Ont.

2150 SAWYER, Thomas Jason (1921-)
SBHCGRM, 125.

WWIR (1975-1976), 500.
CG (A)
Pastor, college prof., denominational admin., author
b. Oct. 17, 1921, Springfield, Tn.

2151 SCARBOROUGH, Alexander J.
CHCCH, 53.
MBaC, CGIC, CChr (H)
Pastor

2152 *SCHAMBACH, Robert W. (1926-)
HATAP, 74, 137, 216-217, 292.
SFH, 42, 82.
AGGC, I
Evangelist
b. 1926, Harrisburg, Pa.

2153 Blau, Eleanor
Tent shelters sounds and spirit of an old-time revival, [by]
Eleanor Blau. In New York Times, 121 (Aug. 25, 1972), 35.

2154 Winship, Michael
Salvation in a canvas cathedral, [by] Michael Winship. In
Washington Star-News, 121 (Aug. 1, 1973), E1.

2155 *SCHMELZENBACH, Elmer F. (1911-)
CN
Pastor, missionary
b. June 1911, near Pigg's Peak, Swaziland

2156 Schmelzenbach, Elmer F., 1911-
Sons of Africa: stories from the life of Elmer Schmelzen-
bach, as told to Leslie Parrott. Kansas City, Mo., Beacon
Hill Press of Kansas City, c1979. 217 p. DLC, OkBetC

2157 Missionary to South Africa defends apartheid system.
In Kansas City Star (Mar. 15, 1961)

2158 SCHOOLER, Alexander R.
GBPAW, 4, 56.
GHPAW, 71, 72, 77, 81, 85, 87.
PeAW
Pastor, bishop

2159 SCHULTZ, David Thurman (1889-1972)
GBPAW, 11.
GHPAW, 156, 157.
PeAW
Pastor, bishop
b. 1889, Mayfield, Ky.
d. 1972, Louisville, Ky.

2160 SCOTT, Alfred J. (1913-)
        WWABA (1985), 743.
        TCKGIC
        Barber, pastor, bishop
        b. Oct. 30, 1913, Gordon, Al.

2161 SCOTT, Booker T. (1905-)
        WWIR (1977), 598.
        PeAW
        Pastor, evangelist, district elder
        b. Oct. 25, 1905, Bullard, Tx.

2162 SCOTT, Floyd Claude (1900-1979)
        CGH, 26, 93.
        WWIR (1977), 598.
        CLGCWFF
        Evangelist, pastor, editor, chief bishop, author
        b. Nov. 11, 1900, Corsicana, Tx.
        d. Aug. 19, 1979, Oklahoma City, Ok.

2163 Bishop Scott dies, funeral Saturday.
        In Black Dispatch (Oklahoma City), 65:14 (Aug. 23, 1979)

2164 SCOTT, Nathaniel T.
        FBHCGA
        Pastor, bishop

2165 SCOTT, Phillip Lee (1907-)
        GBPAW, 45.
        GHPAW, 153, 157.
        PeAW
        Pastor, district elder, bishop
        b. 1907, Greenwood, Ms.

2166 SCOTTON, Marvin Theodore (1925-)
        MOM (1975), 161.
        CGP
        Pastor
        b. Dec. 13, 1925, Liberty, N.C.

2167 SCOTTON, Ralph C. (1909-)
        HWSBM, 95.
        MOM (1975), 161.
        CG (T), CGP
        Pastor, district overseer, evangelist
        b. Feb. 5, 1909, Siler City, N.C.

2168 SELBY, W. M.
        AAOLSJC
        Pastor, bishop, general overseer

2169 SELLERS, Asbury R.
         CG (C)
         Pastor

2170 SEXTON, Clarence Lewis (191-)
         WWIR (1977), 603.
         CGIC
         Pastor, district supt., state coordinator
         b. July 21, 1919, Bamberg, S.C.

2171 SEYMOUR, Delegal (1923-)
         MOM (1975), 315.
         CGP
         Pastor
         b. July 10, 1923, Cat Island, Bahamas

2172 SEYMOUR, Jennie Evans Moore (1883-1936)
         AVOD, 70.
         BPM, 48.
         AFM
         Mission worker
         b. 1883
         d. July 2, 1936, Los Angeles, Ca.

2173 SEYMOUR, William Joseph (1870-1922)
         ATF, 27-28
         AVOD, 47, 60-61, 62, 65-70, 89, 123, 140, 160, 162, 167,
      174, 188-189
         BDARB (1977), 407.
         BHPM, 20, 29, 31-32, 34-40, 43-44, 48, 53-54, 196, 197
         BSFH, 35-38, 44, 48, 60-62, 100, 154
         BTHS, 48
         CLMA (1977), 25
         CPH, 95-96
         DBWS, 62-66, 77, 82
         FWSF (1946), 31-38
         HP, 22, 24, 27, 43, 338, 350, 495
         KMA, 18, 36, 38, 156
         KPF, 64-67, 77
         KWGHW, 25
         MATS, 48-54, 57, 61, 76, 85
         NP, 32-34, 62, 81, 83
         QNC (1983), 28-30, 31, 33, 42, 88, 210, 234
         SAOPCO, 2, 12, 29, 52, 91-92, 125, 131-138, 140, 198,
      201
         SCHG, 113, 114-116
         SHPM, 103-108, 116, 123, 148-149, 168, 178, 221
         SOTP, 104-105, 107-108, 112, 137, 138
         AME, Evening Light Saints [i.e. CG (A)], AF
         Evangelist, pastor, editor
         b. May 2, 1870, Centerville, La.
         d. Sept. 28, 1922, Los Angeles, Ca.

2174   Nelson, Douglas J., 1931-
       The black face of church renewal: a brief essay examining
       the meaning of the Pentecostal-charismatic church renewal
       movement, 1901-1985, by Douglas J. Nelson. Arlington, Va.,
       1981. 18 l. CCmS

2175   Nelson, Douglas J., 1931-
       For such a time as this: the story of Bishop William J.
       Seymour and the Azusa Street revival; a search for Pente-
       costal/charismatic roots, [by] Douglas J. Nelson. Birmingham,
       1981. 363 l. Thesis (Ph.D.)--Birmingham University. UkBU

2176   Tinney, James Steven, 1942-
       Who was William J. Seymour? [By] James S. Tinney. In
       Tinney, J. S., ed. In the tradition of William J. Seymour:
       essays commemorating the dedication of Seymour House at
       Howard University. Washington, 1978, 10-20.

2177   Tinney, James Steven, 1942-
       William J. Seymour: father of modern-day Pentecostalism,
       [by] James S. Tinney. In Journal of the Interdenominational
       Theological Center, 4 (Fall 1976), 34-44; reprinted in Burkett,
       R. E., ed. Black apostles: Afro-American clergy confront
       the twentieth century. Boston, c1978, 213-225.

2178   SHARPTON, Alfred (1954-)
       CGIC
       Evangelist
       b. 1954, New York, N.Y.

2179   Gillespie, Marcia, 1944-
       Young ideas: Alfred Sharpton, [by] Marcia Gillespie. In
       Essence, 2 (Mar. 1972), 32-35.

2180   *SHELHAMER, Julia Arnold (1879-1981)
       FMCNA
       Evangelist, teacher, author
       b. Sept. 14, 1879, Sycamore, Il.
       d. June 2, 1981, Nicholasville, Ky.; buried Warsaw, In.

2181   Shelhamer, Julia (Arnold), 1879-1981.
       Trials and triumphs of a minister's wife, [by] Julia A. Shel-
       hamer. Atlanta, Repairer Publishing Co., 1923. 223 p.
       KyWAT

2182   Hayes, Sharon (Boyd)
       Julia Shelhamer: little old lady in gospel shoes, [by]
       Sharon Boyd Hayes. In Light and Life, 114 (Feb. 1981), 14-
       16, 30-31.

2183   Lord Jesus will answer.
       In Time, 57 (Feb. 12, 1951), 69-70.

2184 Williamson, Glen, 1909–
      Julia: giantess in generosity; the story of Julia Arnold
      Shelhamer, [by] Glen Williamson. Winona Lake, In., Light
      and Life Press, c1969. 118 p. IGreviC, KyWAT

2185 SHELTON, Maceo (–1974)
      CLJCAF
      d. Sept. 1974

2186 White, Maurice F.
      Maceo Shelton, Anita Munz, buried; died in plane crash,
      [by] Maurice F. White. In Philadelphia Tribune (Sept. 28,
      1974), 1, 16.

2187 SHELTON, S. McDowell (1929–   )
      BDNM (1975), 457.
      RWWAS, 71, 129.
      WWABA (1985), 755.
      CLJCAF
      Evangelist, radio preacher, editor, bishop, denominational
      executive, author
      b. Apr. 18, 1929, Philadelphia, Pa.

2188 Lear, Len
      Philadelphia's Bishop Shelton: prophet or profiteer? [By]
      Len Lear. In Sepia, 27 (Jan. 1978), 56–61.

2189 Vietcong invitation only to black bishop.
      In Kansas City Call (Feb. 16, 1972), 12.

2190 SHEPPARD, Horace W.
      CG (A)
      Pastor

2191 SHORT, David William
      MHPD, 119–126
      NP, 132
      MBaC, OCSC, NDSTCCU
      Pastor, evangelist, archbishop, author

2192 SHORT, Stephen N.
      I
      Pastor, university chaplain, author

2193 SHORTER, Florence Simpkins (1910–1978)
      Ba, HC
      Janitor, singer, pastor, bishop
      b. 1910, Aiken, S.C.
      d. Dec. 17, 1978, Washington, D.C.

2194 Bishop Florence Shorter, church founder, pastor.
      In Washington Post, 102 (Dec. 21, 1978), B6.

2195 SHORTER, Wesley (-1973)
         HC
         Janitor, minister

2196 SHOUSE, Elaine Marie (1948-)
         PeAW

2197 Shouse, Elaine Marie, 1948-
         An analysis of the poetry of three revolutionary poets:
         Don L. Lee, Nikki Giovanni and Sonia Sanchez, [by] Elaine
         Marie Shouse. Urbana, 1976. iv, 187 1. Thesis (Ph.D.)--
         University of Illinois. IU

2198 SHOWELL, Cornelius
         BWCOLJCWW
         Pastor

2199 Sibley, Wallace Jerome (1938-)
         WWIR (1985), 354.
         CG (C)
         Pastor, state overseer, author
         b. June 30, 1938, St. Marys, Ga.

2200 Sibley, Wallace J.
         Hopes of a black minister, [by] Wallace J. Sibley. In
         Church of God Evangel, 61 (Feb. 28, 1972), 13.

2201 *SIPES, James Leo (1893-1961)
         GBPAW, 15.
         GHPAW, 125.
         PeAW
         Pastor, bishop
         b. 1893, Martin County, In.
         d. 1961, Bedford, In.

2202 SKINNER, Arturo (-1975)
         DEC
         Pastor
         d. Mar. 2-, 1975, Newark, N.J.

2203 Skinner, Arturo, -1975
         Deliverance. Newark, N.J., Deliverance Evangelistic Cen-
         ters, 1969. 52 p. Autobiography.

2204 Apostle Skinner rites draw thousands.
         In Newark Afro-American (Mar. 29, 1975), 1, 2.

2205 SMALL, W. S. (-1941)
         TDOOP, 180, 181.
         PHC
         Pastor
         d. Jan. 1941, Caruthersville, Mo.

2206 Prayer needed.
       In Pilgrim Holiness Advocate, 21 (Jan. 23, 1941), 7.

2207 SMITH, A. B. (-1956)
       CHCCH, 279-280, 281, 282.
       CChr (H)
       Pastor, bishop
       b. 19--, Arkansas
       d. 1956

2208 SMITH, Amanda Berry (1837-1915)
       NAW (1607-1950), III, 304-305.
       NYT (Mar. 6, 1915), 11:6.
       WWOCR (1915), 246.
       AME
       Evangelist, missionary
       b. Jan. 23, 1837, Long Green, Md.
       d. Feb. 24, 1915, Sebring, Fl.

2208a Smith, Amanda (Berry), 1837-1915.
       Amanda Berry Smith. In Loewenberg, B. J., ed. Black
       women in nineteenth-century American life. University Park,
       Pa., c1976, 142-173. DLC, OkU

2209 Smith, Amanda (Berry), 1837-1915.
       Amanda Smith, the King's daughter; an autobiography, [by]
       Amanda Smith. Abridged by E. & L. Harvey. Greencastle,
       In., Harts-Flame Publications, 1977. 159 p. KyWAT

2210 Smith, Amanda (Berry), 1837-1915.
       An autobiography: the story of the Lord's dealings with
       Mrs. Amanda Smith, the colored evangelist; containing an ac-
       count of her life work of faith, and her travels in America,
       England, Ireland, Scotland, India and Africa, as an indepen-
       dent missionary. With an introd. by Bishop Thoburn. Chi-
       cago, Meyer & Brother, 1893. 506 p. DLC, FTaSU, IEG,
       MB, MH, OO, OU, PP, TNF, TxU, ViU

2211 Smith, Amanda (Berry), 1837-1915.
       An autobiography: the story of the Lord's dealings with
       Mrs. Amanda Smith, the colored evangelist; containing an ac-
       count of her life work of faith, and her travels in America,
       England, Ireland, Scotland, India and Africa, as an indepen-
       dent missionary. With an introd. by Bishop Thoburn. Chi-
       cago, Christian Witness Co., c1921. 506 p. Reprint of 1893
       ed. CU, DLC, WaS

2212 Smith, Amanda (Berry), 1837-1915.
       An autobiography: the story of the Lord's dealings with
       Mrs. Amanda Smith, the colored evangelist; containing an ac-
       count of her life work of faith, and her travels in America,

England, Ireland, Scotland, India and Africa, as an indepen-
dent missionary. With an introd. by Bishop Thoburn. Miles,
Mi., Newby Book Room, 1962. 506 p. Reprint of 1893 ed.
NjMD

2213 Brown, LeRoy Chester, 1908-
      On whom the fire fell: testimonies of holiness giants, [by]
      LeRoy Brown. Kansas City, Mo., Beacon Hill Press of Kansas
      City, 1977. 56 p. "Amanda Smith: twice bought and paid
      for": p. 22-29. OkBetC

2214 Cadbury, M. H.
      The life of Amanda Smith, "the African sybil, the Christian
      saint," [by] M. H. Cadbury. With an introd. by J. Rendel
      Harris. Birmingham, Cornish Bros., 1916. 84 p. NIC, NN,
      Uk

2214a Kletzing, Henry Frick, 1850-1910.
      Traits of character illustrated in Bible light, together with
      short sketches of marked and marred manhood and womanhood,
      [by] H. F. Kletzing and E. L. Kletzing. 3d ed. Naperville,
      Il., Kletzing Brothers, 1899, c1898. 371 p. "Mrs. Amanda
      Smith, formerly a slave": p. 290-291.

2214b McLeister, Clara (Orrell), 1882-1958.
      Men and women of deep piety, by Mrs. Clara McLeister.
      Edited and published by E. E. Shelhamer. Syracuse, N.Y.,
      Wesleyan Methodist Publishing Association, 1920. 512 p.
      "Amanda Smith": p. 384-393.

2215 Taylor, Marshall William, 1846-1887.
      The life, travels, labors, and helpers of Mrs. Amanda
      Smith, the famous Negro-missionary evangelist, [by] Marshall
      W. Taylor. With an introd. by J. Krehbiel. Cincinnati,
      Printed by Cranston & Stowe for the author, c1886. 63 p.
      IEG

2216 SMITH, David E. (-1974)
      RWWAS, 43-44.
      CG (AP)
      Pastor, bishop
      d. Dec. 1974, Beckley, W. Va.

2217 SMITH, Elias Dempsey (-1920)
      CSSIA (1965), 129.
      MHAFY, 60.
      TCKGIC
      Evangelist (elder)
      d. 1920, Addis Ababa, Abyssinia (Ethiopia)

2218 SMITH, Francis L. (1915-)
      GBPAW, 49.

GHPAW, 153, 157.
HP, 398, 551.
RWWAS, 53.
PeAW
Pastor, district elder, presiding bishop, author
b. Dec. 18, 1915, Ironspot, Oh.

2219   SMITH, Goodwin C.
CG (C)
Pastor
b. 19--, Bermuda

2220   Dirksen, Carolyn
In Harlem's ghetto, [by] C. D.   In Church of God Evangel,
61 (Feb. 28, 1972), 16-17.

2221   SMITH, John C. (1931-   )
MOM (1975), 213.
CGP
Pastor, district overseer
b. Mar. 14, 1931, Fitzgerald, Ga.

2222   SMITH, Karl Franklin (1892-1972)
CUWS, 70-71, 75-76.
GBPAW, 12, 14, 49.
GHPAW, 153, 157, 162.
PeAW, PeAJC, PeAW
Pastor, denominational officer, author
b. Oct. 5, 1892, Roseville near Zanesville, Oh.
d. Jan. 22, 1972, Columbus, Oh.

2223   Full proof of his ministry: a memorial of 35 years of gospel
work by Karl F. Smith.   Columbus, Oh., 1954.   [54] p.
Sponsored by the Personal Interest League of Church of
Christ of Apostolic Faith.

2224   SMITH, Lucy (1874-   )
Ba, I
Pastor, evangelist, dressmaker
b. 1874, Georgia

2225   Faith healer.
In Ebony, 5 (Jan. 1950), 37-39.

2226   SMITH, Rudolph (1930-   )
WWIR (1977), 624.
CG (A)
Pastor, national asso. officer
b. Oct. 19, 1930, Glenwood, Ga.

2227   SMITH, Rufus J.
BWTS, 263, 276.

CTTR, 550.
SBHCGRM, 122.
CG (A)
Evangelist, pastor, association pres.

2228 SMITH, William Lujene (1907-)
GBPAW, 56.
PeAW
Pastor, bishop
b. 1907, Montgomery, Al.

2229 SMITH, Willie Mae Ford (1906-)
HGS (1975), xxxi, 4, 27, 62, 63, 85, 107, 181, 187-189,
193, 196-203, 217, 251, 299, 302, 304, 307, 309, 313, 327,
328, 330, 337, 338.
NBaC, CG (AP)
Evangelist, singer
b. 1906, Rolling Fork, Ms.

2230 SMOOT, J. D. (1877-1947)
CTTR, 167, 547.
SBHCGRM, 122, 124.
FWBaC, CG (A)
Pastor
b. Nov. 1, 1877, near Tuskegee, Al.
d. 1947, Detroit, Mi.

2230a [Massey, James Earl], 1930-
J. D. Smoot, 1877-1947. In Massey, J. E. Three black
leaders of the Church of God reformation movement. Anderson, In., c1981, 1-5.

2231 SOLES, Henry

Journalist, publisher
b. 194-, Alabama

2232 Soles, Henry
My hang-up was white people, [by] Henry Soles, as told
to Stanley C. Baldwin. In Adair, J. R., ed. Brothers black.
Grand Rapids, Mi., c1973, 18-22. OkT, OU

2233 SPARKS, Ella V. Dancy
MHAFY, iii, 129
CGIC
Editor

2234 SPENCER, Keith Collins (1936-)
BDNM (1975), 478.
CG (A)
Pastor, Bible institute instructor
b. Feb. 1, 1936, Barbados, W.I.

2235 SPENCER, Willie
      CG (C)
      Pastor

2236 Sibley, Wallace Jerome, 1938-
      Black churches of U.S. origin, [by] W. J. Sibley. In
      Church of God Evangel, 68 (May 22, 1978), 6-8.

2237 SPOONER, Geraldine M. (1873-197-)
      CPHC, 348, 349, 355, 564, 570.
      PeHC
      Missionary, author
      b. Aug. 9, 1873, Bristown, Barbados
      d. 197-, Rustenburg, Tvl.

2238 Duncan, Florine (Freeman), 1925-
      You gave, yet Africa calls, [by] Florine and Montgomery
      Duncan. [Franklin Springs, Ga.], Advocate Press, 1959.
      106 p. On Geraldine M. Spooner: p. 86-92.

2239 From the field: "missionary mother" in South Africa.
      In Helping Hand, 10 (May 1963), 6.

2240 King, Blanche Leon (Moore), 1897-1984.
      "Being very godly ... (they) read the word and prayed
      together daily," [by] Blanche L. King. In Helping Hand, 15
      (Apr. 1968), 4-5.

2241 SPOONER, Kenneth E. M. (1884-1937)
      CPHC, 348-350, 355-356, 564, 570.
      SOTP, 199.
      CE, PeHC
      Missionary
      b. Jan. 8, 1884, Barbados, W.I.
      d. Feb. 28, 1937, Rustenburg, Tvl.

2242 Spooner, Geraldine M., 1873-197-.
      Sketches of the life of K. E. M. Spooner, missionary,
      South Africa. Material collected and arranged by Mrs.
      K. E. M. Spooner, A. E. Robinson [and] P. F. Beacham.
      [Franklin Springs, Ga., 1945] 108 p.

2243 SPRIGGS, Robert (1928-   )
      WWIR (1985), 369.
      CGIC
      Pastor
      b. Jan. 7, 1928, Greensboro, N.C.

2244 SPURLOCK, Nathaniel Samuel (1893-   )
      CGH, 33.
      Ba, CLGCWFF

Pastor, evangelist, overseer, bishop
b. Mar. 22, 1893, Lovelady, Tx.

2245 STAFFORD, Arlinar A. (1930-)
MOM (1975), 382.
CGP
Evangelist, pastor
b. Nov. 19, 1930, Wyatt, Mo.

2246 STARNES, W. D. (1900-1954)
CGH, 25, 56.
CLGCWFF
Pastor, vice chief bishop
b. July 5, 1900, Williamson County, Tn.
d. 1954, Chicago, Il.

2247 STEINBERG, Martha Jean Jones
RC, I
Model, evangelist, radio preacher
b. 19--, Memphis, Tn.

2248 Happy family.
In Ebony, 8 (Oct. 1953), 91.

2249 Lane, Bill
Queen of the evangelists, [by] Bill Lane. In Sepia, 27
(May 1978), 20-25.

2250 STEPHENS, Bessie (1916-)
MOM (1975), 383.
CG (T), CGP
Evangelist, pastor
b. Aug. 16, 1916, Virginia

2251 STEWART, E. B.
CP, 69, 88.
MHAFY, 89, 91.
CGIC
Pastor, bishop

2252 STREET, Archie J. (1898-)
GBPAW, 40.
GHPAW, 153, 157.
PeAW
Pastor, district elder, bishop
b. 1898, Ramer, Tn.

2253 STREITFERDT, Thomas (1929-)
GBPAW, 47.
GHPAW, 153, 157, 171, 172.
WWIR (1985), 377.

PeAW
Pastor, radio preacher, district elder, bishop, editor, author
b. Feb. 10, 1929, Warren, Oh.

2254 STROBHAR, Walter Nathaniel (1900-)
WWIR (1977), 645.
UHGA
Pastor, bishop, denominational pres.
b. Jan. 31, 1900, Savannah, Ga.

2255 STUCKEY, James Ferry Fulton (1860-1939)
CGH, 23.
Ba, CLGCWFF
Pastor, evangelist, chief bishop
b. Apr. 7, 1860, Kibbler, Ar.
d. July 10, 1939, Kansas City, Ks.

2256 *STULTZ, Bob
OBSC
Farmer, machinist, pastor, youth leader, author

2257 Stultz, Bob
White black man, [by] Bob Stultz [and] Phil Landrum.
Carol Stream, Il., Creation House, c1972. 172 p. Autobiographical.

2258 SWAN, T. W.
CGICI
Pastor, editor

2259 TALIAFERRO, Hobart Samuel (1896-1968)
GBPAW, 37.
GHPAW, 153, 157.
PeAW
Pastor, district elder, bishop
b. 1896, Harriman, Tn.
d. 1968, Atlantic City, N.J.

2260 TALLEY, Theodore Roosevelt (1906-198-)
AOHUTR
PeAW
Pastor, district elder
b. May 25, 1906, Arkin, Ar.
d. 198-, Ecorse, Mi.

2261 TANN, Rosa Lee Burnham (1948-)
WWIR (1977), 653.
CGIC
Teacher
b. May 4, 1948, Norfolk County, Va.

2262 TATE, M. L. Ester (1870-1930)
        PPIB, IV, 110.
        CLGPGT
        Evangelist, chief overseer
        d. 1930, Nashville, Tn.

2263 Church of the Living God, the Pillar and Ground of the Truth.
        Seventy-fifth anniversary yearbook of the Church of the
        Living God, the Pillar and Ground of the Truth, Inc., 1903-
        1978: Mary Magdalena Tate, revivor and first co-revivor and
        bishop. [Helen Middleton Lewis and Meharry H. Lewis,
        editors]. Nashville, c1978. 65 p. DLC

2264 TAULBERT, Mary
        I
        Evangelist
        b. 19--, Mississippi

2265 Gott, Helen T.
        Mary Taulbert tells of healing love, [by] Helen T. Gott.
        In Kansas City Star, 95 (Aug. 30, 1975), 3.

2266 TAYLOR, James M. (1875-1941)
        CGH, 25.
        CLGCWFF
        Pastor, overseer, evangelist
        b. 1875, Pine Bluff, Ar.
        d. Dec. 22, 1941, Chattanooga, Tn.

2267 TAYLOR, John Emmanuel (1932-)
        MOM (1975), 324.
        CGP
        Evangelist, constable
        b. Aug. 19, 1932, Turks Island, Bahamas

2268 TAYLOR, Nathaniel (1904-)
        MOM (1975), 173.
        CG (T), CGP
        Pastor, district overseer
        b. Aug. 5, 1904, Rum Cay Island, Bahamas

2269 *TAYLOR, William (1821-1902)
        DAB
        NYT (May 20, 1902), 9:5.
        WWWA (1897-1942), 1221.
        WWWCH (1968), 398.
        ME
        Pastor, evangelist, missionary, editor, bishop, author
        b. May 2, 1821, Rockbridge County, Va.
        d. May 18, 1902, Palo Alto, Ca.

2270   Taylor, William, 1821-1902.
       Christian adventures in South Africa, [by] William Taylor.
       London, Jackson, Walford and Hodder; New York, Carlton &
       Porter, 1867. xiv, xv, 557 p. CtY-D, ICU, MH, NjPT

2271   Taylor, William, 1821-1902.
       The flaming torch in darkest Africa, [by] William Taylor.
       With an introd. by Henry M. Stanley. New York, Eaton &
       Mains, 1898. 675 p. CtY-D, GEU, IEG, IU, OrU, OU, WU

2272   Taylor, William, 1821-1902.
       My Kaffir sermon, [by] William Taylor. n.p., 189-. 42 p.
       Cover title. KyWAT

2273   Taylor, William, 1821-1902.
       Story of my life: an account of what I have thought and
       said and done in my ministry of more than fifty-three years
       in Christian lands and among the heathen, by William Taylor.
       Edited by John Clark Ridpath with original engravings and
       sketches by Frank Beard. New York, Hunt & Eaton, 1895.
       750 p. DLC, GU, IU, MSohG, NcD, OCl, PP, PPT

2274   Taylor, William, 1821-1902.
       William Taylor of California, bishop of Africa. Revised with
       a preface by the Rev. C. G. Moore. London, Hodder and
       Stoughton, 1897. xii, 411 p. CtY-D, GU, NcD, NcU, OMtvN

2275   Davies, Edward, 1830-
       The bishop of Africa; or, The life of William Taylor, D.D.
       With an account of the Congo country, and mission. [By]
       E. Davies. Reading, Ma., Holiness Book Concern, 1885.
       192 p. "Published for the benefit of the building and transit
       fund of William Taylor's missions." DLC, IEG, IEN, IU,
       KyWAT, MB, NcD, NjPT, NN, WHi

2276   Davies, Edward, 1830-
       The bishop of Africa; or, The life of William Taylor, D.D.
       With an account of the Congo country, and mission. [By]
       E. Davies. Reading, Ma., Holiness Book Concern, 1885.
       216 p. "Published for the benefit of the building and transit
       fund of William Taylor's missions." CBGTU, TNJ

2277   Mills, Wallace George
       The Taylor revival of 1866 and the roots of African national-
       ism in the Cape Colony, [by] Wallace G. Mills. In Journal of
       Religion in Africa, 8:2 (1976), 105-122.

2278   Paul, John Haywood, 1877-1967.
       The soul digger; or, Life and times of William Taylor, [by]
       John Paul. Upland, In., Taylor University Press, c1928.
       318 p. DLC, ODa

2279 Paul, John Haywood, 1877-1967.
      William Taylor, a sketch of his life, [by] John Paul. Kan-
      sas City, Mo., Nazarene Publishing House, 192-. 63 p.

2280 TERRELL, Clifford McCollum (1949-)
          WWIR (1977), 658.
          CGIC
          Pastor
          b. Nov. 11, 1949, Norfolk, Va.

2281 THARPE, Rosetta (1915-1973)
          HGS (1975), xxix, xxxi, 32, 136, 187, 188, 189-196, 203,
      224, 230, 250, 261, 270, 271, 272, 297, 301, 313-316, 322,
      330, 332, 338.
          CGIC, NBaC
          Singer
          b. 1915, Cotton Plant, Ar.
          d. Oct. 1973, Philadelphia, Pa.

2282 Singer swings same songs in church and night club.
          In Life, 7 (Aug. 28, 1939), 37.

2283 20,000 watch wedding of Sister Rosetta Tharpe.
          In Ebony, 6 (Oct. 1951), 27-28, 30.

2284 THOMAS, Freeman M.
          GBPAW, 19.
          GHPAW, 131, 150, 153, 157, 158.
          PeAW
          Pastor, bishop
          b. 19--, Pelham, Ga.

2285 THOMAS, George A. (1882-)
          CHCCH, 300, 301.
          MBaC, CChr (H)
          Pastor
          b. May 15, 1882, Neshoba County, Ms.

2286 THOMAS, Ted (1935-)
          WWIR (1985), 338.
          CGIC
          Pastor, school admin., district supt., bishop
          b. Oct. 19, 1935, Raeford, N.C.

2287 THOMPSON, Brice H.
          MOM (1975), 68.
          CGP
          Minister, overseer, teacher
          b. Aug. 18, 1936, Acklins Island, Bahamas

2288 THURMOND, Willie A. (-1944)
          CHCCH, 280, 281, 282.

CChr (H)
Pastor, bishop. d. 1944, Jackson, Ms.

2289 TINNEY, James Steven (1942-)
        CGIC, I
        WWIR (1985), 391.
        Pastor, editor, college prof. author
        b. May 12, 1942, Kansas City, Mo.

2290 TOBIN, Robert F. (-1947)
        GHPAW, 114, 125, 126, 127, 129, 130.
        PeAW
        Pastor, denominational official, author
        d. 1947, Los Angeles, Ca.

2291 TODD, James H. V. (1916-)
        MOM (1975), 325.
        CGP
        Pastor. b. July 24, 1916, Paget, Bermuda

2292 TORREY, Allen Joseph (1904-)
        CHCCH, 283, 288, 289.
        CChr (H)
        Pastor, bishop
        b. Feb. 29, 1904, Copiah County, Ms.

2293 TRAFFANSTED, Jessie Bell Thurman (1912-)
        WWIR (1985), 394.
        CGIC
        Bookkeeper, clerk
        b. Jan. 30, 1912, Fort Payne, Al.

2294 TROGDON, Barney L. (1937-)
        MOM (1975), 32.
        CGP
        Pastor, teacher, overseer, denominational admin.
        b. Mar. 15, 1937, Randolph County, N.C.

2295 TURNER, La Paula
        UFMCC
        Pastor

2296 Tinney, James Steven, 1942-
        Ministering in a gay church, [by] James S. Tinney. In
        Afro-American (Washington) (Aug. 3, 1974), 12.

2297 TURNER, William Clair, 1948-
        UHCA
        Pastor, editor, seminary prof. and chaplain, author

2298 TURPIN, Joseph Marcel (1887-1943)
        GBPAW, 3, 33.

GHPAW, 53, 67, 72, 77, 82, 87, 90, 155, 157.
RWWAS, 69.
PeAW
Pastor, bishop
b. Jan. 1, 1887, Denton, Md.
d. Mar. 17, 1943, Baltimore, Md.

2299 TWINE, C. A. (1859–1963)
CHCCH, 280, 281, 282.
CChr (H)
Pastor, bishop
b. 1859, Virginia
d. 1963

2300 TWYMAN, Harris J.
RWWAS, 97, 98.
BWCOLJCWW, UWCCChrAF
Pastor

2301 TYSON, James Edison (1927-)
GBPAW, 51.
GHPAW, 157.
PeAW
Pastor, bishop
b. 1927, Johnstown, Pa.

2302 VALERA B., Juan (1937-)
MOM (1975), 70.
CGP
Evangelist, pastor, overseer
b. Nov. 20, 1937, Santo Domingo, Dominican Republic

2303 VANCE, John (-1956)
CHCCH, 48-50.
CChr (H)
Pastor, evangelist
d. May 3, 1956

2304 VARLACK, Adrian Laurence (1944-)
MOM (1975), 32. WWIR (1985), 402.
CGP
Pastor, accountant, bishop, denominational admin.
b. Oct. 24, 1944, Anegada, Virgin Islands

2305 VARNELL, A. F.
GBPAW, 69.
GHPAW, 74, 77, 87.
PeAW
Pastor, bishop

2306 VINCENT, Jean
CG (C)

Pastor
b. 19--, Haiti

2307 WADDLES, Charleszetta Lina Campbell (1912-   )
      BDNM (1975), 515.
      WWABA (1980-1981), 813.
      WWIA (1980-1981), II, 3399.
      I
      Minister
      b. Oct. 7, 1912, St. Louis, Mo.

2308 Davis, James Kotsilibas
      Mother Waddles: the gentle warrior, [by] James Kotsilibas
      Davis. In Life, 66 (Mar. 21, 1969), 87-89.

2309 Edson, Lee
      Mother Waddles: black angel of the poor, [by] Lee Edson.
      In Reader's Digest, 101 (Oct. 1972), 175-178.

2310 Harrington, Jeremy, 1932-
      Jesus! Superstar or savior? Edited by Jeremy Harrington.
      Cincinnati, St. Anthony Messenger Press, 1972. 132 p. On
      Mother Waddles: p. 121-123. DLC

2311 The power of a woman in Detroit.
      In Ladies Home Journal, 89 (May 1972), 24.

2312 [Smith, Vern E.]
      Mother Waddles's mission. In Newsweek, 79 (May 1, 1972),
      123.

2313 Smith, Vern E.
      The perpetual mission of Mother Waddles, [by] Vern E.
      Smith. In Ebony, 27 (May 1972), 50-52, 54, 56, 58.

2314 WADEN, Fletcher (1906-   )
      MOM (1975), 216.
      CG (T), CGP
      Pastor
      b. Sept. 9, 1906, Richland County, S.C.

2315 WADEN, Sally Robertson (1927-   )
      MOM (1975), 386.
      CG (T), CGP
      Pastor
      b. May 14, 1927, Chesterfield, S.C.

2316 WAGNER, Norman Leonard (1942-   )
      WWIR (1975-1976), 578.
      PeAW
      Pastor, evangelist, youth leader, district elder, author
      b. Jan. 14, 1942, Youngstown, Oh.

2317 I'm saved and I'm proud.
      In Ebony, 30 (June 1975), 84-86, 88, 90, 92.

2318 WALKER, Eddie Lee
      RFSTGA, 49.
      CN
      Pastor

2319 WALKER, Maggie Laura (-1979)
      DEC
      Bible institute prin.
      d. 1979, Newark, N.J.

2320 WALLACE, George A.
      CLMA (1977), 411.
      CG (C)
      Pastor, overseer

2321 WALLACE, Wendell
      JCITCC, 11-12, 28-30
      CG (A), I
      Pastor, evangelist, author
      b. 19--, Kansas City, Mo.

2322 Wallace, Wendell
      Born to burn, [by] Wendell Wallace, with Pat King. Spe-
      cial charisma ed. Watchung, N.J., Charisma Books, 1972,
      c1970. 103 p. Autobiography. DLC

2323 Wallace, Wendell
      Born to burn, [by] Wendell Wallace, with Pat King. Plain-
      field, N.J., Logos International, c1970. 95 p. Autobiography.
      ODa, Wa

2324 WALTERS, Alexander (1858-1917)
      NYT (Feb. 3, 1917), 13:5.
      WWIAM (1916), 232-233.
      WWWA (1897-1942), 1295.
      AMEZ
      Pastor, bishop, author
      b. Aug. 1, 1858, Bardstown, Ky.
      d. Feb. 2, 1917, New York, N.Y.

2325 Walters, Alexander, 1858-1917.
      My life and work, [by] Alexander Walters. New York,
      F. H. Revell Co., c1917. 272 p. DHU, DLC, IEG, MB, NN

2326 WALTERS, Norman Noel (1903-)
      GBPAW, 68.
      PeAW
      Pastor, bishop
      b. 1903, Kendal, Jamaica

2327 WALTON, Marguerite Cooper (1910-)
      WWIACUA (1970-1971), 557.
      WWOAW (1974-1975), 1005.
      CGIC
      Teacher, college admin.
      b. May 16, 1910, Lexington, Ms.

2328 WARD, Andrew
      CGIC
      Evangelist, editor

2329 WARMSLEY, Ernestine Laura Walker (1930-)
      WWIR (1985), 412.
      CGIC
      Social worker, editor
      b. Feb. 20, 1930, St. Louis, Mo.

2330 WASHINGTON, Earnestine Beatrice Thomas
      HGS (1975), xxxi, 191, 194, 195, 224, 330, 335.
      CGIC
      Singer
      b. 191-, near Cotton Plant, Ar.

2331 WASHINGTON, Fred Willis (1943-)
      WWIR (1977), 584.
      CGIC
      Pastor, laboratory technician
      b. Mar. 19, 1943, Fairbanks, La.

2332 WASHINGTON, Frederick Douglas (1913-)
      HGS (1975), 191.
      HP, 494.
      MHAFY, 76, 90, 91, 135, 136, 137.
      WWIR (1975-1976), 584.
      CGIC
      Pastor, bishop, author
      b. Jan. 1, 1913, Dermott, Ar.

2333 WASHINGTON, William Alexander (1886-1949)
      CHCCH, 271-272, 435-437.
      CChr (H), ACChr (H)
      Pastor, bishop
      b. 1886, Carroll County, Ms.
      d. May 1949, Los Angeles, Ca.

2334 WATERS, Charles E. (1917-)
      PPIB, III, 149.
      AOPeCA, TFPeCA
      Pastor, overseer

2335 WATKINS, Charles William (1923-)
      GBPAW, 53.

GHPAW, 177.
PeAW
Pastor, district elder, bishop
b. 1923, Richmond, Va.

2336   WATSON, James Thomas (1911-)
MLMR, 149.
WWIR (1985), 414.
CGIC
Pastor
b. Mar. 19, 1911, Harvey, Il.

2337   WATSON, William Henry (1943-)
WWIR (1985), 414.
CGIC
Pastor
b. May 17, 1943, Arkansas City, Ks.

2338   WAULS, Robert Allen (1914-)
GBPAW, 38.
GHPAW, 153, 157.
PeAW
Pastor, district elder, bishop
b. 1914, San Antonio, Tx.

2339   WEATHERS, Joseph
RWWAS, 40, 67-68.
WCCChr, HTCChr
Pastor, bishop

2340   WEBB, W. E. (-1964)
CGH, 25.
CLGCWFF
Pastor, overseer

2341   WEEKS, Thomas J. (1916-)
GBPAW, 41.
GHPAW, 153, 157.
PeAW
Pastor, bishop
b. 1916, Montserrat, W.I.

2342   WELLS, Wyoming
CP, 79, 87, 88, 92, 96.
MHAFY, 88, 90, 91, 135, 136, 141
CGIC
Pastor, bishop

2343   WHARTON, Compton (1946-)
MOM (1975), 72.
CGP

Pastor, overseer
b. June 21, 1946, Georgetown, Guyana

2344 WHITE, A. H.
WWIR (1985), 420.
HGWCLGPGT
Pastor, bishop, editor

2345 WHITE, Andrew M. (1913-1955)
CHCCH, 280, 281, 282.
CChr (H)
Pastor, bishop
b. July 13, 1913, Yazoo City, Ms.
d. Sept. 22, 1955, Los Angeles, Ca.

2346 WHITE, Charley C. (1885-   )
CGIC
Pastor, author
b. Sept. 10, 1885, near Shelbyville, Tx.

2347 White, Charley C., 1885-
No quittin' sense, [by] C. C. White and Ada Morehead
Holland. Austin, University of Texas Press, 1969. xi, 216 p.
The author's life story, based on tape recordings of his own
narrative, and written down in book form by A. M. Holland.
DHUD, DLC, ICU, NN

2348 Holland, Ada (Morehead)
It's always Christmas at God's Storehouse. Text and
photos by Ada Morehead Holland. In Texas Magazine (Houston) (Dec. 19, 1965), 4, 6-7, 9.

2349 [Holland, Ada (Morehead)]
One-man war on poverty. In Ebony, 20 (Feb. 1965), 77-
78, 80, 82, 84.

2350 Sapper, Neil Gary, 1941-
A survey of the history of the black people of Texas, 1930-
1954, [by] Neil Gary Sapper. Lubbock, 1972. v, 549 1.
Thesis (Ph.D.)--Texas Tech University. On Charley C.
White: 1. 519-521. TxLT

2351 WHITE, G. B.
AFCG
Pastor, presiding bishop

2352 WILEY, George H.
RWWAS, 74, 75-76, 90-91.
ACChrG, MHATOLJAF
Pastor, bishop

2353 WILLIAMS, A. D.
          CHCCH, 283, 288, 289.
          CChr (E)
          Pastor, bishop

2354 WILLIAMS, Archie
          BCUC, 48.
          CN
          Pastor

2355 WILLIAMS, Donald Eugene (1929-)
          WWABA (1985), 899.
          WWIR (1977), 715.
          CG (A)
          Pastor, denominational admin., author
          b. Jan. 4, 1929, De Land, Fl.

2356 WILLIAMS, Douglas
          RWWAS, 99, 100.
          HChrCChr, RAJCA
          Pastor, bishop

2357 WILLIAMS, Edward Lee (1922-)
          WWIR (1985), 425.
          CGIC
          Pastor, teacher
          b. Feb. 5, 1922, Columbus, Ga.

2358 WILLIAMS, Emery Columbus
          WWIR (1977), 715.
          CG (A)
          Pastor, Bible institute pres., evangelist
          b. May 3, 19--, Eastman, Ga.

2359 WILLIAMS, Frank W.
          PPIB, III, 200-201.
          AFMCG
          Evangelist, bishop

2360 WILLIAMS, Franklyn Rudolph (1930-)
          MOM (1975), 73.
          CGP
          Pastor, overseer
          b. May 11, 1930, Turks Islands

2361 WILLIAMS, Frederick Ezekiel (1877-1943)
          CHCCH, 54, 121, 223, 264.
          TDOOP, 180-181.
          CChr (H)
          Pastor
          b. Aug. 3, 1877, Gordonsville, Al.
          d. Nov. 14, 1943, Indianapolis, In.

2362   Wolfe, R. W.
           One of our foremost colored preachers called to his reward,
           [by] R. W. Wolfe. In Pilgrim Holiness Advocate, 23 (Dec. 2,
           1943), 7.

2363   WILLIAMS, Hudson A. (1947-   )
           MOM (1975), 333.
           CGP
           Evangelist, pastor
           b. Oct. 14, 1947, Bahamas

2364   WILLIAMS, James

2365   Williams, James
           From Frogtown to freedom. San Diego, Ca., Vision Publi-
           cations, 1977. 65 p. Autobiography.

2366   WILLIAMS, L. W.
           CSSIA (1949), 128.
           Ba, LHLFAPCMAF
           Pastor, bishop

2367   WILLIAMS, Linda Colene Nelson Selby (1921-   )
           BDNM (1975), 546.
           [HGW]CLG[PGT]
           Pastor
           b. July 4, 1921, Laurens, S.C.

2368   WILLIAMS, McKinley (1901-   )
           BDNM (1975), 546.
           RWWAS, 79, 80, 83, 85.
           COLJCAF, BWCOLJCWW
           Pastor, bishop
           b. Feb. 17, 1901, Albany, Ga.

2369   WILLIAMS, Marie (1920-   )
           MOM (1975), 388.
           CG (T), CGP
           Pastor, evangelist
           b. Feb. 1, 1920, Fredericksburg, Va.

2370   WILLIAMS, Riley F. (1897-1952)
           MHAFY, 64, 110-115.
           CGIC
           Pastor, bishop, builder, evangelist

2371   WILLIAMS, Smallwood Edmond (1907-   )
           BDNM (1975), 548.
           RWWAS, 59, 79-85
           WWIAP (1977-1978), 1076.
           WWIR (1985), 426.

COLJCAF, BWCOLJCWW
Pastor, evangelist, bishop, radio preacher, author
b. Oct. 17, 1907, Lynchburg, Va.

2372 Williams, Smallwood Edmond, 1907-
This is my story: a significant life struggle; autobiography
of Smallwood Edmond Williams. Washington, Wm. Willoughby
Publishers, c1981. vi, 195 p.

2373 Top radio ministers.
In Ebony, 4 (July 1949), 56-61. On Smallwood Edmond
Williams: p. 58.

2374 WILLIAMS, Smallwood Edmond (1930-)
BWCOLJCWW
Musician
b. 1930, Washington, D.C.

2375 Williams, Smallwood Edmond, 1907-
My son was a dope addict, [by] Smallwood E. Williams. In
Ebony, 7 (Sept. 1952), 31-32, 34-38.

2376 WILLIAMSON, Linnette
I
Dressmaker, missionary, pastor
b. 19--, Kingston, Jamaica

2377 Ayo, Foluso
Linnette Williamson, [by] Foluso Ayo. In Essence, 5 (Oct.
1974), 15.

2378 Browne, J. Zamgba
Rev. Lennette Williamson, [by] J. Zamgba Browne. In
New York Amsterdam News, 70 (Nov. 12, 1977), 12.

2379 WILLIS, Andrew Hopewell (1937-)
WWIR (1977), 718.
CGIC
Pastor, seminary admissions counselor, editor
b. Aug. 13, 1937, Philadelphia, Pa.

2380 WILLIS, Levi E.
MHAFY, 90, 91.
CGIC
Pastor, bishop, banker, mortician, publisher

2381 Bishop buys 73-year old Norfolk Journal-Guide.
In Jet, 43 (Mar. 15, 1973), 31.

2382 WILSON, Quander L.
GEAC
Pastor, bishop

2383 WINLEY, Jesse (1920-1980)
      AME, SSS
      Laborer, pastor, general overseer, author
      b. Sept. 20, 1920, Georgetown, S.C.
      d. June 20, 1960, New York, N.Y.

2384 Winley, Jesse, 1920-1980.
      Jesse, [by] Jesse Winley, with Robert Paul Lamb. Spring-
      dale, Pa., Whitaker House, c1976. 223 p. Autobiography.

2385 "Victory celebration" held in memory of Bishop Jesse Winley.
      In International Pentecostal Holiness Advocate, 64 (Aug.
      10, 1980), 11.

2386 WINSTON, Dora Catherine (1924-   )
      WWIR (1977), 722.
      CGIC
      Evangelist missionary, singer, pianist
      b. Aug. 1, 1924, Norfolk, Va.

2387 WITCHER, Randle E.
      CG (C)
      Pastor

2388 WOOLARD, Lucy
      FBHCGA
      Pastor, domestic, taxi driver

2389 Banks, Carolyn
      The fire, [by] Carolyn Banks. Photographs by Margaret
      Thomas. In Potomac (Mar. 10, 1974), 16-17, 30, 32.

2390 WORD, Timothy (1900-1974)
      MOM (1975), 217.
      CG (T), CGP
      Pastor
      b. Nov. 25, 1900, Franklin County, Ga.
      d. Nov. 7, 1974

2391 WORD, Vina M. Sturivant (1905-   )
      MOM (1975), 390.
      CG (T), CGP
      Evangelist, pastor
      b. Sept. 2, 1905, Charlotte, N.C.

2392 YOUNG, D. J.
      FTINS, 47.
      MHAFY, 63
      TBPALM, 94.
      CGIC
      Pastor, evangelist, editor, publisher
      d. 19--, Kansas City, Ks.

2393   YOUNG, Elzie
          RWWAS, 79.
          PeCAFA
          Pastor, bishop

2394   YOUNG, Toni
          I
          Pastor, author

2395   Young, Toni
          Toni: the story of a black saint, [by] Toni Young, as
       told to Jean E. Jolley.   San Diego, Ca., Vision Publications,
       1976.   Autobiography.

2396   ZIGLAR, James R.
          RWWAS, 96, 97.
          ACChrG, UCJA
          Pastor, bishop

Numbers refer to bibliographical or directory entries unless
preceded by "p." which indicates page(s).

Flame (Kansas City, Mo.) 681
Florida 269, 526, 631-632, 1193-
    1194, 1199, 1547; p. 92, 93,
    96-97, 112, 122, 126, 206
Florida Bible Institute 1193-
    1194
Flowers, S.L. see Flowers,
    Sumpter Lee (1881-1945)
Flowers, Sumpter Lee (1881-
    1945) 338
Fluker, Samuel Anthony (1937-)
    1574
Flynn, John Thomas (1882-1964)
    1279
Foggs, Edward L. (1934-)
    380, 1575; p. 48
Fonville, C.E. see Fonville,
    Cephus E.
Fonville, Cephus E. 1576
Foote, Julia A.J. (1823-)
    1577-1580
Forbes, J.A. (1914-) see
    Forbes, James Alexander
    (1914-)
Forbes, J.A. (1935-) see
    Forbes, James Alexander
    (1935-)
Forbes, James Alexander
    (1914-) 774, 785, 1581;
    p. 125
Forbes, James Alexander
    (1935-) 53-54, 87, 578,
    780, 790-791, 1582-1583
Ford, Anna Mae (1916-)
    1584; p. 119
Ford, Eddye Betty Chambers
    (1911-) 1585
Ford, Mrs. Frank Curtis see
    Ford, Eddye Betty Chambers
    (1911-)
Ford, George L. 833
Ford, Mrs. Robert L. see
    Ford, Anna Mae (1916-)
Forman, James (1928-) 491
Forson, N.M. p. 167
Fort Wayne, In. p. 38
Fort Wayne College see Taylor
    University
Fort Worth, Tx. p. 63
Foster, Fred J. 868-869, 990
Foursquare Gospel Church see
    International Church of the
    Foursquare Gospel
Fowler, C.J. see Fowler,
    Charles J. (1848-1919)
Fowler, Charles J. (1848-1919)
    997

Francis, Silburn B. (1932-) 1586
Franco, Sergio 478-479
Franklin, Robert Michael 3
Fraser, C. Gerald 1503
Fraser, Wilhelmina (1904-) 1587-
    1588
Frazee, J.J. 1589; p. 172
Frazier, E. Franklin see Frazier,
    Edward Franklin (1894-1962)
Frazier, Edward Franklin (1894-
    1962) 158-159
Free Christian Zion Church of
    Christ 536; p. 75
Free Church of God in Christ 737;
    p. 113
Free Church of God True Holiness
    p. 113, 116
Free Gospel Church of Christ 941;
    p. 166-167
Free Methodist Church of North
    America 540-547, 1182; p. 76-78
Freedom Chapel Pentecostal Ortho-
    dox Church of Christ p. 167
Freeman, Mrs. Harry see Free-
    man, Mary Jayne Hill (1918-)
Freeman, Mary Jayne Hill (1918-)
    1590
Freemasonry p. 59
Freire, Paulo (1921-) 575
Fresno, Ca. p. 64
Frodge, Harold C. 481
Frodsham, Stanley Howard (1882-
    1969) 283
Full Gospel Holy Temple Churches
    754; p. 119-120
Full Gospel News (Portland, Or.)
    755
Full Gospel Pentecostal Association
    755; p. 120
Fuller, M.K. p. 76
Fuller, W.E. (1875-1958) see
    Fuller, William Edward (1875-
    1958)
Fuller, W.E. (1921-) see Fuller,
    William Edward (1921-)
Fuller, William Edward (1875-1958)
    1591; p. 84, 111, 126
Fuller, William Edward (1921-)
    1592; p. 112
Fuller Normal and Industrial Insti-
    tute 731, 1195-1196; p. 111
Fundamental Bible Seminary and
    College 1197
Furbee, Jack W. 514
Furnas, J.C. see Furnas, Joseph
    Chamberlain (1905-)
Furnas, Joseph Chamberlain